Changing Identities
in Early Modern France

Michael Wolfe, Editor

Changing Identities in Early Modern France

With a Foreword by Natalie Zemon Davis

Duke University Press Durham and London

1997

© 1996 Duke University Press *All rights reserved*

Printed in the United States of America on acid-free paper ∞

Typeset in Garamond 3 by Keystone Typesetting, Inc.

Library of Congress Cataloging-in-Publication Data appear

on the last printed page of this book.

Foreword

❧ *Changing Identities in Early Modern France* is published as a tribute to the life and work of Nancy Lyman Roelker. In the sixteenth-century France she knew so well, books were dedicated to important personages who had supported or encouraged the author in the past and whose name, it was hoped, would protect the book as it ventured into the world of readers. If this were the custom today, Nancy Roelker's study would have been piled from floor to ceiling with dedicated volumes, so numerous were the historians, young and old, who benefited from her scholarly generosity. She listened to countless thesis and book proposals, pored over manuscripts, suggested major revisions with the utmost of tact, and offered cheer when there were snags. Over fifty years of teaching she made history live for her students, telling the story with empathy or laughter or wise insight into human ambition. Along the way her scholarly publications made a signal contribution to our understanding of early modern France.

Born in Rhode Island, Nancy Roelker was linked through her mother to the founders of the Massachusetts Bay Colony and through her father to the early settlers who made Rhode Island a haven for dissenters. Educated at Radcliffe and Harvard in both philosophy and history, she went on to teach history at the Winsor School in Boston and then at Tufts and Boston University, with visiting stints at Stanford and at Brown.

Already before World War II, she had traveled to France, the first of many visits in which she rummaged in archives and libraries, took in the wine harvest in the Bordelais, and found time to organize a campaign to restore the important Paris library of the Société de l'histoire du protestantisme français. Her love of France was always seasoned with an amused appreciation for what the French were up to and coupled with a concern for international exchange and peace. In 1963, as a participant in Harvard's Center for International Relations, she translated and edited works on twentieth-century politics by Jean-Baptiste Duroselle and François Goguel; in 1982–1985, when the world was still in the grip of the cold war, she was the United States representative to the International Committee of Historical

Sciences. Both in the academy and without, she sustained a balanced and humane liberalism, defending freedom of inquiry and expression against bigots who would curtail it.

Her publications on sixteenth-century France explore religious belief and political culture and their interconnection in actual events: in the drama of a religious conversion, the challenge of a legal sentence, the decision to make war. Her *Paris of Henry of Navarre* (1958) recreated that city and its politics in the late sixteenth-century through the diary–memoirs of Pierre de l'Estoile, an important office-holder in the royal courts. From this study emerged a picture of "news," of how information was collected and disseminated through gossip and the ever-more-active printing presses of Paris. With her 1968 volume, *Queen of Navarre Jeanne d'Albret, 1528–1572,* Nancy Roelker pioneered the study of female rulership. Jeanne d'Albret's conversion to Protestantism, her emergence as a major leader of the Reformed cause, and her unswerving focus on her son Henri as the dynastic hope of France are shown to be products both of family political values and of Jeanne's own self-fashioning. The relations between women—Jeanne and her mother Marguerite de Navarre, and Jeanne and her rival Catherine de Médicis—are analyzed both as intimate psychological events and as public events of great consequence.

Nancy Roelker's *One King, One Faith* (1996) portrays the mental world of the judges of the Parlement of Paris as they decided cases of heresy and political-religious disorder throughout the entire sixteenth century. In her earliest work she quoted an arresting sentence from the journal of Pierre de l'Estoile: "I will cling to this old trunk of the Papacy . . . though she be a harlot . . . still she is my Mother." In this last magisterial synthesis, Roelker examines the mainstream of centrist judges: men who stayed Catholic, clinging both to Mother Church and to the Gallican Liberties of the French Church, which for them were inseparably entwined. Relatively tolerant humanists within the walls of their personal libraries, these *parlementaires* kept to a sterner but still middle course in their judicial chambers, holding France in rightful legal bounds against the deviations of Protestants and of radical ultramontane Catholics. Here the interplay between personal belief, public commitments, and changing circumstances is strikingly displayed.

Nancy Roelker dedicated *One King, One Faith* to a cluster of younger scholars whose work had nourished her own. One of them was Michael Wolfe, author of an innovative book on the conversion of Henri IV and editor of this volume. Wolfe and his collaborators have identified major issues in early modern political, social, and cultural history, some of them stretching across the Atlantic to France's "New World." Although Nancy Roelker knew that this book was underway, she died in late 1993 before it could be placed in her hands. All the contributors have been in long dialogue with Nancy Roelker over the years. In her absence, they hope to pass on to readers the spirit of her generosity and scholarship.

Natalie Zemon Davis, *Princeton University*

Contents

Michael Wolfe

Introduction: Becoming French in Early Modern Europe

Historical hindsight offers a deceptive prescience when we are interpreting how people in past societies coped with the myriad problems
that beset them individually and communally. Knowing how the story
eventually turns out often leads us to impute, however falsely, a certain
inevitability or sense of process to actions taken long ago. Thus the historicist trap is sprung, snaring us along with our readings of the past. Escaping
this dilemma requires a long, hard look at our basic operative assumptions,
among them the notion that modern national identities represent the
culmination of long-term developments that stretch back seamlessly to the
Middle Ages. We do well to recall the revisionist critiques of Whiggish
historians a generation ago, who were taken to task for positing a linear
trajectory in the emergence of British parliamentary institutions over the
past millennium, or the ongoing debate over the German *Sonderweg,* tied as
it is to the twentieth-century experience of National Socialism.[1] Such examples of presentist special pleading could easily be multiplied.

For the French, the perennial question asked long ago by Michelet and
since revisited in *Les lieux de mémoire* revolves around determining whether
the historical emergence of a French identity was an antecedent or a consequence of the politics of state building under first the monarchy and then,
after 1789 (definitively after 1871), a succession of republican regimes.[2]
One school of thought on the subject, which might be called the apolitical
and is epitomized in the now classic studies of Fernand Braudel, sees
"Frenchness" as an almost ecological condition growing out of the very soil
of the country. Politics becomes almost incidental as *histoire événementielle*
pales before the deeper currents of demography, geography, and the environment. The resulting unity was at once resilient enough to embrace regional
distinctions, yet transcendent enough to establish a paramount sense of
unity joining Picard, Provençal, and all the others to form *les* France.[3] Other
scholars, such as Charles Tilly, take a contrary view that emphasizes the
essentially political and class dynamics, underpinned by materialistic factors, which have animated evolving notions of what it means to be French.

They see French identity as an alloy forged by centuries of violent contention both before and after the French Revolution of 1789, wherein differences—cultural, social, and political—far from being accommodated, have instead been overwhelmed or at best partially absorbed by hegemonic groups who claim the right to define Frenchness. Evaluating the construction of this collective identity therefore requires us to be attentive not only to the groups who have fitted into it, but also to those who historically have been excluded.[4]

The essays in this volume grapple with the problem of French identity from the outbreak of the Hundred Years' War up to the consolidation of the monarchy under the Bourbons. Such focused studies can eschew the otherwise natural tendency of historians to connect, if only rhetorically, the present age with times long ago. In the process, they enable us to probe more deeply the unique dynamics of identity formation among discrete groups under specific circumstances, with no compelling necessity to construe strained lineages with the modern nation. Drawing on a rich variety of interdisciplinary methods, these essays probe different aspects at play in the concatenation of Frenchness during the early modern period.[5] In this they reflect the spirit of Nancy Roelker's lifelong pursuit of recapturing in all its complex ambiguity what it meant to be French to powerful women such as Jeanne d'Albret, to proud jurists of the Parlement of Paris, and to keen yet opinionated observers of contemporary society such as Pierre de l'Estoile.[6]

The collection begins with five essays devoted to the complex interplay between the key ideologies and institutions that have long framed discussions of what makes French history distinctly French. John Salmon's bold foray into the nineteenth-century romantic attitudes toward the Renaissance reminds us that our vision of the past passes through many other filters besides those of the present. The contrary assessments of the French Middle Ages and Renaissance proffered first by *philosophes* and then by romantic authors, poets, and historians remain a standard feature of textbooks.[7] Where the *philosophes* saw the Middle Ages as a time of intellectual darkness and clerical obscurantism, the romantics viewed it as a great age of faith and virtue. Similarly, for men like Voltaire, the Renaissance marked a return of learning and liberty to Europe, whereas romantics characterized it as an era of irreligion and vice. However, Salmon's close examination of the relationship between the political, cultural, and aesthetic currents of the time reveals deep-seated ambivalences in romantic attitudes toward the Renaissance. One group, styled "ironists" by Salmon, championed what they saw as the initial liberalism of the Renaissance as it had developed in Italy before spreading to France in the sixteenth century. While celebrating this progressive impulse, writers such as Stendhal, Musset, and Saint-Beuve were nevertheless troubled by some of the unethical tendencies of Renaissance secularism; they also lamented Richelieu's and Louis XIV's eventual suppression in the seventeenth century of the new freedoms humanism had ushered in. By contrast, Philarète Chasles and Saint-Marc Girardin believed that the new national spirit they saw awakening in sixteenth-century France prepared the way for the glorious triumphs of the country under the Bourbons. Michelet and Quinet, who represent another group of romantics, termed "symbolists" by Salmon, embraced a more historicist stance in judging the universal significance of the Renaissance (and Reformation) in the development not just of the French, but of all humanity. Anticipating Jacob Burckhardt's view of the Renaissance as the birth of modernity, Michelet and Quinet related the intellectual progressivism they saw in the sixteenth century to the emergence of a strong centralized state and the bourgeoisie—a conclusion Karl Marx also reached during the 1840s. Especially pronounced in the work of French romantic historians was their strong anticlericalism and ongoing reevaluation of the respective merits of monarchy and republicanism as forms of government. Thus again did contemporary concerns about ideology and ethics enter into historical discussions. Salmon's analysis of the conjunction of high culture and amoralism found in French romantic views of the Renaissance reflects at base the self-referential nature of any attempt to characterize the spirit—and thus identity—of a shared past.[8]

The ways that aesthetics, politics, and culture worked to construct early modern French identity form the thrust of Lawrence Bryant's essay as well. While focusing on France, Bryant delves into the general Renaissance concern with forms of government from the vantage point of extant collections of accounts relating the performances of princes in public assemblies. Motivated mainly by questions of protocol, these accounts show that the stimulus for dividing questions of power into political theory or history developed as officials and courtiers faced a tangle of customs and practical problems in staging public displays of royal majesty. Aspects of this topic have been treated in terms of major ceremonies such as the royal funeral rites and the *lit de justice;*[9] however, the role of Renaissance ceremonialism—and the humanist, literary, and artistic forces advancing it—has not been considered as an agent in the transformation of French political culture into the monarchical and protonational form so evident under the Bourbons. The appearance of powerful groups in public performances composed an image of authority in much the same way that a Renaissance artist drew together the elements of a painting or other artistic work. Once composed, the image signaled as well as scripted the various roles assigned in public performances of power. Yet, like actors, participants in such affairs constantly reinterpreted (or perhaps better, renegotiated) their parts—a tendency most alive in the case of France, as Bryant shows, during the turmoil of the Wars of Religion. Similarly, an attempt to fix in "perfected" form the rules of order, hierarchy, and sovereignty was mounted in officially sponsored publications and debates in French academies, which promoted the idea and then the practice of royal majesty under the Bourbons that profoundly colored contemporary understandings of France's history and political culture; in short, what it meant to be French.[10]

The grounding of the legitimacy of French political institutions and official ideologies in canonical texts forms the subject of Sarah Hanley's fascinating investigation into the concoction of the much vaunted French Salic law during the fourteenth and fifteenth centuries. Asserted after 1550 as a fundamental law of the kingdom, a contention long reiterated in modern studies of the French monarchy, the Salic law excluded women from the royal succession based on practices that legists believed went back to the early Franks. Hanley retraces the tortuous, and hitherto untold, story of how this purportedly most ancient of French public laws actually came to be formulated by legal scholars during the Hundred Years' War. Compounding this discrepancy was the fact that sixteenth-century legists who researched the matter discovered this to be the case but chose to disregard the evidence in favor of what Hanley calls the "misogynist litany."[11] Its standing as a French public law dissipated once it became clear that the Salic law was merely a private law from an early medieval Franco-Germanic code. The original documents long advanced to substantiate female exclusion by the Salic law were in reality forgeries from the 1400s into which words had been interpolated to make the law French and to make its regulation constitutional. Especially fascinating in Hanley's study is the fact that the initial interpolations by Jean de Montreuil and others in the late fourteenth and early fifteenth centuries did not go unchallenged at the time. Christine de

Pizan, in particular, attacked the underlying misogynist assumptions animating these purposeful and, in her estimation, unethical manipulations of France's history and legal traditions.[12] Pizan's objections carried little weight, however, and in time were conveniently forgotten, even when rediscovered in the sixteenth century. Indeed, by that later date, legal scholars and political theorists wished to refashion the old Salic law into the French royal (Salic) law, rooted not in history but in natural law. This became particularly pressing in the aftermath of the 1593 leaguer Estates-General, when a faction of militant Catholics advanced the candidacy of the Spanish infanta over the dynastic claims of Henri de Navarre. It was hoped that in resolving the long-standing contradictions inherited from the Salic law's sordid past, the permanent exclusion of women from government in France could be established. In this light, the rise of the French state was predicated on a hardening of attitudes—and laws—restricting the place of women at all levels of French society.[13]

The consolidation of prominent social groups accompanied the establishment of reigning royal ideologies and dynastic houses during these centuries, argues Robert Descimon in his study of the birth of the robed nobility in the Parlement of Paris. Members of the Parlement of Paris have commonly been regarded as noble, even though the status of individual councillors along with the corporate eminence of the parlement as a whole did not fully coalesce as a distinct social category before the end of the sixteenth century. Indeed, the term *noblesse de robe* first appeared in 1607, in the index of Estienne Pasquier's *Recherches de la France.* Descimon reexamines what jurists had to say about the social identity of the robed nobility as revealed in juridical decisions handed down by the parlement dealing with cases that impugned the social standing of individual magistrates. The Parlement of Paris also provides an excellent vantage point from which to chart the ongoing evolution of urban society during the Wars of Religion.[14] Here Descimon focuses not only on the high robe of *premiers présidents,* who split off from the urban patriciate, but also the changing hierarchy within the parlement itself. Evidence indicates that the parlement became closed and hostile to social affiliations that might compromise its status. It fiercely protected its members' economic interests in judicial office as an investment, reconciling itself between 1543 and 1583 to a growth in the number of offices in exchange for a hike in the fees it charged to plaintiffs; it also mounted an ardent defense of the *droit annuel,* which guaranteed judges the right to bequeath their office, even though later, in 1604, the parlement opposed this practice.[15] As a result of these attitudes and behaviors, the robed nobility had become a clearly identifiable sociopolitical category in France by the early seventeenth century, as can be seen in Charles Loyseau's *Traité des ordres et simples dignités* (1610). The link between these changes and the political evolution of the monarchy from Valois to Bourbon rule, regardless of the new directions undertaken by French society after the final defeat of the Catholic Holy League in the 1590s, also powerfully influenced the development of the robed nobility as a self-conscious, well-defined group whose role in the politics of Paris, the court, and the realm at large would be decisive until 1789.[16]

Distinguishing social groups—and their composite identity—can be carried a step further when gender is factored into the equation. A case in point can be found in Kristen Neuschel's analysis of the involvement of noblewomen in both carrying out and protecting themselves and their families against the violence that was ordinarily a part of aristocratic life. Surviving documentation reveals that noblewomen, who had traditionally taken a strong hand in managing family property, frequently helped prepare their households for war by securing weapons and supplies. They also occasionally became involved in actual acts of war—an opportunity available to women in the lower orders, too.[17] Aristocratic women, such as the unidentified Catherine scrutinized so closely by Neuschel, commonly possessed more than a passing familiarity with the use and maintenance of weapons, from cannons to harquebuses. They could also under special circumstances act as military leaders, ordering action by subordinates to seize disputed property, quash rebellion, or even deploy troops in the field, as they did during the Wars of Religion. Especially interesting, as Neuschel points out, was not only men's reliance on noblewomen's expertise in these matters, but also their unthinking acceptance of it. Both routine aristocratic violence and warfare in general were far less "gendered" than historians have previously thought—a finding that raises significant questions about the process of state formation in France. As seen in Hanley's work, the consolidation of state power under the monarchy was in part grounded in the formal exclusion of women from holding public authority; yet as late as the 1570s, this process had not markedly affected the organization and activities of aristocratic households. Thus, unlike the country's rulers, noblemen did not need to have their authority propped up by newly rigid gender roles—at least not yet. These apparent disparities at the level of social and gender self-identity reflect the complexity of state formation in France and the corresponding emergence of a set of attitudes and behaviors sufficiently unified to mark the French as a distinct people.[18]

The interplay of class and gender in defining the boundaries of dissent and deviance in early modern France is explored in the essays in part 2. Building on Nancy Roelker's now classic study of aristocratic women and religious choice in the French Reformation, Charmarie Blaisdell explores from the Catholic viewpoint the ways that class, education, the high moral cause of religious reform, and sometimes widowhood empowered aristocratic women in convents to defy royal and ecclesiastical authority.[19] Focusing on the aunts, sisters, cousins, and nieces of Catholic and Huguenot elites from the late fifteenth to the late sixteenth centuries, Blaisdell reconstructs how women in religious communities experienced the swelling calls for Catholic renewal and eventual Protestant reform. While theoretically subordinate due to the restrictions imposed by their vows, aristocratic women in convents often displayed as much willfulness about how they wished to live their lives and faith as did their female relatives at court. Many nuns refused to accept attempts to reassert secular and ecclesiastical authority over their lives, often being so bold as to take their cases to the law courts. Royal convents in particular, because they recruited their members almost exclusively from the aristocracy, provided a platform from which nuns could display a remarkable independence at the risk of sometimes harsh discipline. In this regard, they hardly differed from the aristocratic women who chose Calvinism after 1550. Blaisdell examines the impact that growing demands for religious reform had on nuns and convent life, considering the various factors that led some to resist change while others embraced it wholeheartedly. Records from the Parlement of Paris, ecclesiastical visitations, and town councils throughout France recount numerous examples of the interplay of religion, gender, and class among women whose actions from the outset contested the boundaries men in authority tried to impose on them.

The readiness of Catholic women to assert themselves politically and religiously continued during the Wars of Religion and the century of Catholic renewal that followed. The women who became swept up in the religious enthusiasm of the times have been virtually ignored—an oversight Barbara Diefendorf begins to rectify in her essay on Parisian women and the

Holy League. These women shared in the fierce Catholic militancy that dominated Paris between 1588 and 1594, and patronized the ascetic new religious orders, such as the Capuchins and Feuillants, frequently associated with Catholic activism. The political involvement of highly placed aristocratic women, particularly from the Guise family, has long found a place in popular histories of the League.[20] Diefendorf, however, shows that such activism cut across class lines by focusing on women from bourgeois and magisterial families—women like Marie du Drac, Louise Sevin, Barbe Acarie, and Madeleine Luillier. Unfortunately, the available evidence does not allow us to calculate what proportion of Paris's female (or male) population supported the league. Diefendorf therefore proceeds by asking a series of questions about key women whose affiliation with the league can be demonstrated. Interestingly, Diefendorf shows that many of the same factors encouraging activism among leaguer women also animated the devotional actions of women whose families supported the royalist cause. Political differences could therefore be subsumed in shared religious goals related to promoting Catholic reform. Indeed, after 1594, Parisian women whose families had earlier been divided now worked together to found new religious orders, open hospitals, and encourage right religion. Activism among women who had found ample opportunities to become involved in public affairs during the Wars of Religion persisted into the seventeenth century. From this perspective, the defeat of the Catholic League was primarily confined to its political objectives, not its religious ones.[21]

Although women in the aristocracy and urban notability enjoyed a surprising measure of independence on matters of politics and religion, the same cannot be said of women from lower down the social ladder. Denis Crouzet's essay recounts the bizarre fate of Nicole Obry, whose purported possession by the Devil in 1566 became a cause célèbre throughout France, in the process serving almost as a parable of the wider confessional struggles then rocking the kingdom. Crouzet peels away the many layers of opinion and perception that textured the affair, highlighting in particular the liturgical and eschatological dimensions shaping the *déroulement* of Nicole's possession and subsequent public exorcism in Laon.[22] The case inspired several publications at the time, most notably Jean Boulaese's seven-hundred-page tome relating in sometimes gruesome detail the poor woman's experiences. Drawing on this evidence, Crouzet discovers the complex dialogue that developed between the clergy of Laon and Satan. During these exchanges, Satan revealed that his minions at large in the world were in fact the Huguenots. Prevailing demonological beliefs established a script for Nicole and other participants that was as influential as it was predictable.[23] Charles IX himself attended the proceedings during which this damning avowal against the French Calvinists occurred. What clearer sign from God did he and all other good Catholics need to wage pitiless war against the heretics? Indeed, Crouzet detects from the outset of the affair a mounting fervor on the part of Catholics to redress the setbacks they had suffered at the hands of the Huguenots during the first civil war. The strange case of Nicole Obry, whose own identity became caught up in currents of personal self-delusion and the brewing devotional militancy, helped to rally French Catholics in their quest not only to eradicate heresy, but also to establish definitively the religious foundation of the *bon François*.[24] In this instance, local forces pressured the crown ultimately to pursue policies it might otherwise have been loath to adopt. A young woman's experiences thus encapsulated the tensions roiling the country and helped to set the stage for the new series of violent clashes between confessional factions that broke out in later years.

Instances of demonic possession and the ensuing attempts to suppress them have long intrigued historians, who have studied witch hunts to explore the complex formation of European identities during the early modern period. Richard Golden's essay offers a global overview of recent research on this problem, systematically examining the intensity of witch hunting from Iceland to the Urals. Most studies of European witchcraft concentrate on western and central Europe; widening our ken, however, enables us to place the phenomena of black magic, demonic possession, and pre-Christian folkloric traditions into a broader perspective that does not privilege the experiences of the modern "great powers" of Great Britain, France, and Germany. Golden carefully determines the extent (numbers executed) of witch hunting in relation to population sizes so as to measure its severity more accurately, and thus reassesses the areas of Europe that experienced severe, moderate, or minimal witch hunting. In addition, Golden estimates the number of alleged witches killed in different areas of Europe. One of his most interesting findings in this regard is the extremely localized nature of the witch hunts, with specific concentrations in select locales that necessarily distort interpretations when transposed to a "national" setting.[25] Witch hunting in France was largely confined to its northern, eastern, and southwestern peripheries; the vast majority of the country actually experienced little in the way of sustained campaigns against suspected witches. In terms of the total number of witches executed in relation to total population, France took a remarkably mild approach to handling witches. There was no "witch-craze" in France. Golden accounts for the discontinuous character of the witch hunts by focusing on the activities of individual witch hunters and rogue judges. Degrees of state control or religious fervor set the stage for potential witch scares, but the witch hunters themselves often triggered the actual witch panics. It was therefore primarily individuals who shaped the geography of witchcraft persecutions by acting as catalysts who took advantage (or chose not to) of opportunities offered by misogyny and criminal procedure to root out evil from the local community.

Witch hunting was far from the only occasion to attack people (usually women) who lived on the margins of Old Regime society. Alfred Soman's pathbreaking essay on infanticide in early modern France, based on twenty years of research in the criminal archives of the Parlement of Paris, indicates that infanticide was by far the most important capital offense committed by women in France during the sixteenth and seventeenth centuries.[26] The number of women executed for this crime far outnumbered those who perished as condemned witches. The frequency of verdicts handed down for infanticide does not necessarily mean that child killing was a common occurrence, however. An average of ten hangings a year over the period 1565–1690, when the infanticide "craze" reached its height, represents 50 to 90 percent of all women hanged, and 15 to 34 percent of all hangings under common law (men included). Soman reviews the legal and procedural grounds shaping infanticide prosecutions, as well as the broader religious and social attitudes about female sexuality, children, and public order. Unsurprisingly, the majority of women condemned for murdering their children were from the popular classes and unmarried. Initial evidentiary problems were solved when the crown ruled in 1557 that a woman's guilt could be established if she had tried to hide her pregnancy to salvage her honor; if for any reason her child subsequently died—a common enough occurrence at the time—the courts considered her culpable. After setting these general parameters, Soman shifts his attention to the case of a particular woman, one Marie-Jeanne Bartonnet, who was tried at the Châtelet of Paris in 1742 for infanticide. Related in compelling, often poignant detail, Bartonnet's experience illustrates many of the themes raised earlier by Soman, who ends by suggesting that in the eighteenth century, a new, sympathetic sensibility began to be felt toward abandoned women like Marie-Jeanne, whose status as victim rose as the number of infanticide trials diminished. The shifting boundaries of deviance and dissent, not only for poor women but for other groups as well (Jews, Protestants, peasants) during the Enlightenment signaled a deeper transformation of French society and culture at large, one which in time expanded in a more inclusive fashion the shared attributes that together defined the French as a nation.[27]

The last part of this collection explores the shifting contours of identity in light of overseas discoveries, rising sectarian disputes, and the growth of royal government in the French provinces. Donald Kelley begins it by assessing the impact of the discovery of the New World on Spanish and other European writers during the sixteenth century. Like so much else about sixteenth-century Europe, European historiography was a mixture of old and new—medieval chronicles and universal histories drew as many readers (perhaps more) as the works using new methods and ideas to animate humanist and antiquarian scholarship. Old myths such as the *translatio imperii* persisted in coloring European intellectuals' view of the new lands and peoples of the Americas, while new ideas like the notion of Progress took hold in the attempt to measure as favorably as possible the level of "civilization" in Europe over against the "obvious" barbarity of the Amerindians. In the case of Spain, first, and later other colonizing European powers such as the French, English, and Dutch, the New World discoveries fitted into these long-standing myths and traditions about Providence and imperial destiny that for the most part confirmed, rather than altered, how the Europeans viewed themselves and the world at large. Yet, as Kelley points out, seeds of change were sown that in time transformed the historiographical valuation placed on the New World discoveries by Spanish writers, such as Bartolomé de Las Casas, who brought into the discussion an early formulation of the kinds of interracial and intercultural questions so familiar to us today. In the end, Kelley argues that the discoveries and the ensuing formation of New Spain—to be followed in time by a New France and a New England—forced significant adjustments to the old tradition of Eurocentric and Euromorphic historical writing.

Perhaps no writer in the sixteenth century evidenced these complex mental changes more clearly than Michel de Montaigne, whose essay "Des cannibales" (essay 31) marked a mighty step forward in the history of European self-criticism. Montaigne's preoccupation with the quotidian reflected his unique search for principles of order in the ordinary as France sank into seemingly perpetual civil war.[28] William Bouwsma's essay builds on the extraordinary recent flowering of Montaigne studies by attempting to describe the new *forma mentis* now emerging for Montaigne. This recent work presents us with a Montaigne who brought what was most profoundly radical in Renaissance rhetorical tradition to a kind of grand climax. The essential thrust of this tradition—and central to Montaigne's quest for self-understanding—was its denial of the ontological status of all hierarchies.[29] This position, as Bouwsma then points out, made possible the sense of the significance of the ordinary and of everyday life that is so conspicuous in Montaigne. Bouwsma recognizes this sense as a peculiarity of *modern* culture, as do Mikhail Bakhtin, who nevertheless failed to extend his insights into Rabelais and the novel to Montaigne's oeuvre, and the Canadian philosopher Charles Taylor.[30] Bouwsma explores the intriguing anomaly of earlier readers of Montaigne, in the main shaped by an aristocratic culture that could value only the extraordinary, who failed to recognize—perhaps because of Montaigne's extensive classical quotations and allusions—this crucial aspect of his thought as revealed in the *Essais.* Similarly, Bouwsma offers a critique of the Annaliste school, which until recently, at least, greatly underestimated in favor of serial history what intellectuals like Montaigne have to say (and teach us) about *Alltagsgeschichte.*[31]

Montaigne's inability to escape the fractious politics of late sixteenth-century France forms the subject of Zachary Schiffman's essay. Schiffman begins by framing the problem of the intellectual *engagé* in terms of Thomas More's consideration of the issue as set forth by Hythlodaeus in book 1 of *Utopia.* More's pessimistic conclusion that intellectuals could only affirm the madness of kings and princes, not change them for the better, resonates with anyone who has read Montaigne.[32] Nevertheless, like More, Montaigne lived a public life with all the attendant responsibilities (and liabilities) that it entailed. During his career as a *parlementaire,* Montaigne—much like his good friend Étienne de la Boétie—behaved like an intellectual in politics, seeking a rational solution to the problem of religious strife through such works as his translation of Raymond Sebond's *Natural Theology,* which completed La Boétie's civil plan for church reform as outlined in his *Memoir on the Edict of January.*[33] Montaigne's disillusionment, especially acute after his failure to mend relations between Henri de Navarre and Henri de Guise after the Saint Bartholomew's Day massacre, led him to imitate Hythlodaeus's withdrawal from politics, culminating in his extended trip to Italy. Yet political duties dogged him, for during this trip the king "invited" him to become mayor of Bordeaux, a position he subsequently held for two terms, from 1582 to 1586. Schiffman examines Montaigne's mayoralty in light of the recent history of that institution and the political situation in Guyenne after 1578. Montaigne's initial success in maintaining his political aloofness broke down during his second tenure as mayor when he became involved in the ongoing dispute between Navarre and the maréchal de Matignon, who also acted as royal provincial governor, over Huguenot *places de sûreté* such as the strategically located town of Mont-de-Marsan. Montaigne's success in this delicate affair may even have contributed to Navarre's crucial victory at Coutras on October 20, 1587. His success also represented, Schiffman argues, a solution to the problem posed by Hythlodaeus, one that helped to establish a new role for the intellectual in politics and perhaps even a new model of political behavior.[34]

Just as Montaigne could not find permanent refuge in his *arrière-boutique,* so too did early French colonial forays to the New World fail to escape the fractious confessional politics back home. Most recent studies of the European explorations quite rightly concentrated on Europe's confrontation, if not collision, with the New World—its people, wildlife, and terrain—and the different reactions this experience fostered among the colonizing states.[35] But, as Silvia Shannon argues in her close look at the ill-fated 1555 mission to Brazil led by Nicolas Durand de Villegagnon, the patterns of conflict between Catholics and Protestants so typical of the Wars of Religion can be discerned in the earlier struggles attending the founding of Fort Coligny. Shannon carefully sorts out the secular motivations at play in the venture from the potent myths later spun by Calvinist writers about the colony's significance as a religious refuge. Jean de Léry's famous account of the Tupinamba Indians, extolled by Claude Lévi-Strauss as the anthropologist's breviary, construed the mission to the New World as an attempt by the Reformers—with the support of the crown—to spread the renewed Gospel message.[36] Likewise, Catholic apologists emphasized the confessional aspect by insisting that blame for the mission's failure rested squarely with the heretics. As a result, interpretations of the French colony in Brazil as a refuge have persistently—and wrongly—been viewed through the prism of the later Wars of Religion. Shannon revises these views by focusing on the colony's leader, Villegagnon, who is particularly vilified in the Protestant accounts. A staunch Catholic, Villegagnon nevertheless welcomed Calvin's Reformers to his colony, in large part because the confessional situation in France was still so fluid in the mid-1550s. In time, however, the Reformed ministers challenged his authority, sparking conflicts that ended in violence and recrimination. In his later recollection of events, written in the 1560s, Villegagnon retreated from this initial openness; like other participants in the venture to Fort Coligny, Villegagnon's problems of self-perception and ultimately identity became swept up in the struggle during the Wars of Religion to define the confessional underpinnings of what it meant to be French.

These factors worked to change provincial identity as well, as Mack Holt demonstrates in his essay on the "Frenchness" of sixteenth-century Burgundians.[37] The incorporation of the duchy of Burgundy into the kingdom of France in 1477, after the death of the last Valois duke of Burgundy, Charles the Bold, sharpened the perception of Burgundian identity and raised the possibility of particularism and exclusion if the duchy failed to accommodate itself to the sense of Frenchness that was growing in the sixteenth century. That the process of integration and assimilation went relatively smoothly was due largely to the fact that Burgundy was already culturally French. One of the principal components of French identity that appealed to Burgundians was the strong sense of the crown's ties to the Catholic church and the way the sacral French monarchy reinforced these bonds. When in the course of the sixteenth century the crown began to stray from this legacy of the *rex christianissimus* by legally recognizing the Huguenots in a series of edicts of pacification, Burgundian pressure to return to this common Catholic identity became intense.[38] The speeches and writings of three prominent Burgundians during the religious wars—Jean Bégat, a judge in the Parlement of Dijon; Pierre de St.-Julien, a cleric and historian from Chalon; and Étienne Bernard, an *avocat* in the Parlement of Dijon—make it clear that the legal and clerical elites of Burgundy considered Catholicism an integral part of French identity. By contrast, to be Protestant, they thought, was to be "foreign."[39] Holt shows that even though much of the rhetoric was couched in terms of provincial particularism, each man made it clear that he considered Catholicism a vital part of French identity. As Catholic identity itself evolved during the Wars of Religion, especially during the period of the Holy League, Burgundian support for the crown depended in great measure on how strongly the king was willing to defend this Gallican legacy. Only when the crown returned to its traditional moorings with the abjuration of Henri de Navarre in 1593—symbolized for the Burgundians when he publicly took communion on his entry into Dijon in 1595—were amicable relations between the crown and the province restored. The Burgundian experience suggests that French resistance to Protestantism during the sixteenth century sprang from the fact that for many, at all social levels, the French mentality began in a Catholic cast.

In my essay on Protestant reactions to the conversion of Henri de Navarre in 1593, I approach the confessional dynamics present in French identity at this time from the standpoint of French Calvinists. The difficulties French Calvinists faced in coming to grips with Henry IV's abjuration marked a crucial turning point in their quest for recognition. While the king's conversion was not the foregone conclusion that Catholics at the time and nationalist historians later construed it to be, it did become a more attractive option to Henry as his Protestant supporters among the nobility and in the towns struggled after 1584 to bring traditional royalism and religious dissent into harmony.[40] The polemic surrounding the royal conscience after 1584 presaged the arguments and concerns raised in the next century's religious wars and imposed peaces in France up to the revocation of the Edict of Nantes in 1685. At the heart of the Huguenots' tragic story was the impossibility of reconciling traditional royalism with religious dissent in a country where the popular majority and major institutions still remained committed to confessional uniformity—a situation that did not change with the Edict of Nantes. Rather than leading them to a New Jerusalem, the path of loyalism brought Huguenots steadily diminishing political options once their protector became heir presumptive to the French throne in 1584. Ultimately, French Calvinists suffered so much in the next century because they had tied their existence, as enshrined in the Edict of Nantes, not to principles of religious liberty and toleration (which they valued as little as the Catholics), but rather to the sufferance of the crown held by their *bon* Henri. In the 1580s and early 1590s, however, few French Calvinists dared to contemplate, let alone ask, whether Henri de Navarre and his successors could still be *bon* once they became Catholic.

The individual explorations of Frenchness assembled in this volume offer a wide variety of angles from which to analyze the historical genesis of French identity. Perennial problems relating to the interplay of politics, religion, gender, class, and order marked the experience of men and women from all walks of life during the early modern period as they struggled to situate themselves in relation to the established, but by no means stable, heritage of French identity that emerged from the late Middle Ages.[41] Historians who probe the different dimensions of this subject do well to recall the contingent nature of what lay ahead for France once the Bourbons came to power in 1589, and the fact that no matter how deeply ingrained the sense of Frenchness became in the centuries to come, the ineluctable patterns of conflict over French identity examined in this collection have remained essentially unresolved. Witness the explosive potential of nearly anything relating to Vichy, as in François Mitterrand's revelation of his short-lived collaboration and long-term friendships with some high officials of the regime.[42] Should the conflict over defining what makes the French unique ever be settled, the question of French identity would cease to be problematical for both the French and the historians who study them. Thankfully, however, just as the debate over the bicentennial of the French Revolution has recently highlighted, the French—and those who study them—still fail to agree on what has made them a nation.[43] *Vive la controverse!*

Notes

1. I thank Richard Golden for kindly assisting me with this introduction. With the end of the cold war and the publication of such books as Francis Fukuyama's *The End of History and the Last Man* (New York: Free Press, 1992), there has been a recrudescence of what might be called neo-Whiggery. For example, see J. H. Hexter, ed., *Parliament and Liberty from the Reign of Elizabeth to the English Civil War* (Stanford: Stanford University Press, 1992), which forms the first installment of the multivolume series auspiciously entitled *The Making of Modern Freedom.* In Germany, the recent controversy known as the *Historikerstreit* has reopened discussion of Germany's "special" path to modernity, particularly poignant since the reunification. For English-language discussions of this controversy, see Richard Evans, *In Hitler's Shadow: West German Historians and the Attempt to Escape the Nazi Past* (New York: Pantheon Books, 1989); Charles Maier, *The Unmasterable Past* (Cambridge: Harvard University Press, 1988); and Harold James, *A German Identity, 1770– 1990* (London: Routledge, 1989).

2. Pierre Nora, ed., *Les lieux de mémoire,* 3 vols. (Paris: Gallimard, 1984–). An excellent review essay on the subject is David Bell's "Recent Works on Early Modern French National Identity," *Journal of Modern History* 68 (1986): 84–113. Also well worth consulting are two books that appeared twenty years ago, which

consider the topic, respectively, in terms of the impact of modern industrialism and by reference to political culture and state building: Eugen Weber, *Peasants into Frenchman: The Modernization of Rural France, 1870–1914* (Stanford: Stanford University Press, 1976); and Orest Ranum, ed., *National Consciousness, History, and Political Culture in Early Modern Europe* (Baltimore: Johns Hopkins University Press, 1975).

3. Among Fernand Braudel's many works, see in particular *L'identité de France*, 2 vols. (Paris: Arthaud, Flammarion, 1986); English edition: *The Identity of France*, trans. Siân Reynolds, 2 vols. (New York: Harper & Row, 1988–90), vol. 1, *History and Environment*, vol. 2, *People and Production.*

4. Charles Tilly, *The Contentious French* (Cambridge: Harvard University Press, 1986). On the resurgence—and perhaps even reinvention—of regional identities and conflicts over "Frenchness" sparked by modern industrialization and communications, see Willaim Brustein, *The Social Origins of Political Regionalism in France, 1849–1981* (Berkeley: University of California Press, 1988); and Anne-Marie Thiesse, *Écrire la France: Le mouvement littéraire régionaliste de la langue française* (Paris: Presses Universitaires de France, 1991).

5. Recent collections exploring different dimensions of French identity in the early modern era include *Culture and Identity in Early Modern France (1500–1800): Essays in Honor of Natalie Zemon Davis,* ed. Barbara B. Diefendorf and Carla Hesse (Ann Arbor: University of Michigan Press, 1993); *Society and Institutions in Early Modern France,* ed. Mack Holt (Athens: University of Georgia Press, 1991); and *Politics, Ideology, and the Law in Early Modern Europe: Essays in Honor of J. H. M. Salmon,* ed. Adrianna Bakos (Rochester: University of Rochester Press, 1994).

6. See Nancy L. Roelker, *Queen of Navarre, Jeanne d'Albret, 1528–1572* (Cambridge: Harvard University Press, 1968); Roelker, *One King, One Faith: The Parlement of Paris during the Sixteenth Century* (Berkeley: University of California Press, 1996); and, as editor and translator, Roelker, *The Paris of Henry of Navarre as seen by Pierre de l'Estoile: Selections from His Mémoires-Journaux* (Cambridge: Harvard University Press, 1958).

7. For another recent analysis of the romantic encounter with the past, in this case medieval architecture, see Tina Bizzarro Waldeier, *Romanesque Architectural Criticism, a Prehistory* (Cambridge: Cambridge University Press, 1992). On the contrast between Enlightenment and romantic thought, see Nader Saiedi, *The Birth of Social Theory and Social Thought in the Enlightenment and Romanticism* (Lanham, Md.: University Press of America, 1993).

8. These questions are explored further in Laurence Lockridge, *The Ethics of Romanticism* (Cambridge: Cambridge University Press, 1989); and Steven E. Alford, *Irony and Logic in the Romantic Imagination* (New York: Peter Lang, 1984), which concentrates on Friedrich von Schlegel and William Blake.

9. The Neoceremonialist school can be traced back to the seminal work by Ernst Kantorowicz, *The King's Two Bodies: A Study in Mediaeval Political Theology* (Princeton: Princeton University Press, 1957). Its principal exponents today include

Ralph Giesey, author of *The Royal Funeral Ceremony in Renaissance France* (Geneva: Droz, 1960) and *Cérémonial et puissance souveraine: France, XVe–XVIII siècles* (Paris: Armand Colin, 1987); Richard Jackson, who wrote Vive le Roi! *A History of the French Coronation Ceremony from Charles V to Charles X* (Chapel Hill: University of North Carolina Press, 1984); and Sarah Hanley, author of *The Lit de Justice of the Kings of France: Constitutional Ideology in Legend, Ritual, and Discourse* (Princeton: Princeton University Press, 1983). For a recent critique of Hanley's book, see Elizabeth A. R. Brown and Richard C. Famiglietti, *The* Lit de Justice: *Semantics, Ceremonial and the Parlement of Paris, 1300–1600* (Simaringen: Jan Thorbecke Verlag, 1994). For a general critique of the neoceremonialists, see Alain Boureau, *Le simple corps du roi: L'impossible sacralité des souverains français, XVe–XVIIIe* (Paris: Armand Colin, 1989).

10. Henry Mechoulan, ed., *L'état baroque: Regards sur la pensée politique de la France du premier XVIIe siècle* (Paris: J. Vrin, 1985).

11. For contrasting approaches to the study of Renaissance law, see Donald R. Kelley, *Foundations of Modern Scholarship: Language, Law, and History in the French Renaissance* (New York: Columbia University Press, 1970); and Nancy Struever, *The Language of History in the Renaissance: Rhetoric and Historical Consciousness in Florentine Humanism* (Princeton: Princeton University Press, 1970).

12. See the recent collection of essays in *Politics, Gender, and Genre: The Political Thought of Christine de Pizan,* ed. Margaret Brabant (Boulder: Westview Press, 1992).

13. On the evolving place of women in early modern French society, sometimes referred to as the *querelle des femmes,* see Carolyn Lougee, Le paradis des femmes: *Woman, Salons, and Social Stratification in Seventeenth-Century France* (Princeton: Princeton University Press, 1976); and, more recently on women in the eighteenth century, Dena Goodman, *The Republic of Letters: A Cultural History of the French Enlightenment* (Ithaca: Cornell University Press, 1994).

14. Descimon's earlier works on the robed nobility and Parisian society in general during the sixteenth century include *Qui étaient les Seize? Mythes et réalités de la Ligue parisienne, 1585–1594* (Paris: Klincksieck, 1984) and, with Elie Barnavi, *La Sainte Ligue, le juge, et la potence* (Paris: Hachette, 1985).

15. On the evolving practice of the sale of office, the best book to consult is still Roland Mousnier, *La venalité des offices sous Henri IV et Louis XIII,* 2d ed. (Paris: Presses Universitaires de France, 1970).

16. On this crucial dynastic shift, see Keith Cameron, ed., *From Valois to Bourbon: Dynasty, State, and Society in Early Modern France* (Exeter: University of Exeter Press, 1989).

17. Images of women in war abound in J. R. Hale, *Artists and Warfare in Renaissance Europe* (New Haven: Yale University Press, 1990).

18. These themes will be more fully explored in Hanley's *State Building in Early Modern France: Law, Litigation, and Local Knowledge* (Princeton: Princeton University Press, forthcoming).

19. Nancy L. Roelker, "The Appeal of Calvinism to French Noblewomen in the Sixteenth Century," *Journal of Interdisciplinary History* 2 (1972): 391–418.

20. See, for example, Louis Maimbourg, *The History of the League,* trans. John Dryden (London, 1684); and Louis Anqueil, *L'Esprit de la Ligue ou, Histoire des troubles en France pendant le XVIe et XVIIe siècles,* 5th ed., 3 vols. (Paris, 1808). On the Guise family, see Jean-Marie Constant, *Les Guise* (Paris: Gallimard, 1984).

21. Orest Ranum discusses the ensuing "generation of saints" in *Paris in the Age of Absolutism: An Essay* (New York: John Wiley & Sons, 1968).

22. This approach characterizes Crouzet's two major works, *Les Guerriers de Dieu: La violence au temps des troubles de religion ver 1525–vers 1610,* 2 vols. (Paris: Seyssel, 1990), and *La Nuit de la Saint-Barthélemy: Un rêve perdu de la Renaissance* (Paris: Fayard, 1994). On possession and exorcism in France at the time, see D. P. Walker, *Unclean Spirits: Possession and Exorcism in France and England in the Late Sixteenth and Early Seventeenth Centuries* (Philadelphia: University of Pennsylvania Press, 1981).

23. For an overview of belief in witches and the judicial procedures used against suspected witches, see *Teufelsglaube und Hexenprozesse,* ed. Georg Schwaiger (Munich: C. H. Beck, 1988). For France, see in particular Robert Mandrou, *Magistrats et sorciers en France au XVIIe siècle: Une analyse de psychologie historique* (Paris: Seuil, 1980); and Robin Briggs, *Communities of Belief: Cultural and Social Tension in Early Modern France* (Oxford: Clarendon Press, 1989).

24. On the evolving status and meaning of citizenship, see Charlotte Wells, *Law and Citizenship in Early Modern France* (Baltimore: Johns Hopkins University Press, 1995).

25. Borderlands have been treated recently by Peter Sahlins in *Boundaries: The Making of France and Spain in the Pyrenees* (Berkeley: University of California Press, 1989).

26. On infanticide in the Anglo-Saxon world at the time, see Peter C. Hoffer and N. E. H. Hull, *Murdering Mothers: Infanticide in England and New England, 1558–1803* (New York: New York University Press, 1981).

27. For a recent study of criminality in sixteenth- and seventeenth-century rural France, see Malcolm Greenshields, *An Economy of Violence in Early Modern France: Crime and Justice in the Haute Auvergne, 1587–1684* (University Park: Pennsylvania State University Press, 1994). Recent works on the emancipation of Jews and Protestants in eighteenth-century France include Simon Schwarzfuchs, *Napoleon, the Jews, and the Sanhedrin* (Boston: Routledge & Kegan Paul, 1979); and Geoffrey Adams, *The Huguenots and French Opinion, 1685–1787: The Enlightened Debate on Toleration* (Waterloo, Ont.: Wilfrid Laurier University Press, 1991).

28. On Montaigne's relationship with contemporary events, see Géralde Nakam, *Les Essais de Montaigne: Miroir et procès de leur temps, témoignage historique et création littéraire* (Paris: Nizet, 1984). On the ethical implications of political engagement and detachment in the Renaissance, see Nancy Struever, *Theory as Practice: Ethical Inquiry in the Renaissance* (Chicago: University of Chicago Press, 1992).

29. Another thinker at the time also involved in critically leveling such differ-

ences was Peter Ramus, who perished in the 1572 Saint Bartholomew's Day massacre in Paris. On his thought and work, see Kees Meerhoff, *Rhétorique et poétique au XVIe siècle en France* (Leiden: E. J. Brill, 1986).

30. Mikhail Bahktin, *Rabelais and His World,* trans. Hélène Iswolsky (Bloomington: Indiana University Press, 1984). On Charles Taylor, see in particular his *The Ethics of Authenticity* (Cambridge: Harvard University Press, 1991) and *Philosophical Arguments* (Cambridge: Harvard University Press, 1995).

31. See Alf Lüdtke, *The History of Everyday Life: Reconstructing Historical Experience and Ways of Life,* trans. William Temple (Princeton: Princeton University Press, 1995).

32. Baldesare Castiglione likens the courtier serving an evil prince to a "caged bird" (p. 130). See in particular book 4 of *The Book of the Courtier,* trans. George Bull, 6th ed. (New York: Penguin Books, 1983).

33. Étienne de la Boétie, *Mémoire sur la pacification des troubles,* ed. Malcolm Smith (Geneva: Droz, 1983). A translation of his more famous "De la servitude volontaire" is available in *The Politics of Obedience: The Discourse of Voluntary Servitude,* trans. Harry Kurz, intro. Murray N. Rothbard (New York: Free Life Editions, 1975).

34. On the continuing development of the role of the intellectual *engagé* in early modern France, see Orest Ranum, *Artisans of Glory: Writers and Historical Thought in Seventeenth-Century France* (Chapel Hill: University of North Carolina Press, 1980).

35. On the French encounter with the New World, see Frank Lestringant, *L'atelier du cosmographe* (Paris: Albin Michel, 1991); English translation: *Mapping the Renaissance World: The Geographical Imagination in the Age of Discovery,* trans. David Fausett (Berkeley: University of California Press, 1994). Among the best treatments on the wider impact of the European discoveries is the classic study by Alfred W. Crosby, *The Columbian Exchange: Biological and Cultural Consequences of 1492* (Westport, Conn.: Greenwood, 1972).

36. Claude Lévi-Strauss, *Triste tropiques* (Paris: Plon, 1955), pp. 2–3.

37. Among the fine regional studies in English that have appeared over the past decade or so are William Beik, *Absolutism and Society in Seventeenth-Century France: State Power and Provincial Aristocracy in Languedoc* (Cambridge: Cambridge University Press, 1985); Daniel Hickey, *The Coming of French Absolutism: The Struggle for Tax Reform in the Province of Dauphiné, 1540–1640* (Toronto: University of Toronto Press, 1986); and David Potter, *War and Government in the French Provinces: Picardy, 1470–1560* (Cambridge: Cambridge University Press, 1993).

38. Joseph R. Strayer, "France: The Holy Land, the Chosen People, and the Most Christian King," in *Action and Conviction in Early Modern Europe: Essays in Memory of E. H. Harbison,* ed. Theodore Rabb and Jerrold E. Seigel (Princeton: Princeton University Press, 1969), pp. 3–16.

39. On the continuing polemical conflict between the confessions over the next century, see Bernard Dompnier, ed., *La controverse religieuse,* 2 vols. (Montpellier: Université de Montpellier, 1980).

40. For a contrary view of the relationship between Henry IV's faith and his

politics, see Ronald S. Love, "The Religion of Henry IV: Faith, Politics and War, 1553–1593" (Ph.D. diss., University of Southern California, 1986).

41. See Colette Beaune, *Naissance de la nation de France* (Paris: Gallimard, 1985); English translation: *The Birth of an Ideology: Myths and Symbols in Late-Medieval France,* trans. Susan Rose Huson, intro. Frederic L. Cheyette (Berkeley: University of California Press, 1991).

42. It took Robert O. Paxson, in his pathbreaking book *Vichy France: Old Guard and New Order, 1940–1944* (New York: Knopf, 1972), to break nearly thirty years of silence on these dark years. The trials of Klaus Barbie and, more recently, Paul Touvier have kept alive the debate over collaboration and collective guilt. For a recent consideration of this subject, see the essays in *Le régime de Vichy et les Français,* ed. Jean-Pierre Azema and François Bedarida (Paris: Fayard, 1992). Then there was the recent revelation in Pierre Péan's *Une jeunesse française: François Mitterrand, 1934–1947* (Paris: Fayard, 1994) of not only François Mitterrand's brief dalliance with the Pétainists, but his continuing friendship with high-ranking officials of the Vichy regime into the 1980s.

43. See Steven L. Kaplan, *Adieu 89,* trans. André Charpentier and Rémy Lambrechts (Paris: Fayard, 1993). Although Kaplan deplores the infighting among French intellectuals and politicians over the legacy of the Revolution, he cannot resist occasionally entering the fray himself, especially when it concerns the revisionary opinions of François Furet.

I

Ideologies and

Institutions

J. H. M. Salmon

The French Romantics and the Renaissance

The philosophic historians of the Enlightenment—Voltaire, Robertson, and Gibbon—judged the past by the civilized standards of the eighteenth century and found the medieval centuries wanting. They clarified their distaste for barbarism and superstition by defining an end to medievalism and a beginning for modern times, a beginning associated with the printing press, the fall of Constantinople, the discovery of America, and the French invasion of Italy, together with less tangible developments in classical humanism, art, and science. It seems logical that romanticism, reacting against the Enlightenment and the more regulated classicism it had inherited, should rehabilitate the Middle Ages, exalting the chivalric ethos, heroic poetry, crusading fervor, Catholic piety, and corporate life. It also seems to follow that romanticism should disparage a Renaissance that apparently negated these concepts. Such indeed was the legacy of Chateaubriand, who viewed the French sixteenth-century nobility as corrupted by Italian manners and thought that the feuds of the Guise and the Châtillon repeated those of the Pazzi and the Medici.[1] Such also was the trend of the German contribution to French romanticism, with its suggestion that the vigor and emotion of the north, purified by Christianity, were superior to the tired rationalism of the classical south. Friedrich Schlegel, for instance, discerned a subversive paganism in Italian art from the time of Raphael and deplored the pernicious effects of the movement to imitate the classics stimulated by Petrarch.[2]

Some liberals, even less inclined than Chateaubriand to hold a brief for the Renaissance, disagreed with his taste for chivalry and Catholicism, and differed even more emphatically with his politics. Sismondi, Thierry, and Mignet discerned the birth of political liberty in the medieval commune and lamented its decay in the early modern period. While declaring chivalry to have existed only in fiction, Sismondi deplored the revival of the classics, criticized William Roscoe's idealization of the Medici, and saw the Renaissance as the triumph of despotism.[3] In their younger days Thierry and Mignet—the one with an abiding sympathy for *les vaincus,* the other with a seeming impartiality sprung from the iron laws of social revolution—held the medieval French monarchy to be the ally of the communes against an oppressive feudal aristocracy. Hence in their eyes the development of absolutism in early modern times constituted a betrayal, resulting in the destruction of both monarchy and nobility in the Revolution. In political terms, at least, liberals of this kind, and also of the more conservative variety represented by Guizot, had no wish to dwell on Renaissance France. Guizot's 1828 lectures collected in *The History of Civilization in Europe* brush quickly over the standard generalizations about the beginning of modern times. While he admitted that the Renaissance constituted a revolution in ideas, he condemned its moral climate as "soft, idle and licentious," and marveled at "the mixture of sybaritism and intellectual development, of enervated morality and boldness of mind."[4] He chose to end his next course of lectures at the Collège de France in the fourteenth century, although it was entitled *The History of Civilization in France since the Fall of the Roman Empire.* Moreover, he invited his audience to acknowledge the bias against the medieval centuries in Voltaire's *Essai sur les moeurs:* "You will see that Voltaire incessantly applied himself to the task of extracting all that is gross, absurd, odious and calamitous in this epoch."[5] In his later general history of France, Guizot insisted on the superiority of the Middle Ages to the Renaissance in originality, brilliance, and ultimate influence, and inserted in the section on the Renaissance a long digression on the achievement of medieval literature and philosophy, including a six-page quotation from the *Chanson de Roland.*[6] To Guizot's fellow doctrinaire, Barante, who in terms of Chateaubriand's classification of the new history was the leader of the "narrative" school (just as Guizot led the "philosophical" one), the revival of classical learning resulted in an age of historical pedantry.[7]

This is the negative side of the question. There were abundant reasons for the romantics to ignore, decry, or lack sympathy with the Renaissance. Yet there are two other kinds of romantics who possessed initially, or later developed, a strong aversion for medievalism and clerical Catholicism and found a positive focus in the Renaissance. The first are the ironic romantics, who concentrated either on sixteenth-century Italy (Stendhal and Musset) or on sixteenth-century France (Nodier, Mérimée, and the young Sainte-Beuve); the second are the two symbolists Michelet and Quinet, the former somewhat overrated in this context, the latter unduly neglected. There was also, of course, a great deal of romantic writing on the France of the religious wars, but much of it was in the vein of adventure and the macabre, and had little to do with the concept of the Renaissance. The ideas concerning the French Renaissance to be considered here have been limited to Sainte-Beuve's study of sixteenth-century French literature and the controversy concerning the role of Francis I.

Sainte-Beuve's youthful work was begun at the time he entered the charmed circle of Victor Hugo. In literary terms he saw the sixteenth century as inheriting the common touch of mocking Gaulois tradition from the *fabliaux,* the *sotties,* and from François Villon. His work experienced an infusion of classical ideas through Guillaume Budé, Joachim du Bellay, and Jean Dorat, culminating in the school of Ronsard. In an argument reminiscent of Du Bellay himself, Sainte-Beuve claimed that the French had imitated the Romans as the Romans had the Greeks, digesting and converting what was best to their own context. Yet the triumph of the Pléiade scarcely outlived the century, for Malherbe tamed the revolutionary consequences of blending classicism with a popular native tradition by eliminating the latter. There followed a regime of literary pedantry and *politesse courtisane* institutionalized by Richelieu and completed by the sterile regulation of the arts under Louis XIV.[8]

As Sainte-Beuve put it, the French Renaissance superseded a world of barons, monks, and serfs, a world in which liberty was denied and poetry depended on the gallant deeds and broken lances of the elite, a world symbolized by crusades and pilgrimages to Calvary, a Catholic world in which cathedrals were a constant reminder of the insignificance of man.[9] Unfortunately the Renaissance had proved short and abortive, and was succeeded by "a monarchy that was brilliant, ephemeral, artificial and superficial, lacking any real ties with either the past or the future of France."[10] Sainte-Beuve compared the period between the Holy League and the Revolution to a capricious interval between the acts of a drama, bearing no relation to the action of the play. In another image he likened it to an elegant and fragile bridge flung over an abyss, carpeted with gold and silk and ornamented with statues "des beaux génies du grand siècle." His own age was resurrecting the inspiration of Ronsard in the school of Hugo. As the Italians had returned to Dante and the English to Shakespeare, so the French romantics were breaking out of the mold established in the time between Malherbe and Boileau, and going back to Du Bellay, Mlle Gournay, d'Aubigné, and Regnier, uniting the free Gaulois tradition with the Renaissance in an audacious and insouciant style without rules and scruples.[11]

This attempt to associate romanticism with the Renaissance did not pass unheeded in the *cénacles*. Even before it was published in 1828 with a selection of Ronsard's poetry, the guests at Nodier's entertainments in the Arsenal had already signed their names in the copy of a more venerable edition that reposed there. Echoes may be heard in a snatch of salon conversation inserted in Balzac's *La peau de chagrin:* "I should hope you haven't adopted the barbarous language of this new school that thinks it has done marvels by resurrecting Ronsard."[12] The speaker on this occasion presumably sided with two other works on sixteenth-century French literature jointly awarded the prize offered by the Académie Française in 1826, for which Sainte-Beuve had originally intended to compete.[13] Despite differences between their arguments, neither Philarète Chasles nor Saint-Marc Girardin had disappointed the intentions of the Académie. The former observed that Italy had provided *le premier éveil* and argued that Renaissance France was so corrupt in its manners and so gross in its literary traditions that it was necessary for Malherbe to impose a restraining hand and point the way to true classicism. Girardin, on the other hand, saw the French Renaissance as a preparation for the age of Corneille and Racine, and he remarked also that a new national spirit in the sixteenth century had enabled despotism to destroy the outdated feudal and bourgeois liberties of the Middle Ages. From the time of Francis I, politics and literature had become closely associated, and the outcome, he believed, was the foundation of a new liberty in literature.[14]

So paradoxical a conclusion may be associated with the contemporary debate about the reputation of Francis I, despot and *roi chevalier,* patron of the arts and importer of the Italian Renaissance. He received a far less favored place in Sainte-Beuve's *Tableau* than did that universal hero of the time, Henry IV. He was mentioned briefly in terms of the poetry that honored his accession in 1515 and the patronage he had accorded Clément Marot, and that was all.[15] To the many who were familiar with such popular legends as Bayard's knighting of the king after Marignano, and, equally, to the few who knew the details of his familiarity with the erudite Budé, this must have seemed a deliberate slight. Charles Lacretelle, whose coldly academic prose was in marked contrast to the chivalric effusions of such writers as Mme de Genlis and Mme Amable Tastu, associated the two strands when he stated that *le roi chevalier* had refined chivalry by reconciling it with learning. According to Lacretelle, the new chivalry had been "l'orgueil et le bonheur de la nation."[16] This sentiment was so widely held that even Stendhal, no friend to kings, suggested in the first part of *Racine et Shakespeare*

(1823) that the reign "du noble François 1er" would make a suitable subject for patriotic national drama.[17] A year later, reviewing the remarkable development of the new French historiography for the English press, Stendhal favorably compared the refinement of language and manners at the court of Francis I with the repressive pomp of Versailles under Louis XIV.[18] The honor of *le roi chevalier* obliged the public to overlook the scandals of his court. Paul Lacroix, the prolific historical popularizer, inserted a scene in his romance *Les deux fous,* featuring Francis I and Triboulet, in which the king reproves ribald talk about women.[19]

The best known exposure of *le roi chevalier* is, of course, *Le roi s'amuse* (1832), which Victor Hugo derived from Lacroix, but reversing the roles to make the king a monster of callous lechery. The play provoked a ban by the July monarchy no less firm than that which Hugo had experienced under Charles X, when *Marion de Lorme* presented Louis XIII in a negative light. An earlier and even more forthright denigration of Francis I came from the pen of Pierre-Louis Roederer, whose chequered career included the escorting of the royal family to the Legislative Assembly on the tenth of August, the patronage of Napoleon, a retreat from politics to history and literature under the Restoration, and a return to the House of Peers under Louis-Philippe. As a historian, Roederer tried to elevate Louis XII to the role of father of constitutionalism and simultaneously to demote his licentious successor to corrupter of the monarchy: "The oppression of this voluptuous—indeed, dissolute and debauched prince—knew no restraint. His iniquity was boundless, his cruelty frightful. He was not content merely to exercise tyranny: he wanted to institutionalize it and transmit it to his successors by a court system intended as its permanent instrument. His oppression of liberties was not, perhaps, the most deplorable calamity he made the nation suffer. He distorted and depraved its morals, and made their debasement incurable through this same court system, which he designed to be perpetually corrupt and perpetually corrupting."[20]

The relevance of this debate lies in the conjunction of cultivated immoralism and patronage of literature and the arts. Musset hinted at the problem in an unfinished play of 1830, *Les derniers moments de François 1er,* in which he combined all elements in the debate by depicting the king dying of venereal disease while he recalls past battles and listens to the singing of joyous songs. Musset made it a little more precise in *André del Sarto,* in which the painter loses his artistic integrity by accepting a pension from Francis I, and he returned to the theme in *Lorenzaccio.*[21] In the context of the Italian Renaissance, the problem appears in rather different guise in Stendhal, and then again, this time in terms of class war and moral indignation, in Quinet's *Révolutions d'Italie.*

Begun under Napoleon, Stendhal's *Histoire de la peinture en Italie* is in no sense as scholarly a book as the multivolume works on the history and literature of Italy conceived or completed in that period by Sismondi and Ginguené.[22] He tried to explain Renaissance art by the history and character of the Italian people, but his history, like that avowed by his friend Mérimée, was of the anecdotal kind.[23] The part of the book that he rushed into print in 1817 (a large proportion remained unpublished until 1932) is similar in composition to his contemporary guidebook *Rome, Naples et Florence en 1817.* It was hastily put together and includes half-confessed passages of plagiarism.[24] The introduction is a paraphrase of Robertson's preface to *Charles V,* sprinkled with aphorisms redolent of Gibbon ("Vinrent les barbares, ensuite les papes").[25] Nevertheless, *Histoire de la peinture* contains a strong, if captious, thesis. It is the first expression of "Beylism," the dynamic and amoral pursuit of power or success for its own sake, here applied to the artists and despots of late fifteenth- and early sixteenth-century Italy.

Stendhal's view of the Renaissance contains various dissonances that become more comprehensible in the light of his background and personality. The intensity of his emotions is evident from his outbursts in the salon of his friend Delécluze, his professed atheism, his denunciation of Mme de Staël and the old aristocracy in the margins of his copy of her *Considérations sur la Révolution française,* and his vilification of her acolyte Wilhelm Schlegel—indeed of the entire clan of the German Romantics. He was both a passionate Jacobin and an idolater of Napoleon. It has been said that Julien Sorel in *Le Rouge et le Noir* is a self-portrait of Stendhal as he really was, and Fabrice del Dongo in *La Chartreuse de Parme* of Stendhal as he would have liked to have been.[26] A taste for order, represented incongruously by both his Bonapartism and his defense of Louis XVIII's charter, was mingled with his urge to dominate regardless of the issue at stake, as seen in his altercations with Victor Cousin. His spiritual home was Italy, and his romanticism was derived from his friends and acquaintances among the Italian romantics, who included Manzoni, Monti, and Pellico. The two parts of *Racine et Shakespeare* revamped the ideas that Manzoni had already published, although it may have been Claude Fauriel, the romance philologist, who suggested them to

Manzoni in the first place. Fauriel and Stendhal were older than the romantic generation, and both were indebted to the ideologues under Napoleon's regime. Both associated themselves with the literature of the south, but they chose to differ in their attitudes to Mme de Staël. Whereas Fauriel was primarily a medievalist, Stendhal identified himself with the Renaissance.

Stendhal had as much to say about the tyrants as he had about the painters of the Italian Renaissance, and it is the former who fixed the character of an age for which he chose Cesare Borgia as the typical representative. Spirit and superstition, atheism and assassination, poison, passion, and pride were declared by Stendhal to be the stock-in-trade of his heroes.[27] He had no respect for popes in general, but two in the period attracted his admiration: Alexander VI as "the only man, with the exception of Cesare Borgia, who united a vast genius to the most dissolute morals and the blackest of vices," and Julius II as "inspired by an insatiable thirst for glory, undeviating in his plans and indefatigable in executing them, magnanimous, imperious, greedy to dominate—a great soul born to shatter the conventions both of old age and of the Holy See."[28] He praised those who set aside Christian morality, and he blamed religion for setting art on a false trail, likening it, in his bitterest imagery, to a diseased mother who, in feeding her children, infected them with an incurable malady.[29]

To make art the plaything of changes in the political and religious climate of the times suggests the kind of relativism associated with all historical explanation of the aesthetic. This was certainly not a pose that Stendhal maintained consistently. In one passage he sneered at Italian painting before the end of the thirteenth century by calling it inferior to the crude colored prints sold at modern country fairs for peasants to kneel on in church.[30] In another place, where he suggested that the highest perfection in art conveyed something nature did not provide, he criticized the painters of the fifteenth century as so spellbound by natural beauty that they were no more than faithful mirrors.[31] He admired Da Vinci, Michelangelo, and Raphael almost unreservedly. He listed them beside his models of men of power as unparalleled in their possession of "de l'esprit et de l'énergie," yet somehow lacking "la science des idées" required to attain the sublime.[32] Machiavelli, whose name appears beside the Borgias and the artists in this context, did not fulfill Stendhal's need either, but the author of *The Prince* did not come to the general attention of the romantics until the subsequent decade.[33] To a point Stendhal was anticipating Burckhardt's chapter on the state as a work of art, for he clearly thought that both statesman and artist in this time were men not only of passion and impulse, but also of practical calculation.

A year after Stendhal published his history of Italian painting, Victor Cousin was lecturing on the unity of truth, beauty, and morality at the Sorbonne.[34] Clearly Stendhal preferred to explain Renaissance art by its amoral and relativist association with high politics rather than in terms of the sublime. In this his text often bore a close resemblance to Voltaire's discussion of the Renaissance in *Essai sur les moeurs.* His attitude to Voltaire was not unlike his view of Mme de Staël, for while he declaimed against him vigorously he often borrowed his facts and ideas, sometimes twisting them in the process. Voltaire dwelt on the crimes and artifices of Alexander VI and Cesare Borgia, who, he said, had employed as much skill to subdue the towns of the Romagna as had Alexander the Great, Genghis Khan, and other conquerors in subduing vast areas of the world;[35] Stendhal referred to Cesare Borgia in similar terms as some kind of Alexander or Genghis *in parvo.*[36] Voltaire praised the patronage of the Medici and compared fifteenth-century Florence with the court of Louis XIV, and Stendhal observed that Europe still celebrated "la magnificence désintéressée et les vues libérales des premiers Médicis."[37] However, Stendhal also argued that large absolutist monarchies inhibited art, whereas the regime of petty Renaissance despots had encouraged it. Seeing the Renaissance as a unique age, he was more careful in his analogies than the historians of the eighteenth century, and he derided the depiction by Robertson and Roscoe of Cosimo de' Medici as a kind of early George Washington.[38] Stendhal believed that the greatest art arose at a time of insecurity when the ruler's dynamic urge to achieve much in a brief period was communicated to those he protected. Thus, while Stendhal praised the ability of Lorenzo, Cosimo's grandson, to maintain peace and stability and to patronize both painters and scholars, he noted that it was not in Lorenzo's time, but rather in the Italian wars of the succeeding age that high art flourished "au milieu des batailles et des changements du gouvernement."[39] This, too, resembles a passage from Voltaire: "And almost everything [in the glory of Italian art] was carried to perfection while the armies of Charles V were sacking Rome, while Barbarossa was ravaging the coasts, and while the dissensions of princes and republics troubled the interior of the country."[40]

The unpublished part of *Histoire de la peinture* develops further views of Italian history and the place of art within it. Taking his facts from Sismondi while reversing the latter's interpretation, Stendhal described the struggles of the city republics of the twelfth and thirteenth centuries as conflicts in which liberty was never secure, and fear and suspicion were always present. The Italian character formed in this period was unruly, cruel, and vengeful. In later ages the object of the rulers was to encourage political indifference by turning emulation toward the beaux-arts, and pacifying violence by means of "la volupté."[41] Art had become the opium of the people. In the macabre stories of sixteenth-century Italy later known as *Chroniques ita-liennes,* written in the late 1830s, Stendhal returned to his theory of art and violence. The introduction to his *Abbesse de Castro* describes "the deep hatred and unending distrust that gave so much spirit and courage to the Italians of the sixteenth century, and so much genius to their artists."[42] In Italy passion had not, as in France, been transmuted into gallantry and thereby been stifled. The rich and powerful oppressors, of whom the Medici had been the least warlike but the most hypocritical, had tried to seduce "le bas peuple" with the arts. The Medici and their like had covered their deceits with official histories glorifying their regimes. None of the authors of these works could be trusted, least of all Guicciardini, who had sold himself to the rulers of Florence. In the eighteenth century, Stendhal claimed, the histories derived from such suspect sources by Robertson and Roscoe repeated the lies of the apologists for despotism.[43] Stendhal's Jacobin sympathies had been translated wholesale to the Renaissance. His final step was to associate them with the romantic vogue for banditry. Bandits, the true republicans, were heroes of the people who had fled to the woods to oppose tyrants.

After the triumph on the stage of his own bandit, *Hernani,* Victor Hugo went on to set other melodramatic plays in the Renaissance, including *Le roi s'amuse* (1832), *Lucrèce Borgia* (1833), and *Angelo, tyran de Padoue* (1835). The prefaces to the two latter plays assert that the audience will find them instructive historically. They certainly contain the trappings Stendhal had thought typical of the Renaissance, but neither in event nor in background do they reflect historical truth. A critic of *Le roi s'amuse* remarked that "M. Hugo's play has nothing to do with history, and springs entirely from his unfettered fantasy."[44] Like Hugo's *Cromwell,* Musset's *André del Sarto* (1833) and *Lorenzaccio* (1834) were not written to be performed, despite their dramatic qualities, and the events they describe are reasonably close to the sixteenth-century sources on which they were based. *André del Sarto* elaborates an incident from Vasari's life of the artist, while *Lorenzaccio* deals with the 1537 assassination of Alessandro de' Medici by his distant cousin, Lorenzo (Lorenzaccio), following closely the contemporary account by Benedetto Varchi, although telescoping into a few days events that were in reality spread over several years. In *Lorenzaccio* Musset inserted many extraneous historical details from Varchi, and he also consulted Cellini, Vasari, and Machiavelli in order to convey the artistic and political climate of the age.[45] This was, indeed, a deliberate attempt at what romantic historians called *couleur locale,* in the serious sense of writing history "as it really was," and not in the pejorative sense used later by Musset in his satirical *Lettres de Dupuis et Cotonet.* In the play itself Musset put into the mouth of Lorenzaccio his belief that his method could convey truths that ordinary history could not: "It is not men themselves that I distrust; it is the books and the historians who err by showing them differently from the way they really were."[46] *Lorenzaccio* stands halfway between romantic drama and the genre of *scènes historiques* practiced by Mérimée, Vitet, and Roederer, aimed at presenting genuine history by imagined dialogue.

The plot of *André del Sarto* is a strange anticipation of the outcome of Musset's affair with George Sand, for the play recounts the artist's betrayal by his mistress and his disciple. Sand was herself an enthusiast for the Italian Renaissance, and in the early stages of her association with Musset she gave him the draft of six scenes she had written on the theme of *Lorenzaccio.* She has received little credit in the making of the play Musset wrote just before their ill-fated journey to Italy in December 1833, yet it is she who provided the essential theme of the character of the assassin and the reasons for his deed.[47] Lorenzaccio, whom Musset invested with aspects of his own character, has won the confidence of his intended victim by becoming the master of the duke's debauches, only to discover a basic corruption in himself that inhibits action, and a wider decadence in society that suggests the futility of his purpose. His own plot marches in parallel with two others—that of Piero Strozzi to restore the republican regime, and that of papal envoy Cardinal Cibo to impose the tyranny of Rome. In the outcome, no one within the city save a few students is prepared to act after the death of the duke, and the new despot, Cosimo de' Medici, takes over. Musset depicted the consequences of tyranny on all strata of society, and also suggested a parallel with the July revolution, when the popular forces were deprived of the fruits of victory and a new bourgeois oligarchy acquired power.

Not only did Musset re-create Stendhal's Renaissance of passion, bloodshed, and conspiracy, he also raised the problem that haunted Stendhal in his history of Italian painting: the link between the tyrant and the artist. Musset had intended to put Cellini himself on stage, but in his final draft he substituted an imaginary pupil of Raphael and admirer of Michelangelo, Tebaldeo Freccia. Freccia declares that the pictures of his masters inspire "a singular ectasy . . . I believe to see there the glory of the artist." His faith is "the holy religion of painting." His vocation is to "realize dreams, that's the life of a painter." When Lorenzaccio asks him to enter his service, he replies: "I belong to no one; when thought seeks to be free, the body must be so as well." Questioned further as to why he should stay in a city where daily assassination occurs at the caprice of the ruler, he answers: "I love my mother, Florence." Finally, he responds to the demand: "Are you republican? Do you like the princes?" with: "I'm an artist; I love only my mother and my mistress."[48] The exchange allowed Musset to present the artist as idealist, in contrast with the cynical self-interest of the men of power. Freccia is a remnant of another romantic attitude, that of the "noble" Renaissance, encapsulated in Abel-François Villemain's fictitious *Lascaris,* in which the Greek scholar, fleeing from captured Constantinople, is welcomed by the Medici to begin "this noble mission of Greek genius in the midst of Italy."[49] The episode was as false historically as the theory that the Turkish conquest of Byzantium generated the Renaissance as an intellectual movement. Musset, like Stendhal before him, had no sympathy for the roseate view of the Renaissance Italy of which this was a part. He used its reflection in the moral freedom of the artist to underline the corruption of the times.[50] *Lorenzaccio* deserves the acclaim it has received from modern critics, not least for its historical depiction of Renaissance attitudes remarkably close to those later defined by Burckhardt.

While Musset was writing *Lorenzaccio,* Michelet was composing his sweeping synthesis of medieval French history. The sixth volume, ending with Louis XI, appeared in 1843, after Michelet had published, this time in collaboration with Quinet, an attack on the Jesuits. By this time he had broken with the conservative liberal establishment that had promoted his own academic career, and had moved toward a radical social romanticism. His faith reposed infallibly on the genius and spirituality of the French people, and he came closer and closer to the conclusion that the church, far from fulfilling the true aspirations of the people in the Middle Ages, had frustrated and exploited them. Thus in 1846, when brooding over his rhapsodic invocation, *Le Peuple,* and grieving for the loss of his father, he confided to his journal his renunciation of his romantic medieval ideal: "What did I do when I embellished the ideal of the Middle Ages? Did I hide the reality? I have labored against myself and against the world's progress. How vital it is that I continue to live so that I may weaken those unfortunate prejudices that I supported without realizing what I was doing."[51] In the following year he published the first volume of his history of the Revolution, and it was not until 1855 that he brought out of the seventh volume of his *Histoire de France,* the volume devoted to the Renaissance.

The Renaissance now appeared to Michelet as the denial of the long centuries he had come to detest: "That bizarre, monstrous and prodigiously artificial period we call the Middle Ages has no argument in its favor save its extreme length and its obstinate resistance to the return of nature."[52] The French people, alienated from nature, could now march forward again, but they did so initially not through the collective forces evident in modern times but by discovering the strength and self-reliance of individualism, epitomized in the adage borrowed by the renaissance from Protagoras, "man the measure of all things." In this vein Michelet apostrophized his readers: "You overconfident generations who comprise the greatness of the nineteenth century, come and see this living source through which humanity receives new strength, the source of the individual soul that feels it is greater than all the world and expects no external aid to achieve its salvation."[53] The Renaissance, in the celebrated formula, was "the discovery of the world and of man." Michelet's idealist historical vision was thronged with spirits—the spirit of the ages, the spirit of the peoples, the spirit of the nations—each personified and represented by its own symbols. The spirit of the Renaissance was heroic: "heroism of action, heroism of creativity. . . . The sixteenth century is a hero." The attempt to proscribe nature and science by medieval culture, with "its terrorism, its police, its execution stakes," could not break humanity, which emerged from its bondage to find freedom through reason.[54]

In chapter 17, where Michelet returned to these introductory remarks, he tried to define the character of the Renaissance in the early sixteenth century with rather more precision, and admitted the difficulty. In art, Da Vinci, Michelangelo, and Raphael were the phenomena of their age, but to explain their achievement was another matter. In an earlier passage he had made the bizarre suggestion that Da Vinci's drawing of Leda and the swan represented the integration of humanity in nature, and, in an equally fanciful flight of the imagination, he depicted the artist freeing caged birds as the symbol of his passion for liberty (fig. 1). Michelangelo, Michelet's prophet of the new age, was depicted as a Cyclopean figure working through the night with a lantern strapped to his forehead as he frenetically attempted to release the ideal form from a block of stone (fig. 2). Michelangelo's contempt for worldly authority was conveyed in the story of the artist's attempt to prevent Pope Julius II from inspecting his work on the ceiling of the Sistine Chapel by obliging the pontiff to climb a perilous scaffold (fig. 3).[55]

The Renaissance was something specifically Italian, and its inspiration was the revival of antiquity, the two familiar themes stressed again by Burckhardt. But for Michelet there were two antiquities—that of the Bible and that of Greece and Rome—and they were to wage war by medium of the printing press until what Michelet discerned as the classical message, "return to Nature," triumphed. "This is the welcome the Renaissance offers us. It is the first word which it addresses to us, and it is the final word of reason."[56] The symbols of the movement were Columbus, Copernicus, and Luther. In considering the latter Michelet reverted to one of his early preoccupations. In 1828, on his way to join Quinet in Heidelberg, he had written to his friend that all his studies were concentrated on "the great revolution of the sixteenth century."[57] The Reformation was still of primary interest to him. Besides, he was writing a history of France, not of Europe or Italy, and he paid more attention to the religious wars than to the Renaissance as such.

Quinet's highly original views on the Italian Renaissance were developed in the course of his anticlerical lectures at the Collège de France, where he joined Michelet in 1841. He adopted a quasi-religious vision of the Renaissance not only as the liberation of human reason but also as its reunion with what Quinet conceived as the true message of Christianity. Thenceforth social justice was seen as possible on earth, and the Renaissance became the harbinger of the French Revolution.[58] Quinet developed his radical attitude to the Renaissance while writing his *Révolutions d'Italie* during the Revolution of 1848 and its aftermath. Quinet did not attempt to hide the fact that he saw the Italian past through the distorting lens of current politics. Indeed, he inserted a note to say that the events of February 24 had interrupted him after writing the following: "It seems to me that the *popolani grassi* of our time are doing something not just unprecedented but also foolhardy in relying upon nothing else save money; for to abandon to their adversaries

1. Da Vinci releasing caged birds so that he might share the joy
of their freedom. (Engraving from Jules Michelet, *Histoire de
France*, Paris, F. Rouff, c.1885, v.2, p. 1073)

God, the fatherland, humanity, heroism, beauty, science and art, is to de-
prive themselves immeasurably, and to hand over too large a share to the
little people [*peuple maigre*] impatiently awaiting their turn."[59] This makes
it seem that the French *haute bourgeoisie* suffered by comparison with their
Italian counterparts in earlier times, for the latter had, in Quinet's eyes, been
responsible for the art and science of the Renaissance. So, indeed, they did.
But Quinet's main theme was that the *popolani grassi* had for six centuries
exploited and repressed the lower classes of Italy, as their French equivalent

2. Michelangelo working frenetically on a statue at night. Engraving from Michelet, *Histoire de France,* Rouff edition, v.2, p. 1033)

3. Pope Julius II obliged by Michelangelo to climb a perilous ladder to inspect the ceiling of the Sistine Chapel. (Engraving from Michelet, *Histoire de France,* Rouff edition, v.2, p. 1037)

had exploited the people for the past fifty years. While they could be credited with the Renaissance, aesthetic considerations were not Quinet's principal concern. He wanted to show why popular nationalism had been so long delayed in the Italian context.

The concept of renaissance was not, for Quinet, limited to early modern times. It was the germ of Italian nationality, the memory of the remote classical past that had enabled the cities to escape from barbarism. If England had attained liberty through aristocracy, the Italian communes had sought it through the distant and democratic memory of ancient Rome. Yet terror, not liberty, had dominated the medieval republics. The few months of butchery experienced in the French Revolution had stretched into centuries for the Italians. Quinet, who claimed to scorn past official histories and their modern exegetes, cited the words of the fourteenth-century chronicler Matteo Villani to describe the implacable misanthrophy in which faction killed faction like animals in a slaughterhouse, and terror fed on terror.[60] The wealthy middle class that had absorbed the nobility used craft and cruelty to repress the challenge from below, and, when necessary in face of factionalism and social revolution, had not hesitated to replace oligarchy with despotism. Dante had been the mirror of Italian popular aspiration.[61] Petrarch had broken away from the corporate pressure imposed by church and state to express, like some fourteenth-century Chateaubriand, the moral anguish of the solitary individual mind, and in so doing to introduce something unknown in antiquity.[62] Boccaccio was the spokesman for bourgeois equality who mocked the feudal myths of the past and introduced the concept of *l'art pour l'art.*[63]

Quinet's chair at the Collège de France was in the field of southern languages and literature, and it can be seen how indefatigably he adapted the great names of Italian letters to his schema of social revolution and anticlericalism. It was for this reason that an intense controversy arose among the professors of the Collège as to whether they could be compelled to lecture within the orthodox confines of their subject, leading to Quinet's resignation in 1846.[64] If the Revolution of 1848 seemed in its first months to justify his stand, the publication of *Les révolutions d'Italie* appeared as a harbinger of subsequent disappointment. After the failed social revolution of the Ciompi in 1378, according to Quinet's interpretation, the Florentine fiscal revolution of the *catasto,* a tax proportionate to wealth, enabled the Medici to pacify the people and to postpone their aspirations indefinitely.

The flowering of the artistic Renaissance helped to lull the popular conscience, and, although the artists themselves remained free, the writers were chained to the artificial courts of the despots. Like a tree detached from its roots, the *popolani grassi* lost their instinct for nationality and patriotism. The bourgeoisie had destroyed the old principle of chivalric heroism, and under the Medici the alternate principle of popular heroism had no opportunity to express itself.[65] Confident in their cultural superiority, the rulers of Italy disarmed, and Italy became the battleground of foreign powers. Quinet, like Stendhal, noted the coincidence of high art and military destruction: "Incredible as it may seem, it is at this very time that the masterpieces of Leonardo da Vinci and Michelangelo are achieved. The still-damp frescoes of Raphaël are blackened by the smoke of the soldiers who are sacking the Vatican."[66] At this moment, too, arose someone who, for Quinet, was the first literary genius since Boccaccio. Machiavelli accomplished in terms of the real what the great painters achieved in terms of the ideal. While Michelangelo renewed art from the wellspring of pagan antiquity, Machiavelli devised a theory of politics from the study of ancient Rome: "Michelangelo and Machiavelli, contemporaries who seem to be worlds apart, are both closely possessed by the same instinct for antique form. The first attains the furthest edge of the ideal, the second descends deeper than any man into the abyss of the real."[67]

Machiavelli apart, the giants of the Renaissance seemed to Quinet to be citizens of the world, not Italians. Their lack of national patriotism was evidence to him of the death of popular sentiment. This absence of national aspiration was the outcome of a social revolution frustrated by the bourgeois elite and the diversionary tactics of high culture. It was also the by-product of papal opposition to a strong secular state, indeed of Catholicism in general: "When the citizen's conscience has been deadened in this way by the men of politics, it is the business of the priest to complete the process by putting his heart to sleep. Always and everywhere, after Machiavelli comes Loyola."[68] This analysis of the past was intended to convey a message to the present. In the mid-nineteenth century, Quinet called for the social resurrection of Italy, the advent of democracy, and the rejection of Catholic authority.

In this reappraisal of French romantic views of the Renaissance a common element emerges, the conjunction of high culture and political amoralism.

It lurks behind the controversy about Francis I. It was expressed as a cult of energy by Stendhal, who added a note of social protest to be taken up in more explosive terms by Quinet. Its psychological ramifications were explored by Musset in *Lorenzaccio*. It serves to distinguish the ironic from other varieties of romanticism, and it reveals the extent to which the more traditional romantics could be radicalized. In 1823 Stendhal spoke in *Racine et Shakespeare* of measuring romanticism by the amount of pleasure it provided for the generation at which it was aimed, and in 1836 Théophile Gautier introduced *l'art pour l'art,* a theory of aesthetic amoralism, in the preface of *Mademoiselle de Maupin.* On the one hand, the more skeptical of the romantics had come to apply the climate they discerned in the Renaissance to their own age: on the other, the most influential of the romantic historians had imposed a revolutionary social romanticism on the Renaissance.

Notes

1. F.-R. de Chateaubriand, *Études ou discours historiques,* 4 vols. (Paris, 1831), 1:cxl.

2. Wallace K. Ferguson, *The Renaissance in Historical Thought: Five Centuries of Interpretation* (Cambridge, Mass.: Houghton Mifflin, 1948), p. 151.

3. J. C. L. Simonde de Sismondi, *Histoire des républiques italiennes du moyen âge,* 8 vols. (Zurich, 1807–9); *De la littérature du midi de l'Europe,* 4 vols. (1813; Paris, 1819); *Histoire des français,* 31 vols. (Paris, 1821–44). William Roscoe's *Life of Lorenzo de' Medici* was published in 1796, his *Life and Pontificate of Leo the Tenth* in 1805.

4. François Guizot, *Histoire de la civilisation en Europe depuis la chute de l'Empire romain jusqu'à la Révolution française,* ed. Pierre Rosanvallon (Paris: Hachette, 1985), p. 252.

5. François Guizot, *Historical Essays and Lectures,* ed. Stanley Mellon (Chicago: University of Chicago Press, 1972), p. 357.

6. Guizot, *The History of France from the Earliest Times to 1848,* trans. Robert Black, 8 vols. (New York, n.d.), 3:109–28.

7. G.-P. Brugière de Barante, *Mélanges historiques et littéraires,* 3 vols. (Paris, 1835), 2:27.

8. C.-A. Sainte-Beuve, *Tableau historique et critique de la poésie française et du théâtre français au seizième siècle,* 2 vols. (Paris, 1828), 1:331–33.

9. Ibid., pp. 361–62.

10. Ibid., p. 365.

11. Ibid., p. 368.

12. Honoré de Balzac, *La peau de chagrin* (1831; Paris: Livre de Poche, 1972), p. 252.

13. Philarète Chasles, *Tableau de la marche et des progrès de la langue et de la littérature françaises depuis le commencment du seiziéme siècle jusqu'en 1610* (Paris, 1828); Saint-Marc Girardin, *Tableau de la marche et des progrès de la littérature française au seizième siècle* (Paris, 1828).

14. Girardin, *Tableau,* pp. 3, 69.

15. Sainte-Beuve, *Tableau,* pp. 15–24.

16. Charles Lacretelle, *Histoire de France pendant les guerres de religion,* 4 vols. (Paris, 1814), 1:iii.

17. Stendhal [Henri Beyle], *Racine et Shakespeare,* ed. Henri Martineau (1823; Paris: Le Divan, 1928), p. 3.

18. Stendhal, *Courrier anglais: lettres à Stritch,* ed. Henri Martineau, 5 vols. (Paris: Le Divan, 1935), 1:111. On the other hand, in an article on Andrea del Sarto published in 1821, Stendhal remarked that, for all his sensitivity to art, Francis I lacked the qualities of a great king. See the editor's note in Stendhal, *Écoles italiennes de peinture,* ed. Henry Martineau, 3 vols. (Paris: Le Divan, 1932), 1:23.

19. Paul L. Jacob [Paul Lacroix], *Romans relatifs à l'histoire de France aux XVe et XVIe siècles* (Paris, 1838), p. 645.

20. *Oeuvres du comte P.-L. Roederer,* 8 vols. (Paris, 1853), 2:154.

21. Philippe van Tieghem, *Musset* (Paris: Hatier, 1969), p. 27. Cf. Alfred de Musset, *Lorenzaccio,* ed. Bernard Masson (Paris: A. Collin, 1978), p. 236: "The French king protecting Italian liberty is just like a highwayman protecting a pretty woman on the road from another robber. He defends her until he's ready to rob her."

22. See the Sismondi works cited in note 3, above; and P.-L. Ginguené, *Histoire littéraire d'Italie,* ed. P.-C.-F. Daunou, 8 vols. (1811–19; Paris, 1824).

23. "The only thing I like in history are anecdotes, among which I prefer those which make me imagine I have found a true portrait of the mores and characteristics of a given era" (Prosper Mérimée, *Chronique du règne de Charles IX,* ed. Maurice Rat [1829; Paris: Garnier, 1949], p. 1).

24. Stendhal, *Histoire de la peinture en Italie,* ed. Henry Martineau, 2 vols. (1817; Paris: Le Divan, 1929), 1:ix; Paul Arbelet, *L'Histoire de la peinture en Italie et les plagiats de Stendhal* (Paris: C. Lévy, 1914).

25. Stendhal, *Histoire,* 1:70.

26. Joanna Richardson, *Stendhal* (New York: Coward, McCann, & Geoghagan, 1974), p. 270.

27. Stendhal, *Histoire,* vol. 1.

28. Ibid., p. 260.

29. Ibid., p. 55.

30. Ibid., p. 16.

31. Ibid., p. 189.

32. Ibid., pp. 195–96.

33. See the new translation by J.-V. Peries, *Oeuvres complètes de Machiavel,* 12 vols.

(Paris, 1823–26). The translator stressed the scientific aspect of Machiavelli's works and arranged them topically (*histoire, politique, art militaire,* etc.). Reviewing this edition in the *Courrier Français* (July 23, 1825), Mignet remarked on the value of Machiavelli as one who observed human behavior without moralizing and appreciated that history consisted of inexorable chains of cause and effect. See Yvonne Knibiehler, *Naissance des sciences humaines: Mignet et l'histoire philosophique au XIXe siècle* (Paris: Flammarion, 1973), p. 110. Ginguené wrote a long account of Machiavelli in the eighth volume of *Histoire littéraire* (1819). Numerous articles about Machiavelli in the Parisian journals in the early 1830s are mentioned by Bernard Masson, *Musset et le théâtre intérieur: Nouvelles recherches sur* Lorenzaccio (Paris: A. Collin, 1974), p. 92.

34. Victor Cousin, *Cours de philosophie professé à la Faculté des Lettres pendant l'année 1818 sur le fondement des idées absolues du vrai, du beau et du bien* (Paris, 1836).

35. "There was no act of violence, artifice, bravura, or villainy which Cesare Borgia did not embrace. To invade eight or ten small towns or dispose of several petty lords, he used more artfulness than Alexander, Genghis, Tamerlane, and Mohammad together used to subjugate the greater part of the world" (*Essai sur les moeurs et l'esprit des nations et sur les principaux faits de l'histoire depuis Charlemagne jusqu'à Louis XIII,* ed. René Pomeau, 2 vols. [Paris: Garnier, 1963], 2:96).

36. Stendhal, *Histoire,* 1:19.

37. Ibid., p. 138.

38. Ibid., p. 44.

39. Ibid., p. 41.

40. Voltaire, *Essai sur les moeurs,* 2:168.

41. Stendhal, *Écoles,* 1:60–62.

42. Stendhal, *Chroniques italiennes,* ed. Beatrice Didier (Paris: Garnier Flammarion, 1977), p. 66.

43. Ibid., p. 4.

44. Gustave Planche in *Revue des Deux Mondes,* December 1, 1932. See Masson, *Musset et le théâtre intérieur,* p. 99.

45. Bernard Masson, *Musset et son double: Lecture de* Lorenzaccio (Paris: Minard, 1978), pp. 9–11; and Joyce G. Bromfield, *De Lorenzino de Médicis à Lorenzaccio* (Paris: M. Didier, 1972), pp. 139–68.

46. *Lorenzaccio,* p. 154. Ceri Crossley's *Musset:* Lorenzaccio (London: Grant & Cutler, 1983), p. 38, suggests a different interpretation: that Tebaldeo represented for Musset a retreat from reality.

47. See George Sand's lines to this effect published as an appendix by Masson in *Lorenzaccio,* p. 308.

48. *Lorenzaccio,* pp. 92–98.

49. Abel-François Villemain, *Lascaris* (Paris, 1825), p. 97.

50. Cf. Masson, *Musset et le théâtre intérieur,* p. 102.

51. Jules Michelet, *Journal, 1828–1848,* ed. Paul Viallaneix, 4 vols. (Paris: Gallimard, 1959), 1:658.

52. Michelet, *Histoire de France: Renaissance et Réforme,* ed. Claude Mettra (1855; Paris: R. Laffont, 1982), p. 36.

53. Ibid., p. 38.

54. Ibid., p. 80.

55. Ibid., pp. 212, 174, 176.

56. Ibid., p. 210.

57. Michelet, *Journal,* 1:705.

58. Ceri Crossley, *Edgar Quinet (1803–1875): A Study in Romantic Thought* (Lexington: French Forum, 1983), p. 56; and *French Historians and Romanticism: Thierry, Guizot, the Saint-Simonians, Quinet, Michelet* (London: Routledge, 1993), pp. 153–54, 161.

59. Edgar Quinet, *Les Révolutions d'Italie,* 5th ed. (1848; Paris, n.d.), p. 179.

60. Ibid., pp. 177–78.

61. Ibid., p. 125.

62. Ibid., pp. 128–29. "The moral anguish which the author of René has likened to a vague sense of melancholy begins above all with Petrarch."

63. Ibid., pp. 135–46. This chapter is entitled "L'art pour l'art: Boccace."

64. Richard Howard Powers, *Edgar Quinet: A Study in French Patriotism* (Dallas: Southern Methodist University Press, 1957), pp. 124–28.

65. Quinet, *Révolutions,* p. 176.

66. Ibid., p. 233.

67. Ibid., p. 277.

68. Ibid., p. 456.

Lawrence M. Bryant

Making History: Ceremonial Texts, Royal Space, and Political Theory in the Sixteenth Century

Early modern political culture, and with it the early modern state, emerged, as Howell A. Lloyd noted, "from the social groups constituting the society of Renaissance France, a product of the consciousness that informed both it and them." Lloyd showed how "men in groups" and "the practice of government" worked in creative tension to shape the state in the sixteenth century; how politics were discussed in terms of the abstraction *corpus mysticum reipublicae* and were represented in communities and assemblies that were superior to the king or any individual group.[1] Ceremonial performances were the heart of political life, and much of late medieval and early sixteenth-century public history consists of chronicles and lists of ranks, meeting places, forms of address, and procedures in a vast number of ceremonial assemblies.

The first successful project for bringing the records of these assemblies together into a single overview of French history took place under the royal sponsorship of the research of Jean du Tillet, the chief clerk of the Parlement of Paris between 1530 and 1570. His *Recueil des roys de France* and *Recueil des rangs* were being collected and used by the monarchy at least thirty years before they were first printed in 1578 and 1580.[2] Like the work of a royal apostle (which he was), Du Tillet's published works established the canon of French ceremonies, and therefore a frozen model of the past to guide the dynamic present. However, as Du Tillet knew, the advent of print and publicity greatly altered the mystery and dynamics of traditional assemblies and ceremonies. Before print, ceremonies had served as a kind of local knowledge that defined membership in the community and was used by rulers for administrative purposes. When print—as Roger Chartier wrote— "penetrated the entire web of social relations . . . and lodged in people's deepest self as well as claiming its place in the public scene," assemblies, groups, and individuals performed with a greatly heightened self-consciousness of the meaning of their acts as repetition of past events and as models for future events.[3] Performances in assemblies ceased to be scripted according to the vagueness of institutional memories or local customs and took on new, multiple ideological meanings as they were researched, as they accrued in time, as they received more extensive publicity, and as they became spaces for enlarging the circulation of ideas. After being staged, any assembly's importance depended on the place it eventually came to occupy in public memory. In political life, people remembered an event—that is, placed in a context and a time—in terms of the spectacle that accompanied it. Warfare and penal justice, by their very nature, created theaters of glory, noble deeds, or horror and had been reported by chroniclers for centuries. Advocates of peace and public order, as these two complementary things became disengaged from the monopoly of the church and its social theories, had fewer antecedents to rely on and began inventing new ceremonial traditions and theaters in order for institutions and people to publicize their roles and rights in what the French called the *bien publique.* In the fifteenth century, ceremonies and assemblies—long associated with feudal counsel, taxation, and religion—took on a new identity as places of public business. By the seventeenth century, the decorum of assemblies, rather than their business, came to be of prime importance. For example, Théodore Godefroy wrote in *Le Cérémonial de France* (1619) that all well-governed states were founded on exact observance of order in their ceremonies and ranks. Confusion in these, he said, made the government look bad and hurt the reputation of the people whom the ceremonies were established to honor. If ceremony broke down, then so also would the bonds of friendship and concord, followed by the collapse of good government.[4] Print transformed past ceremonies into handbooks and models for early modern sociability, manners, and political culture.

This essay looks at three, from among many, sophisticated performances of what I shall call "assemblies-with-the-king."[5] These assemblies took place in Paris during 1517, 1528, and 1557. Until about 1560—when the styles of performances underwent a major shift along with the meanings that contemporaries assigned to such assemblies—"a good deal of backstage negotiation" had been carried out to ensure the on-stage image of collaboration and cooperation for meetings of estates and other gatherings.[6] The costuming, the choreography, and the placement of those who gathered around the king were subject to political interpretations. The potential power of such assemblies was evident in the ever-increasing involvement of the urban elite, the desire of the high nobility to participate, and the growth of royal patronage in the staging of such events. By about 1500, a larger public than ever before in French history followed monarchical politics. This public attention brought additional weight to the traditions of assemblies and gave an impetus for the shaping of a unique French style of what has been tagged "the new European ceremonialism."[7] The impetus resulted in ceremonial performers undertaking research into the precedence, ranks, and designs of ritual theaters.

J. Russell Major recognized the importance of ceremonialism in his analysis of assembling and ruling as central to Renaissance political history. He wrote that to rule, French kings utilized the "officials of the estates and other popular institutions [since] . . . the modest size of their armies made it advisable for them to rule by persuasion rather than by force." These assemblies, he said, should not be confused with modern notions of representative government, because "the concept of representative government was not invented until the creation of the Dutch republic near the close of the Renaissance; until then, kings rarely saw reason to fear representative institutions."[8] Other historians also have noted that kings used assemblies to reach a world that did not know them; as Montaigne put it, "our laws are free enough, and the weight of sovereignty is felt by a French nobleman barely twice in a lifetime."[9] However, kings rarely wasted these twice-in-a-lifetime encounters and developed ways of expanding their public impact.

Assemblies-with-the-king are, I propose, a good source for marking the twisted historical route by which the figuration of participants in the decentralized politics of the early sixteenth century was transformed into a model for a more centralized seventeenth-century form of political sociability.[10] While recent scholarship has overthrown Norbert Elias's view that the nobility was weakened by being divided into court and country factions, his work remains important for his way of viewing society "as neither an abstraction of attributes of individuals existing without society, nor a 'system' or 'totality' beyond individuals, but the network of interdependencies formed by individuals."[11] In this essay, I recount the figuration of participants and networks of interdependencies in assemblies-with-the-king through their dramatic and representational actions. Such a study of the dynamics of these assemblies will enable historians to integrate the history of the period's prodigious ceremonies with the history of its political struggles and thought; it will clarify the cultural processes and political forces that shaped the transition in images of rulers and theories of rulership from the sixteenth-century image of assemblies-with-the-king to the

seventeenth-century king-presiding-at-court.[12] I will show that the sta-
bilizing and consistent theory in the transition was the new humanist notion of an active ruler whose image and rationale were those of the orator-
prince rather than of the sacerdotal or juridical king. This essay looks at
Renaissance assemblies as theaters for accommodating the traditions of
rulership to the new and widely embraced Renaissance idea that good
princes ruled by persuasion and consensus.[13] The importance of the king or
his chancellor as orator in the assemblies, not the mere fact of assembling,
which already had a long history,[14] is critical to our understanding of both
Renaissance assemblies and drama.

A Trajectory for Studying Assemblies-with-the-King

Four images illustrate the stages of the change of both political thought and
artistic technique and styles of deportment: the woodcut from the 1519
frontispiece to Claude de Seyssel's *La Grant monarchie de France* (fig. 1), two
examples from Jacques Tortorel and Jean Perrissin's 1570 *Forty Scenes* (figs. 2
and 3), and the frontispiece to André du Chesne's *Les Antiquitez et recherches de
la grandeur et majesté des roys de France* (fig. 4). A major shift in conceptions of
the relationship of society, politics, and ceremony was necessary for the
latter portrait to serve as public art and an image of state.[15] In each case, the
king's costume characterizes his role in the assembly. Figure 1 reflects a
dying form of royal representation since the king and others have no individualized physiognomy. Identity is revealed through robes of office and
royal paraphernalia; the dynamic of discussion is seen through traditional
hand gestures. Louis XII had already propagated his natural likeness in a
variety of forms without royal accoutrements: as warrior, in court dress, and
in assemblies.[16]

Figures 2 and 3 are from the *Forty Scenes* produced in Geneva in 1570 by
the Huguenots Tortorel and Perrissin. They represent two views of the
Mercuriale in the Parlement of Paris on June 10, 1559, when Anne du
Bourg pleaded against persecution of the Huguenots. Henry II is identified
as the king by his physiognomy and placement rather than by any royal
symbolism. The gestures reveal the dispositions of the participants and
Henry II's angry response. The story continues outside the window, where
Du Bourg and another of the four magistrates arrested with him are being

1. Assembly-with-the-King. Frontispiece of
Claude de Seyssel's *La Grant Monarchie de France.*
(Paris: Regnault-Chauldiere, 1519)

(*Facing page–top*) 2. Assembly-with-the-King. Plate III,
"La Mercurialle tenue aux Augustins à Paris, le 10 de Iuin. 1559,
ou le Roy Henry 2 y fut en personne." (*Les Grandes Scènes
historiques du XVIe siècle reproduction fac-similé de J. Tortorel et
J. Perrissin,* published under the direction of Alfred Franklin,
Paris: Librairie Fischbacher, 1886)

(*Facing page–bottom*) 3. Assembly-with-the-King. Plate IV,
"La Mercurialle tenue aux Augustins à Paris, le X. de Iuin. 1559,
la ou le Roy Henry ii y fut en personne." (*Les Grandes Scènes
historiques du XVIe siècle reproduction fac-similé de J. Tortorel et
J. Perrissin,* published under the direction of Alfred Franklin,
Paris: Librairie Fischbacher, 1886)

Figure 4. Court and Royal
Family with the King.
Frontispiece of André
du Chesne's *Les Antiques et
recherches de la grandeur et
majesté des roys de France.*
(Paris: Jean Petit-Pas,
1609, with permission of
the Newberry Library)

led to the Bastille. In the second scene (fig. 3), a dramatic close-up shows
Du Bourg in three poses: submitting to the king, being seized by the duc de
Guise, and, through the window, being led to prison. The solemn assembly
of figure 1 has become an image of a world confused. Although the king is
shown in the assembled Court of Parlement, the caption contrasts human
justice and divine judgment:

> When Du Bourg remonstrated that all human force
>
> Against God and his Law can only be in vain,
>
> But for having spoken honestly, he was sent to prison:
>
> The place was open to Force and not to Reason.

This clever piece of Huguenot propaganda—which claimed to follow eyewitness accounts and to be truly portrayed—illustrates the full dramatiza-
tion and with it the personalizing of politics that had taken place by the
1550s.

More than new productive and artistic techniques contributed to this new image of assembling. The political and cultural trajectories of the change are evident in the genealogy and credentials that Théodore and Denis Godefroy gave to the 1649 *Le Cérémonial françois* when they began their two volumes with copies of Henry II's 1548 commission for Jean du Tillet to research "solemn assemblies" and Henry III's commission creating the *grand maistre des cérémonies de France* in 1585 (Appendix).[17] Godefroy father and son clearly found in these two moments the impulse that culminated in *Le Cérémonial françois.* Their collection brilliantly supplies the documents, taxonomy, and narrative foundation for interpreting the rebellious and violent period between 1560 and 1652 within the seamless web of ceremonial development that reflected the French monarchy's growth to perfection. In fact, both Du Tillet's commission and Henry III's effort to reform ceremony resulted from political conflicts. Jean du Tillet knew more about public assemblies than any other person in France.[18] He had been the clerk of the Parlement de Paris for thirty years and under Francis I's patronage had researched the ancient registers of the parlement and other archives. Henry II's December 1548 commission was very specific: "We wish to know and understand what rank and order, from the times of our predecessors until the present, were preserved in all grand and solemn assemblies [of] the Princes of our Blood; likewise the Dukes, Counts, and other Princes of our kingdom; Dukes, Counts and others of lesser title and dignity; as well as the Constables, Marshals, and Admiral of France."[19] This commission and the wide circulation in six printings of the *Recueils* attest to Du Tillet's standing as the major figure in the first phase of ceremonial research and royal historiography. The Godefroys saw the next phase in (1) Henry III's 1583 query to an Assembly of Notables on whether to undertake research on "ranks and seances . . . of princes, dukes, officers of the crown"; (2) the approval for making such a register; and (3) that king's edict of 1585 establishing the office of *grand maistre des cérémonies de France.* Since the Godefroys were concerned with precedents for ceremonial study, and not with the context for their documents, they did not bother to mention that Henry III was acting because Du Tillet's political views and plain historical narratives (now widely known from the published versions of the *Recueils*) were outdated and inapplicable among the rhetorical and aesthetic styles favored by the court and government of Henry III.[20]

Henry III's political project endeavored to combine the occasional forms culled out of the traditions for assemblies-with-the-king with the permanent etiquette of the royal aesthetics of the court. The tensions between the king's public and personal authorities were subjects of intense debate over styles of ruling that Ralph Giesey analyzed in terms of " 'Majesté' des juristes et 'Majesté' des courtisans."[21] Du Tillet in his prefaces had separated ceremonies from the business of government. In the 1560s he wrote that "what is divulged in council in monarchies is for the most part only false or . . . only contains the plain narrative of what actually happened without any certitude or intelligence of the business or [its] progress."[22] Assemblies were not for attending to public affairs, according to Du Tillet, but for showing right order and ranks according to the command of the king. The speeches that he had recorded and collected during his long career represented "only false" adornments incidental to what really happened. In the breakdown of institutions in the 1560s, Du Tillet witnessed the collapse of government that balanced solemn assemblies and discussion of public business. Even among leading *parlementaires* and French *avocats,* procedures based on the foundations of traditional French laws and precedents were being replaced by argumentation according to the grand style of eloquence inspired by classical rhetoric and philosophy.[23]

The major intermediary between Du Tillet's ceremonial researches and the Godefroys' *Cérémonial françois* was André du Chesne, who applied the theory of a royal aesthetic and the grand rhetorical style to the monarchy in his *Les Antiquitez et recherches de la grandeur et maieste des roys de France* (1609),[24] a work that established the view of France from the "interior," or the physical and moral center of the monarch and his court. The idea of the king as embodying the nation emphasized his personal power to overawe subjects and thus make them obedient. Like Du Tillet, Du Chesne dismissed politics in public assemblies; but unlike the *greffier,* he embraced royal ceremonies as a substitute for politics. He established government on the principles of aesthetics and unchanging "ideal types."[25] He also publicized the monarchy's status as first family, not its relationship to assemblies. The frontispiece to his book (fig. 4), for example, clearly illustrates the king on a throne with crown, robe, and scepter. The setting is his *maison* with his queen, their children, royal bastards, and other members of the household. The dynastic and historical basis of this orderly family scene is depicted in the kings who represent the dynasties prior to the Bourbon line. Clovis appears particularly fanciful with a closed imperial crown and fleurs-de-lis scepter, while Charlemagne with sword and orb corresponds more closely to traditional representations. Hugh Capet is distinctly unroyal in his plain hat and simple robe, whereas Louis IX strikes a royal juridical pose, having a coronet on his head and the Hand of Justice and fleurs-de-lis scepter in his hands.

By the end of the sixteenth century, representations of the king as judge, leader of armies, or saintly body had ceased to be the primary symbolic way of describing his relationship to government and society.[26] Rather, as seen in figure 4, the king increasingly was represented in natural settings of home and family rather than in tribunals, leading armies, or performing religious rites; his identity was established by a true-to-life figure who sported with domesticated nonchalance the customary accoutrements of his office. The past image of majesty had been synthesized with the domesticated image of family. The image of the ruler broke free from politico-juridical assemblies and was restated as an idealized and paternal gathering. This new image of the ruler and the shift in theories about assemblies represented a rejection of ways of thinking about society that was represented in the brief flourishing of Renaissance experiments with assemblies-with-the-king.

Historians today generally agree that in France—from the recovery starting with Charles VII to the taming of princely houses by Louis XI, followed by the rising demands of the Italian and Habsburg wars from Charles VIII to Henry II—royal administration underwent profound transformation by bringing new men and ideas into royal government. These men, particularly jurists associated with the French parlements and a refashioned nobility, shaped a new kind of administration according to a synthesis of humanist ideas about the courtier, the citizen, and the subject.[27] All depended on the monarch for their salary and/or patronage, influence, status, and the public visibility that constituted reputation.[28] At the same time, the king's need for public support and money encouraged experimentation with new forms of persuasion. On the one hand, assemblies provided the king with a forum to imitate classical orators and emperors; on the other, they appealed to those who sought to publicize the political sphere as the places where advice and counsel were given to the king. Such performances compelled Frenchmen to reflect on the true duty of royal officials and the political traditions of the French monarchy. Accordingly, in Renaissance assemblies orators shared center stage with rulers, and in humanist teachings, the ideal orator should be the ruler. Ruler-orators were to embody universal learning in order to persuade society to join them in their civilizing mission.[29]

The solemn assemblies of the French kings in 1517, 1528, and 1557 illustrate the appeal and the precarious nature of the turn to orator-kings. These assemblies can best be thought of as experiments in forms of government that took place before assemblies were differentiated and historicized into monarchical and national institutions in the 1560s and 1570s. The process of historicizing assemblies-with-the-king into national tradition is a factor in analyzing particular assemblies, since the sixteenth-century French invention of assemblies-with-the-king as normal politics is like the English project of the same period. G. O. Sayles demonstrated how the focus of English assembling traditions only fortuitously settled on Parliament. In the early sixteenth century this institution could have disappeared without much notice had not Henry VIII, "faced with other possibilities, deliberately selected parliament in 1529 as an instrument to his liking and set it upon a new career as a legislative assembly, with the commons as a pliant but necessary tool for his purposes."[30] Only after 1529 did political discourse insulate Parliament from "the passage of time and the alteration of circumstances."[31] As mentioned earlier in the discussion of books of ceremony, traditions of assembling took another direction in France. To take Quentin Skinner's words, "the nature and limits of the normative vocabulary available" to French political actors included many traditions of assembling but did not settle in any one institution. If it were true, as Skinner put it, "that the developing theory and practice of the Valois monarchy in the first half of the sixteenth century had already made it an object of hostility and disillusionment amongst important sectors of the French ruling class," the disillusionment resulted from the monarchy's efforts to shape and define institutions where none was fixed, rather than from any subversion of permanent institutions.[32] The dialectic of king versus national or representative assemblies makes no sense in contexts before the 1560s at the least, and probably the 1540s.

Three Solemn French Assemblies: 1517, 1527, 1557

From the late fifteenth century onward, many, frequently contradictory, examples of ideal kingly conduct circulated throughout Europe. In cases of war, the king's deportment could signify the difference between life and death: for example, whether he entered a rebellious city in armor and permitted a sack or wore robes and gave the officials and people a hearing in an assembly. Other reasons also determined deportment; for example, Louis XII's refusal to sit in staged thrones in triumphal celebrations in Milan and Lyons because he reportedly saw such spectacle as detracting from God's role in military victories. However, occasional art, medallions, and epithets glossed over the traditional claims of the "très chrétien" king with "le hubris antique."[33] In Italy, Charles VIII regularly used assemblies-with-the-king to show his legitimacy. The Italians had different forms in these assemblies from the French and sometimes challenged the king, as when Piero Capponi tore up a treaty diminishing Florentine liberty "in front of the King's eyes." Capponi set civic liberties against royal force: "since such shameless demands are being made, you sound your trumpets and we will sound our bells."[34] Louis XII convoked assemblies wherever he claimed sovereignty, most notably in his dealings with Milan and Genoa.[35] Louis XII also adhered to the importance of assemblies, from his support of the Estates-General of 1484 to his reign's many assemblies, most notably the 1506 one that voted him the sobriquet "father of the People." His most recent biographer asserted with good evidence that "the consultative aspect of the French monarchy reached its peak in the Renaissance under Louis."[36] Francis I, however, was the king who most fully dramatized the king's embodiment of occasional *topoi* and dress in his assemblies and public art. In this way, he directed procedures that were becoming institutionalized into matters of theater and empathy rather than law and justice.

In 1516, Francis I returned victorious from the invasion of Italy, boasting that he had made peace and reformed the French church. However, he needed money to pay for his wars and support for his new Concordat of Bologna with the papacy. His general European peace, he claimed, ended the isolation from Christendom in which he had found France at his succession to the throne two years earlier. The king and his chief representative in legal assemblies, the chancellor, Cardinal Antoine Duprat, used assemblies to persuade different segments among the French to support a tax that would keep the peace. In this campaign of persuasion, an assembly-with-the-king was held at the Palais de Justice, the home of the Parlement of Paris, on February 5, 1517. With the king in attendance, Chancellor Duprat told high-ranking ecclesiastics, representatives of the university, and the Parlement of Paris of the king's successes, of the need for taxes, and of the Concordat.[37] Francis I's short speech chided the court for not supporting him on the Concordat and warned that he might use his special right of *nouvel advènement* to make new ordinances without counsel. The right of *nouvel advènement* was a royal lawyers' invention, based on occasional customs, of a new king's right to tax, abolish, or reform offices and privileges as he saw fit. His proposals received a cold reception. This assembly, however, was a rehearsal for the king's appeal to the towns of the kingdom in a March 21, 1517, Parisian assembly and in a series of provincial assemblies.

Francis I called together fifty-two representatives from the major towns of France because he "wished to enrich his kingdom, to show to the deputies the way this could be done, and to have their advice on making good laws to do it."[38] Despite the explicit exclusion of the Parlement of Paris from the assembly, the deputies met in "the chamber of the parlement, in the presence of the king and of several princes of the realm." They heard the chancellor's oration in defense of the Concordat and of tax reform as parts of a general program to benefit and enrich the whole kingdom: "Now since it has pleased God that we have peace, which is the preamble and foundation of all that the king desires to do, which is to enable his subjects to live in tranquillity and repose and to enrich them. These things come about through policy and good administration of *'la chose publique.'* "[39] The chancellor talked about the king's desire to appoint good judges and remove bad ones, and to reform the kingdom's laws and administration. As to the laws, "he had commissioned some persons to assemble and to look over all the ordinances of his ancestors and predecessors and . . . to take away superfluous ones." The deputies were given copies of the fourteen pages of proposed legislation and sent to meet in the Hôtel-de-la-Ville of Paris to formulate their responses.

In selecting the chamber of parlement as the venue of his assembly and excluding the Parlement of Paris, the king made sure that the assembly was recognized as an alternative to the February one. It did not suffice to raise taxes, because, as the chancellor's secretary, *parlementaire* Jean Barrillon, put it, "such public assemblies" always favored private interest over the public good.[40] The king nevertheless tried to turn the experiment to some good and ordered the deputies to explain his proposals "in full assembly" of each of their towns and to return their responses to the chancellor. When the responses finally reached Paris, they never left the leather bag in which they were kept. However, the experiment still represented an important attempt by the government to reach out to subjects through persuasion, as had been practiced by Louis XII and advocated by Guillaume Budé and other influential humanist reformers.

Powerful institutions like the University of Paris and the Parlement of Paris resisted efforts to enlarge political space through general assemblies-with-the-king, as was made clear in meetings in July and December 1527. The recent controversy over whether or not the July meeting was the "first" *lit de justice* should not distract from the important point for this discussion of the degree to which the whole assembly was stage-managed.[41] In looking from the perspective of assemblies-with-the-king, the July speech of Fourth President Charles Guillart of the Parlement of Paris was ad hoc and planned to defuse the contest over registering the Concordat by establishing the absolute submission of the court to the king and by defining its duties as an institution.[42] Some *parlementaires* might well have known the story circulating among humanists of how Thomas More as Speaker of the Commons had in 1523 defused the demand of the chancellor, Cardinal Wolsey, for a tax subsidy. The cardinal had stage-managed the occasion by coming to Parliament "with his whole train royally . . . there amongst them." More counter-stage-managed by having the Commons remain in "a marvellous obstinate silence" after the cardinal's oration with the excuse that they were "abashed at the presence of so noble a personage" into silence and that they could only discuss matters in the absence of the cardinal's regal aura.[43] The French were no less capable of such playacting. Most likely, Guillart's procedural oration in July 1527 allowed tensions to be defused in preparation for the more important and larger assembly of December 16–20, 1527.

The December 1527 assembly, like the 1517 one, was carefully staged and was innovative in its membership. The king also adopted the new style and spoke at length for himself. The king's and parlement's mutual embrace of oration stimulated new approaches to ceremonial figuration and interpretation. After his defeat at Pavia and captivity in Spain, Francis I was forced by the humiliating Treaty of Madrid to give up French territory and to send his two eldest sons as hostages to Spain. The king desired to break the treaty and to ransom the princes by making an alternative cash payment. (The script was somewhat like that of the large 1506 assembly, which made it appear that Louis XII "had been forced . . . by the people" to break the marriage compact with the Habsburgs and let his daughter Claude marry Francis, then duke of Angoulême.)[44] On December 16, 1527, Francis opened his assembly at the Palais de Justice of the Parlement of Paris before representatives from the other parlements, high clergy, deputies from the towns, and a vast array of other dignitaries.

Francis I "asked counsel at the assembly [on his obligations] to what he had agreed to by the Treaty of Madrid."[45] The king sat above the assembly on a royal throne known as the *lit.* The chancellor declared the assembly a secret meeting and had removed all people who were not "deputies for assisting." Those who remained swore not to reveal what the king said, whereupon the chancellor explained that the assembly had been called because of the king's "duty of his office." The king, he said, had already heard the advice of great and worthy men, but he did not wish to act "without first communicating to his subjects, not in the form of Estates, rather desiring to assemble them in this place, that is, the *Lit de Justice,* hoping for succor, comfort, and aid as well as good and loyal counsel according to their consciences, for the benefit of him, his kingdom, and the *chose publique.*"[46] Seated on the throne, Francis delivered a long and moving speech in which he threatened to resign and return to Spain if full support for him was not forthcoming from all the estates.

The political theater seems very evident. The king desired to break the treaty because it went against his duty as king; the price was to leave two of his children, one the heir to the throne, hostages in Spain. He needed support and money to advance his alternative treaty. If the delegates refused, then they would be blamed for the resignation of the king and the crisis in the monarchy. The king in person persuaded the assembly of his earnestness. Four days later, on December 20, the speakers for the nobility, the clergy, the towns, and the parlements, assembled again before the king to give their counsel and promises of support and money. The Parlement of Paris, in what Sarah Hanley interpreted as a *parlementaire* maneuver to dramatize its constitutional role in interpreting public law, showed in a legal brief the illegality of the treaty.[47] This move to stage the rallying between king and kingdom was reinforced by timing the assembly meeting during the feast of Christmas. As events turned out, this "secret" meeting of representatives from throughout the kingdom succeeded in publicizing the king's need and building national consensus. Francis I's personal touch provided, at least in the eyes of Catherine de Médicis, a model for her son Charles IX during his troubled reign. The lasting message of the assembly was the public accessibility of the monarchy and the very clear conviction that the king's presence at such gatherings could work political miracles.

Francis I continued to experiment with the hitherto undefined and fluid forms of assemblies-with-the-king.[48] Since the 1520s, French offices and institution passed from precarious to protected status, and today's historians are unable to decide whether social, political, or constitutional interpretations best explain the events. The view of this discussion is that stage management—that is, costuming, speaking, listening, and silences—was the business of all assemblies-with-the-king, and, as such, defined relations among different parts of the society and government. Assemblies created a repertoire of procedures and a hierarchy of privileges that strongly delineated the manner in which a king ruled. Even in refusing favor or in punishing the king had to observe norms, as did Henry II in the 1559 Mercuriale where Anne du Bourg spoke for over an hour against the persecution of Lutherans (figs. 2 and 3).[49]

Assemblies-with-the-king became historicized well after their staging, and only when they could be bounded within an institutional history. In 1527, the monarchy and assemblies-with-the-king still had no fixed composition or procedure and were not institutionalized. Only in the second half of the sixteenth century, and not in the beginning, were "the procedure and the professional hierarchy" both fixed among a "Fourth Estate" of lawyers.[50] Russell Major has emphasized that meetings between kings and subjects were "especially frequent during the early stages of the Renaissance monarchy . . . [and] lent a popular flavor to the government, but as no fixed composition or procedure was ever established they never became institutionalized."[51] No one should be surprised that procedure was the point of tension between popular participation and professional administration. Procedures that sufficed without the king's presence became problematic when the king attended an assembly. Where traditional writers held that a king should adhere to customs, reformers and royal officials agreed that the king had a reserved right to alter laws as well as procedures. In a precedent-oriented society, the preservation or change in forms was remembered long after the pressing business of the day was forgotten, at least until a narrative of events developed that was as powerful as institutional memories. Institutional memories preserved forms and procedures; the memory of events existed within a grand narrative of individuals or collective deeds, of causes, and of movements. From Sarah Hanley's constitutional perspective, the 1527 assembly in the Parlement of Paris had as its first concern the performance for the record of what the King's men constructed as a fixed and institutionalized procedure of government. In hindsight, the king in parlement was discovered to be an institution called the *lit de justice.*[52]

Francis I's success in 1527 probably inspired other such assemblies, such as the one held by Henry II on January 5, 1557. According to the summons, debts and war had forced Henry II "to renew the practice of his ancestors, to wit, to seek aid and favor of his people, to whom he could not more commodiously declare his necessities and persuade them to furnish out his charge than by calling together the general estates of his realm."[53] The meeting was again in the Palais de Justice, but this time there were two elevated thrones: one for Henry II and one a bit lower for his son the dauphin. The king revealed his weakness by asking for money to launch a war to bring general peace and restore prosperity. Yet, he also pledged never again to impose new taxes in "his public promise and in his son's presence to the end that both of them might thereby be included and bound to the performance of the same."[54] In an unexpected way, the 1557 assembly takes on aspects of the family portrait of royal authority that Du Chesne used for his frontispiece in 1609. In 1557, speakers for each of the four estates (church, nobility, parlements, and *villes*) responded with promises of support, though the effort failed because the towns insisted that a list of grievances be considered and that the amount of their contribution be cut.

The assembly of 1557 embellished the gestures and protocols of the 1517 and the two 1527 assemblies-with-the-king. The individual gestures and dress had become almost formulaic by 1557 in establishing rank, who knelt, who removed hats (and when), and who spoke. In 1557, Jean du Tillet, who attended the meeting, wrote: "Since it pertains to the Secretary of State and of Finances to keep the register of the Assembly and is not my duty, it is enough for me to have researched the order and *séance* of the assembly that will remain in the *registre du Parlement,* to make use of when it will be needed."[55] Du Tillet perhaps acted peevishly because other ceremonial organizers intruded on his monopoly as chief clerk of the Parlement of Paris and recorded the official business conducted there. But his careful description of the staging of the assembly—the placement of the furniture, the ornamentation, the order of entrances, and the seating arrangements—showed the coming of age of a formal etiquette for governing relations among the estates and offices. His corresponding neglect of the speeches illustrates the importance of an enduring "order and *séance,*" not the particular business of a day, in shaping monarchical traditions. In assemblies-with-the-king, the ranks were preserved as examples to the future, but not the matter of business as revealed in orations.

Assemblies and Orators

Particularly noteworthy in the above sample of assemblies is the broad application of a sense of ruling through persuasion and spectacle that displayed the new emphasis on the power of speech and oration. Rulers saw in assemblies great rhetorical potential which gave legal and constitutional weight to words. The ideal of the orator-king came from Italy to France in the early sixteenth century.[56] Other examples exist of assemblies designed for kings or chancellors both to persuade and to command in person. They demonstrate rulers' direct involvement in governing through spectacle and persuasion. Noteworthy and distinct in the French examples are the experimentations with the orator-king as fundamental to the French monarchy.[57]

The orator-king dramatically personalized politics at a time when theory and institutions were in enormous flux. His constant travel to take part in these dramas enhanced the king's effectiveness by enabling many of his subjects to experience his real presence among them at least once. Royal entries became extended rhetorical devices for turning the more structured assemblies to specific political purposes. At once ludic and serious, the king-among-the-people image came to embody heroic, divine, and legal-traditional attributes associated with the late sixteenth-century idea of royal majesty. This tangle of elements combined with ancient and medieval practices to establish the rules of deportment an individual must observe when before the king, and the king when before the people.

From Francis I's reign onward, *rhétoriqueurs* at court and throughout the cities of the kingdom closely resembled humanists who praised the heroic king as part "of a mission of public morality."[58] Through such praise they explained to the king what "the French in general and the inhabitants of towns in particular expected of him." By acknowledging this praise verbally, the orator-king conformed to a civic ethic that evaluated the worthiness of the ruler's manner of life. According to this code, he was expected to be seen among his people, who in turn were to demonstrate their natural love for him.[59] The problem of disobedience—of which there was plenty—

was addressed paternally in the form most capable of reconciliation and public healing: the king had not been heard or his intentions had been misunderstood. In the first half of the sixteenth century, the assemblies-with-the-king promoted a new consciousness of state by conveying the king's will directly from his mouth to his subjects' ears; in response, his subjects demonstrated a willingness to obey in gestures and words. The humanist image of this relationship was the Gallic Hercules, an image that appealed to king and subjects alike because it tended to personalize the king's exchanges with his subjects.[60] This personalized image of the orator-king existed in uneasy tension with the ideology of impersonal juridical monarchy shaped by lawyers and *parlementaires*. In an edict of 1523, Francis I propagated a clear statement of his ideal of kingship in which he highlighted the dependency and needs of "le plus humble et plus bas," for whom the king had a unique responsibility.[61] The personal image was necessary to reinforce a patriarchal hierarchy that the impersonal juridical image undermined.

The growth and increasing ceremonial complexity of the royal court complicated the new ideal of the orator-king. However, as Gaston Zeller has noted, the separation between king and subjects was less than in other European countries, and this closer rapport between them was "a reason why the royal institution was profoundly popular."[62] In the king's court, the Venetian ambassador wrote in 1561, "no one is excluded from his presence. The lackeys themselves and men of the lowest condition dare to penetrate in the secret cabinet of the King, in order to see all that happens there, to understand all that is said. This great familiarity makes, it is true, the subjects insolent, but it also makes them loyal and devoted to their King."[63] Zeller credited the great drift toward a highly personalized royal cult and ceremonial isolation to Henry III's reign. If this is true, it is ironic that Henry III, more than any other king since Louis XII, tried to rule through assemblies, even though the greatest observer of his reign, Michel Montaigne, tended to see this king as isolated more from too much ceremony rather than too little of it. In his essay "Ceremony of interviews between kings," Montaigne wrote that "not only each country but each city has its particular forms of civility, and so has each occupation."[64] This diversity was problematic when political practices had to reconcile images and theories of authority. But, as demonstrated in the 1517, 1527, and 1557 assemblies-with-the-king, the objective was to generate an empathetic understanding between king and people that enabled the king to recast the laws and institutions of France in a manner that overrode older legal and natural law arguments. In France, the "new ceremonialism" treated the successful staging of an event as being sufficient to legitimize its procedures forever afterward. In recycling a new form, an order was quickly fashioned into an old model for ranks and orders. More than an invented tradition, the French monarchy stumbled onto staging history. The assemblies-with-the-king were so successfully promoted as events in the kingdom's history that by the seventeenth century the national past came to be primarily the one discovered in the forms of celebrating the majesty and grandeur of the French kings. Ralph Giesey noted that it was "the absence of a lasting momentum of representative institutions, at the national level, that made possible the growth of absolutism in France."[65] To this, I would add that what also made it possible was the impossibility of imagining assemblies-without-the-king, as, in very different ways, the experiences of the Huguenots and the Holy League showed. This topic, however, requires another essay.

This essay has called attention to the importance of the turn to ceremonies and the rhetorical impetus embodied in the orator as cultural hero as keys for understanding sixteenth-century political history and thought.[66] All historians, to some degree, find moments and events, such as assemblies-with-the-king, that they elevate from anecdotal to representational history, fashioning them into symbols that frame their particular narrative of an age. A central historiographical problem concerns the process through which any event first becomes publicized and then is incorporated as a privileged moment in history. Nancy L. Roelker once reminded us of the weight that style bears in reconstructing history by citing the prologue from Shakespeare's *Henry V* to begin her definitive (and very style-conscious) study of Jeanne d'Albret, queen of Navarre:

> Into a thousand parts divide one man . . .
> For 'tis your thoughts that now must deck our kings,
> Carry them here and there, jumping o'er times,
> Turning the accomplishment of many years
> Into an hour-glass.[67]

The hourglass stands as a metaphor for the condensation of kingly acts into the stuff of historical narrative; or, to follow Nancy Roelker and Shakespeare again,

a Muse of fire, that would ascend
The brightest heaven of invention,
A kingdom for a stage, princes to act,
And monarchs to behold the swelling scene!

This essay has examined the shaping of assemblies-with-the-king primarily as the invention of rulers and their "artisans of glory," who strove to have others see and hear kings as they wished to be seen and heard.[68] Once assembly traditions were discovered and then subjected to taxonomies, ceremonial collectors from Jean du Tillet to Théodore and Denis Godefroy could give narrative form not simply to a single king but to the entire French monarchy. This convergence of assembly, rhetoric, and print required people to think in a new way about the various styles, forms, and images that informed the public conduct of French kings. Central to these new perceptions was the question of what was appropriate in kingly demonstrations of paternal love, piety before God, and empathy before subjects over against the conscious manipulation of honor, ambition, and greed to serve princely interests. Thomas More and Niccolò Machiavelli offered later generations of French readers contrasting examples of how to select and include events into assembly traditions by expanding the legal element represented in "majesty" to encompass rhetorical, biological, and political concepts of "embodied majesty."[69] Valois assemblies-with-the-king naturally adapted the new ceremonialism of Italian civic culture—which synthesized concerns about legitimacy, renown, and communal traditions—to French conditions, all the while preserving as the leitmotif the desire to stage an event so authentically and impressively that it absorbed past traditions and supplied the form and critique for future performances. Thus, through performance, remotely connected events became fabricated into an apparently seamless web of history that was at base fictive. The French became persuaded that the web was the monarchy as embodied in the king, though by comparison, we do well to remember that the English eventually became dissuaded that the monarchy existed solely in the person of the king.

It is also worth noting that between 1550 and 1600, another form of spectacle—theater—competed with and eventually superseded assemblies-with-the-king. The speeches of actors on stages dramatized the manner in which pretended kings of yore grappled with political dilemmas. In early seventeenth-century France, theatrical productions reflected many aspects of contemporary political thought, though, interestingly, the growing appeal of actor-kings in classical drama drew inspiration from the eloquent speeches and lavishly staged spectacles of real sixteenth-century kings. The earlier humanist ideal of the orator-king transformed nobles and townspeople into auditors; it converted places of assembly into tribunals and theaters of power, and it urged the public to interpret highly charged political gestures and symbols. In a variety of ways, the programs of sixteenth-century French kings to act and to persuade in public ceremonies prepared people to become audiences, to respond to drama and grandeur, to see history in staged events, and—most important—to be ruled. The widespread use of print and pre-scripted ceremonies encouraged the French people collectively to imagine new kinds of politics and drama. However, as seventeenth-century politics became steadily reduced to royal spectacle, so too did words, along with the ideal of the orator-king, lose their public power in affairs of state. Rather than directly shaping the policies and institutions of royal government, rhetoric instead enriched the new public taste for theater and literature, nourishing in the process the emergence of a public sphere during the eighteenth century that stood apart from the monarchy.

Appendix: Documents of Royal Approval for Research on French Ceremonial Traditions, printed at the beginning of Théodore and Denis Godefroy's *Le Cérémonial François,* 2 vols. (Paris: Sebastien Cramoisy, 1649).

DE LA NECESSITE DE FAIRE VN *Recueil des Rangs & Seances* entre les Princes, Officiers de la Couronne, & autres grands Seigneurs du Royaume de France. *Necessité de faire vn Recueil touchant les Rãgs desGrands de France.*

Et la Commiſsion donnée à ce ſuiet par le Roy Henry II. en 1548.

E iourd'huy vingt-deuxiéme iour de Decembre, mil cinq cens quarante-huit, A moy Iean du Tillet, Protonotaire & Secretaire du Roy, Greffier Ciuil de ſon Parlement à Paris, a eſté apportée par vn Cheuaucheur de l'Eſcurie dudit Seigneur la Commiſſion, de laquelle la teneur enſuit. *1548.*

HENRY par la grace de Dieu Roy de France, A noſtre amé & feal Protonotaire & Secretaire; Maiſtre Iean du Tillet, Greffier Ciuil de noſtre Cour de Parlement à Paris, Salut & dilection: Pource que nous deſirons ſçauoir & entendre quel rang & ordre, du temps de nos predeceſſeurs Roys de France iuſques à huy, ont tenu en toutes grandes & ſolennelles Aſſemblées les Princes de noſtre Sang, tánt Ducs que Comtes, & les autres Princes de noſtre Royaume, Ducs, Comtes, & autres de moindre titre & dignité; & ſemblablement les Conneſtable, Mareſchaux, & Admiral de France: A cette cauſe nous vous mandons & commettons, que tous autres affaires ceſſans & poſtpoſez, vous ayez tant par vous que par ceux que vous commettrez ſous vous à bien voir & viſiter les Regiſtres de noſtredite Cour de Parlement, faiſans mention de ſemblables choſes: Et ſur iceux feſiez bons & loyaux Extraits de ce que verrez appartenir à la verification de ce que deſſus; leſquels Extraits feront mention ſpeciale de la qualité de l'Aſſemblée, & ſi elle eſtoit ſolennelle en forme d'Eſtats, ou d'Entrées des Roys nos anteceſſeurs en leurs Villes, ou en tenans le Lict de la Iuſtice, ou autres ſolennelles Aſſemblées, eſquelles les Rangs & ordres ſe ſoient gardez, & aſſignez à vn chacun, & de quels temps, & ſous quels Roys elles auront eſté faites: & ſi vous connoiſſez que pour plus ample intelligence, & verification de tout ce que deſſus, il ſoit requis voir aucuns Regiſtres eſtans, ſoit en noſtre Chambre des Comptes, ou au Treſor de nos Chartes audit Paris, vous vous retirerez par deuers les Gens de nos Comptes, & Treſorier de noſdites Chartes; Auſquels nous mandons & enioignons vous exhiber & repreſenter, ou faire exhiber & repreſenter ſi toſt que requis en ſeront par vous leſdits Regiſtres, pour ſur iceux faire faire ſemblables Extraits: Tous leſquels Extraits qui ainſi ſeront par vous faits, vous ferez tenir és mains de noſtre tres-chet & feal Chancelier incontinent, & le plus diligemment qu'il vous ſera poſſible: Car tel eſt noſtre plaiſir. De ce faire vous auons donné, & donnons plein pouuoir, puiſſance, authorité, commiſſion & mandement eſpecial. Donné à Sainct Germain en Laye le vingt-vniéme iour de Decembre, l'an

Le Rang des Princes, Ducs, Comtes, & Officiers de la Couronne.

Ce Recueil ſe deuoit faire du Greffe Ciuil de la Cour de Parlement.

De la Chambre desComptes Et du Treſor des Chartes.

Les Extraits deuoiẽt eſtre deliurez, és mains du Chancelier.

é iiij

de grace mil cinq cens quarante-huit; & de nostre Regne le deuxiéme. Ainsi signé, Par le Roy, *De l'Aubespine.* Et seellé à simple queuë de cire-iaune. Pour executer le contenu de laquelle Commission, ie me suis transporté au Greffe Ciuil dudit Parlement, celuy de la Chambre des Comptes, & au Tresor des Chartres dudit Seigneur: Et aprés la plus diligente visitation & perquisition que possible m'a esté, i'ay assemblé & collationné fidelement les Extraits & Copies par l'ordre & en la forme qui ensuiuent, &c.

1583. *Les Articles, & Propositions du Roy Henry III. à l'Assemblée des Princes, Officiers de la Couronne, Conseillers de son Conseil, & des Presidens, Conseillers, & autres Officiers, tant de la Cour de Parlement de Paris, que de la Chambre des Comptes, & autres Cours Souueraines, à Sainct Germain en Laye, l'an mil cinq cens quatre-vingts trois.*

La Proposition du Roy. SI l'on doit resoudre les Rangs & Seances tant des Princes, Ducs, Officiers de la Couronne, qu'autres qui en doiuent auoir, comme les Compagnies; A sçauoir ceux du Conseil du Roy, les Parlemens, Chambres des Comptes, & autres Cours & Corps, pour éuiter la contention & confusion que souuentefois l'on voit artiuer en tous lieux, où lesdits Rangs & Seances se doiuent tenir; & en faire vn Registre autentique, pour à l'aduenir estre obserué.

L'aduis de l'Assemblée.

Response à icelle Proposition. COMBIEN que l'ordre qui paroist és choses exterieures & publiques soit vn grand indice de la disposition des plus particulieres, & que pour cette occasion il fust tres-expedient pour la reputation de ce Royaume, de pouruoir à l'incertitude des Rangs & Seances, qui rend nos Ceremonies (qui sont d'ailleurs tres-belles & bien establies) toutes confuses & imparfaites; toutesfois parce que ce seroit vn œuure grand, plein d'épines, & qui ne se peu pas acheuer promptement, lesdits Sieurs ont estimé qu'il suffira, quant à present, d'y donner quelque commencement. *Rang des Grands.* Et à cette fin qu'il plaise à sa Maiesté commander au Maistre de ses Ceremonies de luy recueillir vn Memoire bien ample de toutes les disputes qui sont entre les Princes, Officiers de la Couronne, & autres grands Seigneurs pour raison desdits Rangs; ensemble de ce qu'il trouuera sur les Registres & Memoires concernans lesdites disputes, pour auec le temps y estre pouruen par sa Maiesté comme elle verra bon estre. Et *Rang des Communautez.* pour le regard des disputes qui sont pour lesdits Rangs entre les Communautez, tant de Gens d'Eglise, Cours Souueraines, qu'autres particuliers Officiers de sa Maiesté; qu'il est bien expedient de les vuider dés à present, & pour ce faire en retenir la connoissance en son Conseil, ou l'attribuer à tels autres Iuges qu'il plaira à sa Maiesté choisir, & deputer.

Creation, & inſtitution de la Charge de Grand Maiſtre des Ceremonies de France, par le Roy Henry III. & les Lettres de Prouiſion d'icelle en faueur du ſieur de Rhodes, l'an 1585.

DE PAR LE ROY.

1585.
2. Ianuier.

GRAND MAISTRE de France, Maiſtres ordinaires de noſtre Hoſtel, & vous Maiſtre & Controlleur de noſtre Chambre aux Deniers, Salut : Comme pour le ſingulier deſir que nous auons que toutes choſes ſoient conduites & maintenuës en noſtre Cour auec l'ordre requis pour y faire reconnoiſtre la dignité, & ſplendeur conuenable à noſtre Royale Grandeur, nous ayons fait pluſieurs beaux Reglemés*, pour l'execution d'aucuns deſquels nous auons par exprés voulu & ordonné, que le ſieur de Rhodes Guillaume Pot, Preuoſt & Maiſtre des Ceremonies de nos deux Ordres, ſoit ordinairement, où le plus ſouuent qu'il pourra à noſtre ſuite, afin de faire & accomplir ce qui dependra de ſa Charge ſelon noſtre intention : Et tout ainſi que ce nous ſera beaucoup de contentement de voir cette Charge dignement deſſeruie, auſſi voulons nous bien l'honorer le plus que faire ſe pourra. Sçauoir faiſons, que nous pour ces cauſes, & autres bonnes conſiderations à ce nous mouuans, & ayans égard meſmement aux continuels & agreables ſeruices qu'il nous a cy-deuant faits en icelle, comme nous eſperons qu'il nous continuëra de bien en mieux : Auons iceluy ſieur de Rhodes fait, creé & inſtitué, faiſons, creons & inſtituons par ces preſentes Grand Maiſtre des Ceremonies, pour par luy doreſnauant en cette qualité nous ſeruir audit Eſtat, & en iouyr & vſer aux honneurs, authoritez, prerogatiues, preeminences, franchiſes, libertez, & droicts qui y appartiennent, & aux gages de mil eſcus par an, que nous luy auons ordonnez & attribuez, ordonnons & attribuons par ces preſentes tant qu'il nous plaira. Si vous mandons que ſans prendre dudit ſieur de Rhodes autres nouueaux Sermens que celuy qu'il a cy-deuant fait & preſté, Vous, cette preſente creation & inſtitution de Grand Maiſtre des Ceremonies feſiez enregiſtrer és Regiſtres, papiers & écrits de noſtre Chambre aux Deniers, & dudit Eſtat & Charge feſiez, ſouffriez, & laiſſiez iceluy ſieur de Rhodes iouyr, & vſer pleinement & paiſiblement, & à luy obeyr & entendre de tous ceux, & ainſi qu'il appartiendra és choſes touchans & concernans icelle. Mandons en outre aux Treſoriers de noſtre Eſpargne, qu'ils payent, ou par les Treſoriers de nos Officiers domeſtiques chacun en l'année de ſon exercice, faſſent payer audit ſieur de Rhodes leſdits gages de mil écus doreſnauant par chacun an, ſelon & enſuiuant les eſtats qui en ſeront par nous faits, & qu'il eſt accouſtumé en ſemblable : Car tel eſt noſtre plaiſir. Donné à Paris ſous le ſeel de noſtre Secret le deuxiéme iour de Ianuier, l'an mil cinq cens quatre-vingts cinq. Signé, *Henry* ; Et plus bas, Par le Roy, *Brulart*, auec vn paraphe.

*Ils ſe verront dans le troiſiéme volume.

Notes

I thank the National Endowment for the Humanities; California State University, Chico; and the Folger Shakespeare Library Institute for making it possible for me to spend my sabbatical year 1993–94 as an NEH Fellow at the Folger Shakespeare Library. In the ideal research conditions of this library I worked on this essay, and I first presented parts of it at a Folger Institute luncheon seminar. I also appreciate the helpful comments of colleagues at the Folger: Nancy Kline Maguire, Patricia Springborg, and Richard Helgerson. Marcia Langley Bryant made valuable suggestions and corrections as well. I greatly appreciate Michael Wolfe's many efforts—as a diligent editor, careful reader, and learned critic—to improve the essay. I, of course, am responsible for any shortcomings it may have.

1. Howell A. Lloyd, *The State, France, and the Sixteenth Century* (London: George Allen & Unwin, 1983), pp. 47, 21–47.

2. The standard studies in English on Du Tillet are Donald Kelley, *Foundations of Modern Historical Scholarship: Language, Law, and History* (New York: Columbia University Press, 1970); and Sarah Hanley, *The Lit de Justice of the Kings of France: Constitutional Ideology in Legend, Ritual, and Discourse* (Princeton: Princeton University Press, 1983), pp. 102–25. This paper also benefits from discussions over the years with Elizabeth A. R. Brown. I read an early version of her book on Jean du Tillet and his *Recueils* for the kings of France and have drawn from her introduction to the edition of *Jean du Tillet and the French Wars of Religion: Five Tracts, 1562–1569* (Binghamton, N.Y.: Medieval and Renaissance Texts and Studies, 1994). I was not able to obtain a copy in time for consideration in this essay of Brown and Richard C. Famiglietti's *The Lit de Justice: Semantics, Ceremonial, and the Parlement of Paris, 1300–1600,* Beihefte der Francia, Deutsches Historisches Institut Paris (Sigmaringen: Jan Thorbecke, 1993).

3. Roger Chartier, ed., *The Culture of Print: Power and the Uses of Print in Early Modern Europe,* trans. Lydia G. Cochrane (Princeton: Princeton University Press, 1987), p. 1. I apply to ceremonies the notion that Henri-Jean Martin began his discussion of the printing revolution with: "From our standpoint, Europe must be considered as one area, not only of production, but also the circulation of goods and people. Therefore, it was also an integrated whole in terms of the spread of information and cultures" (*Histoire de l'édition française,* ed. Henri-Jean Martin and Roger Chartier, 4 vols. [Paris: Promodis, 1983], 1:145).

4. Théodore Godefroy, *Le Cérémonial de France, ou description des Ceremonies, Rangs, & Seances observées aux couronnements, Entrées, & Enterremens des roys & Reynes de France & autres Acts et Assemblées Solemnelles* (Paris, 1619), preface.

5. For a recent review of thoughts on late sixteenth-century assemblies, see Sarah Hanley, "The French Constitution Revised: Representative Assemblies and Resistance Rights in the Sixteenth Century," in *Society and Institutions in Early Modern France,* ed. Mack P. Holt (Athens: University of Georgia Press, 1991), pp. 36–50. For some sense of the scale of assembling, see Léonce Anquez, *Histoire des Assemblées*

politiques des Réformés de France: 1573–1622 (Paris, 1859); Frederic J. Baumgartner, *Radical Reactionaries: The Political Thought of the French Catholic League* (Geneva: Droz, 1976); J. Russell Major, *Representative Government in Early Modern France* (New Haven: Yale University Press, 1980).

6. J. H. Shennan, "The Political Organization of the Estates," in *Government and Society in France, 1461–1661* (New York: Barnes & Noble, 1969), p. 33, refers specifically to meetings of the three estates.

7. Richard C. Trexler, *The "Libro Cerimoniale" of the Florentine Republic* (Geneva: Librairie Droz, 1978), p. 10; and L. M. Bryant, "Configurations of the Community in Late Medieval Spectacles: Paris and London during the Dual Monarchy," in *City and Spectacle in Medieval Europe,* ed. Barbara Hanawalt and Katheryn Reyerson, Medieval Studies at Minnesota 6 (Minneapolis: University of Minnesota Press, 1994), pp. 3–32.

8. J. Russell Major, *Representative Government in Early Modern France,* pp. 257, 160–204.

9. *Essays,* 1:42, as cited in Robert Mandrou's *Introduction to Modern France, 1500–1640: An Essay in Historical Psychology,* trans. R. E. Hallmark (London: Edward Arnold, 1975), p. 124.

10. J. Russell Major, *From Renaissance Monarchy to Absolute Monarchy: French Kings, Nobles, and Estates* (Baltimore: Johns Hopkins University Press, 1994), p. xx and passim.

11. Norbert Elias, *The Civilizing Process:* vol. 1, *The History of Manners;* vol. 2, *State Formation and Civilization,* trans. Edmund Jephcott (Oxford: Basil Blackwell, 1978, 1982), 2:7. For a recent assessment, see Jean-François Solnon, *La Cour de France* (Paris: Fayard, 1987); and Roger Chartier, *Cultural History: Between Practices and Representations,* trans. Lydia G. Cochrane (Ithaca: Cornell University Press, 1988), pp. 71–94.

12. I am indebted to several important studies that acknowledge the place of performance in understanding shifts in mentalities and the shaping of institutional identities. First among them are the works of Frances A. Yates, including the essays in *Astraea: The Imperial Theme in the Sixteenth Century* (London: Ark Paperbacks, 1975), *The French Academies of the Sixteenth Century* (London: Studies of the Warburg Institute, vol. 15, 1947), and *The Valois Tapestries,* 2d ed. (London: Routledge & Kegan Paul, 1975). The literature on ceremony and public life is surveyed in Roy Strong's *Art and Power: Renaissance Festivals, 1450–1650* (Berkeley: University of California Press, 1984). For an update to Strong's bibliography, see Robert Baldwin, "A Bibliography of the Literature of Triumph," and other essays in *"All the World's a Stage . . ." Art and Pageantry in the Renaissance and Baroque,* ed. Barbara Wisch and Susan Scott Munshower, Pennsylvania State University Papers in Art History 6 (University Park: Pennsylvania State University Press, 1990), pp. 360–85. French ceremonies and political thought are surveyed in Ralph Giesey, "Models of Rulership in French Royal Ceremonial," in *Rites of Power: Symbolism, Ritual and Politics since the Middle Ages,* ed. Sean Wilentz (Philadelphia: University of Pennsyl-

vania Press, 1985), pp. 41–64. The construction of an ideal for the "new" Stuart monarchy is well considered in Malcolm Smuts, *Court Culture and the Origins of a Royalist Tradition in Early Stuart England* (Philadelphia: University of Pennsylvania Press, 1987).

13. For example, see the section "Sous le signe de Mercure: le thème du roi-orateur et l'emblème au caducée composé pour Louise de Savoie," in Anne-Marie Lecoq, *François Ier imaginaire: Symbolique et politique à l'aube de la Renaissance française* (Paris: Éditions Macula, 1987), pp. 421–33; also, L. M. Bryant, "Politics, Ceremonies, and Embodiments of Majesty in Henry II's France," in *European Monarchy,* ed. Heinz Duchhardt, Richard A. Jackson, and David Sturdy (Stuttgart: Franz Steiner Verlag, 1992), pp. 127–54.

14. See Joseph Strayer, "France: The Holy Land, the Chosen People, and the Most Christian King," in *Action and Conviction in Early Modern Europe,* ed. J. K. Rabb and J. E. Seigel (Princeton: Princeton University Press, 1969).

15. Claude de Seyssel, *La Grant monarchie de France* (Paris, 1519); J. Tortorel and J. Perrissin, *Quarante tableaux ou histoires diverses qui sont Mémorables, touchant les guerres, massacres et troubles advenus en ces dernières années* (Geneva, 1570); André du Chesne, *Les Antiquitez et Recherches de la Grandeur et Majesté des Roys de France* (Paris, 1619).

16. Robert Scheller, "Ensigns of Authority: French Royal Symbolism in the Age of Louis XII," *Simiolus* 13 (1982): 75–141; and Frederic J. Baumgartner, *Louis XII* (New York: St. Martin's Press, 1994), particularly pp. 153–68.

17. Théodore Godefroy and Denis Godefroy, *Le Cérémonial françois,* 2 vols. (Paris, 1649).

18. See note 3 above.

19. Godefroy and Godefroy, *Cérémonial françois,* vol. 1, introduction; see also Hanley, *The* Lit de Justice, p. 107.

20. Jean François Solon, *La Cour de France* (Paris: Fayard, 1987), pp. 126–59.

21. Giesey, *Cérémonial et puissance: France, xve–xviie siècles* (Paris: A. Colin, 1987), pp. 56–61.

22. I use the Folger Shakespeare Library 1579–80 edition entitled *Recueil des Roys de France, leurs couronne et maison, ensemble le rengs des grands de France, par Jean du Tillet, sieur de la Bussiere, Protonotaire et Secretaire du Roy, Greffier de son Parlement Plus Une Chronique abbregée contenant tout ce qui est advenu, tant en fait de Guerre, qu'autrements entre les Roys et Princes, Republique et Potentats estrangue: Par M. I. du Tillet, Evesque de Meaux freres* (Paris, 1580), p. 332. The Folger 1578 edition is entitled *Les Memoires et Recherches de Jean du Tillet, Greffier de la Cour de Parlement à Paris, Contenans plusieurs chose memorables pour l'intelligence de l'estat des affaires de France,* and it was printed in Rouen by Philippe de Tours in 1578. The introductions in the two texts differ in ways that suggest they both were translated from a Latin original and that the translators had different views of the French monarchy. I use the 1580 Paris edition because it was expressly stated to be the one approved by Du Tillet's family and the Parlement of Paris.

23. Tacitus's appeal to sixteenth- and seventeenth-century public figures is based on the fact that he opened a place to rhetoric as literature and preserved an ideal of eloquence in face of institutional forms that greatly restrained candid speech; see Salmon, "Cicero and Tacitus in the Sixteenth Century," *American Historical Review* 85 (1980): 63–70; and M. Fumaroli, *L'Age de l'Eloquence: Rhétorique et "res literaria" de la Renaissance au seuil de l'époque classique* (Geneva: Droz, 1980), pp. 425–705.

24. This book's companion (and more frequently published) volume looks at the other France in *Les antiquitez et recherches des villes, chasteaux et places plus remarquables de toute la France* (Paris, 1609). A century later, Piganiol de la Force organized his popular *Nouvelle Description de la France* according to this same division.

25. Giesey, *Cérémonial et puissance,* pp. 50–56.

26. A sample of studies on the changing images of French kings includes Claire Richter Sherman, *The Portraits of Charles V of France: 1338–1380* (New York: New York University Press, 1969); Robert W. Scheller, "Ensigns of Authority"; Scheller, "Imperial Themes in Art and Literature of the Early French Renaissance: The Period of Charles VIII," *Simiolus* 12 (1982): 5–69; Scheller, "Gallia cisalpina: Louis XII and Italy: 1499–1508," *Simiolus* 15 (1985): 5–60; Jean Boutier, Alain Dewerpe, and Daniel Nordman, *Un Tour de France Royal: Le Voyage de Charles IX (1564–1566)* (Paris: Aubier, 1984), pp. 325–45. Also, see Lecoq, *François Ier imaginaire;* Michael Tyvaret, "L'Image du roi: Légitimité et oralité royale dans les histoires de France au XVIIe siècle," *Revue d'histoire moderne et contemporaine* 21 (1974): 521–47; and Peter Burke, *The Fabrication of Louis XIV* (New Haven: Yale University Press, 1992).

27. Lloyd, *The State,* pp. 49–83, authoritatively and persuasively updates and analyzes the issues and literature of the "crisis" interpretation of the period, and also discusses the political and legal side of problems of performance in the exaltation of the king and association of offices with the king; see pp. 146–58.

28. Donald R. Kelley, *The Beginning of Ideology: Consciousness and Society in the French Reformation* (Cambridge: Cambridge University Press, 1981), pp. 178–85; George Huppert, *The Idea of Perfect History: Historical Erudition and Historical Philosophy in Renaissance France* (Urbana: University of Illinois Press, 1970). Major reviewed the recent literature that established the nobility as "the most dynamic element in the society of that day" in *From Renaissance Monarchy to Absolute Monarchy,* pp. xvii–xx.

29. These views are summarized in François Belleforest's introduction to his *Harangues militaires et concions de princes, ambassadeurs,* but he was already losing faith in the ideal. On the primacy of rhetoric in Renaissance views of society, see Brian Vickers, *In Defence of Rhetoric* (Oxford: Clarendon Press, 1988), pp. 255–93; Marc Fumaroli, "Rhetoric, Politics, and Society: From Italian Ciceronianism to French Classicism," in *The Theory and Practice of Renaissance Rhetoric,* ed. James G. Murphy (Berkeley: University of California Press, 1983), pp. 253–47; J. H. M. Salmon, "Cicero and Tacitus," pp. 307–31. On orator-princes, see my summary in "Politics, Ceremonies, and Embodiments of Majesty," pp. 128–54.

30. G. O. Sayles, *The King's Parliament of England* (New York: W. W. Norton, 1974), p. 134.

31. Ibid., p. 7.

32. Quentin Skinner, *The Foundations of Modern Political Thought*, 2 vols. (Cambridge: Cambridge University Press, 1978), 1:xi, 2:255.

33. Lecoq, *François Ier imaginaire*, p. 488; R. Doucet, *Les Institutions de la France au XVIe siècle*, 2 vols. (Paris: A. & J. Picard et Cle, 1948), 1:76.

34. Francesco Guicciardini, *The History of Italy*, trans. Sidney Alexander (New York: Collier, 1969), pp. 63–65.

35. As recounted by Jean d'Auton, for example, in *Chronique de Louis XII*, ed. R. de Maulde-la-Clavière, 4 vols. (Paris, 1889–95). These chronicles were edited and published by Théodore Godefroy in 1615 and utilized extensively as sources in his compilation of French ceremonies. For the ceremonies of the kings in Italy, but without much analysis of the political context, see Bonner Mitchell, *The Majesty of the State: Triumphal Progresses of Foreign Sovereigns in Renaissance Italy (1494–1600)* (Florence, 1896).

36. Baumgartner, *Louis XII*, p. 84.

37. R. J. Knecht, *Francis I* (Cambridge: Cambridge University Press, 1982), pp. 55–58; Jean du Tillet, *Recueil des Roys de France, leurs Couronne et maison, ensemble le reng des grands de France* (Paris: Jacques du Puys, 1579–80), pp. 420–21.

38. Jean Barrillon, *Journal*, ed. Pierre de Vaissière, 2 vols. (Paris, 1897), 1:273–305.

39. Ibid., p. 279.

40. Ibid., p. 303.

41. This contentious assembly of July 1527 and the December one Sarah Hanley saw as the origins of the *lit de justice* as a constitutional forum; see Hanley, *The* Lit de Justice, pp. 48–85.

42. See R. J. Knecht, "Francis I and the '*Lit de Justice*': A 'Legend' Defended," *French History* 7.1 (1993): 43–83, which calls attention to the importance of stage management: "Historians have traditionally assumed that [President of the Parlement of Paris] Guillart's speech and the king's response to it were spontaneous. However, we cannot be sure that stage-management was absent from the proceedings in the Grand'Chambre on 24 July" (p. 67). Guillart's speech is reprinted in this article. I think that Professor Knecht should follow his insight into stage management; as it is, his view of the day remains even more "unduly selective" (his words) than Sarah Hanley's interpretation. The narrow historicity of the July assembly that he presents is distinctly different from the way Du Tillet and others fitted them into a chain of history that is the point of Hanley's interpretation.

43. William Roper and Nicholas Harpsfield, *Lives of Saint Thomas More*, ed. and intro. E. E. Reynolds (London: Everyman's Library, 1963), pp. 10–12, 70–72.

44. Baumgartner, *Louis XII*, pp. 146–47.

45. Godefroy and Godefroy, *Cérémonial françois*, 2:478–90; also Knecht, *Francis I*, pp. 215–17.

46. Godefroy and Godefroy, *Cérémonial françois*, 2:478–91.

47. Hanley, *The* Lit de Justice, p. 82.

48. Bryant, "Politics, Ceremonies, and Embodiments of Majesty," pp. 128–54.

49. Kelley, *The Beginning of Ideology,* pp. 171–77.

50. Ibid., p. 180.

51. J. Russell Major, "Popular Initiative in Renaissance France," in *Aspects of the Renaissance: A Symposium,* ed. Archibald R. Lewis (Austin: University of Texas Press, 1967), p. 32.

52. Hanley, *The* Lit de Justice, pp. 102–22.

53. Lancelot Voisin, sieur de la Popelinière, *The Histoire of France: The Four First Books* (London: John Winder, 1595), p. 242.

54. Ibid.

55. Godefroy and Godefroy, *Cérémonial françois,* 1:380, also 2:380–82.

56. See Vickers, *In Defence of Rhetoric,* pp. 254–93.

57. See note 28 above.

58. Lecoq, *François Ier imaginaire,* p. 493, and "Épilogue," pp. 482–94, is the major source for this paragraph. The author included a discussion of "the panegyric of the sovereign" delivered to or about the sovereign which needs to be analyzed as the companion of the oration made by the prince in a kind of elaborate political and rhetorical game.

59. The issue is reviewed in Boutier et al., *Un Tour de France royal,* pp. 286–91. On how access to the king figured in the architecture of the Louvre, see David Thomson's *Renaissance Paris: Architecture and Growth, 1475–1600* (Berkeley: University of California Press, 1984).

60. Lecoq, *François Ier imaginaire,* pp. 421–33; Bryant, "Politics, Ceremonies, and Embodiments of Majesty"; M. R. Jung, *Hercules dans la littérature française du XVIe siècle* (Geneva: Librairie Droz, 1966).

61. Isambert et al., *Recueil général des anciennes lois françaises* (Paris, 1928), vol. 12 (1514–1546), pp. 216–17.

62. Gaston Zeller, *Les Institutions de la France au XVIe siècle,* 2d ed. (Paris: Presses Universitaires de France, 1987), p. 97.

63. Ibid. The "love" of the subjects for their kings has almost become a fixture of French historiography and needs to be examined as a historical creation rather than an explanation of events and behavior. For example, see Mandrou's *Introduction to Modern France* on the topic (pp. 101–31).

64. Michel de Montaigne, *The Complete Essays of Montaigne,* trans. Donald M. Frame (Stanford: Stanford University Press, 1965), 1:13, p. 32.

65. Giesey, "La Société de Cour," in *Cérémonial et puissance souveraine,* p. 86.

66. On this point, see Alison Brown, "Platonism in Fifteenth-Century Florence and Its Contribution to Early Modern Political Thought," *Journal of Modern History* 58 (1986): 383–413; Marc Fumaroli, "Rhetoric, Politics, and Society: From Italian Ciceronianism to French Classicism," in *Renaissance Eloquence: Studies in the Theory and Practice of Renaissance Rhetoric,* ed. James J. Murphy (Berkeley: University of California Press, 1983), pp. 253–73.

67. Nancy Lyman Roelker, *Queen of Navarre: Jeanne d'Albret, 1528–1572* (Cambridge: Harvard University Press, 1968), p. 1, citing Shakespeare's *Henry V.*

68. Orest Ranum, *Artisans of Glory: Writers and Historical Thought in Seventeenth-Century France* (Chapel Hill: University of North Carolina Press, 1980).

69. See Bryant, "Politics, Ceremonies, and Embodiments of Majesty," pp. 128–54.

Sarah Hanley

Identity Politics and Rulership in France: Female Political Place and the Fraudulent Salic Law in Christine de Pizan and Jean de Montreuil

In France amid the growing national consciousness and establishment of a public realm in the 1200s–1400s, through the period of
nascent state building and centralization of the 1500s–1700s, two juridical
frameworks shaped political identity. The first, a resurrected *French Salic law*
(Salic Law Code, 500s–800s), briefly mentioned in 1358, was alleged in the
1400s to be a public law excluding women (and their sons) from rule in a
body politic represented as "the king's one body." The second, a *French Law
Canon* (civil law and public law) rooted in natural law, was formulated from
the 1550s to the 1650s establishing a monarchic state that privileged the
male right to rule in state (king) and household (husband) through a parallel
system of marital regime governance.[1] Reflection on the history of those law
partners reveals the contested processes through which political identity
was culturally configured in late medieval and early modern France. The
curious odyssey of the Salic law offers an interesting trajectory given its
failure to attract attention (1358–1400), debated validity (1400s–1480s),
tempered success (1480s–1530s), and awkward collapse (mid-1500s) under
the accumulated weight of forgery and fraud.

In the 1400s some writers held that an ancient Salic ordinance juridically
established the exclusion of women from rule in the kingdom of France. The
truth is quite the contrary.[2] The Franco-Germanic Salic Law Code, rendered
in a Merovingian redaction (c. 507–11) and then an expanded Carolingian
one (802–3),[3] did not contain an ordinance regulating succession to realm
and rule. When the text of a Salic ordinance (title *De allodio,* article 6) was
resurrected in the 1400s, therefore, it proved unyielding on that point. A
Carolingian redaction reads as follows: "Indeed concerning Salic land no
part of the inheritance may pass to a woman, but all the inheritance of land
goes to the virile sex."[4] Standing alone, that civil ordinance is perplexing; in
context, it is less so. An integral part of a section titled *De allodio* ("On
allodial [lands]"), the ordinance (article 6) was mediated, even contradicted,

by others in that title and in other titles. Taken as a whole, Salic laws permitted women to inherit allodial lands (essentially family farms), sometimes favored transmission through female lines, and also allowed other lands held in grant from rulers to pass (in the absence of males) to females.[5] That said, around 1000, when Salic laws and Roman laws had meshed through concurrent usage, the Salic Code disappeared.

In northern France in the 1100s–1300s, a fusion of laws—Salic, Roman, and feudal—produced regional customary laws (*coutumiers*), written laws collected by jurists and treated as "French common laws" applied in a kingdom deemed a public realm regulated by public law.[6] Official compilations were ordered by kings in 1454, 1494, and 1509, then redacted in the *Coutume de Paris* (1510, revised 1580).[7] In accordance with French customary law, women succeeded to lands, including duchies, fiefs, and appanages, and rendered homage for them; and some women who did not inherit directly passed inheritance rights to successors, as practiced in the Paris region.[8] Contrary to false allegations made in the 1400s, those practices prevailed throughout this period until the early 1500s.[9] As a result, the attempt to transform the Salic ordinance from a civil law of the Salian Franks (regulating inheritance of allodial lands) into a public law of the French kingdom (regulating succession to monarchic rule) met with contextual and textual obstacles that triggered a protracted political debate over female exclusion from rule (1400s–1530s).[10] The analysis presented here recounts the opening phase of that political debate, which took place in 1400–29, when Jean de Montreuil responded to a challenge launched by Christine de Pizan.

The contested precept of female exclusion was mired in a troubled political past. In 1317 an Assembly of Notables approved the exclusion of a young Capetian royal daughter, Jeanne of France (sole surviving issue of Louis X, son of Philip IV), who was pressed into renouncing her succession rights in 1316 and bypassed by her uncles, Philip V and Charles IV. Charles IV died without male issue in 1328, and another Assembly of Notables approved the exclusion of his sister, Isabelle of France (now the sole surviving issue of Philip IV, queen in England since 1308), along with her young son, Edward III (king in England, 1327). Thus a Capetian first cousin, the Valois Philip VI, was crowned. At the time, however, the Notables offered no grounds in law, or even in reason, for such momentous decisions, and did not allege a Salic law in either case.[11] Grounds justifying these moves excluding women were supplied later, from hindsight.

The cleric and historiographer Richard Lescot (1329–1358), who held a royal commission to investigate the succession claim of Charles II (son of Jeanne), apparently found a Carolingian redaction of Salic law in the archives of his abbey, Saint-Denis. In a Latin tract entitled *Genealogia aliquorum regnum Francie . . .* (Genealogy of the Kings of France, 1358),[12] Lescot referred to "Salic law" by name (for the first time) and attached his comment about its Merovingian and Carolingian origins to his genealogy of French kings. But he gave no text for perusal.[13] The resulting subterfuge implied that the custom of male rule (observed in the royal genealogy) was prescribed by an ancient Salic law (founding the kingdom).[14] But Lescot's alleged Salic law was ignored at the time, or even rejected, in official circles.[15] Perhaps the settlement of Charles II's claim in 1359 was a factor. Or perhaps the Salic law text had been shown to jurists in the Parlement of Paris and been judged inapplicable to royal succession. Whatever the case, French *ordinances* took no notice either. In both the Parlement of Paris and the Royal Council, Charles V and Charles VI held *royal séances,*[16] at which they promulgated ordinances (1375, 1392, 1403, 1407) regulating succession to rule: father-king to eldest son–dauphin regardless of age.[17] Two of the ordinances (1403, 1407) referred to that system of male preference obliquely as a "right of nature," but none established strict female exclusion or cited a Salic law prohibiting succession of royal daughters (and their sons) should no royal sons survive. Aside from a few stray rumors about a missing law,[18] therefore, the only grounds sanctioning strict female exclusion in the 1300s and up to 1409 were sporadic and vague references to custom.[19] The compelling silence in juridical and royal quarters confirms that Salic law was unknown—or, if known, had no standing in official circles. That silence further suggests that succession of royal daughters (or sons through them) was possible in the absence of royal sons.

The prelate, politician, and diplomat Jean de Montreuil (c. 1361–1418), secretary to Charles V, *prévôt* of Lille, and humanist literary figure in the reign of Charles VI, was uneasy with the silence. Determined to remove a vague precept on exclusion from the risky arena of custom (subject to change through usage), he sought juridical confines in a fixed Salic law (founding the kingdom). In his works Montreuil fastened on a popular theme invented by French propagandists: the illusion of English designs on the French crown (supposedly stemming from 1328).[20] But his noteworthy introduction of a Salic law text actually was provoked by events in French circles, especially by Christine de Pizan's case, made in 1405, for a custom of female inclusion. In his treatise *A Toute la chevalerie* (To All the Knighthood, 1409–13),[21] written in French for a wide audience, Montreuil claimed to have read a Latin copy of the "Salic law," pronounced it a founding "constitution and ordinance" that sanctioned the exclusion of women in 1328, and held that Charlemagne excluded the women's sons as well. What he offered, however, was a Latin fragment written by him in 1406 and taken, it appears, from a manuscript of the 1390s: "Indeed no part *in the realm* may pass to a woman."[22] That alleged Salic law fragment, moreover, contains a misleading interpolation, the phrase "in the realm," which is not found in the Salic ordinance. Montreuil's interpolated passage and commentary in *Knighthood* thus accomplished the work of a forgery, albeit one swiftly repaired.

Right away in all three versions of his *Traité contre les Anglais* (Treatise against the English, 1413, 1415, 1416),[23] Montreuil replaced the forged fragment with a fuller, correct Latin passage (although the first clause, "Indeed concerning Salic land," is still missing). In the 1413 *Treatise,* written in French to ensure the wider audience, he cited the ordinance: "No part of the inheritance may pass to a woman but all the inheritance of land goes to the virile sex";[24] then he attempted to cover the textual loss ("in the realm") and other lacunae with commentary. Accordingly, Montreuil attached to the end of the Salic law text his own opinion stating that this law absolutely "excludes and prevents women from any and all ability to succeed to the crown of France." And he repeated his addendum excluding their sons.[25] In the *Treatise,* therefore, he maintained the substance of the forgery just corrected in *Knighthood.* He also chose his audience carefully. In his 1415 *Treatise,* written in Latin and destined for the entourage of Queen Isabelle of Bavaria, regent for the incapacitated Charles VI, Montreuil removed his spurious opinion forbidding rule to women.[26] Finally, in his 1416 *Treatise,* also written in French for a larger audience, Montreuil again attached to Salic law the same opinion definitively excluding women from rule in France.[27] Yet once the correct text appeared in 1413, manipulated or not, it was clear that Salic law did not prohibit women from monarchic rule in any realm, and certainly not in the kingdom of France.

This experienced politician and humanist writer deliberately chose to privilege forgery over philological integrity, his own legal opinion against the text of the Salic ordinance. Those who followed him did the same. Textual evidence to the contrary, what sustained their unequivocal stance that women were legally excluded from rule in the French realm? The exclusionists, it may be argued, grounded their arguments primarily in the weighty moral injunctions of the ubiquitous *defamation litany* that always supported their case,[28] not in the weak text of a Salic law that constantly fell short. Stamped with the imprimatur of Greek and Roman writings, the medieval defamation litany, cited and re-cited over centuries, constituted a body of knowledge in itself. Subscription proved exclusion. Genre and trope in form, misogynist dicta designated women as generic *woman,* removing from each the human essence of individuality.[29] Readings of Aristotle and Ovid informed a model of "male mastery" of women (their bodies, knowledge, words) aimed at removing women from learned disputation.[30] Lessons from the defamation litany, inflated and politicized in the 1400s, thus supported a model of male command of the body politic aimed at the exclusion of women from succession to rule.

The defamation litany attained a political thrust in two ways. Interpretations of *nature* and *woman* took on public dimensions in the move from person to polity; and the "right of nature," which signaled only male preference in succession (ordinances of 1403 and 1407), was aligned with an alleged Salic law that dictated strict female exclusion. A few examples suffice. Ovidian literary lessons, rooted in nature, reduced woman to mindless animal prey driven by wanton lust and stalked and captured by men.[31] Reshaped, those lessons linked female deficiency, body and mind, with incapacity for governance of self and polity. Above all, Aristotelian biological lessons, dictates of nature, posited defective woman imperfectly reproduced, deficient in body and mind, and passive in propagation (lacking the force of generative male seed).[32] Reshaped, those lessons linked female deficiency with incapacity for rule in a body politic. Finally, Salic law, a product of the combined forces of defamation that induced moral certainty and legal evidence fabricated to conform with moral certainty, was drawn into the litany in the early 1400s. A presumptive body of knowledge, the defamation litany shaped political identity in an era when political thinkers postulated metaphysical notions of the French kingdom as a body politic generated by male-to-male transmission of seed: that is, a series of related kings biogenetically incorporated in *the king's one body* regenerated over time.[33] Germane to this discussion of Pizan and Montreuil are several propagators of defamation whose serial reach colored notions of governance.

In his famous dialogue between Genius and Nature, Jean de Meun, cleric and teacher at the University of Paris and an author of *The Romance of the Rose* much indebted to Ovid, pronounced the body of woman, root of female inconstancy, to be the implacable enemy of mind. A popular work praised by writers, including Matheolus, Jean Le Fèvre, and Jean de Montreuil, some later copies of *The Romance of the Rose* contained miniatures illustrating misogynist invectives.[34] The cleric and lawyer Matheolus, author of *The Book of the Lamentations of Matheolus*,[35] borrowed from Aristotle, Ovid, Theophrastus, and Meun's *Romance*. Matheolus warned notable men active in public life, including the chancellor and councillors in the Parlement of Paris, against the carnal appetites of women that ensnare men and the frightful woes of marriage. He capped his warnings with expressions of disgust for the female body, graphically described in salacious and sordid terms.[36] Jean Le Fèvre, a cleric and a lawyer in the Parlement of Paris, translated Ovid and praised Meun's *Romance,* borrowing excerpts from the Genius and Nature dialogue. An open admirer of Matheolus, Le Fèvre translated the *Lamentations* into French; and at least one copy contained miniatures depicting the female body as a gross monstrosity.[37] Finally, Jean de Montreuil praised and defended Jean de Meun and his *Romance of the Rose,* calling it an ornament of poetic genius and a focus of humanist adulation. Yet by the 1400s there was more at stake than mere defamation. Poetics served politics in that a priori injunctions on female incapacity upheld political exclusion far better than vague memories of an alleged custom or readings of a Salic law text that collapsed under historical and philological scrutiny. That Pizan divined.

The prolific writer Christine de Pizan (c. 1364–c. 1431) was the daughter of an officer in the court of Charles V, the spouse (and widow) of a notary-secretary for Charles VI, and the mother of a son, also a notary-secretary for that king, and a daughter in a convent. An active author from 1390 to 1429, Pizan was commissioned to write the biography of Charles V, wrote political missives to Queen Regent Isabelle of Bavaria, and composed her last work early in the reign of Charles VII. At home in political circles and law courts, archives and libraries, she understood the moral intent of female defamation and its negative political ramifications. Pizan wrote (and illustrated) a treatise entitled *Le Livre de la Cité des Dames* (The Book of the City of Ladies, 1405),[38] which records and validates rule by women in the world over time. Recognizing no custom or law excluding women from governance, *City of Ladies* pointedly addresses the unholy alliance, then in progress, of female defamation and female exclusion from rule.

Pizan denounced the defamatory impulse calibrated by ancient and medieval writers and defended women's capacity for intellectual pursuits and talent for governance. She exposed the array of misogynist injunctions repeated over the ages—the malicious slander of women as *woman,* the trumpeting of female inferiority—as unworthy of learned men. "Like a gushing fountain, a series of authorities" who appear to "speak from one and the same mouth" demean women whose perfections are legion.[39] She charged defamers with fabricating lies about nature and woman for personal reasons, not learned ones. Some of the worst attacks, she said, were fueled by sex-based jealousy actually born of male imperfections, as exemplified by Aristotle, whose ugly body seeded his malice toward women, and Ovid, whose castration spurred his anger toward them.[40] If the learned writer Jean de Meun, purveyor of "badly colored lies," the mediocre writer Matheolus, "an impotent old man filled with desire," and a contemporary writer (Jean de Montreuil) who "*mis*-takes the situation" in praising Meun's work sought truth, Pizan said, they would employ their own critical faculties, distinguish fact from fiction, and commend the admirable "natural behavior and character of women." Instead they maliciously turned woman, the "entire feminine sex," into "monstrosities in nature."[41] In *City of Ladies* she unmasked by name and association a lineage of public defamers: Aristotle, Ovid, Meun, Matheolus, and Montreuil. She also reversed the thrust of misogynist dicta by recasting the defamers as writers who lacked critical faculties, men whose self-proclaimed expertise issued not from universal strength of mind but from individual sexual weakness of body, hence mind. And she demanded an end to the defamation litany: "Let all of them be silent." "From now on let them keep their mouths shut."[42] This condemnation set the groundwork for a discussion of good governance of self and polity.

Pizan took a historical stance for her discussion of governance by women. She refused the reduction of individual women to generic *woman* and offered historical proof of women active in politics, past and present, named and placed in legend and life. Denying the body-mind distinctions applied to learning, judging, and governing, she declared that "a woman's mind is fit for all tasks" when properly educated. She objected to the definition of public officeholding, judicial and military, as male exercises in judgment and prowess requisite for rule. Admitting that only men were taught such skills and exercised those offices, she insisted that women, too, could be taught and readied for office should they be called and invested with authority because women had demonstrated a "natural sense for politics and government" abroad and at home.[43] Women rulers such as Semiramis, queen of the Assyrians, and Dido, founder of Carthage, built, ruled, and defended empires and cities with political astuteness, military might, and spiritual merit.[44] Queens in France, including Fredegund, Clotilda, Jeanne, Blanche, and Isabelle of Bavaria, "reigning now," had served well as consorts, rulers, and regents in the kingdom.[45] Noblewomen in France, wives and widows such as the late duchess of Anjou, who quelled a revolt in Provence, and presently Anne of Bourbon, a "most great landowner" and a "good and wise ruler," had demonstrated women's capacity for governance over vast principalities.[46] Pizan drew a striking conclusion: women are capable of learning the rudiments of good governance, have ruled, do rule, and in the future may rule in empires, cities, kingdoms, and subaltern principalities.[47] Moving on, she addressed spiritual matters no less political.

In the last book of *City of Ladies,* which seems anachronistic,[48] Pizan aligned women's spiritual roles with political ones, actually amending a current tenet of political thought that seriously threatened her case. Familiar with the way the polity was represented as a body politic (head and members),[49] she probably knew the body politic–body mystic analogy on rulership as well. Recently rendered in a popular marriage metaphor, that analogy likened the political marriage of prince and realm (a body politic) to the spiritual marriage of prelate and church (a body mystic).[50] And the ritual tie common to both was the anointment (with holy oil) of French kings in the coronation ceremony and bishops in the ordination. Pizan created an alternative. She introduced a range of holy women whose spiritual roles benefited humanity and the polity, whose spiritual merits matched those of men.[51] That spiritual body is governed by God's specially crowned and anointed ruler, Mary, queen of heaven and head of the feminine sex, who could have been called (as any woman) to terrestrial rule and is called by Reason, Rectitude, Justice, and Nature to rule the *City of Ladies.*[52] The superior edge given that female body mystic headed by Queen Mary (notably anointed and crowned by God) compared with the male one headed by bishops (merely anointed and mitred by other men) was intended, as was the route thus opened for anointment of a queen called to coronation. *City of Ladies* appeared just after Pizan's serious dispute with Montreuil over defamation.

From 1399 to 1404 Pizan indicted and judged Meun a public defamer, calling his *Romance of the Rose* "a doctrine full of lies"; it was a charge she also applied to Montreuil (Meun's defender) and repeated in *City of Ladies*.[53] During an epistolary quarrel in the years 1401–4, Montreuil denounced "that woman Christine," who was purportedly incapable of comprehending the *Romance,* and likened her to a courtesan for criticizing the great teacher Meun and "taking her writings to the public."[54] Undeterred by the defamation,[55] Pizan around 1403 rhetorically situated herself in the office of a judge capable of rendering ethical and political opinions infused with civic import.[56] She moved the issue of defamation, a charge akin to the crime of libel,[57] from the literary quarter to political ones, including councillors in the Parlement of Paris, the provost of Paris, and the circle of Queen Regent Isabelle of Bavaria. By 1404 Montreuil had lost the quarrel in an embarrassing denouement witnessed in theological, literary, and political circles.[58] At this point (1404–5) Pizan composed *City of Ladies,* unmasking the union of female defamation and political exclusion, and circulated it in prime political circles over the next ten years, while Montreuil, from 1406 onward, held a fragment of Salic law in the wings.[59] Neither kings nor queens had ever acknowledged the strict exclusion of women from rule, and Pizan capitalized on that profound political silence witnessed in recent French ordinances. *City of Ladies,* unprecedented in tone and topic, launched a full-scale public challenge to writers currently maneuvering to exclude women from political rule by resorting to defamation. The twin charges struck home.

In this milieu of legal doubt and moral certainty, the actions of Montreuil are instructive. During the anxious years shadowed by Charles VI's incapacity and Isabelle's regency, Montreuil took up the political cause of exclusion. As *City of Ladies* circulated, between 1405 and 1415, Montreuil at some point, probably around 1409, decided to refute its arguments. He did so in his *Treatise* (1413, 1416), in which he addressed *City of Ladies* in content but did not acknowledge it by name (admitting its repute). The route followed by the refutation is traceable. First, Pizan lauded queen Semiramis and also French queens, queen regents, and noblewomen involved in governance, including Queen Regent Isabelle. Montreuil dismissed the exploits of Semiramis, alleging that the widowed queen sometimes donned "the clothing of a man and pretended to be the king's son," so no one could know whether it was a man or a woman who accomplished the deeds. He negated the example anyway as merely a "particular [local] case which established neither law nor custom" there or anywhere.[60] While he mentioned some French noblewomen, including daughters of kings, he denied them the status of rulers in principalities "great and small." One moment he reversed himself and admitted that women had held lands (some in benefice) in the French kingdom; the next moment he insisted that women cannot exercise authority over others, so they cannot succeed to the crown of France.[61] Mired in confusion, Montreuil turned to defamation.

Second, Pizan denounced the defamation litany and its corollary, exclusion of female rule, and focused on the natural courage and capacity demonstrated by women rulers already charged with governance. Montreuil identified governing authority as a male prerogative and drew on the litany for proof. He charged that women, who by nature suffer ungovernable carnal passions, often marry men of lower status, an act of derogation most unworthy in a queen. Worse, rule by a queen who by nature lacks "virility" (generative male seed) would undermine the exalted royal lineage "descending from male to male" and always observed in France.[62] Those politicized proofs drawn from the litany sustained Montreuil's view that a queen cannot govern herself, let alone a polity; that a queen in office would disembody a body politic incorporated in the king's one body.

Third, Pizan negated male definitions of public office, judicial and military, as prerequisites for rule, and stressed the ability of women to exercise offices when taught and readied for them. Montreuil adamantly prohibited women from holding judicial, military, or royal office by resorting to moral injunctions. Woman's innate "instability," body and mind, and her consequent inability to separate mundane personal passions from public political interests, render her incapable of rule.[63] Officeholding in both polity and church, Montreuil held, adheres to the male principle.

Fourth, Pizan circumvented the male body politic—body mystic analogy by positing a worthy female body mystic enabling anointment and coronation of a queen called to rule. Montreuil focused on the dearth and minor status of church offices open to women, reminded readers that women cannot be anointed, cannot hold either papal office (head of the church) or bishoprics (head of sees), and cannot take part (as prelates in church councils) in appointing popes. Conflating coronation (king) and ordination (bishop) as unique male exercises marked by anointment,[64] he held to the male correspondance between body politic and a body mystic and repudiated any female surrogate.

Fifth, Pizan did not deny male preference in rule observed in France but staunchly held that circumstances might call a woman to rule (as queen or as regent) and recognized no custom or law prohibiting such assumption of office. Around 1409, Montreuil introduced his trump card, the Salic law he had held in the wings since 1406. First he gave a forged rendition of the Salic ordinance, which he amplified in *Knighthood;* then he gave the correct text, which he suitably altered in *Treatise* to exclude women (and their sons) from rule in France. Montreuil's fraudulent French Salic law represented his last hope for defeating Pizan's influential argument validating rule by women in *City of Ladies* and his best hope for restoring his own reputation, damaged by the earlier conflict with Pizan over defamation now recorded in that treatise.

This opening phase in the political debate over female exclusion ended in 1418 with the Burgundian attack on Paris, when Pizan took up residence in a convent and Montreuil was killed. Pizan composed the final footnote, *The Story of Joan of Arc* (1429),[65] which instantiated her political stand in a living example: the patriotic and valiant Joan, called by God and king (Charles VII) to serve the polity, a woman whose political purpose and military prowess saved France.

There is no doubt that Christine de Pizan, whose *City of Ladies* in 1405 instigated a long political debate over female exclusion from rule, earned the status of political author, then and now. Modern scholars who exclude the treatise from a canon of political writings—judging it antihumanist, or moralist, or prudish—should reassess views still held in thrall to the judgments of the medieval writers Pizan opposed. In this debate over political identity and governance of a body politic, Pizan was the critical political thinker, and Montreuil and his humanist cohorts the moralists. Then and later, in the 1430s and 1460s, when a French Salic law dictating female political exclusion was put to the test and failed, subscription to defamatory moral injunctions kept the false juridical claim afloat in forgery. Reciting Jean de Montreuil and disputing Christine Pizan, other exclusionists reaped some rewards when that Salic law, albeit still contested, achieved popularity through blatant forgery set in print in the 1480s–1530s. The time for reckoning arrived in the mid-1500s when the Salic law collapsed and jurists scrambled to extricate the French monarchy from the grip of forgery and fraud. They did it by suppressing the fraudulent Salic law and introducing a French Law Canon, which juridically designed the early modern monarchic state as a marital regime system of governance privileging male right in parallel realms, household and state, a system that was contested in turn.[66]

Notes

Discussions with Nancy Lyman Roelker led to this essay; the penetrating skepticism of Marilyn Hanley drove the analysis; colleagues at the Institute for Advanced Study contributed insights; and the Guggenheim Foundation generously supported the larger project.

1. For the complete study, see Sarah Hanley, *State Building in Early Modern France: Law, Litigation, and Local Knowledge* (forthcoming); Hanley, "The Monarchic State: Marital Regime Government and Male Right," in *Politics, Ideology, and the Law in Early Modern Europe,* ed. Adrianna E. Bakos (Rochester: University of Rochester Press, 1994); and Hanley, "Engendering the State: Family Formation and State Building in Early Modern France," *French Historical Studies* 16.1 (1989): 4–27. All italics are mine.

2. Hanley, "La Loi Salique," in *Encyclopédie politique et historique des femmes,* vol. 1, ed. Christine Fauré (Paris: Presses Universitaires de France, 1996).

3. See Katherine Drew, *The Laws of the Salian Franks* (Philadelphia: University of Pennsylvania Press, 1991); for Latin text, see Karl August Eckhardt, *Monumenta Germaniae Historica, Leges Nationum Germanicarum* (Hanover: Historisches Institut des Werralandes, Göttingen, 1962, 1969), *Pactus Legis Salicae* [Merovingian], vol. 4, pt. 1 (1962); and *Lex Salica* [Carolingian], vol. 4, pt. 2 (1969).

4. Drew, *Salian Franks,* p. 198 (*Lex Salica,* title 34, art. 6 [Systematic Version]; this is title 62, art. 6 [Standard Version]); Eckhardt, *Monumenta,* vol. 4, pt. 2, p. 214: "De terra vero Salica nulla portio hereditatis mulieri veniat, sed ad virilem sexum tota terre hereditas perveniat" (*Lex Salica,* 34:6); my translation retains "virile sex" (Drew's substitutes "male sex").

5. Salic ordinances made no distinction between "allodial land" (i.e., family farms) and "Salic land"; and even if "Salic land" were taken to refer to lands held by special grant from the king, women (in the absence of male heirs) could also inherit lands held by grant; see Drew, *Salian Franks,* pp. 39–45, 149; for examples, see Suzanne Fonay Wemple, *Women in Frankish Society: Marriage and the Cloister, 500–900* (Philadelphia: University of Pennsylvania Press, 1981); and Émile Chénon, *Histoire général du droit français public et privé des origines à 1815,* 2 vols. (Paris: Société Anonyme du Recueil Sirey, 1929), vol. 1, no. 178: "the exclusion of women was only relative and not absolute"; "they were not incapable of inheriting paternal land."

6. François Olivier-Martin, *Histoire de la coutume de la prévôté et vicomté de Paris,* 21 vols. (Paris: Éditions Cujas, 1922), 1:86–88, 99–101; Pierre Petot, "Le Droit Commun selon les coutumiers," *Nouvelle revue historique du droit français et étranger* 28 (1960): 412–29; and Chénon, *Histoire,* vol. 1, nos. 194–95, regarding inalienability of a public realm.

7. François André Isambert et al., eds., *Recueil général des anciennes lois françaises depuis l'an 420 jusqu'à la revolution de 1789,* 21 vols. (Paris, 1821–33), Charles VII: 9:252, art. 125; Charles VIII and Louis XII: 11:292, 457–61; on redactions, see Olivier-Martin, *Histoire de la coutume,* vol. 1, chap. 2, pts. 1–3; and chap. 2, pt. 4.

8. Charles T. Wood, *The French Apanages and the Capetian Monarchy, 1224–1328* (Cambridge: Harvard University Press, 1966), chaps. 1–5, Philip's scheme in 1314 to set Jeanne aside.

9. In error, Alain Chartier (secretary to Charles VI and Charles VII), said (as did Baldus) that feudal law prevented women (and their sons) from succeeding to noble fiefs. The mistake was corrected later by Charles Dumoulin (*Commentaire*, chap. 14, no. 20), citing cases where women (in the absence of men) transmitted succession rights to sons; see Antoine Loisel, *Institutes coutumières,* ed. André Dupin, 2 vols. (Paris, 1846), vol. 2, no. 325. Removal of the ritual kiss from homage acts is traced in J. Russell Major, "Bastard Feudalism and the Kiss: Changing Social Mores in Late Medieval and Early Modern France," *Journal of Interdisciplinary History* 17 (1987): 509–35.

10. Hanley, "La Loi Salique."

11. The case made for the absence of Salic law in official circles (1300s) still holds; see Paul Viollet, "Comment les femmes ont été exclues en France de la succession à la couronne," *Mémoires de l'Académie des Inscriptions et Belles-Lettres* 34.2 (1895): 125–78; John M. Potter, "The Development and Significance of the Salic Law of the French," *English Historical Review* 52 (1937): 235–53; Ralph E. Giesey, "The Juristic Basis of Dynastic Right to the French Throne," *Transactions of the American Philosophical Society,* n.s., 5.5 (1961): 3–42; and Kathleen Daly and Ralph E. Giesey, "Noël de Fribois et la Loi Salique," *Bibliothèque de l'École des Chartes* 151 (1993): 5–36.

12. Richard Lescot, *Genealogia aliquorum regum Francie per quam apparet quantum attinere potest regi Francie rex Navarre* (1358), pp. 173–78, in *Chronique de Richard Lescot, Religieux de Saint-Denis (1328–1344),* ed. Jean Lemoine (Paris, 1896). On the commission from a councillor in the Parlement of Paris, see Lemoine, pp. vi, xiii, 173.

13. Lescot, *Genealogia,* p. 178: "Legem vero salicam" linked with Clovis, Childebert, Clothaire; "Item legis salice, id est francisce" with Charlemagne and Louis; a Carolingian copy of Salic law (see note 4) was in the Saint-Denis archives (Bibliothèque Nationale [hereafter BN], MS Latin 4628A).

14. In 1410 Lescot was accused by the monks of Notre Dame of earlier forgeries and interpolations; see Lemoine, *Chronique,* pp. vi–viii.

15. The Anonymous manuscript (c. 1390–99, Bibliothèque Royale, Brussels, 10306) does not claim a Salic law–public law connection. But the author referred to (Lescot's) discovery of a "loy salica," claimed to have read it in this "exact form," and gave a fragment with an interpolation, "in the realm" (not found in the original; see note 4): "Indeed, no part *in the realm* may pass to a woman" (Mulier vero nullam *in regno* habeat portionem); Lemoine, *Chronique,* pp. xiv–xv; see note 3 on Montreuil's repetition of this passage (cf. note 22).

16. Sarah Hanley, *The Lit de Justice of the Kings of France: Constitutional Ideology in Legend, Ritual, and Discourse* (Princeton: Princeton University Press, 1983; French ed., Paris: Aubier, 1991), see chap. 1, on the *royal séances* of 1375, 1392, and 1407;

table 1 distinguishes between medieval *royal séances,* held in both royal councils and parlement, and later innovative *lit de justice* assemblies, first convened in 1527 (and given fictive medieval origins in the 1300s), defined as constitutional assemblies, and convoked only in parlement thenceforth.

17. *Ordonnances des Roys de France de la Troisième Race,* ed. Eusèbe de Lauriére et al., 21 vols. (Paris, 1723–1849), 6:26–32, 45–49 (1374, rev. 1375); 8:518 (1375); 7:530–38 (1392); 8:581–83 (1403, Royal Council); 9:267–69 (1407).

18. The attempt of Collette Beaune to accord Salic law recognized status in the 1300s based on several rumors about such a law (unnamed with no text) and Lescot's work is not convincing; see Beaune, *The Birth of an Ideology: Myths and Symbols of Nation in Late-Medieval France,* trans. Susan Ross Huston (Berkeley: University of California Press, 1991), pp. 249–52 (with mistaken pagination on Lescot).

19. Potter, "The Development and Significance of the Salic Law," see pp. 235–53, regarding Pope Benedict XII (1340) and Baldus de Ubaldis (1377) on custom; Viollet, "Comment les femmes ont été exclues," pp. 139–41, on the absence of Salic law despite Lescot's naming it to support the Valois right.

20. Peter S. Lewis, "War Propaganda and Historiography in Fifteenth-Century France and England," *Transactions of the Royal Historical Society,* ser. 5, 15 (1965): 7–13; the weak and sporadic English claims were aimed at securing French lands, not the crown.

21. Jean de Montreuil, *A Toute la chevalerie* [hereafter *Knighthood*] (c. 1409–13, in French, no. 220, pp. 89–149), in *Opera: L'Oeuvre historique et polémique,* vol. 2, ed. Ezio Ornato, Nicole Grévy, and Gilbert Ouy (Turin: B. Giappichelli, 1975). But his lines 1284–1489 including Salic law date to 1406; see ibid., *Opera,* introduction, pp. 10–12; *Knighthood,* p. 131a. Parts of *Knighthood* (written after the Latin, *Regali ex progenie,* c. 1408, with no Salic law) are repeated in *Treatise* (1413); *Opera,* introduction, 12n.4, 21–22.

22. Montreuil, *Knighthood,* pp. 131–32, "loy Salica," "loy salique." But his source was not the Salic ordinance (see note 4), it was the anonymous manuscript (1390–99, see notes 15, 21), from which he copied a long passage, including the interpolated fragment, "Mulier vero *in regno* nullum habeat portionem," and through which he insinuated (by repeating the words of that author) that he (Montreuil) had read the Salic law in this "exact form."

23. Montreuil, *Traité contre les Anglais* [hereafter *Treatise*], in *Opera,* vol. 2, written in three stages: (1) c. 1413 in French, no. 222, pp. 159–218; (2) c. 1415 in Latin, no. 223, pp. 219–61; (3) 1416 in French, no. 224, pp. 262–313.

24. Montreuil, *Treatise* (1413), p. 168: "Nulla portio hereditatis mulieri veniat sed ad virilem sexum tota terra perveniat" (cf. note 4); *Opera,* preface, p. xiv, notes that Montreuil made the correction but does not analyze his ensuing fabrication.

25. Ibid., p. 168: "qui exclut et forclot femmes de tout en tout de pouoir succeder a la couronne de France, comme icelle loy et decret die absolument que femme n'ait quelconque portion ou royaume (c'est a entendre a la couronne de

France)"; p. 209. He transposed "[allodial] land" into the "kingdom of France" (the public domain) and "inheritance" (in families) into "succession" to the "crown of France."

26. Montreuil, *Treatise* (1415), pp. 226–27, presented to the dauphin (Charles VII). Charles VI (king, 1380–1422) suffered crippling bouts of dementia from 1389; Isabelle (queen, 1385) acted as regent intermittently and was officially appointed in 1408.

27. Montreuil, *Treatise* (1416), p. 274: "qui exclut et forclot femmes du tout en tout de pouoir succeder a la couronne de France."

28. My term, inspired by Pizan, denotes a body of politicized defamatory injunctions that through rote repetition and rare intervention assumed moral stature that was used to define political command. Helen Solterer, *The Master and Minerva: Disputing Women in French Medieval Culture* (Berkeley: University of California Press, 1995), recounts the defamation dilemma: women (slandered) were warned against critical response by subtle threats to charge them as defamers if they disputed the authors.

29. See R. Howard Bloch, *Medieval Misogyny and the Invention of Western Romantic Love* (Chicago: University of Chicago Press, 1991), showing how courtly love literature followed suit.

30. Solterer, *The Master and Minerva*, chap. 1, on that model and the Aristotelian shift discussing woman as a "thing."

31. Ovid, *The Art of Love*, trans. J. H. Mozley (Cambridge: Harvard University Press, 1985), book 1, lines 22–51, 89–159, 257–87 on prey; and 318–50 on lust and crimes against famous men; book 3, lines 118–75, 772–806, on female cunning, secrets, stealth, deception, adultery, and seduction.

32. Aristotle, *The Generation of Animals*, trans. A. L. Peck (Cambridge: Harvard University Press, 1943), book 4, pt. 3, on biology; and pt. 6, on woman as a deformity.

33. French writers molded an Aristotelian-oriented one-body concept based on male generative capacity (male replication in propagation) likewise reflected in the body politic (male replication in succession); see Hanley, "La Loi Salique," and "The Monarchic State." Ernst H. Kantorowicz, *The King's Two Bodies: A Study in Mediaeval Political Theology* (Princeton: Princeton University Press, 1957), pp. 332–33, notes that the two-bodies concept (prince and office), well developed in England, was absent from France, but does not treat French alternatives or Salic law.

34. Jean de Meun, *Le Roman de la Rose*, wrote the second part (c. 1275–80); see lines 16293–676.

35. Matheolus (or Mathieu), *Liber Lamentationum* (c. 1298), trans. c. 1371–72 by Jehan Le Fèvre de Resson, *Les Lamentions de Matheolus et Le Livre de Leësce*, ed. A. G. van Hamel (Paris, 1892), vol. 1, *Lamentations;* vol. 2, *Leësce*.

36. Ibid., van Hamel's analysis of *Lamentations*, a work unknown before Le Fèvre's translation, is in vol. 2, pp. lxviii–cvii; notes on Matheolus (defrocked for marrying), pp. cvii–clxxiv, and some of the worst terms applied to his wife.

37. Ibid., notes on Le Fèvre, 2:clxxv–ccix.

38. Christine de Pizan, *Le Livre de la Cité des Dames* (December 1404–April 1405); I used *The Book of the City of Ladies,* trans. Earl Jeffrey Richards (New York: Persea Books, 1982), books I–III.

39. Pizan, *City of Ladies,* quotes: I.1.1, I.2.2.

40. Ibid., Aristotle: I.14.1–3, I.9.2, I.14.1–3, and book III; Ovid: I.9.2, II.54.1, III.19.6; passages covertly related: I.8.4–5, I.8.7–9, I.14.1, linking Aristotle, Ovid, Matheolus (and Meun).

41. Ibid., lies: I.1.1, II.68.2; Meun and Matheolus, fact and fiction: I.1.1, I.2.2; Matheolus: II.19.1; impotence: I.8.5. She named Meun and the *Romance* (II.25.1) and covertly referred to her own criticism of Montreuil for defending it (1401–4) in the remark on men "naturally given to slander" who "*mis*-take the situation—as I well know!" I.8.9–10; cited her poem against slander, *Letter by the God of Love* (May 1399), and covertly referred to her earlier writings castigating Ovid and Meun, and by association Montreuil, in II.54.1 (cf. note 53).

42. Ibid., quotes: I.38.4–5; her call for men to "keep their mouths shut" mimics and defies Montreuil's earlier abusive letter [Eric Hicks, *Le Débat sur Le Roman de la Rose* (Paris: Éditions Honoré Champion, 1977), letter 154, cf. note 54].

43. Ibid., on mind: I.13.8; political sense: I.11.1.

44. Ibid., Semiramis: I.15.1–2; Dido: I.46.1–3, II.54.1; both Pizan and Montreuil used legend and history.

45. Ibid., queen regents in France: Fredegund (for Clotaire II): I.13.1, I.23.1; Clotilda (saint, wife of Clovis I): II.35.1; Blanche (of Castile, for Louis IX, saint): I.13.2, I.13.7, II.65.1; Jeanne (of Evreux, third wife of Charles IV), Blanche (of Navarre, second wife of Philip VI), Blanche of France (daughter of Charles IV, wife of Philip d'Orleans), and Isabelle of Bavaria (for Charles VI): II.68.1.

46. Ibid., on noblewomen, I.13.1–8, as follows: duchess of Anjou (daughter of Saint Charles of Blois, duke of Brittany; widow of a brother of Charles V): I.13.6; Anne of Bourbon: I.13.7, II.68.10; and others "well-informed in government": II.68.1–10.

47. Ibid., I.11.1, I.13.8.

48. Richards, *City,* p. 269, suggested that Mary fits into a universal history of women.

49. Pizan, *The Book of the Body Politic* [*Le Livre du corps de policie,* c. late 1404–7], ed. and trans. Kate Langdon Forhan (Cambridge: Cambridge University Press, 1994), books I.1, III.1.

50. Lucas de Penna (1320–c. 1390), *Commentaria in Tres Libros Codicis:* "Just as there is contracted a spiritual and divine marriage between a church and its prelate, so there is contracted a temporal and terrestrial marriage between the prince and the realm"; cited in Kantorowicz, *The King's Two Bodies,* pp. 221–23; see Hanley, "The Monarchic State," for its redefinition as a marital maxim.

51. Pizan, *City of Ladies,* book III; the list of women (married, single, secular, and religious) includes two monks (women disguised as men) lauded for (male) constancy by other monks (III.12.1, III.13.1).

52. Ibid., on monks: III.1.1–3; on Mary: III.2.1.

53. Hicks, *Le Débat,* letters and analysis: Pizan called *Romance* a "gross" work that "accuses, blames, and defames women," and indicted Meun (and Montreuil by association), a "public defamer" who "dares to defame and blame one entire sex without exception" (letter V, pp. 11–22); and cf. note 41.

54. Ibid., his *Letter,* no. 154, disparages woman; invokes the Greek courtesan Leuntion, who criticized Theophrastus (a student of Aristotle); and complains it is impossible "to close the mouths of those who say unjust things" about great works. A cohort, Col, pronounced Pizan (as woman) lacking reason and crazy, and demanded she retract her erroneous charges (6:23–24).

55. Ibid., disdaining defamation aimed at her as woman denied the "faculty" of "reason" and censuring letters "reproaching my feminine sex which you say is passionate by nature."

56. Solterer, *The Master and Minerva,* chap. 6, treating *L'Epistre au Dieu d'Amours,* the epistolary quarrel, and especially *Le Livre du chemin de long estude* (1402–3).

57. Hicks, *Le Débat;* like Pizan, Jean Gerson complained that some defamers added to "defamatory libels" indecent pictures in "miniatures" (pp. 63, 72, 209).

58. Ibid., pleading for supporters (*Letters,* pp. 27–45).

59. Richards, *City,* pp. xliv–xlv.

60. Montreuil, *Treatise* (1413), pp. 173–74.

61. Ibid., pp. 169–71, 173.

62. Ibid., pp. 167, 172.

63. Ibid., pp. 171–73.

64. Ibid., p. 173.

65. Pizan, *Le Ditié de Jehanne d'Arc* (July 31, 1429), the only French work honoring Joan written before her death.

66. Hanley, "Social Sites of Political Practice in France: Law, Litigation, and the Separation of Powers in Civil Society and State Government," *American Historical Review* (forthcoming).

Robert Descimon (*Translated by Orest Ranum*)

The Birth of the Nobility of the Robe: Dignity versus Privilege in the Parlement of Paris, 1500–1700

A fourth estate, which having charge of the laws and sovereign authority over property and life, forms a body apart from that of the nobility? (Whence it comes about that there are two sets of laws, those of honor and those of justice, in many matters quite opposed.)—Montaigne, *Essais* (Frame translation), 1:23

The definitions of the French nobility that we inherited from the eighteenth century are inadequate, as historians who study the sixteenth century are well aware. First of all, it is necessary to deconstruct the Colbertian idea of nobility and discern the social dynamics that culminated in the compromises of the later seventeenth century. The impulses toward nobility that were creatively and continually at work in the society carried with them a cultural struggle toward imposing some values and rejecting others.[1] In this sense "nobility" was not at all a juridical essence; it expressed itself in the heterogeneous sphere of the elites, where it contributed to establishing the boundaries, but it never succeeded in subsuming the whole elite sphere.[2]

Considering noble identity as a product of historical change flies in the face of the older notion that it reflected an innate, natural condition; it thereby forces us to examine more closely the evolution of early modern society and the construction of what Federico Chabod called a "state constituted of offices" (*État d'offices*).[3] Ennoblement, especially ennoblement through office, constitutes one of the best observation points for studying the mutations that took place in the noble order between the end of the Middle Ages and the personal reign of Louis XIV. And recall that the idea of nobility can never morally be separated from notions of service and civic duty, behind which may be discerned the political concept of service, or "office," in its most general meaning.

The relation between noble office and noble order must be understood if we hope to comprehend the changing sense of what it meant to be noble in early modern France. I hope to show in the following pages that this relation was considered first as the creator of a *statut viager,* or lifetime "personal" nobility; that "legal science" then imposed a conception of "perfect nobility" transmitted by the high-ranking offices that reflected princely majesty; and that the absolute monarchy finally imposed a hybrid joining of the two in "gradual nobility," or nobility established over several generations.

Personal Nobility

Since the glossators of the Middle Ages, a large consensus among jurists placed the nobility within civil law rather than natural law, with the result that the idea of nobility was historicized and relativized. The monarchy's actions, justified by the phrase "the king alone can ennoble in France," became an established legal concept in jurisprudence as a result of both fiscal practices and hierarchical impulses. The distinction between customary ennoblement and legalized ennoblement that developed in March 1600 as a result of the promulgation of the *édit des tailles,* which defined who had to pay the *tailles,* was a remarkable historiographical accomplishment,[4] and is the point of departure for our current reflections on the subject.

The phrase "nobility of the robe" as something opposed to "nobility of the sword" appeared at the beginning of the seventeenth century in a rather harsh climate of political struggle,[5] thus beginning a deceptive symmetry. Much to be preferred is the phrase "political nobility" or "civil nobility," a concept forged by early jurists, notably Bartolus, who was careful not to use Aristotelian political terminology "Nobilitas est politica seu civilis prout differt nobilis a plebeio" (Nobility is political or civil as it distinguishes the noble from the plebian).[6] The discussions about the *civis* by the postglossators clarified juridical views on the problem of nobility that are grounded on the distinction between *originarius* and *accidentalis.* Like citizenship, nobility could be either inherent in the person or accidental. In the latter case, it was acquired through a legal fiction that had the same juridical powers as nature, but it remained extraneous to the person. No one had the power to cast off his origins by himself. As God was the master of nature, the sovereign was the master of legal fictions, but these fictions were supposed to imitate nature.[7]

Humans were therefore thought to have a natural character that could be modified by a fictive character. But legal thought only appeared to form a link with noble ontology. "Nature," in the juridical sense, did not in fact derive from divine right or from Platonic essences; it was a historical sedimentation, the result of seigneurial associations that tied a man to a piece of land, be he the master of it or the subject. Jurists typically thought as André Tiraqueau did (*De nobilitate,* 1549, 4:4): "Quod ad jus naturale attinet, omnes homines aequales sunt" (With respect to natural law, all men are equal). The historian must ponder the scandalous alterity—compared with his ways of thinking—of the master molds of classification in corporatist societies. By contrast, early modern jurists only worked out a systematic theory through topological reasoning in which *quaestiones* were discussed. Their exploration of *loci communes* led them to develop arguments that, taken out of context (*topos*), would be contradictory; for example, "Is one noble by nature?" If the question was whether one should prefer nobility to nonnobility, juridical science replied yes; but if it was a question of whether or not nobility had to be proved, this same juridical science replied no, since according to the *Digest* all men were presumed to be equal. Juridical thinking was therefore slanted toward the naturalist ontology of the military nobility, that is, the "hereditary nobility"; it accepted presuppositions only for the benefit of common sense.[8] Cardin Le Bret, the well-known author of *De la Souveraineté du roi* (1632), offered a characteristic example of the juridical art of equivocation on the word *nobility.* As *avocat général* in the Cour des Aides, he pled in 1598 that "nobility is nothing other than the enhancement of the race, which has its source and its roots in the paternal family"; in another passage, however, he equivocated by saying that "nobility depends less on law than on nature, that is to say, on the law of nations and on a series of degrees of consanguinity." In 1601 he took the seemingly contradictory position that liberty "is derived from the pure law of nature that has led us all to be born free, at just the point where nobility is grounded only on the rights of mankind." A bit further on still, he abandoned the juridical scientific perspective in order to sketch an attempt at a compromise typical of the sort grounded on common sense, writing: "In short, since the rules about noble rights were created by men, so they derive their origins from the same nature that, having caused some to be born stronger, happier, and wiser than others, by and by caused the nobility to be born."[9] Le Bret was not contradicting himself. His thought had not evolved between 1598 and 1601. He was simply arguing in a different way about cases involving different questions and different ways of stating the law (that is to say, fundamentally *suum cuique tribuere*).

The interplay between nature and civil law was thus a way of asking the essential question: How was noble status created? In answer we could content ourselves with the banal but dearly loved formulas stated by the jurists: "Scientia confert nobilitatem" (Knowledge confers nobility), "Scientia est regina divitiarum" (Knowledge is the queen of possessions), "Vir sapiens est vir nobilis" (A knowledgeable man is a noble man), and so on. From these formulas it is evident that the idea of a nobility of the robe was already established by the second half of the fifteenth century.[10] Françoise Autrand's study rests on a semantic analysis of the words *noblesse* and *noble* as used in pleas before the Parlement of Paris from the fourteenth century on. These words appear in a variety of usages, but only rarely do these have to do with what would seem to us to be the traditional definition of nobility: "Ex nobili et militari genere progenitus" (Sprung from a noble and military race) (1418). Again the use of arms and the military vocation are linked only to an *état* and to its *vertu,* not to a hereditary character. Most of the legal investigations in the fifteenth century allude to *living* nobly, and only secondarily to blood and heredity.[11]

Is one then obliged to support the idea of a triumphant nobility of the robe based on a term-by-term comparison between the privileges of nobles and *parlementaires* from the fifteenth century on? Exemptions from the *aides,* exemptions from the *tailles,* exemptions from the *ban* and the *arrière-ban* form the image of the prestigious status of those making up the parlement. But it would be just as pertinent to compare *parlementaires'* privileges in this early period with those of the *bourgeois de Paris,* which were scarcely less than those of nobles.[12] Still, the bourgeois would certainly not be considered nobles, and for an obvious reason: they did not live nobly. *Bourgeois de Paris* were nevertheless exempt from the *franc fief,* the tax with commoner connotations that was so symbolic for Tocqueville. Even the highest-ranking royal officials in the sixteenth and seventeenth centuries clung to the title *bourgeois de Paris* in order to be exempt from the *ban.*[13]

In 1596, the *maître des comptes,* Antoine Lecoigneulx, obtained a famous decree from the Cour des Aides declaring that he was exempt from paying the *tailles* on land he owned and had improved at Saint-Cloud, near Paris, because he was a *bourgeois de Paris.*[14] Not one of these cases mentions the privileges that went with robe noble status or with an office in the sovereign courts. Thus it is possible to say, regarding the *parlementaires'* privileges, that "all this was worth as much as nobility"; but one can also say that "all this was worth as much as the bourgeoisie."

Did the parlement think of itself as part of the Second Estate? In the fourteenth century it considered itself to be a "microcosm of French political society." Indeed, as Autrand observed, "one of its functions was to represent each of its elements before the king. Clerks, nobles, bourgeois, individuals from the 'various countries' of the realm, each group of notables, in other words the only ones that counted in the polity, had some representation in the parlement," a "representative function," she added, that undoubtedly diminished over time.[15] But this function was certainly not forgotten because of its usefulness to the parlement in its struggle with the Estates-General. For example, a president in the Cour des Aides of Montferrand noted, concerning a passage in the 1561 *ordonnance* of Orléans that purported to force these magistrates to pay the *tailles:* "I do not know whether or not it is because the sovereign courts are composed of individuals from the three estates, that is to say the church, the nobility, and the popular, that the said presidents and councillors [of the parlement] are linked to their immediate [social] condition regarding the payment of the *tailles,* be they commoners or exempt, be they nobles or priests."[16] The Parisian lawyer Julien Peleus, who penned an essay praising First President Nicolas de Verdun, likewise wrote: "Thus we know that the authority of the estates of the realm is condensed in this venerable body, in order to be able to hold conveniently the reins of the state." Elsewhere he said that "the parlement must contain the flower of everything that is the most exquisite in the world, because therein lies the honor of all the other estates."[17] During the Estates-General of 1614, and also during the preparations for the aborted estates called during the Fronde, the parlement did not fail to make its superiority emphatically known by claiming that it alone was the true representative of the realm. After this, the next logical conclusion would be to claim the magistrate's superiority over the *gentilhomme.*

To be sure, the magistrate was perfectly noble by reason of his office, which, according to *avocat général* Jacques Cappel in 1535, was "by explicit privilege included *in corpore juris.*" This was one of the most strongly grounded commonplaces of Roman jurisprudence. Magistrates repeated it ceaselessly down into the seventeenth century. The nobility of the *parlementaires* was, of course, a necessary condition for their being able to judge *gentilshommes.* But nobility derived from royal office no longer seemed completely sufficient by the end of the sixteenth century. In 1598, *procureur général* Jacques de la Guesle, who came from an old but not particularly illustrious Auvergnat line himself, scolded his colleagues: "Think of how the nobility judges the children of their tenants and other persons of low rank who obviously were born and raised on their sharecropping farms, and whom they later see raised up to hold royal office. Will the nobility willingly accept to be bridled and corrected by such people?"[18] It was therefore preferable for royal judges to be not only noble *ex officio,* but also noble *ex genere,* at least by a legal fiction.

What was the nature of the nobility that the magistrate received from his office? Many jurists denied that such nobility was in any way transmissible, "it being acquired by rank and office, because it is for the life of the officer and does not pass to his heirs,"[19] wrote Guy Coquille at the beginning of the seventeenth century. At the end of that century, having demonstrated that he was thoroughly familiar with the terms of the problem developed by medieval juristic science, Gilles-André de la Roque added: "It is necessary to note that, in the past, officers were satisfied to enjoy the exemptions that nobles have in exercising their offices, not thinking about whether this would ennoble them. . . . The person of the officer was ennobled, but his children were not. He lived as a noble . . . , but he died as a non-noble."[20] Charles Loyseau, a well-known jurist during Henry IV's reign, came around to seeing things this way (*Offices,* 1:9, 42–43) when he compared the nobility derived from office to that of a common woman married to a noble. This use of the political marriage metaphor attributes the active role to the office, and the passive one to the officeholder.

In the court cases that we shall soon consider, the barristers representing younger sons emphasized the accidental character of the nobility that an officeholder received by reason of his office. Thus one barrister asserted in 1573 that "the rank of councillor was only a personal one, and its noble privileges did not extend to heirs." The same lawyer argued before Parlement that the realm was "divided into three estates," and that "when the nobility was called up [for the Estates-General], the parlements were not summoned; to the contrary, this summons was made before the provosts and the seneschals." These arguments were accompanied by social observations: far from living nobly, magistrates lived like bourgeois, and "the wives of Messieurs of the Court or of masters of requests, were seen wearing cloth hoods."[21] In other words, the nobility of the *parlementaires* was only an "honorary order" (according to Loyseau), like that of the lawyers who used "noble man Master" in front of their names. Many jurists refused to think in any other way. In

1660, *avocat général* Bignon (the younger) opposed the opinion that nobility "is only accidental to the officer, [and therefore] external, accessory and indirect, since it is not attributed to his person internally and primarily because of what this nobility is, but by a means that is external to him, which is his office."[22] And, in 1675, a lawyer pled that nobility was a privilege accorded to the office before it was accorded to the officer, and that the office was the secondary passage by which this privilege reached the officer.[23]

Perfect Nobility

How should we understand the link between the ennobling office and the ennobled officer? This was one of the troubling questions taken up by Charles Loyseau. His reflections center on dignity, which he considered to be the common feature of the three legitimate forms of public duty: office, lordship, and order. The last form of duty, order, is strictly a personal dignity because it requires nothing more than aptitude. By contrast, lordship and office are "real," in that they transmit dignity to those who hold them. In other words, "order is still more inherent to the person than to the office" (*Ordres*, 1:23). As a result, order can be lost only with difficulty, the important exception being "the order, which has occurred only because of office." Loyseau then took up the example of the officer "who is a commoner by ancestry and who loses his ennobling office" (*Ordres*, 1:53), which he solved in a way generally favorable to the magistrates: "Nobility is not like a simple privilege that is inherent and inseparably attached to office . . . , it is a true order and absolute quality." Nobility proceeds from the office, but it is "directly attached to the person of the officer who has been found worthy of holding an ennobling office, through which it consequently forms and imprints the order and condition of nobility, . . . it being therefore true to say that nobility, like any other order, is an absolute quality that is not limited by time or by other conditions, any more than other legitimate acts by law" (*Offices*, 1:ix, 37). The relation between office and officer therefore derived from a difficult dialectic between "personality" and "reality," as Jean Domat still stressed during the reign of Louis XIV: "One generally calls the honors that duties attract the 'dignity of office,' and that dignity can be considered either in the persons of the officers who hold offices, or in the offices themselves."[24] This was the traditional view, for Florentin de Thierriat had already written, in 1606: "Civil or political nobility is divided into two parts: one is personal and concerns the ennobled person; the other is real and concerns the fief or dignity."[25]

There was not only equivocation in the theory, there was ambiguity in society. If one considers, for example, the status of Councillor François Thomas, seigneur de la Roche Thomas, whose estate became the occasion for a spectacular shift in jurisprudence between 1595 and 1607, one finds certain evidence of confusion. La Roche Thomas was noble by virtue of the office of lay councillor that his father-in-law, Pierre Viole, seigneur d'Athis, had ceded to him by his daughter's marriage contract. In other words, the young councillor became a noble through an intermediary: his wife, Jacqueline Viole. La Roche—whose cousin's (Councillor Clerk Robert Tiercelin) family had encountered no difficulty in being considered a *noble de race* at the end of the sixteenth century—granted his wife the right to reside in one of his castles and seigneurial houses in the event of his death. This was a privilege held by the widows of *gentilshommes*. And so, even though the La Roches held commoner offices, they had been living nobly in the province of Maine, and the family's outward signs of nobility were worth as much as those of the Violes, an old robe family of Paris.[26] According to custom, the ennobled person ought not be concerned about how he had become noble— by office, by fief, or by a combination of the two.[27] The solution for these uncertainties was found by the parlements themselves. The judges were better placed than anyone else for imposing their nobility on the law and society. It certainly seems appropriate to think that the "idea of self-referencing or autopoietic systems can translate into the fact that the jurists had the mastery over the criteria of their own identity." The use of the adjective *autopoietic* with reference to the theories developed by Niklas Luhmann and Gunther Teubner, among others, does not imply the adoption of a concept of law as a closed and autonomous system.[28] From my perspective, the concepts of self-referentiality, self-organization, and autopoiesis permit the linkage between the topical structure of judicial reasoning in the sixteenth and seventeenth centuries and the formation of relatively closed social and cultural worlds—what Durkheim referred to as the "polysegmental" character of traditional societies. The above concepts that focus on the self have the merit of breaking away from the lazy interpretations such as historiographical "commonsense," notions of "interest," and "discursive constructions" to which cultural facts are sometimes reduced.

The question of the transmission of status involved less the fiscal privileges of officials than the transmission of their property as nobles when they
died. Fiscal exemption certainly played a determining role in the development of the consciousness of the noble order, but this exemption was not
the exclusive preserve of nobles. On the contrary, the crown was inclined
to assess the *tailles* on sovereign-court judges who then claimed other
exemptions, especially those accorded to *bourgeois de Paris* or to bourgeois from other free cities. The magistrate who paid the *tailles* was
like a museum piece, very rare indeed. By contrast, there were numerous
court cases about paying the *tailles* in which *parlementaires'* descendants
were involved, especially those inhabiting lands or towns that were not
exempt. It is important to stress here that the jurisdictions on this matter belonged to the Cour des Aides, and that the procedures regarding
who was obliged to pay and who was exempt were determined by royal legislation, and never by customary law. The jurists did not hide their irri-
tation over the question of tax payment that resulted from the close
link that venality of office established between public debt and the creation
of a privileged state apparatus. Thus Jérome Bignon, senior, drawing on the
procureur général's opinions from 1637, wrote: "Saying that the nobility of a
parlement councillor's son is not true nobility, because it has no effect nor
even the tiniest consequence such as exemption from the *tailles,* results not
from a lack of nobility but from the multiplication of officials and the
venality of offices, as well as the amount of the *tailles* and the burden they
place on the people. But fundamentally it is true nobility acquired by the
value of merit."[29]

On the other side of the taxation issue, assimilating a councillor's inheritance to that of a *gentilhomme* was a customary avenue completely controlled
by the parlement. The court constructed a remarkable jurisprudence *per
jura*—that is, by juridical arguments. To litigious articles in customary law
and to inquiries *par turbes* ostensibly conducted to clarify them, it applied
principles from Roman law to clarify royal legislation. (The *turbe* inquiry
consisted of a solemn questioning of at least ten legal practitioners, who had
to reply unanimously to confirm the claim of notoriety that a litigant might
make about a custom.) The exception to this pattern was the legislation on
the *tailles* in Dauphiné of April 15, 1602, which had philosophical underpinnings similar to the jurisprudence of the Parlement of Paris. The process
presupposed two parallel evolutions: the shift from giving priority to mov-

able property to giving priority to real property,[30] and the consolidation of the notion that an office is a legal entity and a fictive real property.[31] Jurisprudence attributing nobility in the first degree to a councillor in the parlement was not exclusive to the Parlement of Paris. A decree promulgated by the Parlement of Bordeaux, its members garbed in the red robes reserved for special events, declared a lawyer noble simply because he was the son of a deceased councillor in the parlement.[32]

Noble privilege in Paris also involved the termination of a couple's joint ownership of movable property. The *préciput* of a noble spouse (which consisted of the right to take all movable goods in return for paying all debts) was the only undeniably noble element in an inheritance. Widows of councillors' sons won this privilege (but not without challenges) thanks to a well-known decree dating from 1540.[33] Obviously, fortunes consisting principally of personal property were more likely to be held by ennobled Parisians than by the nobles of rural areas of the Île-de-France. But for the dominant social groups as a whole, movable property became economically less and less important over the course of the sixteenth century.

The important issue was noble heritability, a rather well-known phenomenon, though less studied than commoner inheritance.[34] For Paris, noble inheritances were not an issue because the Parisian customary laws were grounded on a notion that the land's status and person's status were not linked. Thus Parisian custom required both nobles and bourgeois to transmit the fiefs nobly and all *censives* commonly, regardless of the owner's social rank. But the Parlements of Paris and Rennes drew a considerable number of members from regions where Ligerian and Poitevin customary law prevailed, which, like the customary law of Brittany, required property to be transmitted according to the owner's personal status.[35] In other words, the social status of the person involved determined whether the inheritance would be treated as a noble or a common one. The economic effects of this were considerable, since the share of the estate transmitted to the oldest son increased to two-thirds of the total. These customary laws also included distinctions between noble inheritance and ennobled inheritance, a far cry from the fortunate silence of Parisian custom on such matters. The Parlement of Paris rendered judgments on cases involving these matters by deciding that magistrates were noble, not ennobled.

The autopoietic construction of robe nobility as perfect and transmissible nobility is shown in table 1.[36] The jurisprudence thus established in the

Table 1. Principal Judgments Establishing the Nobility of the Robe Founded on Dignity

Date	Estate	Custom	Type of Succession	Status
Feb. 26, 1547 (new style)	Delamothe estate	customary law of Poitou	direct descent	councillor, Parlement of Paris
May 8, 1573	Mesnager estate	customary law of Poitou	collateral descent	councillor, Parlement of Paris
Sept. 7, 1595	La Roche estate	customary law of Maine	collateral descent	councillor, Parlement of Paris
Dec. 22, 1607	La Roche estate		decree annulling preceding judgment and ordering a commoner inheritance	
July 7, 1597	R. Garnier estate	customary law of Maine	direct descent	councillor, Grand Conseil
July 18, 1600	Challopin estate	customary law of Anjou	direct descent	councillor, Parlement of Rennes
Mar. 24, 1603	Marie Molé estate	customary law of Maine	direct descent	daughter of a councillor, Parlement of Paris
Aug. 29, 1626	Besnard estate	customary law of Touraine	direct descent	councillor, Parlement of Paris
Aug. 14, 1635	Pierre Legras estate	customary law of Maine	direct descent	councillor, Grand Conseil
May 26, 1637	Charles de Bordeaux estate	customary law of Troyes	collateral descent	son of councillor, Parlement of Paris
Mar. 15, 1645 (?)	Gazet estate (father and son)	customary law of Brittany	direct and collateral descent	the father: councillor, Parlement of Rennes; the son: councillor, Parlement of Rennes
May 22, 1660	Lelou estate	customary law of Brittany	direct descent	master, Accounts, Nantes
Mar. 6, 1675	Lefebvre estate	customary law of Brittany and Anjou	direct descent	auditor, Accounts, Nantes

Parlement of Paris was founded on the notion of dignity, as opposed to privilege.[37] The commentators say as much when writing about the Mesnager decree: "The quality and the dignity of councillor in a sovereign court is entirely different from that of the councillors and *échevins* of the city of Poitiers, who are ennobled by privilege, just as the king's secretaries are, . . . and the councillors of the sovereign courts are ennobled by the dignity of their offices."[38] In the end, they went so far as to argue that the "dignity of the magistracy makes a deeper mark on the true character of the nobility of blood" than do letters bestowing nobility issued by the chancery. As a result, it became unacceptable to juxtapose the person ennobled by letters patent with the "radiant star of the sovereign authority that communicates its brilliance and splendor."[39]

That dignity came to prevail over privilege was certainly manifest in the crucial decree of March 24, 1603, concerning the estates of Jean Gauchery, who died in 1559, and Marie Molé, his wife. His estate, despite his office as king's secretary, was judged to be common; hers, as daughter of a councillor in the parlement, but also half-sister of Edouard Molé, president since 1602, was declared noble. The jurists who commented on this decree justified the decision by noting the Grand Conseil's late acceptance (1576) of the rights that Charles VIII had bestowed on the king's secretaries in 1485 and that Henry II confirmed in 1549. This acceptance, which was granted *only* in the Grand Conseil, took place after Gauchery's death.[40] In fact, the nobility of the king's secretaries had not been generally accepted by jurists, and the parlement still refused to accept the decree. Cardin Le Bret observed in 1593: "Albeit that the dignity of a king's secretary is not as noble and splendid as the other, [that is, of a councillor in the Grand Conseil], . . . we should have no doubts that this office is noble and dignified enough to begin to assure, for the posterity of those who hold it, a preliminary degree of true and entire nobility."[41] This great absolutist jurist could find no better way of saying that offices emanating from the chancery did not provide a perfect nobility to their holders and, indeed, were less ennobling than offices in the sovereign courts, despite what the royal decrees stated.

The idea of *dignitas* was an important topic in political philosophy; for jurists, some offices were ennobling and others were not: "All the juridical doctors who have recognized what the dignity of this great office of councillor was worth, have unanimously agreed that it conferred true nobility."[42] The grounds for the nobility of the major offices was their proximity to royal majesty, for these dignities were little more than the small change of majesty. "A magistrate is a star lighted by the rays of the majesty of our visible God."[43] Ennoblement did not therefore result from the royal will, it "occurred without any particular statement from the sovereign in favor of the person himself, but is a necessary result of the right that is attached to the office."[44] This ennoblement was *taisible;* that is, it occurred and was maintained without anything being said. In some ways, it was a juridical ennoblement not founded on royal favor, in contrast to the type of ennoblement obtained by the king's secretaries through special right. Indeed, "the administration of justice was the thing that most closely approached divinity. . . . The quality of sovereign prevailed over and surpassed that of nobility," stated the lawyer in the Mesnager trial, pleading the case of the older of the litigants.[45] *Parlementaire* jurists took quite literally the title "sovereign courts" as the mark and insignia of the princely authority that had been conferred on them. Like the king, the magistrate did not have an heir, he had a successor. In fact, this was a familiar theme restated from Roman law: the parlement, like the Roman Senate, was *pars principis, pars corporis imperialis,* since "the prince holds himself to be of the body of the said court, and also, he truly is its head," as Jacques Cappel recalled in 1535.[46] Citations from Justinian's *Codex* and various testimonials from Roman antiquity were never lacking in jurists' writings. Thus they could conclude that the royal official became a "new man who no longer has a family, other than the *corps* of the Parlement that he has entered." This second birth permitted him to "surpass in dignity" persons noble by birth: "He honors them by becoming their equal." Put another way, "what many generations require to make a *gentilhomme,* the divine character of sovereign magistracy does in a more ample and accomplished way."[47]

Dignity descended through the paternal side, not the maternal, and the dignity of the *parlementaire* councillors extended to their spouses and descendants, since dignity passed from "persons to their property."[48] Speaking about ancient Rome, Loyseau noted that "nobility proceeded from the luster remaining from the ancestor's dignity" (*Ordres,* 4:24). And Claude Gaultier asserted that "the children of councillors in the parlement are made noble by their father's office as much as by his person; it is the title of the dignity that causes nobility to pass to posterity. . . . Thus the title of the paternal dignity passes on, with all its advantages, and makes its mark on the property of the estate and on the persons of the children who inherit the character of a noble inheritance."[49] Le Bret made a brilliant link between the Roman law tradition and the dynastic feature of nobility through dignity of office: "And if we grant them this quality of nobility, as truly nobility, coessential, joined and annexed to their dignities like the light of the sun, how can their children be denied it when, even during their father's lifetime, they are deemed and reputed by law to be lords and masters over the properties, titles, and honors of their families?"[50] It was in this way that the "proposed error" that ended in the reforming decree of 1595 concerning La Roche Thomas was explained:

And there is a remarkable distinction that these customary laws make between children and the collateral heirs of an ennobled person: the latter inherit customarily because they have nothing *citra nomen haeredis* . . . (nothing closer than the heir's quality). The prerogatives of dignity and nobility of the person from whom they are inheriting cease as far as they are concerned and die with the person, but children, held and reputed to be one and the same person as their father, whose memory as a public servant is holy and worthy, enjoy the same prerogative of nobility that their father has acquired, owing as much to his quality and dignity as to respect for his virtue and merit, and this nobility continues in the person of the children: and, at that, they are not called to become nobles because they are heirs, but by right of blood and filiation.[51]

The reasons that prevailed to make direct descent noble and collateral descent common in the same customary law were apparently genuinely philosophical,[52] and as such were comparable to the philosophy underlying the statutory law regarding succession to the crown.[53]

This philosophy with *dignitas* at its center was nevertheless coming apart at the very same time that it was taking shape. In its fundamentally Roman law mode,[54] the *parlementaire* theory regarding the nobility of the robe built up two nobilities of equivalent status: on the one hand, the logical sequence between military service, birth, and chivalry; and, on the other, the logical sequence of judicial duty, dignity, and the senate. This was the aim. But the movement drew too much on self-interested reasoning, and the unfavorable political environment prevented its success.

Gradual Nobility

The Parlement of Paris had established its jurisprudence without considering either the jurisprudence of the Cour des Aides or the royal *ordonnance* promulgated by the Council of State. At the same time, for fiscal reasons there came to be elaborated a notion of gradual nobility, an intellectual curiosity that absolutist legislation obliged respect for as a golden rule. "The trivial maxim *a patre et avo* [from father and grandfather]" had, according to an excellent jurist working in the reign of Louis XIV, "weak beginnings," and, he continued, citing Livy, had "scarcely any relation to our nobility." It is, of course, possible and more plausible to refer to the *Codex,* about *de dignitatibus* (on dignities): "et avum consularem et patrem praetorium virum habuistis . . . claritatem generis retinetis" (If one had a grandfather who was a consul and a father who was a prætor, one should retain the honor of the race).[55] In fact, however, this maxim was a French one dressed up to look Roman; it became forceful in the edict on the *tailles* promulgated in 1600, and *avocat général* Cardin Le Bret seems to have inspired it. In his seventh plea (the one on which the decree of April 1593 was grounded), Le Bret extended the jurisprudence of the Cour des Aides in direct opposition to Roman law, in other words against the *parlementaire* jurisprudence concerning noble inheritance. For Le Bret, as well as for the royal *ordonnances* promulgated in the sixteenth century, there were only two ways to acquire nobility: "to be of noble descent," and through the "formal action [*rescript*] of the prince"—in other words, by nature and through an explicit fiction not a tacit legal fiction. Drawing an analogy with the customary proofs of nobility from noble descent, which must be "taken from the paternal grandfather and father," Le Bret elaborated the concept of a gradual nobility for the councillors in the sovereign court. They were noble only if they were both the children and the grandchildren of a councillor.[56] But the edict on the *tailles* did not have an immediate influence on *parlementaire* jurisprudence, which continued to develop systematically. The concept of a gradual nobility did not convince the adepts at Roman law (nature was presumed, but not the legal fiction), and it seemed illogical even to the theorists who formulated the legislation for the *recherches* of false nobles under Colbert. Thus Belleguise brought up the case of a councillor whose son was a councillor, while another son was not: "Since children are by law considered to be the same person as the father, it seems strange to have one son noble and other common, and that the blood in the same body is not of equal purity."[57] The idea of gradual changes in nature was, however, well anchored in customary law, where—in a striking parallelism—nobility was defined by possession for one hundred years, with property being inherited nobly on the *tierce foi* (that is, on the third homage sworn, in other words, after the third-generation transmission of property).

The break occurred in 1644, with a royal edict confirming the exemption to the *gabelle* for the officers of the parlement, a right they had been benefiting from since 1520; but now they and their heirs were granted the "same rights as the other nobles by birth, barons and *gentilshommes* of our realm . . . even though," the edict adds, "they are not of noble and ancient birth, and as for those officers who are nobles by birth and descent, we wish the present decree to show our increased generosity toward them." Here was a decree that took everyone's sensitivities into account. This royal generosity was extended to the three other great sovereign courts of Paris.[58] The new legislation did not do much to change practice, and, despite what many historians have asserted, it is not certain that the parlement was generally satisfied by it. In fact, the edict surreptitiously changed the principle of *parlementaire* nobility from a dignity into a privilege. Nobility therefore ceased being customary and became legal. In addition, the edict created a paradoxical distinction between the privileges of the different parlements. In short, the king's generosity could always be withdrawn. This is what happened in 1669, when a new edict (created to make the fixing of office prices more efficient) explicitly imposed gradual nobility and took away from the Parlement of Paris the privilege that the edict of 1644 had *not* given it, since the parlement had possessed it already by reason of its own jurisprudence.

Why was the royal council successful in undermining the autopoietic— that is, the self-referential—definitions that the nobility of the robe had developed? The reasons seem to be every bit as legal as social: the weakening of the philosophy of *dignitas,* the fragility of *parlementaire* jurisprudence in regard to inheritance law, the isolation of the parlement, and the near triumph of the "fiscal state" as opposed to the "judicial state." Turning briefly to this fourth reason, let us note that the *recherches de noblesse* of the 1660s were in fact contracts carried out by tax contractors for both their own and the king's benefit. Financial matters concerning the king's state were judged in the royal council, thereby escaping the jurisdiction of the sovereign courts. It is therefore true to say that the law of the tax contractors and of the royal council shaped the law of nobility beginning with the reign of Louis XIV.[59] The eighteenth century bequeathed this law to today's *juges d'armes.* This little juridical revolution had been coming for a long time, and for the first three reasons noted above.

The tension between dignity and privilege no longer appeared in all its logic after the first decade of the seventeenth century. A legal brief drafted in 1634 by or for François Legras, a councillor in the Grand Conseil and the son of François Legras the elder, also a councillor in the Grand Conseil, dictated that any increase in favor of the eldest son was grounded on the equivalence of ennoblement by office and ennoblement by letters patent from the royal chancery (the latter being revocable for monetary reasons, but not being of the gradual nobility type, since if it had been, no one would have wanted the letters). The brief cited a decree of February 26, 1628, which ordered an inquiry *par turbes* into the customary law of Maine in order to learn "if the inheritance of a man newly ennobled by office or by letters patent should be divided among his children nobly or commonly for the first time." "The court, by this link, made it known that it had placed the two types of ennoblement in parallel and had judged them to be equal, with each being as perfect as the other."[60] However, in the two cases in question (1628 and 1634) the parlement's decrees could not serve as precedents because the litigants reached a compromise.

Indeed, the customary features of the nobility of the robe constantly submitted parlement's decisions for litigants' approval. The most forceful decrees on the matter were undermined by friendly compromises that took little account of learned juridical interpretation. Thus, in the Mesnager case, a high point in jurisprudence, an interlocutory decree recognized that "the said litigants were in agreement that the late Master Jacques Mesnager was a commoner, ceasing to be a councillor in the court of parlement by which the appellant he claims was noble." The litigants agreed that there were no claims to be "noble and extracted from noble lines" other than from their relation with the deceased.

Society therefore posed a crucial question: Was nobility such a desirable possession? The question seems astonishing for a so-called society of orders. The answer reflected the conflicts and divisions within families moved by "the different motivations of honor and interest,"[61] and was, in fact, painfully banal: the oldest children were partisans of nobility, and the younger ones were against it, inasmuch as they sought for themselves the privileges of personal ennoblement that would permit them to avoid the inconveniences that came with old nobility. This is not at all surprising when one considers the devastating consequences that Breton noble-inheritance laws had on the younger children.[62] In addition, relations between brothers and sisters or brothers-in-law were sometimes hostile: they would go to court.

This was the case on July 8, 1535, when lawyer Danguechin made the following accusation about the husband on the opposing side (a councillor in the parlement): "His spouse, who is a woman of courage and honor, declares that she will not admit to being and does not wish to be declared an ignoble commoner by decree, even for such a small sum as two or three hundred livres."[63] Yet in the end the wife did indeed plead, with her husband, to be declared a commoner. In 1626, Councillors Pierre Viole d'Athis and Cyprien Perrot, both magistrates issuing from old robe families, went to court against their brother-in-law, Councillor Pierre Besnard de Rezé, and sought to have the estate of Guillaume Besnard, their father-in-law and father, considered that of an ennobled man, which meant that their wives, Jeanne and Marie Besnard, would be considered merely the daughters of an ennobled person.[64] Councillor Pierre de Briou asked for an equal share in the estate of his father-in-law, François Legras, seigneur of Luart and councillor in the Grand Conseil, and of Diane Garnier, the daughter of Robert Garnier, a playwright and a councillor in the Grand Conseil, his mother-in-law.[65] Lawyers representing eldest children did not fail to "shame" younger ones who tried to pass off their father as a "half noble," thereby dishonoring his "memory by a cowardly act."[66] In other words, the jurisprudence that underpinned the concept of perfect nobility for magistrates did not lack its opponents within the law courts themselves.

Furthermore, the parlement had played a very solitary game. Judges in the Chambre des Comptes who claimed to descend from blood nobility did not hesitate to add the title *écuyer* to their names. The judges in the parlement considered this rank beneath their dignity. There was, indeed, something paradoxical about ennobling graduate judges, but not financial magistrates. Even if they could not claim to be part of the royal political body, other officers also sought noble-type immunities. Elderly jurist Guy Pape granted immunity from excise taxes to councillors in the Parlement of Grenoble (*quaestio* 376) because, thanks to their offices, they were no longer commoners. Such reasoning also held for former councillors (*quaestio* 377), for their widows, and for lesser judges (*quaestio* 378): "quod eo ipso, quod talia officia eis conferuntur desinunt esse plebeii" (as a result of the offices conferred on them, they cease to be plebians) and "dicuntur vivere nobiliter" (are said to live nobly). Pape was aware of the fact that just the opposite rules had prevailed.[67] His reasoning derived from the functionalist logic of the service state (*état d'offices*), even though the creation of social hierarchies out of statutes affecting officeholders actually helped to reinforce the dynastic state.

Not until long after the edicts of 1644–45 did the parlement lend its support to the other sovereign counts that were claiming nobility (although the possibility cannot be ruled out that the magistrates in the Cour des Aides and the Chambre des Comptes never asked for the parlement's support). Bignon the younger argued in 1660 for the unity of all the sovereign courts in the realm, with "one sovereign company, considered to be such, being neither more nor less sovereign than another, just as substances, as substances, are not more substantial than another substance."[68] The belated recognition of noble solidarity in the sovereign courts marked a change in atmosphere.

Still, it is possible to observe that the briefs and pleas produced by lawyers who argued that councillors had only personal nobility were not publicly distributed. On the other hand, collections of legal comments and opinions disseminated the fundamental decrees about the nobility of the robe and the juridical arguments that had prompted them. This fact is sufficient to confirm what has been called the autopoietic nature of the work that the high magistracy was doing for itself, and its acceptance of absolutist legislation in no way changed this. These collections thus omitted the decree promulgated in the region where Angevin customary law applied concerning the estate of Bernardin Cador, a councillor in the Parlement of Rennes (it ordered a distribution of property on commoner terms). In 1678 *avocat général* Lamoignon accounted for this by noting: "This was about a councillor's nobility that was not well founded, . . . with the decision being made on the grounds that Monsieur Cador was not the son of a councillor and therefore could not pass his nobility on to his children according to the French maxim, *Patre et avo.*"[69] It looked as if the earlier jurisprudence of the Parlement of Paris had vanished. Since ennoblement now occurred gradually instead of in the first degree, it was no longer customary, but legal— that is, determined by the king's edicts. And if the parlement decided to return to its former jurisprudence, a decree from the royal council brought it into line. *Parlementaire* ideology, however, continued to survive despite this change.

It is self-evident that nobility that came by gradual steps, over generations, in no way affected the social ranks of the high magistracy. Ever since the establishment of the *droit annuel* in 1604, what can be thought of as a cheap insurance premium had secured for robe nobles the hereditary and venal heritability of their offices. It mattered little whether or not a son succeeded his father in *his* office: he could simply buy another office of equal rank whenever he wished to do so. The new slackening of intellectual qualifications for becoming a judge also did not impede the progress of hereditary succession to the magistracy. Thus the robe controlled both its own perpetuation and the means of its ennoblement. Indeed, an immediate and perfect nobility no longer had the same attractiveness as in the sixteenth century, when inheriting offices depended on royal favor. The inclusion of the parlement into the general venal system compromised robe nobles' claim to hold a supremely high dignity that emanated from the crown. But in exchange for abandoning part of their professional ideology, and with the adoption of the traditional ontological values of the sword nobles, the high robe could identify itself with the *ancienne noblesse*.[70] This is what the Parlement of Rennes did in 1678, when it closed its membership to commoners. It carried out an extraordinary campaign of self-promotion that led to the belief, held to this day, that the Breton (*originaires*) magistrates of the court, and even those who were not Breton (*non originaires*) could claim since the sixteenth century to be old nobles.[71] Certainly the little worlds of the provincial nobility and of the magistracy were not watertight, especially since both were swept up in the games of princely clienteles. But one cannot discern the identities of their family origins if one does not take into account the cultural and social breaks that destabilized the very idea of nobility in the centuries between the reigns of Charles VIII and Louis XIV.[72] In this context, tacit ennoblement was not really a usurpation, and the dignity pertaining to it was not a privilege. The essential split appears (*taisible*) as a totally ideological break culminating in the failure of the Holy League. This break had two far-reaching consequences: the urban patriciate—which until the early sixteenth century had been an unequaled center of political and intellectual vitality—became socially without prestige; and the world of the jurists broke into pieces, and a chasm henceforth separated the judges of the sovereign courts (who were nobles *ex officio*) from the barristers (a profession, however, that did not derogate), to say nothing of the legal professionals, notaries or procurators, whose offices were generally considered to bring derogation from nobility. Having a common culture no longer assured the unity of the various milieux within the long robe. Indeed, the evolution of the barrister's status must be seen as a continual decline that the League proved unable to stop and that came to a head in the barristers' strike of 1602.[73] In the seventeenth century, barristers resorted to compensatory tactics that distanced them from the *vera philosophia* upheld by the *scientia juris* and brought them closer to the doctrine of Reason of State and to erudite libertinage.[74] One cannot overemphasize the importance of the role that legal science—*mos gallicus* and *mos italicus* combined—played in the invention of the "nobility of the robe," for, far more than rhetoric or Ciceronian humanism, it was scholarly law, zealously defended by *parlementaire* remonstrances and *mercuriales* (professional disciplinary speeches), that defined the *heroes togati*—that is, magistrates and no longer barristers.[75]

In short, there were three phases in between which the dominant social ties affecting the robe oscillated: (1) "accidental nobility," which left the magistrates in their original social status, especially the patriciates of the "*bonnes villes*"; (2) senatorial nobility, which tended to make high-court judges into a "Fourth Estate" outside and above the hierarchy of the three orders; and (3) gradual nobility, which approved an identity in the difference between the "nobility of the robe" and the "nobility of the sword." The interpretation sketched out here is not, however, strictly chronological, since the different concepts of civil nobility were not mutually exclusive. Indeed, these conceptions can be likened to the voices of a musical composition, which move from *crescendo* to *decrescendo* with breaks of silence in between, and all end up superimposed in the musical score that is the entire society.[76]

Still, it is possible to say that the differences in emphasis that give such different frameworks to nobility from the fifteenth century to the mid-seventeenth century express the relative political defeat of judicial sovereignty. It is more interesting to inquire into the processes and compromises that were brought into place and, in so doing, to define social dominance more precisely by looking at the evolution of the traditional notion of nobility. Schematically, the parlement rationalized customary law with the help of Roman law, the *ratio scripta*. The royal council, however, proceeded along generally shared views grounded in customary ideology. The solutions coming from the monarchy's efforts to reshape society gave specific content to old sayings such as "If the king wants it, it is the law," or "In France only the king can ennoble." The dominance of the law (as opposed to custom) as the organizing principle for social cohesion, which no longer depended on the autonomy of each corps and college, asserted the generalized power of the king, the great arbiter of society.

So nobility ceased to be grounded in custom, oral culture, and the community, and came under the power of written and transcendent law. Customary tradition had grounded nobility on the relation between the lord and his land; this was the deeper meaning of the "nature" that came to define the "local name lines," rather than noble origins. Attached to this total social structure, the traditional nobility denied the legitimacy of legal fictions. In the meantime the state constructed the relation of office to officer on that of seigneur-seigneury, thus creating two distinct homologous relations, each capable of producing dignities and dignitaries. The equivalences between the respective worths of the person and the "public function" (in the meaning Loyseau gave the expression) remained a categorical imperative. The active and positive side of the relation could only be man and *his* "virtue"—"Non enim res personam nobilitat, sed persona rem" (The thing therefore does not ennoble the person, but the person the thing),[77] a commonplace in the juridical thought of the sixteenth century. This reasoning applied to the fief, and even more to the royal office. The absolute antithesis of this virtuous relationship was venality.[78] Nobility that was *taisible* assumed that the prince tacitly ennobled both when he received homage and invested the commoner and when he received the officer and provided him with the dignity of office. Such princely action owed little to the prince's will, since it was predetermined by custom. The legalization of ennoblement restored the positive legislative powers of the prince, who no longer bore the law "in his bosom" but created it through his full and certain knowledge. This legalization led to the destruction of the relation between the "personal" and the "real" on which dignity was founded and justified. Behind the princely will, however, could be discerned the state and the public good. The state, always preoccupied by urgent financial matters, instituted a widespread sale of public offices. The result was that the dignity of the office survived venality only owing to the interplay of contested new legal fictions. Privilege came to dominate, linked to public credit. The king's secretaries, whose nobility had been considered transmissible by inheritance ever since the reign of Charles VIII, now became the models for political nobility.[79] The gradual ennoblement of the *robins* was a pale substitute for this model. But what difference did it make? The authority of the magistracy would henceforth rest on new grounds: belonging to a nobility that had preceded it and was external to it.

Notes

1. See Ellery Schalk, *From Valor to Pedigree: Ideas of Nobility in France in the Sixteenth and Seventeenth Centuries* (Princeton: Princeton University Press, 1986); Jonathan Dewald, *Aristocratic Experience and the Origins of Modern Culture: France, 1570–1715* (Berkeley: University of California Press, 1993). About *noblesse de robe,* see Albert Hamscher, *The Parlement of Paris after the Fronde, 1653–1673* (Pittsburgh: University of Pittsburgh Press, 1976), pp. 32–38, which offers a careful investigation of *parlementaire* pretensions.

2. Denis Richet, "Autour des origines idéologiques lointaines de la Révolution française: Élites et despotisme," *Annales Économie, Société, Civilisation* 24 (1969), reprinted in *De la Réforme à la Révolution, Études sur la France moderne* (Paris: Aubier, 1991), pp. 389–416; George Huppert, *Les Bourgeois Gentilshommes: An Essay on the Definition of Elites in Renaissance France* (Chicago: University of Chicago Press, 1977).

3. Pierre Bourdieu, *La distinction* (Paris: Editions de Minuit, 1979), p. 124. Federico Chabod, "Y a-t-il un État de la Renaissance?" *Actes du Colloque sur la Renaissance* (Paris: J. Vrin, 1958), pp. 57–78.

4. François Bluche and Pierre Durye, *L'anoblissement par charges avant 1789,* 2 vols., nos. 23 and 24 (La Roche-sur-Yon: Les Cahiers nobles, 1962).

5. Daniel Hickey, *The Coming of French Absolutism: The Struggle for Tax Reform in the Province of Dauphiné* (Toronto: University of Toronto Press, 1986); L. Scott Van Doren, "War Taxation, Institutional Change and Social Conflict in Provincial France—The Royal *Taille* in Dauphiné, 1494–1559," *Proceedings of the American Philosophical Society* 121.1 (1977): 70–96.

6. Jotham Parsons supplied the translations of the Latin passages.

7. Joseph Canning, *The Political Thought of Baldus de Ubaldis* (Cambridge: Cambridge University Press, 1987), p. 164; Diego Quaglioni, "The Legal Definition of Citizenship in the Late Middle Ages," in *City States in Classical Antiquity and Medieval Italy,* ed. Anthony Molho, Kurt Raaflaub, and Julia Emlen (Stuttgart: Franz Steiner Verlag, 1991), pp. 155–67. The rapprochement between nobility and citizenship is justified by the way jurists likened the privileges of the nobility to the *ingenuitas.* From that point on, the question of ennoblement was phrased in the terminology of the *natalium restitutio,* which Budé had used as early as 1508; see Armand Arriaza, "Adam's Noble Children: An Early Modern Theorist's Concept of Human Nobility," *Journal of the History of Ideas* 55 (1994): 385–405.

8. André Devyver's *Le sang épuré* (Brussels: Éditions de l'Université de Bruxelles, 1973), and the fine thesis by Arlette Jouanna, *L'idée de race en France au XVIe siècle,* 3

vols. (Lille: Atelier de Reproduction des Thèses, 1976), did not reach across the heterogeneity of ways of speaking about the nobility that were embedded in the general thought structures and not subsumed by one or another. As a result, it was inevitable that Jouanna would interpret early modern sources in light of the common sense ideology of today.

9. Cardin Le Bret, *Recueil d'aucuns plaidoyez faits en la cour des Aydes* (Paris, 1625), "35ᵉ plaidoyer," fols. 200v, 202; "37ᵉ plaidoyer," fols. 214–15.

10. Françoise Autrand, *Naissance d'un grand corps de l'État: Les gens du parlement de Paris 1345–1454* (Paris: Publications de la Sorbonne, 1981), p. 261.

11. Autrand, *Naissance,* pp. 245–48; and, also by Autrand, "L'image de la noblesse en France à la fin du Moyen Age. Tradition et nouveauté," *Comptes rendus de l'Académie des Inscriptions et Belles Lettres* (1979): 341–54. It is also possible to interpret the arguments used by lawyers pleading before the Cour des Aides in the fifteenth century in the same way. See Étienne Dravasa, " 'Vivre noblement': Recherches sur la dérogeance de noblesse du XIVᵉ au XVIᵉ siècles," *Revue juridique et économique du Sud-Ouest,* judicial series, 17.1–2 (1966): 23–24.

12. Autrand, *Naissance,* p. 239 (table); Joseph di Corcia, "*Bourg, Bourgeois, Bourgeois de Paris* from the Eleventh to the Eighteenth Century," *Journal of Modern History* 50 (1978): 230 (table); Jean-Richard Bloch, *L'anoblissement en France au temps de François Iᵉʳ* (Paris: Félix Alcan, 1934).

13. Archives Nationales [hereafter AN], Minutier Central des notaires parisiens [hereafter MC], études LXXXVI, 46, March 13, 1558, Pierre Hennequin, councillor in the Parlement; and Oudard Hennequin, *maître des comptes,* Bibliothèque Nationale [hereafter BN], Pièces originales 1024, no. 21, February 3, 1641, Claude Ledoux de Melleville, *maître des requêtes de l'hôtel.*

14. Le Bret, *Recueil,* "20ᵉ plaidoyer," fols. 115–22.

15. Autrand, *Naissance,* p. 266.

16. Jean Combes, *Traicté des tailles et autres charges et subsides* (Paris, 1576), fol. 95.

17. Julien Peleus, *Le premier président du parlement de France* (Paris, 1611), pp. 16, 26.

18. Jacques de la Guesle, *Les Remonstrances* (Paris, 1611), pp. 572–73.

19. Guy Coquille, *Les coustumes du pays et comté de Nivernois,* chap. 35, "Du droit d'aînesse," in *Oeuvres,* 2 vols. (Lyon, 1703), 2:372.

20. Gilles-André de la Roque, *Traité de la noblesse* (Rouen, 1734), p. 102.

21. Georges Louet, *Recueil d'aucuns notables arrests donnez en la cour de parlement de Paris,* 11th ed., ed. Julien Brodeau (Paris: Guillemot, 1633), p. 415.

22. BN, Morel de Thoisy 199, fol. 104v.

23. *Journal des principales audiences du parlement,* ed. François Jamet de la Guessière (Paris, 1678), 3:691.

24. Jean Domat, *Le droit public,* 4 vols. (Paris, 1777), chap. 3, p. 160.

25. Florentin de Thierriat, *Trois traictez* (Paris, 1606), second treatise, p. 142.

26. AN, MC, XIX, 86, July 29, 1543, a marriage contract signed under the authority of Barthélemy Faye, well-known Lyonnais jurist. François de la Roche

Thomas was none other than "the barrister who spoke Latin to his chambermaid," calling her "a silly goose" because she failed to understand him. Bonaventure des Périers, *Les nouvelles récréations et joyeux devis* (Lyon: R. Granjon, 1558). This book was published fourteen years after the death of its presumptive author.

27. See Bluche and Durye, *L'anoblissement,* 2:16; and Huppert, *Les Bourgeois Gentilshommes,* passim.

28. Antonio Manuel Hespanha, "L'étude prosopographique des juristes: entre les 'pratiques' et les 'représentations,'" in *El tercer poder: Hacia una comprension histórica de la justicia contemporánea en España,* ed. Johannes-Michael Scholz (Frankfurt am Main: Vittorio Klostermann, 1992), pp. 93–101. For theories about autopoietics, see, for example, *Autopoietic Law: A New Approach to Law and Society,* ed. Gunther Teubner (Berlin: De Gruyter, 1987); Niklas Luhmann, "The Autopoiesis of Social Systems," in *Sociocybernetic Paradoxes: Observation, Control, and Evolution of Self-Steering Systems,* ed. Felix Geyer and Johannes van der Zouwen (Thousand Oaks, Calif.: Sage, 1986), pp. 172–92.

29. Pierre Bardet, *Recueil d'arrests du parlement de Paris,* 2d ed. (Avignon, 1773), p. 261.

30. François Olivier-Martin, *Histoire de la coutume de la prévôté et vicomté de Paris,* 3 vols. (Paris, 1920–30), (reprinted in 2 vols., Paris: Editions Cujas, 1972), 2:212–15, 246–47; Pierre-Clément Timbal and Henri Martin, "Le préciput du conjoint noble dans la coutume de Paris," *Revue historique de droit français et étranger* 48 (1970): 28–63; Autrand, *Naissance,* pp. 203–7.

31. Ralph E. Giesey, "Rules of Inheritance and Strategies of Mobility in Pre-revolutionary France," *American Historical Review* 82 (1977): 271–89.

32. Bernard Automne, *La conference du droit françois avec le droict romain* (Paris, 1644), p. 26, decree in favor of Gabriel de Ciret, lawyer, a councillor's son, April 6, 1583.

33. AN, X1A 1545, fol. 585, August 13; X1A 4898, fols. 515–23, for the pleas about the estate of Antoine Lemaistre, son of *avocat général* Jean Lemaistre. This is the first decree establishing nobility for the members of the corps of the parlement and their descendents, whether they held an office or not.

34. Jean Meyer, *La noblesse bretonne au XVIIIᵉ siècle,* 2 vols. (1966; reprint, Paris: Éditions de l'École des Hautes Études en Sciences Sociales, 1985), 1:111 (map); Emmanuel Le Roy Ladurie, "Système de la coutume," *Annales E.S.C.* 27 (1972), reprinted in *Le Territoire de l'historien,* 2 vols., (Paris: Gallimard, 1973), 1:222–51.

35. Meyer, *La noblesse bretonne,* 1:103–34.

36. In series AN, X1A 189, fol. 155v, February 26, 1547 (on the Tiraqueau report); X1A 1639, fol. 237, May 8, 1573; X1A 266, fol. 216, September 7, 1595 (on the de Chessé report); the decree about the Robert Garnier estate, July 10, 1597, seems to be missing; X1A 279, fol. 12v, July 8, 1600 (on the de Mesmes report); X1A 286, fol. 148, March 24, 1603 (on the Lemareschal report); X1A 1973, fol. 238, August 29, 1626 (on the Loysel report); X1A 2096, fol. 415v, August 14, 1635 (on the de Mandat report); X1A 5611, May 26, 1637; the Gazet

decree of March 15, 1645, has not been located; BN, Morel de Thoisy 199, fol. 102, May 22, 1660; *Journal des principales audiences du Parlement,* ed. François Jamet de la Guessière (Paris, 1678), 3:691–93, March 6, 1675. All this jurisprudence, which was specific to the parlement, contradicted established customary law practices. As a result, the legal professionals in the *présidial* of Le Mans who were involved in Robert Garnier's estate (June 18, 1597) stated unanimously that it was "common and well-known" that the estates of Yves de Rubey, master of *requêtes de l'hôtel,* and of Du Breuil, councillor in the Parlement of Paris, were settled commonly among their collateral heirs. This was also the case for the estate of Michel Quélain, councillor in the Parlement of Paris, which was divided among his children, who "were originally commoners" (BN, Carrés d'Hozier 102, fol. 15, "Le Boindre"). But the persons participating in the *turbe* alleged that no judgment or decree about the case had been promulgated "but simply a dividing-up of the estate," and they asserted that "the judges had simply given their views and not established whether this was a common-law usage" (Louet, *Recueil,* 150).

37. In addition to Louet, cited above, whose numerous editions made public the parlement's jurisprudence, see Claude Leprestre, *Questions notables de droit décidées par plusieurs arrests de la cour du parlement,* ed. G. Gueret (Paris, 1679). These treatises were authorized by the signatures of well-known judges, but the work and the updating were done by the great lawyer-editors. Under Louis XIV, the *Journaux des principales audiences du parlement* were put together by lawyers on the basis of the conclusions drawn up by the *procureur général,* and very probably were supervised by the courts.

38. Louet, *Recueil,* 2:150.

39. Gaultier, *Les plaidoyez* (Paris, 1662), pp. 498, 503.

40. Gaultier, *Les plaidoyez,* p. 547; the decree is cited above in note 36. See also René Choppin, *Commentaires de la coustume d'Anjou,* in *Oeuvres,* 5 vols. (Paris, 1662), 2:147–48.

41. Le Bret, *Recueil,* "7ᵉ plaidoyer," fol. 38r, v.

42. BN, 4° Fm 18667, *Factum pour Jean Legras écuyer;* it concerns the estate of Pierre Legras, councillor in the Grand Conseil (the decree is cited in note 36).

43. Gaultier, *Les plaidoyez,* p. 498. Gaultier pled for the elder children in the Gazet estate case (see note 36).

44. Ibid., p. 513.

45. Louet, *Recueil,* 2:415.

46. AN, X1A 4898, fol. 518v; the case is cited in note 33.

47. Gaultier, *Les plaidoyez,* pp. 499–500.

48. BN, 4° 18667, cited in note 42.

49. Gaultier, *Les plaidoyez,* p. 504.

50. Le Bret, *Recueil,* "7ᵉ plaidoyer," fol. 33v.

51. Louet, *Recueil,* 2:151.

52. Nonetheless not always convincing today's legal historians: Xavier Martin, *Le principe d'égalité dans les successions roturières en Anjou et dans le Maine,* Travaux et

recherches de l'Université de droit, d'économie et de sciences sociales de Paris, série sciences historiques (Paris: Presses Universitaires de France, 1972), pp. 87–88.

53. Sarah Hanley, *The* Lit de Justice *of the Kings of France: Constitutional Ideology, Ritual and Discourse* (Princeton: Princeton University Press, 1983), pp. 231–53.

54. André Tiraqueau's influence needs to be stressed; see *Commentarii de nobilite et jure primigeniorum* (1549; Lyon, 1602), book 6, pp. 21–22, "An consiliarius Parlamentus efficiatur nobilis," p. 51.

55. Claude Pocquet de Livonnière, *Coutumes du pays et duché d'Anjou,* 2 vols. (Paris, 1725), 1:717; BN, Morel de Thoisy 199, fols. 165–73, memorandum for the officers of the Parlement of Dombes.

56. Le Bret, *Recueil,* fol. 35r, v.

57. Alexandre de Belleguise, *Traité de la noblesse et de son origine* (Paris, 1700 [privilege dated 1669]), p. 28.

58. Bluche and Durye, *L'anoblissement,* 2:20–29.

59. On the activities of the tax contractors searching for false nobles, see BN, Morel de Thoisy 199, fols. 175, 372. Merlin, *Répertoire universel et raisonné de jurisprudence,* 5th ed., 15 vols. (Paris, 1830), 9:444, "Nobility," comments on the ruling of the council of February 26, 1697, which ruled that decrees of the sovereign courts could no longer be used as titles of nobility. See, in general, Jean-Marie Constant, "L'enquête de noblesse de 1667 et les seigneurs de Beauce" *Revue d'histoire moderne et contemporaine* 21 (1974): 548–66.

60. BN, 4° Fm 35506 (21) *Factum pour Maître François Legras;* AN, X1A 1991, fol. 114, February 26, 1628, the estate of Claude Le Divin, councillor in the Parlement of Rennes (on the Loysel report); X2B 231 (305), July 4, 1634, the sentence by the Requêtes of the Palais, which ordered the estate of Diane Garnier, daughter of Robert Garnier, councillor in the Grand Conseil, and wife of François Legras, also a councillor, to provisionally be distributed nobly, until a new inquiry *par turbes* at Le Mans reached a decision.

61. Gaultier, *Les plaidoyez,* p. 511.

62. Michel Nassiet, *Noblesse et pauvreté: La petite noblesse en Bretagne XVe–XVIIIe siècle* (Rennes: Société d'Histoire et d'Archéologie de Bretagne, 1993); Meyer, *La noblesse bretonne,* 1:103–34.

63. AN, X1A 4898, fol. 419v.

64. AN, X1A 1973, fol. 238, August 29, 1626, and MC, LIX 59, fol. 600, October 20, 1625, a dividing up of the *rentes* in the estate of Guillaume Besnard, "all of it without prejudice to the dividing up of the other property, both *acquêts* and *conquêts,* of the late sieur and damsel De Rezay, as stipulated by the customary laws of the places where the said property is located and situated."

65. BN, 4° Fm 35506 (21), *Factum pour François Legras.*

66. Gaultier, *Les plaidoyez,* pp. 514–15.

67. Guy Pape, *Decisionum parlamenti Delphinatus pars prima* (Lyon, 1577), pp. 610–14.

68. BN, Morel de Thoisy 199, fol. 105. The lawyer for the younger children pled

the contrary, namely, that the *"chambres des comptes* . . . do not concern themselves with posts that have as much luster and majesty as those of the parlements" (fol. 104v).

69. *Journal des principales audiences,* p. 693.

70. François Bertaut de Fréauville, *Les prérogatives de la robe* (Paris, 1701).

71. Meyer, *La noblesse bretonne,* 2:929–37. John Hurt, "The Parlement of Brittany and the Crown: 1665–1675," *French Historical Studies* 4 (1966): 411–33.

72. Donna Bohanan's *Old and New Nobility in Aix-en-Provence* (Baton Rouge: Louisiana State University Press, 1992) does not escape this criticism; Jonathan Dewald's *The Formation of a Provincial Nobility: The Magistrates of the Parlement of Rouen, 1499–1610* (Princeton: Princeton University Press, 1980), pp. 69–112, would have been entirely satisfactory had he not relied on Frondeville's questionable genealogies.

73. Myriam Yardeni, "L'ordre des avocats et la grève du barreau parisien en 1602," *Revue d'histoire économique et sociale* 44 (1966): 481–507, is still the best analysis. On the break between magistrates, barristers, and legal professionals during the Wars of Religion, see Elie Barnavi and Robert Descimon, *La Sainte Ligue, le juge et la potence* (Paris: Hachette, 1985), pp. 128–77.

74. Donald R. Kelley, *"Vera philosophia:* The Philosophical Significance of Renaissance Jurisprudence," *Journal of the History of Philosophy* 14 (1976): 267–79. Marc Fumaroli, *L'âge d'éloquence* (Geneva: Droz, 1980), pp. 585–622, provides an admirable analysis of the lawyers' new political behavior. Decline stopped in the eighteenth century. See David Bell, *Lawyers and Citizens: The Making of a Political Elite in Old Regime France* (New York: Oxford University Press, 1994).

75. For another analysis—one that conflicts markedly with Fumaroli's—see Jean-Marc Chatelain, *"Heros togatus:* culture cicéronienne et gloire de la robe dans la France d'Henri IV," *Journal des Savants* (1991): 263–87.

76. Albert Cremer, "Religiosität une Repräsentation. Zum Tod der hohen Pariser Magistrate: 2. Hälfte 16. und frühes 17. Jahrhundert," *Francia* 19.2 (1992): 1–22, offers enlightening reflections on the burials of magistrates who gave up their family chapels in Parisian parish churches during the seventeenth century.

77. Jean Bacquet, *Traité des droits de francs-fiefs,* book 2, chap. 20, p. 3, in *Oeuvres* (Paris, 1688), p. 908.

78. Roland Mousnier, "Sully et le Conseil d'État et des finances, la lutte entre Bellièvre et Sully," *Revue historique* 192 (1942): 68–86; J. Russell Major, "Bellièvre, Sully and the Assembly of Notables of 1596," *Transactions of the American Philosophical Society* 64 (1974): 3–34; Jonathan Powis, "Aristocratie et bureaucratie dans la France du XVIᵉ siècle: État, office et patrimoine," in *L'Etat et les aristocraties, XIIᵉ–XVIIᵉ, France, Angleterre, Ecosse,* ed. Philippe Contamine (Paris: Presses de l'École Normale Supérieure, 1989), pp. 231–45; Orest Ranum, "Money, Dignity and Self-Esteem in the Relations between Judges and Great Nobles of the Parlement of Paris during the Fronde," in *Society and Institutions in Early Modern France,* ed. Mack Holt (Athens: University of Georgia Press, 1991), pp. 117–31.

79. David D. Bien, "Manufacturing Nobles: The Chancelleries in France to 1789," *Journal of Modern History* 61 (1989): 445–86; and Bien, "Offices, Corps, and a System of State Credit: The Uses of Privilege under the Ancien Régime," in *The Political Culture of the Old Régime,* ed. Keith Baker (Oxford: Pergamon Press, 1987), pp. 89–114.

Kristen B. Neuschel

Noblewomen and War in Sixteenth-Century France

Nancy L. Roelker often remarked that the piece of scholarship for which she was best known—judging from the comments that found their way back to her—was her 1972 essay on the leading role of noblewomen in fostering Calvinism among the ranks of the nobility.[1] This fact may have become less surprising to her over time as it became clear that the article was a foundational piece that corrected the historical record by adding women to history and thereby helped to reorient concerns within the field. In the more than twenty years since the publication of Roelker's article and other pioneering work in Reformation era women's history, historians and scholars of literature have recovered information about women's lives and in doing so have uncovered a previously hidden history of gender ideology in this period. We now know, for example, that women were active agents of religious reform (both Protestant and Catholic), but we also know that the various Reformation movements both represented and imposed rigid, patriarchal gender ideologies—social roles and power relations founded in gender repression.[2]

Much remains to be done, however, to develop the broader implications of Roelker's 1972 argument that only by studying noblewomen alongside noblemen will we fully understand the development of elite culture and the course of elite political life. Roelker argued that neither contemporary gender ideology nor scholarship on women's roles at the time she wrote reflected noblewomen's actual political power; hence, scholars had not appreciated their leading roles in the French Reformation. The disjuncture between prevailing ideologies about gender—such as in the prescriptive literature Roelker considered—and the lived experience of women and men no longer surprises us. Yet, ironically, recent research on the representations of gender in literature, theater, political theory, and the arts in this era, coupled with feminist theory stressing the power of gender ideology regardless of historical specificity, has made the repressive gendering of early modern culture seem increasingly implacable, and impervious to female agency.[3] As far as political life is concerned, we still know more about ideas of gender than about how men and women actually lived as gendered individuals. Consequently, we have not yet reimagined our consideration of aristocratic politics in a way that integrates gender.[4]

The present essay constitutes one foray in this direction. In it I investigate the role of noblewomen in a preeminently aristocratic activity, warfare. I will argue that making war in sixteenth-century France was a less gendered activity than has been assumed; women participated in both material and symbolic ways. Moreover, their participation was not always tied to an exclusively female-gendered role. Scholars' view of noblewomen and our approach to warfare itself in the sixteenth century, I will argue, should be adjusted as a result. My conclusions must be considered preliminary, as they are the product of ongoing research into the activities of noblewomen across the century. At the moment, they reflect, almost exclusively, the experiences of the most elite noblewomen. My evidence does point unmistakably, however, to the fact that the content of the culture of violence, as well as material support for violence, involved the work of women as well as men.

An examination of the involvement of noblewomen in war making can begin with their roles as property managers, since managing military resources was a dimension of property management. We now have much evidence that, despite legal limitations, noblewomen were practiced and profoundly important managers of property for their families. Though only widows could legally dispose of property on their own, the role of manager was not reserved for widows. Armed with *procurations* authorizing them to act in their husbands' names, noblewomen purchased land, negotiated credit, paid off debts, collected tenants' dues, and carried out virtually any other task that safeguarding the family's property required. The range of their activities and the initiative and decision making called for suggest that the notarized *procurations* enabling them to act were often but necessary formalities. This does not mean that there were not serious conflicts over the disposition of property and over the control of inheritance that pitted husbands against wives, daughters against brothers and fathers—conflicts in which women were systematically disadvantaged in favor of the patriarchal line. Nevertheless, the work of women in leading noble families in managing property seems to have been both ordinary and necessary.[5]

Household accounts document the countless mundane tasks required for the day-to-day running of aristocratic households. These accounts, which survive randomly among prominent noble families' papers, were ephemeral records of cash flow to meet household expenses, intended more to justify the claim of the secretary at years' end than as a permanent record of everyday expenses. Yet the details recorded in them about the material culture of the household are invaluable. They reveal that providing for the needs of the large group of people who might be lodged by or traveling with the noble lord or lady and maintaining all of the equipment in the household were never-ending problems. These tasks demanded the labor power of many employees and dependents and, of necessity, the constant supervision of the noble householders themselves. In short, there was much work to be done— by noble lord and lady, by aristocratic retainers, and by common laborers.[6]

Interestingly, there does not appear to have been a clear gendered division of labor regarding most of the routine needs of the noble establishment; the lord, the lady, and their gentlemen and gentlewomen attendants alike all concerned themselves with buying horses and mules, mending trunks and cartwheels, and procuring food and clothing. Madame purchased cloth for new shirts for her pages, Monsieur placed an order for new stockings for his, when a local seamstress came to work at the château. Monsieur even hired the seamstress. Indeed, the men of the household had much to do with purchasing cloth for tablecloths, kitchen linen, hangings and furnishings for the lord's rooms, and for their own and their lord's clothing. Seeing to the various needs of the household and its members and managing most of its daily affairs was thus within the routine competence of both lord and lady. It is not surprising to discover that this competence included securing adequate supplies of gunpowder, or that, like other such tasks, it might be assumed by either noble lord or lady. There were cannons and, as the century wore on, increasing stocks of small arms—harquebuses and pistols—to provision for the château's defense.[7]

In addition to sharing the workload, the sharing of tasks across what we would consider conventional gender lines accomplished something else for these nobles: it reflected the blend of public and domestic life that distinguished this class and power within it. Being able to make gifts of food or clothing and having one's personal furnishings maintained by others sustained bonds between greater and lesser nobles within the household and between nobles and guests. Significantly, gender distinctions were not highly marked in these roles within the household: it was not in the separation of such activities as hospitality and war making but rather in their combination that the warrior class found its power both constituted and represented.

Other kinds of property records as well as surviving correspondence reveal both noble women and men managing property—including weapons—and concerning themselves with the security of both their estates and their persons. Consider, for example, certain papers generated by a protracted and very bitter fight over the d'Anjou inheritance begun during the late 1520s. Nicolas d'Anjou (b. 1518), the minor heir, was related to the Chabannes family and was descended, in bastard lines, from the Bourbon family and from the counts of Anjou. In the dispute, Nicolas's paternal uncles (by marriage) were pitted against his maternal grandmother, Suzanne de Bourbon, for control of Nicolas's considerable property until he came of age. In the course of one lengthy attempt to counter the grandmother's claim, one of Nicolas's uncles tried to disqualify her by claiming that she and her second husband were bad managers of their own property and could not be trusted with the boy's. One of Suzanne's châteaux was tumbling down, no longer either livable or defensible; she had not even visited another château—also in poor repair—in more than a year, despite the fact that it was one of the traditional residences of her first husband's family.

Among this litany of charges is a particularly interesting one. Further evidence of Suzanne de Bourbon's mismanagement could be found in how she, when first widowed, had managed her daughters' property before their marriages. She had "taken and appropriated all of the movable goods left by [her late husband], excepting none and [she] even took the artillery from the château of Saint Fargeau, which is a *forte place.*" The uncles' charge continues that the artillery could not be considered movable goods, but rather "something forever joined to and applied to the guard of the said place." And, the document continues, Suzanne de Bourbon sold the cannons to a relative and did not even discharge any debts with the 1,200 or 1,400 livres profit.

The removal of the cannons was treated matter-of-factly as simply one further instance of bad management. They were necessary for the protection of the château; only a very poor protector would have removed them and capriciously spent their value on something else. This was an example of wastefulness, exactly like her wastefulness—a charge made elsewhere—in allowing the forests of one seigneury to be overcut for a quick profit. Suzanne de Bourbon is not accused of failing to understand the importance of cannons because she was a woman, and there is nothing in this document, or in the other documents generated by this dispute, that attempts to disqualify her simply because she was a woman and was presumed to lack expertise—or the right—for that reason.[8]

What I find noteworthy here is precisely the lack of noteworthiness, in contemporaries' minds, of women's familiarity with property management generally and with military resources specifically. Indeed, responsibility for property management naturally led to concerns about its security. Françoise d'Amboise wrote to her son, the prince of Porcien, in the early 1560s to enlist his help—in fact, to scold him for his neglect of the family's affairs—as she prepared to depart for Paris to pursue urgent legal business. She is afraid to leave their château; she cannot find enough trustworthy men to guard the estate effectively. Even while she is in residence at the estate, there is trouble, including "great enterprises in the forests." Will he not return "with good company" to enable her to set out on her journey?[9]

Françoise d'Amboise knew that property had occasionally to be protected by force. "Force" also included extraction of wealth from peasants, and noble landholders occasionally needed arms in addition to institutional enforcement to insist on their supremacy. The cannon and small arms housed in many châteaux, of limited use in out-and-out warfare, constituted impressive force on a local scale. And the threat of arms, at least, could be used in property disputes between noble families. When she first heard of the death of Nicolas d'Anjou's father, for example, Suzanne de Bourbon and her husband sent his son and a number of retainers with a procuration to seize the principal château of Saint Fargeau in her name. They used "many grave threats, saying that they intended to enter the said château," though they were, in the end, unsuccessful.[10]

Personal security was also noblewomen's responsibility. Adult noblewomen, married and unmarried alike, often traveled without escort of husbands, brothers, or fathers.[11] In a letter to the young adult Nicolas d'Anjou some years after the legal wrangles described above, his aunt asks him to plan an intended trip to Paris so that he will pass by her residence. These sorts of requests for visits are incessant in noble correspondence and reflect the relational needs of their face-to-face world of honor and status. She also wanted to travel to Paris and thought they could travel together. She says, in the tone of feigned anger typical of requests between intimates, "I will be very angry if it does not please you to make your journey pass by here. I know which roads to take from here to Paris," she continues, "where we will not be in danger." Her offer may have been a gift—also typical of correspondence—intended to elicit reciprocal favors. While we do not know her precise intentions, it is nevertheless striking that she can offer her reassurance in a matter-of-fact way. Like Françoise d'Amboise, she seems accustomed to confronting potential threats to person and property.[12] The mutual involvement of noble women and men in the management and security of the household and in meeting the threats of small-scale violence would have led naturally to their joint involvement in managing actual war. The prosecution of warfare still involved the mobilization of the resources of each noble household, and not simply the nobles' "employment" by the crown. The need for private cash was particularly acute for Huguenot nobles during the civil wars of the second half of the century, but nobles had to mobilize private resources during the wars in Italy and in northeastern France in the first half of the century also, even though the crown sponsored and directed those conflicts.

Members of the *compagnies d'ordonnances,* as most prominent nobles were, received a relatively generous pension of 1,200 livres for their participation; however, payment of pensions was often in arrears. In any case, the nobleman had to provide his own mounts (more than one horse was required for battle), his armor, and his weapons, which could easily cost more than the spasmodic pension would cover.[13] In addition to arms, food and other necessities had to be procured. Provisioning their forces often required ingenuity on the part of commanders; letters to the crown asking that one's pension be paid so that the soldiers in one's company can be fed are not rare. In Nicolas d'Anjou's household accounts, which tally the expenses of his retinue wherever he went, are notations of the money he is forced to spend as he journeys to hold the muster of his royal *compagnie d'ordonnance;* his accounts also record expenses for feeding household members and visitors—those fed at the expense of d'Anjou on this occasion included not only members of his company but also the royal officials sent to monitor and record the muster.[14] Hence even the routine task of holding a muster meant a drain on a noble commander's resources.

Meanwhile, d'Anjou's wife worked to manage the outlay of expenses for war. In a group of letters to a creditor on whom the family had relied again and again is one from 1552. Madame d'Anjou, Gabrielle de Mareuil, writes to put him off again. He has been very patient, she realizes; yet she asks him to be patient once again. At the upcoming feast of Saint Jean she expects to have some money in hand, and "it will be used for nothing if not to satisfy you. And you would already be satisfied," she says, "were it not for the great expenses which are necessary for this journey for the war."[15]

The work of lower-class women as sutlers, laundresses, seamstresses, cooks, and the like was essential to the functioning of early modern armies. Though state-organized efforts at provisioning and lodging soldiers began in the sixteenth century, seeing to the necessities of life for soldiers was still by and large a private business.[16] The noblewomen of the sixteenth century, it seems, like those of the lower class, supported the work of their men in armies *with the work they ordinarily did.* In the case of noblewomen, it was not specifically "female" work as much as the class-based work of property management and protection, which they ordinarily shared with their husbands and sons.

Indeed, the noble household was not merely the source of funds, it was also the staging point for fighting even on the king's business, and hence noblewomen's familiarity with war making extended, as a matter of course, beyond merely finding the resources for it. The rolls of the noble commander's company were filled with his familiars, many of whom were routinely present in his household. They set out for musters and perhaps to battle from the household—their usual residence—in order to take advantage of the commander's bounty along the way.[17] Noblewomen of the household ordinarily worked alongside and, in the case of the lady householder, supervised some of these men in the course of daily life in the household. Their persons, their weapons, their tasks, their concerns would be familiar.

In the following letter we see illustrated the intermingling of nobles' ordinary lives and men's experience in both military camp and in battle, as Nicolas d'Anjou's married sister Edmée writes to him during the conflict in Italy.

Monsieur my brother, I do not know how to tell you of the pleasure that it is for me to have heard your news and I am very sorry that you have been wounded by a pike, even though you say it is nothing; you ask me to return the gloves you lost to you but I have not seen them, except in your own hands and it displeases me very much that you lost them, since you miss them so much they must have been very good ones. I thank you for the ring you sent me and I have never had one that I like as much. You will see [that I have sent you] an ensign which I hope you will carry and I am sorry that it is not prettier, but I beg you to believe that everything I have in the world is yours.[18]

Nicolas's wounds and his lost gloves, wonderfully juxtaposed in this letter, tell us, first of all, that he must have recently visited his sister's household.

This juxtaposition also tells us that no weighty psychological distance now separated them; the battlefield was not, for Edmée, an unknown, foreboding place. It can be discussed in matter-of-fact terms, and in the next breath she can talk about a lost pair of gloves. Further, Nicolas assumes that sending the gloves on to him, should she find them, is something she can readily do. The task of provisioning the warrior could extend from household to battlefield by means of the page who acted as courier of the letter.

In the second part of the letter, Edmée enacts a ritual relationship with her brother around his battlefield experience. Here we are entering the realm of women's symbolic participation in warfare. Mimicking the role of a lady watching a favored knight in a tournament, Edmée gives her brother a token, the ensign, to carry into battle. Her attention to Nicolas and her appreciation of his actions are marked and displayed by material symbols. Her knowledge of his actions, symbolized by his wound, helps to legitimate them. She encourages him with her token. In turn, his wounds, his gift—the war itself as it is defined by these symbols—is for her. This is a staged scene, reminiscent of and substituting for a face-to-face exchange, that designates Edmée as the audience for her brother.

One way to interpret this ritualized moment is to link it to the traditions of tournament practices and courtly literature. The tradition of martial tournaments in France was alive up until the moment of Henry II's fatal wounding at a tournament in 1559. The persistence of tournaments both reflected and in turn helped to sustain the French army's continued use of the heavy cavalry charge in battle. Until they were abandoned after 1559, tournaments thus continued to be a venue for the display and honing of actual military skills.[19]

In this letter, Edmée adopts the position of female audience to the male warrior, Nicolas, whose feats are offered for the lady's recognition and admiration. The lady in both actual tournament and in the romantic literary tradition is the "mirror in which the honor of the knight recognizes itself."[20] Honor, the essential nature of the nobleman and that which justifies his privilege of violence, must be acknowledged in order to exist; in these settings, the audience of noblewomen is essential to the creation of the identity of the warrior. Edmée's letter to Nicolas suggests that this ritualized construction of male honor carried over into actual warfare, that warfare depended not only on noblewomen's routine work but also on their ritualized presence.

But what was the meaning of this presence? Many readings of medieval tournaments and courtly romances emphasize a disequilibrium in the exchange between knight and lady. The lady helps the knight to accomplish his reenactment of honor by witnessing it, but also by being the goal of the knight's quest. As the Other against which male identity is established, she is given the paradoxical role of being both object—the prize to be won—and mirror—the reflector of the male gaze back to itself. The noble lady is not really the equal of the nobleman; she reflects honor, she does not actually recognize it. To recognize honor in another, and thereby be one means of constituting that honor, one must be honorable oneself.[21]

Recent scholarship, however, also warns against a hegemonic reading of tournament practice and courtly literature, pointing, for example, to resistance within the literature itself to the conventionalized categories of male and female created there, thus positing more complex real-life possibilities for aristocratic women and men of the day.[22] One of the valences of rituals surrounding warfare for men and women of the sixteenth-century aristocracy may indeed have been a rigidly dichotomous one, in which men staked out their claim to violence with the collusion of women, who were disempowered by being objectified in the exchange. But what does such an exchange *mean,* particularly when placed within the broader context of women's very mundane and practical involvement in war? In any case, how much weight could a literary and ritual tradition have in determining the gendered meaning of warfare?

In order to answer these questions more effectively, let us compare Edmée's letter with another, written later in the century during the religious wars, which also concerns women's relationship to combat. It is even more striking than Edmée's letter in the detail it renders and the unwitting insight it provides into the culture of warfare. It documents actual participation by a noblewoman in armed conflict—which was infrequent but not uncommon—but, more important, it also reveals the range of symbolic and practical connections by which she was linked to war making. Above all, participation in war required the lady to be honorable.

The author of the letter is an unidentified noblewoman, Catherine, writing to the duke of Nevers for help for her husband, who is trying to hold out in a besieged fortress. The long letter begins with Catherine's assessment of the situation. She has not been able to get the duke's communications through to her husband. Their adversary (also not identified) has posted sentinels all around the fortress and intercepts any messengers trying to get in. She recounts in detail the efforts of one gentleman of her retinue who had tried to get through the preceding evening: he had been wounded so severely in the arm by harquebus fire that his arm had had to be amputated. Catherine describes other efforts she has made to get the duke's letters through (three of them have by now accumulated), but, she concludes, "nothing but the birds of the sky could get into that fortress."[23]

Catherine goes on to describe a face-to-face encounter with their adversary. Two days earlier, she explains, he had sent a herald and two gentlemen with a formal request for a meeting. She agreed.

Seeing him so close by, with all his troops and with eight cannon, even though I was ill, I got myself into my litter and went to meet him . . . and we were together for about an hour, and he began by haranguing me. And in one word I responded: that men give battle but that God gives victory, that I stand with my husband in such honor and repute that he cannot threaten me without causing himself and his whole army shame, and that at this moment his face was giving him away and his men could see him sweat. He said that I was brave and resolute but that nevertheless he would overrun the fortress within ten days, even if it meant losing 3,000 men. I replied that he didn't have that much time at his disposal, that you were such a generous prince that you would give your servants help, so that without so much as a drumroll or a bugle call he would be forced to raise his siege. Whereupon he said that the best I could hope for my husband would be that he would be captured and would have to pay an onerous ransom. And I answered that I would consider myself rich enough merely to have my husband alive, and that I would gladly go about in my underclothes [*chemise*] if necessary in order to pay the ransom and have him back, but that without doubt my husband would rather die than surrender and would fight to the last breath, as any gentleman of honor would, and with that I left.

The letter continues, once again becoming a straightforward plea for the duke's attention and help. Again, Catherine enumerates the enemy's forces for the duke: so many cannon, so much cavalry, so many pikemen. She reminds the duke that however well fortified the castle, "you know that no fortress is impregnable." She pleads that her husband's twenty years of faithful service to the duke not be forgotten.

Catherine ends the letter with a change of rhetorical tack and focuses on herself. She would rather die, she says, than have her husband harmed in any way. She is covered by tears of sadness, the most unhappy woman on earth. Have pity and compassion for me and my children, she asks. In a final gesture, she begs him to take pity on her by saving her husband, fearing a thousand times more that he will be harmed than the possible loss of her life.

This letter constitutes a performance by Catherine for the duke of Nevers. In it, she reprises her defiant encounter with their enemy, but it is the encounter with the duke himself, which Catherine attempts to stage on her terms, that is Catherine's focus. Here, by analyzing her rhetoric we can discern precisely how Catherine sought to represent herself so that the duke would help her—how, in short, she sought to make herself worthy.

In the first place, and without fanfare, she makes the best case she can for herself and her husband by carefully depicting the military situation. She reports the results of the skirmish in which her man was wounded in matter-of-fact terms; more important, she assesses the precise strength of the enemy forces. This knowledge would be essential should the duke decide to send a force to relieve the siege. In this period, when innovations in fortress design had tipped the scales of force in their favor, sieges dominated military strategy, and many of the most important battles occurred between besieging and relieving forces.

Catherine's familiarity with military matters is further demonstrated by her very presence at the site and by the role she attempts to play, despite her lack of sufficient force to break the siege herself. Successfully besieging a fortress involved not only amassing sufficient force to counter any relieving army but also controlling the surrounding countryside in order to secure adequate provisions. Besiegers faced exposure to the elements, inadequate supplies, and potential violence at any time. Death from exposure was not unknown, and desertion was common.[24] Catherine's retinue was making their enemy's work more difficult by their continued efforts to slip through the siege lines. The most important work, ably guided by Catherine, was a kind of psychological warfare. Catherine attempted to prey on the difficulties the besiegers faced by threatening the enemy commander with the specter of a relieving army. "Without so much as one drumroll or bugle call" you will be forced to raise your siege, she threatens. Catherine knew that the outcome of the siege was not guaranteed and hoped to sway the outcome in her husband's favor. (The fact that the enemy seems to seek contact in order to intimidate *her* suggests his vulnerability.)

Her bravado in the face of the enemy has the duke as its ultimate audience, of course. Her goal in the letter is to depict herself and her husband as worthy in the duke's eyes—hence, as *honorable.* In this regard, the letter is a tour de force. Not only does Catherine depict herself as adept at the concrete tasks of surveillance and harassment of the enemy, she also demonstrates that she understands the currency of honor. She agrees to meet the enemy commander face-to-face—a situation that carried great risks, in view of the public nature of honor. What she actually said to her enemy we do not know, but to her ultimate audience, the duke, she renders a brilliant face-off, in which she bests her adversary at every turn. Indeed, she succeeds in shaming him.

Let us pay closer attention to the posture Catherine adopts. She describes herself as weak, ill, lying on a litter. But she is confident in God; she is threatening. Her staged weakness is a valuable tool because it makes her invulnerable. There is nothing you can do to me that will matter, she says, in effect. This is a kind of posturing with which nobles frequently safeguarded their honor: admit no possibility of dishonor, whatever physical disaster may ensue. Indeed, Catherine's words almost echo those chosen by the Huguenot Louis de Bourbon, prince of Condé (d. 1569), during the third civil war. Condé had sought refuge in western France after his estates in the east were overrun by Catholic forces. In a letter to one of his adversaries, the duke of Montpensier, Condé writes that he will take no notice of the continued devastation of his estates at the hand of Montpensier's troops. They had already been sacked, he says, and cannot now be in worse shape than before. Like Catherine, he stands on his honor and insists that attacks against him will merely shame his opponent.

Condé closes his letter by invoking his power once more. "The line from which I am issued, the virtue which has always accompanied me and the means which, though arms, God has equipped me, assure that it is not within the power of all my enemies together to reduce me to poverty or suffering."[25] Here, we begin to detect a difference from Catherine's stance. Though Catherine also invokes God as her source of strength and as a threat to her opponent, she does not depict herself as armed and dangerous, as does Condé. Indeed, she portrays herself as weak—sick, lying on a litter—and ready to sacrifice her own life. Her willingness to depict herself as vulnerable is most dramatically revealed in her pleading with the duke for help. She weeps and begs for his pity. Here, honor based on a show of strength is no longer being exchanged.

Are we looking at a damsel in distress? Is Catherine, like Edmée, the audience for and object of male violence, to be won or, here, saved? Is Catherine willingly accepting that vision of her role here? In part, yes; indeed, Catherine deliberately portrays herself in this way. The entire letter is a highly skilled invocation of the codes of honor; in the end, she offers her desperate plight to the duke as an opportunity for him to be honorable by saving her.

Yet, as we have seen, this is not the only role Catherine gives herself in the letter, and our interpretation of the significance of her "damsel" role must depend on seeing that role in the context of other roles. She is not just an object or a pitiful supplicant, she is also a powerful participant—manager of and contributor to violence. Most significant, those roles are also gendered; she is not in a woman's role only when she is begging for help. Her work as military informant, for example, is consonant with noblewomen's routine familiarity with weapons and with the prosecution of small-scale violence. Her role of watching, harassing, and informing would not be appropriate for a man of comparable rank, since, in itself, it provided no opportunity for military success, and hence honor.

In addition, Catherine's honor as a noble *woman* was fully deployed in this situation and is skillfully highlighted in the letter. She presents herself as unassailable in her honor, she parries all her opponent's verbal thrusts. Her (and through her, her husband's) stated willingness to die, if necessary, is all the more proof of her honor since honor must be considered more important than life itself in order to define identity. But Catherine's image of herself is powerful for still other reasons. She also says that she would be willing to go about in her underclothes (her *chemise*) if necessary in order to pay her husband's ransom. This is an invocation of power because it symbolizes the complete mobilization of her resources for her husband's cause.

To be without accustomed accoutrements—clad only in a *chemise*—meant being without the clothes and jewels a noblewoman customarily wore. Clothing, jewels, and other portable personal effects, such as tableware, were among the most important objects with which nobles displayed their status. They were enumerated piece by piece, often with cash values attached, in inventories, wills, and marriage contracts. These belongings signaled noble status through the preciousness of their materials and in the expert craft labor they represented. Hence, they symbolized both control of material resources and the power to command attention and labor. A noble body was a powerful body, simply by means of its accustomed trappings.

Embodying both material and symbolic value, these belongings were used for both purposes. Clothes were often given as gifts, by noble men and women, thereby reinforcing a link between a lesser noble and one of greater status. Gifts of tableware, common between great nobles, drew much of their significance from their association with the sharing of food and the bonds of mutual trust such sharing implied. Costly jewels and precious metal tableware, particularly, were easily turned into cash for emergency expenses.[26] Thus, when Catherine threatens her adversary with the image of herself virtually naked, without adornment, she is not only restating her invulnerability, she is also menacing him with resources that she can mobilize against him. To the duke, she is saying, in effect, "I am honorable because I know how to do my job."

It is also important to acknowledge, however, the erotic element in this scene. Catherine is, after all, lying on a litter, and she is depicting herself as, potentially, undressed in front of the enemy and his men. She is physically and, potentially, sexually vulnerable. Indeed, the power of her menacing stance *derives* in part from this erotic valence in the scene. The erotic potential heightens her vulnerability, hence her daring. At the same time, this vulnerability—destined for the duke's eyes—could enable her to claim, as she does, that her enemy is shamed by his encounter with her. He sweats because he is shamed by a woman who is simultaneously strong and sexual. It is his own desire that shames him.

Catherine offers this version of herself—sexually and physically vulnerable, facing disaster should her husband be harmed—to the duke in order to secure his help. Her honor, here, is based on her honor as a married woman. She "stand[s] with her husband in honor and repute"; she uses her sexuality as a tool; she says she will sacrifice all for her family. This noblewoman's honor, in other words, is expressed in several different ways, and therefore had several sources. In part, it lay in Catherine's sense of physical courage and in her ability to support her claim to honor with words and threats of force, expressions of honor appropriate to women but common to noblemen as well. She is also honorable because she is acting in other ways appropriate to but specific to noblewomen. She bolsters her husband's honor with her depiction of her private relationship to him; the duke is offered the spectacle of a dependent woman, and the honor of saving her.

As Edmée was for her brother, then, Catherine is in part the sustainer of her husband's honor. Her own honor resides partly in that role. But neither she nor Edmée can be accurately described as a "mirror" reflecting a male relative's honor. Women made their own claims to honor through word and deed. Catherine, particularly, reveals the skill this role could demand. Moreover, just as she helps construct male honor with her recognition, so do men help construct hers. The duke witnesses it as audience to her letter, and so do the men she commands. Nor would this be unusual. In their ordinary management of households, noblewomen of high rank customarily gave orders to male nobles of lesser rank. Or, to put it another way, noblewomen were served honorably by noblemen. Indeed, every noblewoman's household of which I am aware included some men attached to it. Such men derived honor from obeying a woman. A woman's honor resided in an active, powerful body, and not simply a passive, sexualized one.

These observations about the practical and symbolic involvement of noblewomen in war making suggests new possibilities for approaching the military and political history of the sixteenth century—particularly with regard to the problem of interweaving the military history of the period with its social history. The recent burgeoning of social, cultural, and economic studies of the early modern nobility has not yet embraced the new military history of the period; what we know of the noble culture of honor, of nobles' successful estate management, of their attitudes toward the crown and the possibility of resistance to it has not yet been integrated with what we now surmise about the changes in military technology, administration, and battlefield experience that are sometimes dubbed the "military revolution." Indeed, the relationship of war to society has only recently been recognized as an important subject, and both social historians and military historians have begun to consider the subject of war from the perspectives of technology, administration, social organization, and culture. This integrated perspective on social and military history is vital; neither can be understood alone. Historians trying to chart the increased reliance on firepower and the decline of the traditional heavy cavalry, for example, have noted that the cavalry was retained long after its role was thrown into question by newer tactics; only *cultural* factors, such as the power and prestige of the aristocracy, can explain its continued use, as well as help account for the eventual transition to newer tactics.[27]

Tracing the activities of noblewomen in managing family resources will help to address the complex problem of the pace of change in military practices and administration through the early modern period. When did the crown gain definitive control of armies? Scholarly opinion links state control of armies (and concomitant growth of the machinery of state) to the increase in army size—hence, to the increased use of infantry. The process of change was neither simple nor straightforward, however, as the persistence of the heavy cavalry charge attests. Scrutinizing household accounts and other family papers with an eye toward military matters will enable scholars to determine when noblewomen ceased taking joint responsibility for managing the resources for war and when the household ceased to be the staging point for warfare. These indicators, as much as the growth of royal administration or the size or the cost of armies, will reflect the accomplishment of profound change not only in military practices, but also in noble-crown relations and in noble self-identity.

It is in this light that we might speculate further about the significance of Edmée's ritual connection with her brother as a piece of cultural work supporting the prosecution of war. As confusing to historians as the nature of warfare itself in this postmedieval period has been the *meaning* of war. Before the crown gained definitive control of it, warfare was a politically, culturally, psychologically—and historiographically—messy business: how could nobles fight with the crown, then against the crown, seemingly capriciously? How could they engage in systematic violence as horrible as that which the Wars of Religion produced?[28]

As we strive to understand the meaning(s) warfare had for contemporaries, I propose that we seriously consider women's contributions. Edmée's exchange with her younger brother may have reassured Nicolas by providing an intimate purpose for the danger he faced: his sister's admiration and approval. His sister's encouragement may also have helped to sustain the legitimation of violence by providing an erotic goal. But the inappropriateness of making herself the object of her *brother's* quest suggests that our emphasis, here, would be misplaced. Indeed, it is the conventionality of Edmée's exchange that is most telling. The entire tone of the letter, in which the battlefield seems familiar and close at hand to Edmée and the dangers Nicolas faces are muted by both familiarity and ritual, testifies to the cultural work the letter accomplishes. Edmée is helping to construct what we might call an ideology of familiarity with war. The battlefield is not far distant, either in practical or psychological terms. Fighting itself is familiar; Edmée creates the image of fighting-as-tournament by means of her gift "in return" for Nicolas's wounds. This kind of rhetoric, rooted in an actual familiarity with violence, could nevertheless be an attempt to close the distance between expectations about violence and the increasingly out-of-control reality of violence on the early modern battlefield.

Catherine's cultural "work" in support of war seems more straightforward. She mobilizes the various facets of her honor in order to prevail against the enemy. Yet we must not underestimate the importance of her example. In an unusually long narrative, Catherine has given us a chance to glimpse, and to take seriously, the honor of a noblewoman. That the content of this honor included a self-assuredness in her identity and an adeptness at the exchange of recognition and challenge by which honor was protected—these characteristics help account for the political weight all noblewomen carried, as religious leaders, power brokers, and patrons of other nobles.

Catherine's example also may provide an insight into why the routine political importance of noblewomen in sixteenth-century France has seemed obscure for so long, despite the research of Nancy Roelker and others. If women were indispensable as property managers, as patrons and brokers, as practical and psychological helpmeets in war, why do they seem so invisible to historians? That invisibility is partly, of course, the result of our failure to search for the presence of women in the sources, but our ignorance also reflects our discomfort with the tensions about these roles that appear in the sources themselves. The several dimensions of Catherine's honor and her various roles were contradictory. She is sometimes capable of bestowing honor, sometimes almost capable of military prowess, yet at other times she is a sexual object.[29] Catherine's own stance—unlike, say, the prince of Condé's—has to accommodate all of her contradictory roles. To borrow a phrase from Joan DeJean—used to describe the princesse de Clèves's choice of a solitary life in defiance of convention—the full degree of Catherine's power "cannot be narrated."[30]

It will surprise no scholar who has benefited from recent developments in feminist theory to discover women in a given society acting out contradictory roles. But this knowledge does not diminish the importance of the roles they play. To overlook noblewomen's power in the sixteenth century is to forget that, although it was contingent, so too was the patriarchal power that alternately depended on and effaced it.

Notes

1. Nancy L. Roelker, "The Appeal of Calvinism to French Noblewomen in the Sixteenth Century," *Journal of Interdisciplinary History* 2 (1972): 391–418.

2. See, for example, Lyndal Roper, *The Holy Household: Women and Morals in Reformation Augsburg* (Oxford: Clarendon Press, 1989); and Merry E. Wiesner, *Women and Gender in Early Modern Europe* (Cambridge: Cambridge University Press, 1993), especially chap. 6.

3. The vast literature on women and gender in early modern culture may be sampled in *Rewriting the Renaissance: The Discourses of Sexual Difference in Early Modern Europe,* ed. Margaret W. Ferguson, Maureen Quilligan, and Nancy J. Vickers (Chicago: University of Chicago Press, 1986); and *Seeking the Woman in Late Medieval and Renaissance Writings,* ed. Sheila Fisher and Janet E. Halley (Knoxville: University of Tennessee Press, 1989). Anthropological perspectives lead to negative assessments of women's status in Christiane Klapisch-Züber, *Women, Family and Ritual in Renaissance Italy* (Chicago: University of Chicago Press, 1985). "New Historicism" can also deemphasize women's status with its tendency to ground readings of literature in power relations: see Carol Thomas Neely, "Constructing the Subject: Feminist Practice and the New Renaissance Discourses," *English Literary Renaissance* 18 (1988): 5–18; and Carolyn Porter, "Are We Being Historical Yet?" *South Atlantic Quarterly* 87 (1988): 743–86. Important countercurrents exist which emphasize female agency, for example, in Merry E. Wiesner, "Women's Defense of Their Public Role," in *Women in the Middle Ages and the Renaissance,* ed. Mary Beth Rose (Syracuse: Syracuse University Press, 1986), pp. 1–28.

4. Important recent contributions to the history of women in political life, though largely within the bounds of traditional social and political history, include Sharon Kettering, "The Patronage Power of Early Modern French Noblewomen," *Historical Journal* 32 (1989): 817–41; and Barbara J. Harris, "Women and Politics in Early Stuart England," *Historical Journal* 33 (1990): 259–81.

5. This subject deserves further study. After reading extensively in surviving correspondence, personal accounts, and other family papers, I am convinced that women were routinely involved in property management. References to their activities are constant in ordinary correspondence, for example: Bibliothèque Nationale, Manuscrits français [hereafter BN, MS fr.] 3209, fol. 123, Antoinette de la Marck to Mme d'Humières, February 1, 1580, Paris; BN, MS fr. 3188, fol. 16, Antoine de Bourbon to Mme la vidame d'Amiens, December 7, 1561, St. Germain-en-Laye; BN, MS fr. 3632, fols. 50–51v, Françoise d'Amboise to Antoine de Croy, prince de Porcien, June 3, n.y., Paris. My conclusions are supported by Sharon Kettering, "The Patronage Power of Noblewomen," especially pp. 817–26; and Robert J. Kalas, "The Noble Widow's Place in the Patriarchal Household: The Life and Career of Jeanne de Gontault," *Sixteenth Century Journal* 24 (1993): 519–39.

6. Kristen B. Neuschel, "Noble Households in the Sixteenth Century: Material Settings and Human Communities," *French Historical Studies* 15 (1988): 595–622.

7. Archives Nationales [hereafter AN], 90 Archives Privées [hereafter AP] 24, "Mise de Monsieur et Madame de Mezières," June 1557 and May 1560, St. Fargeau; 1 AP 217, "Mise de Gabrielle de Bourbon, dame de La Trémoïlle," August 1512, n.p.

8. This information about Suzanne de Bourbon's managerial shortcomings is in AN, 90 AP 12, Dossier Charles de Boulainvillers, "Inventaire de ce que mectent et produisent par devers [le Parlement] . . . par Louis, seigneur de La Trimoille . . . contre la tutelle de Suzanne de Bourbon."

9. BN, MS fr. 3632, fols. 139r–v, Françoise d'Amboise to Antoine de Croy, March 31, n.y., Renel.

10. AN, 90 AP 12, Dossier de Charles de Boulainvillers, "Contre la tutelle de Suzanne de Bourbon."

11. Household accounts, which note guests fed at the lord and lady's expense, often mention visitors by name; see Neuschel, "Noble Households," pp. 605–6.

12. AN, 90 AP 8, Avoye de Chabannes to Nicolas d'Anjou, October 30, n.y., St. Maurice. Concerning the exchange of gifts and offers of favors in letters, see Kristen B. Neuschel, *Word of Honor: Interpreting Noble Culture in Sixteenth-Century France* (Ithaca: Cornell University Press, 1989), chap. 3.

13. The warhorse required for heavy cavalry was notoriously expensive to purchase and maintain, and could *alone* cost the equivalent of the annual pension. See R. H. C. Davis, "The Medieval Warhorse," in *Horses in European Economic History,* ed. F. M. L. Thompson (Reading: British Agricultural History Society, 1983); and Ronald S. Love, "'All the King's Horsemen': The Equestrian Army of Henri IV, 1585–1598," *Sixteenth Century Journal* 22 (1991): 513–15. I thank Bert Hall for these references.

14. AN, 90 AP 24, "Mise ordinaire de Monsieur de Mezières," June 1565, Poitiers.

15. AN, 90 AP 91, Dossier 3, Gabrielle de Mareuil to Honofré Melun, May 27, 1552, Nieul.

16. Barton C. Hacker, "Women and Military Institutions in Early Modern Europe: A Reconnaissance," *Signs: Journal of Women in Culture and Society* 6 (1981): 643–71.

17. See Neuschel, "Noble Households," concerning the itinerant quality of household life; and *Word of Honor,* chap. 5, concerning the relationship between households and membership in a *compagnie.* For another example of a noblewoman managing expenses for a man's (in this case, her son's) retinue, see MS fr. 3632, fol. 17, Valeray to Duchess of Nevers, May 17, n.y., Mezières.

18. AN, 90 AP 8, Edmée d'Anjou to Nicolas d'Anjou, n.d., n.p.

19. Frederic J. Baumgartner, "The Final Demise of the Medieval Knight in France," in Regnum, Religio et Ratio: *Essays Presented to Robert M. Kingdon,* ed. Jerome Friedman (Kirksville, Mo.: Sixteenth Century Journal Publishers, 1987), pp. 9–18, which notes Henry II's parallel affection for chivalric literature as well.

20. Louise Olga Fradenburg, *City, Marriage and Tournament: The Arts of Rule in Late Medieval Scotland* (Madison: University of Wisconsin Press, 1991), p. 205.

21. Fradenburg, *City, Marriage and Tournament,* chaps. 9–13, passim. Sheila Fisher argued that a woman's token was a sign of her betrayal of men and that romances were intended to protect and celebrate a homosocial world of warrior

men; see Fisher, "Taken Men and Token Women in *Sir Gawain and the Green Knight,*" in *Seeking the Woman in Late Medieval and Renaissance Writings,* ed. S. Fisher and J. E. Halley (Knoxville: University of Tennessee Press, 1989), pp. 71–105. See also E. Jane Burns and Robert L. Kreuger, "Courtly Ideology and Women's Place in Medieval French Literature," *Romance Notes* 25 (1985): 209–37. Concerning the mutual recognition and construction of honor in noble society, see Neuschel, *Word of Honor,* chaps. 3, 4.

22. E. Jane Burns, *Bodytalk: When Women Speak in Old French Literature* (Philadelphia: University of Pennsylvania Press, 1993).

23. BN, MS fr. 3632, fols. 127–28, "Catherine" to Louis de Gonzague, Duke of Nevers, n.d., n.p. The lower portion of the last page of the letter—which included Catherine's surname—has been ripped away.

24. The current lively debate about the role of fortifications in early modern warfare can be sampled in Clifford J. Rogers, *The Military Revolution Debate* (Boulder: Westview Press, 1995). Rich anecdotal evidence of the experiences of besieging and relieving armies is in Geoffrey Parker, *The Dutch Revolt* (London: Penguin Books, 1985).

25. BN, MS fr. 3950, fol. 39, Louis de Bourbon, Prince of Condé, to Louis de Bourbon, Duke of Montpensier, December 8, 1568, "camp a La Fontayne."

26. The princess of Condé, for example, pawned jewels to finance her husband's defense after his arrest for the Amboise affair: Musee Condé, Chantilly, Titres GE5, Eléonore de Roye to Anne de Montmorency, January 15, 1561, and January 22, 1562.

27. See the landmark work, J. R. Hale, *War and Society in Renaissance Europe, 1450–1620* (London: Fontana, 1985). Recent studies of the connections of military and political history include Brian M. Downing, *The Military Revolution and Political Change: Origins of Democracy and Autocracy in Early Modern Europe* (Princeton: Princeton University Press, 1992); and John P. Brewer, *Sinews of Power: War, Money and the English State* (Cambridge: Harvard University Press, 1990). For combinations of military, political, social, and cultural factors affecting the continued use of heavy cavalry, see Baumgartner, "The Final Demise of the Medieval Knight"; Clifford J. Rogers, "The Military Revolutions of the Hundred Years' War," *Journal of Military History* 57 (1993): 241–78; and Bert S. Hall, "Small Arms and the Tactical Revolution of the Sixteenth Century: A Reevaluation," unpublished paper, 1988.

28. Endemic violence and warfare is explained from an ethnographic tack in Neuschel, *Word of Honor.* See also Arlette Jouanna, *Le Devoir de révolte: La noblesse française et la gestation de l'état moderne* (Paris: Fayard, 1989). Other recent arguments point toward religion as the underpinning for the violence of the era: Denis Crouzet, *Les Guerriers de Dieu,* 2 vols. (Paris: Champ Vallon, 1990); Mack P. Holt, "Putting Religion Back into the Wars of Religion," *French Historical Studies* 18 (1993): 524–51.

29. Similar contradictions appear in certain examples of medieval romantic

literature. See Helen Solterer, "Figures of Female Militancy in Medieval France," *Signs: Journal of Women in Culture and Society* 16 (1991): 522–49. My argument here owes much to Solterer's insights.

30. Joan DeJean, *Tender Geographies: Women and the Origins of the Novel in France* (New York: Columbia University Press, 1991), p. 284.

II

Dissent and

Deviance

Charmarie Blaisdell

Religion, Gender, and Class: Nuns and Authority in Early Modern France

For twenty years, historians of early modern Europe have explored the ways in which the Protestant and Catholic reform movements provided women with a basis for the exercise of private and public power. The historical literature on the subject has influenced and enriched our understanding of social roles and the exercise of power, especially among the elites.[1] In a now classic study, Nancy L. Roelker argued that class, education, the high moral cause of religious reform, and, sometimes, widowhood, empowered some French noblewomen to defy secular and ecclesiastical authority by supporting the Huguenot cause.[2] More recently historians have found that convent life was also a source of public empowerment for women in early modern Italy, Germany, and Spain.[3]

This essay examines a group of French aristocratic women whose membership in religious communities shaped their experience of the *préréforme* and *réforme* in France between 1450 and 1600.[4] Like their relatives at court, these nuns demonstrated strong opinions on the issues related to reform in their religious communities as well as the Protestant Reformation. Not without resistance, some convents followed the path of reform blazed by the prestigious and powerful Order of Fontevrault. Others, like the Benedictines of Gif and Yerres, outside Paris, quarreled both among themselves and with outside authorities about who was responsible for the reformation of their houses. Prestigious convents such as the Benedictines of Montmârtre required several official attempts to reform them as the abbesses adroitly stalled the process by raising jurisdictional issues. A mix of complex reasons lay behind the decision of some nuns to flee. Some wanted to avoid the new strictures placed on cloistered life by reform; others embraced Calvinism and went to Geneva. Some returned to their families when their convents dispersed, though a few returned later and rebuilt their communities. Others defied tradition by marrying. These diverse examples raise important questions about a little known period in the history of French female religious communities. The quality of spiritual and intellectual life within convents, the impact of both Catholic and Protestant reforms on convent

life, and who resisted reform or later accepted Calvinism needs to be as-
sessed, as does the desire of some women for a life outside the convent. It is
also important to discern whether different reactions to Catholic reform and
the Reformation existed among the more traditional Benedictine, Cistercian, and Fontevrault houses and the "newer" ones such as the Clarisses,
Dominicans, and secular orders of Augustinians. Understanding the link
between religion and public power during these "lost" years of the history of
French religious orders may shed light on the call for active female aposto-
lates in the early seventeenth century France that defied the decrees of Trent
and traditional subordinate roles assigned to women.[5]

My sample of 150 mostly royal convents between the end of the Hundred
Years' War and the late sixteenth century has necessarily been limited to
convents whose records survived the Wars of Religion, the French Revolution, and two world wars. Despite the lack of statistical accuracy, preliminary generalizations can be made about nuns and convent life prior to the
resurgence of female religious life in the early seventeenth century. In many
convents, especially royal ones that recruited almost exclusively from the
nobility, independent-minded nuns frequently and unabashedly defied secular and ecclesiastical authority, thus risking harsh discipline and imprisonment, much like their Huguenot "sisters."[6] Struggles over reform both
revealed these women's sense of independence and provided them with new
opportunities for action.

Monastic reform was a recurrent issue long before the sixteenth century,
as the records of parlements and town councils reveal. Economic problems as
much as human weakness had contributed to the decline of spiritual life in
religious houses in the late Middle Ages.[7] By 1450, a century of economic
changes, falling agricultural prices, and devastation caused by the Hundred
Years' War had impoverished even the wealthiest religious communities.
Limited revenues curtailed otherwise favorable opportunities to acquire
more land. Abbeys and priories with large landholdings were often unable
to support their members because of unpaid rents or falling agricultural
prices. Some male houses reluctantly permitted their members to work
outside, an option not available to cloistered women. Some convents took in
infants and widows as pensioners, educated aristocratic girls, or sold needle-
work to supplement their incomes.[8] Houses physically deteriorated for want
of money, yet declining numbers since the fifteenth century did not justify
extensive repairs or building programs. The adverse material conditions

eroded enthusiasm for the spiritual mission of many religious communities. Out of necessity abbesses spent more time trying to enforce seigneurial rights and collect rents than attending to the spiritual needs of the community, sometimes selfishly diverting the income of the house for their personal use.[9] The Concordat of Bologna in 1516 further exacerbated the problems of weak spiritual leadership as the king promoted inappropriate candidates to the position of abbess.

The physical deterioration and spiritual decline contributed to a further decline in recruits, although many religious houses still continued to provide a place for "surplus" daughters. Nuns unsuited to the religious vocation frequently and openly defied the principle of claustration, with family complicity.[10] They participated in civic and religious processions, visited other convents, entertained their families and visitors, and raised nephews and nieces placed in their care since infancy. As worldly concerns and legal disputes dominated convent life, the intellectual and spiritual life of the communities declined. By the 1540s, very few nuns could compare with their learned and pious Huguenot relatives at court. Their refusal to observe cloister, accept individual poverty, and share in the community life in the dormitory, refectory, and choir reflected the open decline of monastic discipline. Abbesses and their communities took advantage of competing ecclesiastical jurisdictions to avoid annual visitations. Cistercian male houses had long resented and resisted supervising affiliated nunneries anyway, and female Benedictine houses nominally under the control of an absentee bishop were so rarely visited that when it happened the nuns were not receptive. Like noble wives and widows, abbesses ably managed lands, collected rents and taxes, and administered justice. Convents filled with capable, well-connected women had grown accustomed to an elected abbess managing their day-to-day affairs, with at most the help of a male *procureur*.[11] No wonder that these women resisted outside interference masquerading as reform.

By 1450, monastic reform in France had become a concern of ecclesiastical and secular authorities much as it had in Germany.[12] After initial prodding from the king and local patrons, the abbey of Fontevrault avoided outside interference and preserved its independence by reforming itself, thus becoming a model both for its dependent priories and for houses of other orders.[13] Other religious communities mobilized for reform only when the bishop or town council imposed it. Whatever the circumstances of reform, it was seldom accomplished smoothly or without public incident, and frequently it divided the convent into factions. Resourceful nuns fiercely defended their traditional privileges in ways resembling those used by aristocratic women at court and elsewhere in the realm.[14]

An examination of the century-long reform of Fontevrault reveals issues that consistently reappear in other cases of female monastic reform.[15] It began in 1459 when the abbess, Marie de Bretagne, decided to enforce cloister and restore her traditional authority over the order. Although Pope Pius II intervened and appointed an ecclesiastical delegation to reform the abbey, Marie was determined to achieve the reform alone. She withdrew with six allies from Fontevrault to the priory of Madeleine-les-Orléans, a community severely damaged by the Hundred Years' War that had experienced a decline both in numbers and discipline. She cleverly undermined their potential resistance to her plan with the promise of a pension from her own rents on lands near Nantes.[16] She reformed the priory and rewrote a rule for the entire Order of Fontevrault later approved by the pope and local ecclesiastical authorities.[17] With her death in 1475, the reform temporarily stalled under the weak leadership of Anne d'Orléans, who had secured election through her royal connections. It resumed in 1491 with the election of Renée de Bourbon, who overcame the eleven-year resistance of her nuns with an appeal to Louis XII and the Parlement of Paris. The king's court furnished her with an *arrêt* and appointed several powerful abbots to help her return to Fontevrault to enforce the rule. She replaced the troublemakers with nuns from other reformed houses, reestablished cloister, and disciplined sympathizers in the village who had financially profited from the nuns' rebellion. With order restored at Fontevrault, Renée attempted to reform the male house under her jurisdiction (Saint Jean l'Habitat) a decision that precipitated a struggle with monks who had long resented the abbess's power over them.[18] Renée presented her case to the parlement and, armed with another *arrêt,* forced the monks to accept her authority.[19] Determined to achieve total reform, she sold her silver service to finance a new wall around the abbey, personally laying the first stone. She ordered a grille installed to close the entrance to the choir, preventing the choir nuns from mingling with the villagers during mass, as had been their custom. To reinforce the ideal of cloister, Renée also made a public vow to observe cloister, which two days later the other nuns repeated.[20] Royal support undoubtedly encouraged Renée's zeal, for later, in June 1517, Francis I, accompanied by Queen Claude, Louise de Savoy, and an entourage of noblewomen, honored her with a visit and the responsibility for instructing the king's natural sister, Madeleine (who subsequently became abbess of the prestigious covent of Jouarre).[21]

More priories fell into line under Louise de Bourbon, Renée's successor.[22] By 1558, a hundred years after reform had begun, at least two-thirds of Fontevrault's affiliated houses had experienced both reform and remarkable economic recovery.[23] Out of the story of the Fontevrault reform emerge several patterns common to the history of female religious orders in the sixteenth century. Although the identification and exile of recalcitrants, the promulgation of new rules such as cloistering, and a return to the common refectory and dormitory changed convent life outwardly, there is little evidence of change in the nuns' spiritual life. Rebellious sisters were usually transferred from one house to another, sometimes several times. The power of the Parlement of Paris was frequently used by a reforming abbess to effect an administrative reform to the convent's advantage, or by a recalcitrant abbess and her nuns to protect the convent from ecclesiastical scrutiny through claims of immunity. What is most striking is the worldliness of the abbesses and nuns as they confidently resorted to courts of law and adroitly dealt with legal and ecclesiastical authorities either to reform and renew religious life or to protect the convent from the bishop's scrutiny. The records of the parlement are replete with complaints against worldly abbesses and heretical and renegade nuns, authorities' complaints about the spiritual life of the community, and abbesses' refusal to knuckle under to episcopal authority. Most cases involving reform of the community followed the pattern of Fontevrault, although in the case of other orders the question of who had jurisdiction over the convent—the local bishop, the pope, or the crown—often complicated matters and delayed a decision. Abbesses commonly appealed to the parlement as a stalling tactic to avoid visitation and reform. What is revealing is the righteous and powerful resistance the abbesses and religious communities presented to the authorities.

The reform of religious communities seldom went as smoothly as that of Fontevrault. Often the reform program divided the members of the community against each other; sometimes its rigors drove nuns away. A typical case occurred when the bishop of Paris, Jean Cardinal du Bellay, tried to reform the Cistercian royal abbey of Saint Antoine-des-Champs in Paris. Between 1544 and 1547 this affair came before the parlement at least six times. Like many royal convents, the nuns of Saint Antoine considered themselves exempt from episcopal jurisdiction and the care of the Cistercians. Beyond that, they disagreed about whether the abbot of Clairvaux or Cîteaux was responsible for visitations.[24] The parlement settled the dispute by ordering the abbots of Clairvaux and Fromment to oversee the reform of the house, offering the assistance of the secular arm if necessary, and threatening to confiscate Saint Antoine's Paris properties if the nuns ignored the order.[25] The abbots reportedly discovered scandalous disorder in the convent and, following the usual procedure, sent the troublemakers away to other houses and imposed reform on the remaining compliant members.[26] One exiled nun appealed to the parlement for justice, claiming that the abbots' wrongful treatment of her dishonored her family's reputation.[27] Another exile complained to the court that she was not receiving proper medical attention at the convent of Maubisson, where she had been sent, and asked to return to her convent.[28] In 1559 Saint Antoine came to the attention of the authorities again when the court granted the bishop power to investigate the escape of three nuns.[29] As the case of Saint Antoine-des-Champs illustrates, the reform of religious houses was seldom accomplished simply by one official order and visitation. In 1564, the Parlement of Paris learned that the Benedictines of Beaumont-les-Tours, who had been touched by the Fontevrault reform in 1502 and reformed again in 1532, no longer observed cloister, participated in divine service, or observed the regulations of religious life pertaining to dress, dining, and dormitory. The court ordered the abbot of the prestigious male house of Chezal-Benoît, reformed at the same time as Fontevrault, to investigate and reform the nuns.[30]

The royal Benedictine abbey of Yerres near Versailles presented another troublesome case. In 1513 the bishop of Paris, Étienne Poncher, after prodding from Queen Claude and Marguerite d'Angoulême, introduced reform at Yerres and other abbeys under his jurisdiction, including Chelles and Gif.[31] Determined to succeed, he sent workers from Paris to install a grille, which the abbess and sisters dismantled as soon as he departed. He then ordered fourteen sisters to move from the previously reformed abbeys of Chelles and Malnoue to Yerres.[32] The powerful abbess, the daughter of a distinguished *parlementaire,* confidently appealed to the parlement, only to find that her prestigious connections were no match against the reformist influence of Queen Claude and Marguerite d'Angoulême.[33] Instead the parlement backed the bishop's suspension of the abbess and transferred six of the recalcitrant sisters.[34] The reform at Yerres might have succeeded at that point if Francis I had not in 1544 appointed Marie de Pisseleu, the niece of his paramour Anne and of the Calvinist Péronne de Pisseleu (also known as Madame de Cany), as abbess. In no time, Marie undid the reform. Moreover, her high-handed treatment of the abbey's tenants led to lawsuits, and she also incurred the anger of the local curé when she denied him his share of the parish tax. The mistress of the novices led a faction of nuns who denounced her to the parlement for upsetting the peace of the community, impeding the progress of reform, and holding heretical ideas. Marie obtained court delays which stalled the proceedings until 1548, when the parlement responded to complaints of the local authorities and sent an armed guard to physically remove her from Yerres to the Hôtel Dieu at Saint Gervais.[35] The following year authorities summoned the nuns of Yerres to court for refusing to pay Marie's annual pension of 200 livres. The nuns claimed in their defense that Marie's recent appointment as abbess of Saint Paul, in Beauvais, relieved them of any financial responsibility for her maintenance, especially since that convent was not even reformed.[36]

Since 1472, the bishops of Paris had tried unsuccessfully to reform the royal Benedictine abbey of Gif near Versailles. Rival factions and contested elections of abbesses had kept the convent in a state of upheaval for many years, precluding any reform of the nuns' daily lives.[37] The Parlement of Paris ordered two of its counselors along with two clerics to visit and reform the convent, but they found the situation so bad that they could make little progress.[38] Finally, in 1513–14, the abbey was forced to submit to "temporal and spiritual reform" under a court order to be carried out by the bishop of Paris, Étienne Poncher. Following this, the community elected a series of capable abbesses who improved the fiscal management of convent property, reestablished cloister, encouraged the renewal of vows, and permitted the bishop's annual visitation.[39] in 1543, however, Francis I appointed Jeanne de Blosset, a Dominican, who was accused of undoing the achievements of the previous thirty years by quietly introducing Dominican control with a Dominican spiritual director and confessors. When complaints of irregularities reached the ears of the bishop of Paris, Jean du Bellay, he investigated.[40] Following his visitation, several nuns, including Blosset, complained to their families of the bishop's arrogance. Informed of their grumbling, Du Bellay brought charges against them in an ecclesiastical court. As the court was about to rule in the nuns' favor, he had the case removed to the parlement which, in spite of the nuns' powerful family connections, condemned the women and sentenced them to prison in a neighboring convent for two years.[41] No sooner had Jeanne Blosset returned to Gif after her release than the parlement was asked to investigate a new complaint alleging that she had allowed her sister Nicole, a nun from Moncel and a suspected Protestant, to live at Gif in secular clothes. Furthermore, it was rumored that the authorities suspected that Jeanne was also "infected with the Calvinist heresy" and might introduce it into the convent.[42]

Elsewhere in France between the 1540s and 1570s—in La Rochelle, Bordeaux, Toulouse, Nîmes, the Dauphiné, and the Ardèche, for example— the same problems of community laxity, disputes over authority, dwindling numbers, and nuns in flight occurred with startling frequency.[43] In addition, in the 1540s Protestant ideas began to filter into some convents through preachers, "tainted" confessors, visitors, and other outside contacts. Some nuns attracted to Calvin's message defied authority and tradition and left their communities, an act that required enormous independence and courage. As early as 1521, Marie Dentière, the learned abbess of an Augustinian house in Tournai, left her convent and married Simon Robert, a former priest turned heretical preacher, with whom she fled to Strasbourg and, later, to Berne. Widowed in 1533, she then married Antoine Fromment, an itinerant preacher, and accompanied him to Geneva. She first came to the attention of the authorities when she attempted to convert the Clarisses who spat at her. Forced as a woman to find noninstitutional ways to promote reform through writing and public preaching in taverns and on street corners, she incurred the wrath of Calvin, who publicly discredited her by calling her a heretic.[44]

About 1555 a daughter of the Esternay family, the seigneurs of La Motte–Tilly, left her Clarisse convent of Saint Catherine's near Provins, where sources said she had been corrupted by heretical books and people. Her mother and brothers convinced the prioress of Saint Cyr-au-Val de Galie, near Chartres, to accept her. She remained there without criticism for her "Lutheran" beliefs until 1561, when she left to marry a renegade Cordelier from the vicinity of Provins.[45] The nuns who fled the prestigious royal Abbaye-aux-Dames in Caen for Geneva or their families may have been influenced by Calvinist preaching in Caen.[46] Philippe de Chasteignier, whose community at Thouars near Poitiers was surrounded by Huguenot partisans, had probably heard Calvinist preaching in the vicinity before she began corresponding with Calvin around 1549. She left the convent in 1557 to go to Geneva, accompanied by eight of her nuns.[47]

In 1561, the English ambassador reported an uproar in the prestigious Fontevrault priory of Madeleine near Orléans when Jeanne d'Albret passed through on her way to Poissy. According to Throckmorton, who reported the incident sometime later, one of Jeanne's pastors, Jean de la Tour, preached to the crowds in Orléans so successfully that twenty-five nuns (out of sixty) "threw aside their habits and scaled the walls."[48] The nuns at Madeleine may have been prejudiced by the prior influence of their humanist confessors, Jean de l'Espine and Jean Dampierre, who later converted to Calvinism.[49] At the nearby Benedictine convent of Saint Loup, the abbess, Michelle Goddard, apostatized in 1562 and left for Montargis, a town belonging to the royal Calvinist sympathizer Renée de France, taking with her some leases and revenues from the convent's holdings.[50] Madeleine de la Foix Caraman of Saint Pierre-des-Chazes, in Bourges, announced after hearing Calvinist preaching that she wished to become the abbess and secularize the convent. Failing that, she left and married in 1563.[51] In 1560 the city councillors of Nîmes learned that some nuns at nearby Saint Sauveur-la-Font celebrated Protestant communion.[52]

The independence of nuns could be a source of embarrassment to their relatives at court. There is the notorious case of Charlotte de Bourbon, daughter of Jacqueline de Longwy—an influential woman at Catherine de Médicis court—who, although a Catholic, supported the Huguenot cause. Jacqueline placed the two-week-old Charlotte in the royal convent of Jouarre near Meaux, where she was raised to be a nun, only to shock her family and the court in 1572 by escaping, announcing her conversion to Calvinism, and fleeing to the Palatinate, well beyond her outraged parents' reach. She later married the Protestant prince of Nassau, William of Orange. A deposition by the nuns of Jouarre said that she had frequently received at the abbey "certain persons professing the reformed religion," whom they named; she had also corresponded with Jeanne d'Albret, who, it was rumored, aided her escape.[53] The resistance to reform and authority at the less prestigious convents was less well publicized, although occasionally the nuns there also came to the attention of authorities. At Montélimar in Dauphiné, the town council took up the problem of Marguerite de Nivette, a former Clarisse at Aubenas, who opened a school in town where she reportedly taught "bad doctrine." The council took measures to have her condemned for heresy after learning that she possessed heretical books.[54]

Nivette was unusual in that very few nuns seem to have possessed heretical books. While they clearly shared an independent, indeed often defiant, spirit with their Huguenot "sisters," they seem to have lacked the latter's passion for reading and learning. The few existing inventories of convent libraries list Bibles, lives of saints, writings of the Church Fathers, and books of hours, but hardly any works in either medieval or humanist learning.[55] Apparently few nuns knew Latin. When Henry II nominated Louise de Lingage as abbess of the royal convent of Saint Pierre d'Avenay in Rheims, her ability to write in Latin and translate the Office from Latin into French was exceptional enough to be noted.[56] The correspondence between the abbess of Fontevrault and the theologians at the Sorbonne in 1541 and 1542, which began when she uncovered what she perceived to be heretical ideas in some of her nuns, was conducted in French, not Latin. Her letters, moreover, reflected her inability to distinguish between heretical and correct doctrine, as the holy doctors pointed out in their reply.[57] Except for a few rare individuals such as Claude Bectroz at Saint Scholastica in Tarasçon, there is little evidence in French convents of the literary achievement that had been the case in France in the Middle Ages, or in the sixteenth century in some Italian and Spanish convents.[58] Nor did French nuns compose spiritual writing comparable to that of Marguerite de Navarre, certain Spanish nuns, and Italian aristocratic women. Protestantism seems to have reached French nuns more through reformist preaching than through writing.

Calvinism's appeal in some convents is difficult to assess since religious houses routinely expunged the names of renegades from their records. Moreover, as we have seen, nuns left their convents for reasons besides conversion to Calvinism, including a profound lack of vocation. Some courageously undertook the long, painful process to be canonically released from their vows in order to return to their families or marry. Such was the case with Pierre de Brantôme's sister, Françoise de Bourdeilles, who at the age of ten had been sent to the prestigious convent of Saint Croix La Trinité near Poitiers for the purpose, she thought, "of learning to read, write and embroider according to the custom for young women." Three years after her arrival, according to her testimony, the king and queen of Navarre; Françoise's mother, a lady-in-waiting in Marguerite's entourage; and other *grands* came to the convent and forced her "with an almost cruel insistence to take the veil which she did despite tears and protestations." In 1549, following the death of her family's patroness, Marguerite de Navarre, Françoise threatened her own and her family's reputation by announcing her intention to renounce her vows, a process that took eighteen years.[59] Little wonder that some nuns took advantage of the chaotic times and simply fled from their convents, even though such escapes were routinely reported to the parlement or town council for punitive action.

The authorities sought court action against the nuns at Notre Dame de l'Andecy, a Benedictine priory near Châlons-sur-Marne, when, following a struggle that began in 1558 over an episcopal visit resulting in demands for reform, one sister fled to be with a "certain gentleman" whom she subsequently sued for matrimony.[60] Soon thereafter, the prioress and several sisters fled to parts unknown.[61] But other nuns were not so fortunate in achieving permanent freedom from convent life. According to a deposition following the Edict of Amboise in March 1563, Jeanne de la Riche and Jeanne de Milly left their convent of Grandvilliers, in Étaples, for the Hôtel Dieu, where, according to the abbess, they "lived in apostasy" and ignored her orders to return. On hearing the abbess's case, the parlement ordered the *bailli* and *échevins* of Étaples to take the runaway nuns by force if necessary and deliver them to the convent door.[62] In Toulouse in 1562, the town council ordered several nuns from the Augustinian house of Pantaléon who had recently left the convent and married to be whipped and imprisoned for three years.[63] In 1572, the Parlement of Paris publicly called for the capture and return of the abbess of the Cistercian house of Gômbre near Meaux. Apparently, she hoped to support herself in the outside world by sneaking away with "all she could take from the abbey," including the furniture.[64]

While families habitually ignored strict claustration of their daughters and even supported them in resisting it, nuns who attempted to quit their convents permanently encountered serious obstacles. Abbesses, civil and ecclesiastical authorities, and family members usually closed ranks to force the recalcitrant to return. Escape from a convent so threatened the family's honor that public denunciation of a daughter's behavior could be endured for the sake of her return to her convent. In 1569 the brother-in-law of Magdalene Gilbert, a nun who had left her convent of Malnoue near Paris the previous year after Huguenot forces attacked and burned it and refused to return, revealed where she was and requested the parlement to order her to return. The parlement's threat to imprison her soon led to her return to the convent.[65]

The destruction of convents by Protestant or Catholic troops often forced the departure of the entire community and challenged the ingenuity of nuns suddenly on their own. If they returned to their families, they presented problems touching on family honor, financial support, inheritance, and dowries should they decide to marry.[66] Parents unwilling or unable to support them prodded their daughters to return to their convents when the fighting ended. Such was the case at the Dominican convent of Villemur in Toulouse, which was entirely destroyed by Huguenots, who sacked the interior and used the materials to build fortifications. The Parlement of Toulouse issued a number of decrees for the convent's rebuilding, but the townspeople ignored them and succeeded in chasing the nuns away. Some nuns sought refuge at another convent, while others went home to their families. But when the wars ended, the convent was rebuilt from scratch.[67] Les Ayés, a Cistercian royal abbey near Grenoble, was well endowed and had traditionally enjoyed the special protection of members of the royal family. Yet, it lost everything at the hands of the Huguenots, who ordered the sisters to return to their families and destroyed the abbey.[68] When soldiers attacked and pillaged the prestigious Abbaye-aux-Dames in Caen, some nuns left for Geneva, but others went home to their families.[69] Some nuns, perhaps because they had no place to go, remained at their priories even when their numbers dwindled to two or three. At the priory of Du Boulay in Touraine, the prioress, Renée de la Pommeraye, who had been accused of heresy and interrogated by the officials of the *chambre ardente* in 1549, lived with one sister and a servant while enjoying the income from the priory's benefices until the local curé, whom she had insulted by denying his seigneurial rights, exposed her to the parlement in 1552.[70] Like their aristocratic relatives at court, nuns could sometimes use their status and political connections advantageously to head off trouble from outside. For example, Françoise de la Rochfoucauld, abbess of the royal convent of Saintes near La Rochelle, wrote letters to her brother, a member of Condé's forces, pleading that the Huguenot forces be ordered to spare the convent, which they did.[71]

Several preliminary conclusions can be drawn from this look at sixteenth-century abbesses and nuns. First, the nuns in the priories of Fontevrault apparently reformed themselves with less struggle than the other orders experienced, probably because of the abbess's tighter organization and better control over the subordinate communities. No such generalization can be made for the Benedictines, Clarisses, Dominicans, and Augustinians, because entire communities seldom agreed on the issue of internal reform. As in the world outside the convent, reform frequently divided religious communities in complex ways. The strong resistance of some nuns to reform and claustration undoubtedly sprang from their desire to see their families occasionally. Attempts by ecclesiastical and civil authorities to close convents to the outside world after years of laxity sparked restlessness and even anger among aristocratic women, many of whom lacked any religious vocation in the first place. Reform also affected male communities, albeit less dramatically, since males had more alternatives, such as becoming tutors, secretaries, and pastors. Lacking these choices, a nun who left the convent could either marry or become a financial liability to her family, alternatives that equally threatened family honor and stability. This lack of choices perhaps explains the vehemence of many nuns against reform measures that threatened their lives in new and unacceptable ways.

The female religious orders appear to show no pattern for conversion to Calvinism, which infiltrated communities of all the orders. Geography played some role; convents located in Calvinist strongholds saw more departures from Catholicism than those in the region of Paris, for example. Frequently the only historical source recording the departure of nuns who accepted Calvinism is a casual mention in a journal or regional history written at the time. Usually the male author ascribes the nun's decision to embrace Calvinism or go to Geneva to the desire "to have the freedom to marry." Such was the case, claimed Brantôme, with Madame Usèz, abbess of Saint Honorat in Tarasçon, who escaped her convent when she was fifty in order to marry.[72] Marriage could not have been an easy choice because many nuns, lacking family support, would have been forced to marry beneath their station.

Class interest no doubt strongly influenced nuns' attitudes toward convent, reform, and Protestantism. In the absence of a true sense of religious vocation, some women used the independence and leadership derived from their aristocratic values to challenge any limitation on their convents' traditions by outside authority. Like their noble "sisters" outside, nuns rejected the gender restrictions of sixteenth-century society by demonstrating a remarkable ability to manage their own affairs, ranging from the internal management of their communities, including the financial and judicial tasks that befell them as feudal "seigneurs," to their occasional defiance of traditional secular and ecclesiastical authority. Elite women, lay and religious, eventually lost both independence and power as a result of political and religious changes in the seventeenth century. However, at least for the period between the Hundred Years' War and the end of the sixteenth century, the combination of high social class, religious and political upheaval, and life in a community of aristocratic women seems to have empowered nuns to challenge the traditional boundaries that restricted their independence to govern their lives and to refuse to submit humbly to traditional authority.[73] An outstanding example of women exerting independence is the defiance of the nuns in three Dominican houses in Strasbourg who refused to dissolve their communities when ordered to do so by town officials. Instead they reformed themselves, but in such an austere manner that some nuns left.[74] In the regions of Brunswick and Lunenberg in Germany, women strongly resisted the dissolution of their convents by the Protestant authorities. The distinctive feature in all these cases is that women acted independently and contrary to the expectations of family, community, church, and society.

The similarities of independent action of Catholic and Protestant women, albeit for different causes and in different arenas, suggest that Protestantism was just one of many causes that spurred women to action in early modern France. Women may have found power in the Protestant message, as Roelker argued, but life in a religious community also offered opportunities for the exercise of individual and collective power. In the case of the Brunswick nuns, Merry Wiesner argued for class as an empowering factor for women in religious communities, especially the older, more traditional ones.[75] In a study of female religious communities in early modern Seville, Mary Elizabeth Perry argued that living in a religious community could empower women regardless of their class, because it provided them a measure of independence from their male-dominated families.[76] In early modern France, religious community and class seem to have empowered Catholic women to act independently and in their own interests.

Notes

Earlier versions of this essay were presented at the Sixteenth Century Studies Conference, October 1991, in Philadelphia, Pennsylvania, and at a conference organized by Charles Daniels and Claire Murphy at the University of Rhode Island in November 1991 to fête Père Germain Marc'hadour. I thank Jodi Bilinkoff, Ruth Liebowitz, and the participants at both conferences for their helpful criticism.

1. William Monter, "Protestant Wives, Catholic Saints and the Devil's Handmaid: Women in the Age of the Reformations," in *Becoming Visible: Women in*

European History, 2d ed., ed. Renata Bridenthal, Claudia Koonz, and Susan Stuard (Boston: Houghton Mifflin, 1987), pp. 205–12; Merry Wiesner, "Nuns, Wives, and Mothers: Women and the Reformation in Germany," in *Women in Reformation and Counter-Reformation Europe,* ed. Sherrin Marshall (Bloomington: Indiana University Press, 1989), pp. 8–28; Charmarie J. Blaisdell, "Renée de France between Reform and Counter-Reform," *Archive for Reformation History* 63 (1972): 196–225; Blaisdell, "Calvin's Letters to Women: Courting of Ladies in High Places," *Sixteenth Century Journal* 13.2 (1982): 67–84.

2. Nancy L. Roelker, "The Appeal of Calvinism to French Noblewomen in the Sixteenth Century," *Journal of Interdisciplinary History* 11.4 (1972): 391–418; Roelker, "The Role of Noblewomen in the French Reformation," *Archive for Reformation History* 63 (1972): 168–96.

3. Natalie Zemon Davis, "City Women and Religious Change," in her *Society and Culture in Early Modern France* (Stanford: Stanford University Press, 1975), p. 95; Ruth P. Liebowitz, "Individuals and Convents in Late Renaissance Italy" (paper presented at a conference in honor of Nancy L. Roelker's 75th birthday, Brown University, June 1990); Merry E. Wiesner, "Religion as a Source of Public Authority for Women: Reformed Convents versus the Reformation" (paper presented at the American Historical Association annual meeting, December 1987); Mary Elizabeth Perry, *Gender and Disorder in Early Modern Seville* (Princeton: Princeton University Press, 1990); Laura Mellinger, "Politics in the Convent: The Election of a Fifteenth-Century Abbess," *Church History* 5.4 (1994): 529–39.

4. There are no general studies of French nuns in this period. One might begin with the old standard work by Lina Eckenstein, *Women under Monasticism* (New York: Russell & Russell, 1963, reprint). A recent and useful collection of essays on women and religious life in various parts of Europe, not just France, is *The Crannied Wall: Women, Religion, and the Arts in Early Modern Europe,* ed. Craig A. Monson (Ann Arbor: University of Michigan Press, 1992). Max Josef Heimbucher, *Die ordern und Kongregationese der katholischen Kirche,* 3d ed. (1896–97; Paderborn, 1933–34), is the best survey of monastic and male and female spiritual organizations before and after the Counter-Reformation. See also Denis de Sainte-Marthe, *Gallia christiana in provincia ecclesiasticas distributa qua series Historia* (Paris, 1744–); Pierre Helyot, *Histoire des ordres religieux et militaires et des congrégations seculières,* 8 vols. (Paris, 1792); Ferdinand Hervé-Bazin, *Les Grands ordres et congrégations des femmes* (Paris, 1889); M. Peigné-Delacourt, *Tableau des abbayes et des monastères d'hommes en France avec la liste des abbayes royales des filles* (Arras, 1875); Philibert Schmitz, O.S.B., *Histoire de l'Ordre de St. Benoît,* 7 vols. (Marrédesous: Éditions Marrédesous, 1942–46), vol. 7 is devoted to women's orders; Dom Beaunier, *Abbayes et prieurés de l'ancienne France: Recueil historique des archévêchés, évêchés, abbayes et prieurés de France* (Liguge: Abbaye St. Martin, 1905), in *Archives de la France monastique,* vols. 1, 4, 7, 10, 12, 14, 15, 17, 19, 36, 37, 45; continued by Jean Martial Besse under the same title in the *Revue Mabillon* (Paris: C. Poussielgue, 1905–90), the standard reference for pre-Revolution French monasteries and convents (hereafter

cited as Beaunier-Besse). Jean Becquet, *Abbayes et prieurés de l'ancienne France: Recueil historique des archévêchés, abbayes et prieurés de France*, in *Revue Mabillon* (1970–75), is a further continuation of Beaunier and Besse. Dom Laurent-Henri Cottineau, *Répertoire topobibliographique des abbayes et prieurés de France* (Maçon: Protat, 1939–70); Paul Biver and Marie-Louise Biver, *Abbayes, monastères, couvents des femmes de Paris des origines à la fin du XVIII siècle* (Paris: PUF, 1975).

5. Elizabeth Rapley, *The* Dévotes: *Women and the Church in Seventeenth-Century France* (Montreal and Kingston: McGill-Queens University Press, 1990).

6. My study is based on an examination of 150 royal convents throughout France, identified from the studies of Besse, Bequet, Cottineau, and Biver and chosen because manuscript evidence, although scant, is available for them. The sample includes Benedictines, Cistercians, Fontevrault, Clarisses, Augustinians, and Dominicans.

7. See C. E. Labrousse and Fernand Braudel, eds., *Histoire économique et sociale de la France* (Paris: PUF, 1980), vol. 1, pt. 2, pp. 903–40, for a general discussion of the impact of rising prices. Emmanuel Le Roy Ladurie noted that the years 1526–34 were crisis years for agriculture, on which convents especially depended, in *Les paysans de Languedoc* (Paris: Flammarion, 1969), pp. 156–57 and passim.

8. Francis Rapp, *Réforme et Réformation à Strasbourg: église et société dans le diocèse de Strasbourg, 1450–1525* (Paris: Ophrys, 1975), pp. 249–65; Schmitz, *Histoire*, 3:202–22, 7:94–99.

9. Records of the Benedictine abbey of Saint Croix-de-la-Trinité near Poitiers show that temporal interests dominated the life of this royal convent in the fourteenth and fifteenth centuries; see Louise Coudanne, "Crise et réforme à l'abbaye Sainte Croix de Poitiers," *Bulletin de la société antiquaires de l'Ouest,* ser. 4, 2 (1952–54): 497–506; Coudanne, "Histoire de l'Abbaye Sainte Croix de Poitiers: quatorze siècles de vie monastique," *Bulletin de la société antiquaires de l'Ouest,* ser. 4, 19 (1986–87): 223–67. On November 14, 1485, the Parlement of Paris learned of the abbess's poor administration of the goods of the abbey of Yerres (Paris, Archives Nationales [hereafter AN], X1A 1493, fol. 280r); on April 2, 1494, a similar complaint was made against the abbess of Faremoutiers (AN, X1A 1502, fol. 296r). The registers of parlement in the late fifteenth century are full of examples of complaints against abbesses (and abbots) for mismanagement of convent resources.

10. Examples of families openly supporting their daughters' resistance to claustration occurred in the Cistercian houses of Flines and Marquette; see Ernst Hartcoeur, *Histoire d'église collégiale et du chapitre de S. Pierre de Lille,* 3 vols. (1899), 3:522.

11. See, for example, Claude-Hyacinthe Berthault, *L'Abbaye Pont-aux-Dames* (Meaux, 1878), pp. 115ff.; Berthault, *L'Abbaye Nôtre Dame de Chelles,* 3 vols. (Paris, 1889–94), 1:234; J. M. Alliot, *Histoire de l'Abbaye et des religieuses bénédictines de Nôtre Dame de Val de Gif* (Paris, 1892), pp. 33–77; Alliot, *Histoire de l'Abbaye et des religieuses bénédictines de Nôtre Dame de Yerres* (Paris, 1899), pp. 152–96.

12. Wiesner, "Religion as a Source of Public Authority for Women."

13. Founded as a "double monastery," Fontevrault was still governed by an

abbess in the fifteenth and sixteenth centuries. On the medieval period, see Penny Schine Gold, "Male-Female Cooperation, The Example of Fontevrault," in *Medieval Religious Women,* vol. 1 of *Distant Echoes,* ed. John A. Nichols and Thomas Schank (Kalamazoo, Mich.: Cistercian Publications, 1984), pp. 151–68; Jacqueline Smith, "Robert of Arbrissel's Relations with Women," in *Medieval Women,* ed. Derek Baker (Oxford: Basil Blackwell, 1978), pp. 178–84. The definitive monograph is Simone Poignat, *L'Abbaye de Fontevrault* (Paris: Nouvelles Éditions Latines, 1966). Also see Jean Lardier, "La Sainte Famille de Fontevraud," Archives Départementales du Maine et Loire [hereafter ADM/L], MI 87; Lardier, "Le Trésor de Fontevraud," ADM/L, 101 H153. Although in 1964 the spelling of Fontevraud was established by ministerial decree, scholars continue to insist on the traditional Fontevrault.

14. Kristen B. Neuschel, "The Construction of Gender in Noble Life in Sixteenth-Century France: New Evidence, New Questions" (paper presented at the American Historical Association annual meeting, December 1987, Washington, D.C.); Neuschel, *Word of Honor: Interpreting Noble Culture in Sixteenth Century France* (Ithaca: Cornell University Press, 1989).

15. Louise Coudanne, "De la règle réformé de Fontevrault (1479) aux statuts d'Étienne Poncher: 1505," *Revue Mabillon* 59 (1979): 393–408; Alfred Jubien, *L'Abbesse Marie de Bretagne et la réforme de l'ordre Fontevrault d'après des documents inédits* (Paris, 1872); Armand Parrott, ed., "Mémorial des abbesses de Fontevrault, issues de la maison royale de France," *Mémoires de la société académique de la Maine et Loire* 36 (1881): 1–189; Bernard Palustre, *L'Abbesse Anne d'Orléans et la réforme de l'ordre de Fontevrault* (Paris, 1899); F. Uzureau, "La Réforme de l'ordre de Fontevrault (1459–1641)," *Revue Mabillon* 13 (1923): 141–46; Jean de la Viguerie, "La Réforme de Fontevraud, de la fin du XVIème siècle à la fin des guerres de religion," *Revue historique de l'église de France* 65 (1979): 107–17; H. Nicquet, *Histoire de l'ordre de Font-evraud* [*sic*] (Paris, 1642).

16. Jubien, *L'Abbesse,* p. 16.

17. Bibliothèque Nationale [hereafter BN], Paris, Fonds Français, 1435 and 13885; Fonds Latin, 11077; *Regula Ordinis Fontis-Ebraldi, La Règle de l'Ordre de Font-Evrauld* (Paris, 1642). The rule clearly shows the measures taken to reform life within the convent by reestablishing cloister and common sleeping and eating quarters, reviving the habit, and enforcing silence at night and during meals, regular attendance at mass, regular confession, and strict rules about age of profession.

18. Jubien, *L'Abbesse,* pp. 35–38; Jean de Viguerie "La Réforme de Fontvraud" *Revue d'histoire de l'église de France;* and Simone Poignat, *L'Abbaye de Fontevrault* (Paris: Nouvelles Éditions Latines, 1966), pp. 54–55.

19. The case dragged on for a number of years. On March 18, 1520, Francis I issued an edict giving the abbess absolute power over the nuns and monks at Fontevrault. I was not able to find the *arrêt* of March 1520. A copy is located in *Extrait des registres du grand Conseil du Roy,* Paris, BN Ld16 183. The *arrêt* is referred to in Jean Lardier, "Inventaire des titres du thresor de Fontevraud" a seventeenth-century manuscript in the ADM/L, vol. 1, 795. BN, MS Latin 5480, fols. 333, 359.

Issues relating to the reform of the abbey from 1454 until 1575 appear throughout the registers of parlement for those years.

20. ADM/L, MI 87, Jean de Lardier, "Saincte Famille de Fontevrauld," 3:587–96; Jubien, *L'Abbesse,* pp. 40–43.

21. Jubien, *L'Abbesse,* pp. 40–44. On Louise de Savoy's interest in church reform, see Gordon Griffiths, "Louise de Savoy and Reform of the Church," *Sixteenth Century Journal* 3.10 (1979): 29–36.

22. ADM/L, "Fonds Fontevrault," Serie H: 206 "Blessac"; Beaunier-Besse, *Abbayes et prieurés de l'ancienne France,* 5:216; ADM/L, Serie H: 206 "La Ramé"; Beaunier-Besse, *Abbayes et prieures de l'ancienne France,* 3:240.

23. Jubien, *L'Abbesse,* p. 52.

24. Sally Thompson, "The Problem of the Cistercian Nuns in the Twelfth and Thirteenth Centuries," in *Medieval Women,* ed. Derek Baker (Oxford: Basil Blackwell, 1978), p. 239.

25. AN, XıA 1560, fol. 224r, June 27, 1547; XıA 1560, fol. 326r, September 5, 1547; XıA 1560, fol. 563v, September 1547.

26. AN, XıA 1561, fol. 224r, February 8, 1547–48.

27. AN, XıA 1561, fol. 338v, March 6, 1547–48.

28. AN, XıA 1561, fol. 224r, February 8, 1547–48.

29. AN, XıA 1593, fol. 434r, April 9, 1559–60.

30. AN, XıA 1610, fol. 60r, v, July 11, 1564.

31. AN, XıA 9322, nos. 78, 79, 93, 123.

32. Alliot, *Yerres,* p. 179.

33. AN, XıA 9322, no. 78, September 5, 1515; XıA 9322, no. 79, September 23, 1515; XıA 9322, no. 93, January 4, 1516; XıA 9322, no. 123, January 13, 1516.

34. AN, XıA 8489, fols. 22r–26v.

35. Alliot, *Yerres,* p. 386; AN Paris, XıA 1563, fol. 132r, July 9, 1548; XıA 1563, fol. 199r, July 22–23, 1548; XıA 1563, fol. 272v; XıA 1563, fol. 316v, August 21, 1548.

36. AN, Paris, XıA 1562, fol. 6r, April 12, 1548–49.

37. Alliot, *Val de Gif,* pp. 77–90. Commencing in 1493, the registers of parlement reflect the upheavals at Gif as the nuns resisted reformation; AN, XıA 8329 July 19, 1493.

38. Alliot, *Val de Gif,* pp. 90–92.

39. Ibid., pp. 95–130.

40. Ibid., p. 137.

41. AN, Paris, XıA 1563, fol. 49, July 14, 1548; XıA 1564, January 18, 1548–49, fol. 162r; XıA 1566, January 4, 1549–50; XıA 1568, fol. 82, January 5, 1550–51.

42. Abbé LeBeuf, *Histoire de la ville et tout le diocèse de Paris,* 5 vols. (Paris, 1863–67), 3:390; *Gallia christiana,* 8:596; and Pierre Pithou, *Preuves des libertés de l'église gallicane,* 2 vols. (n.p., 1639), 2:1175.

43. La Rochelle: Bibliothèque Municipale de La Rochelle, MS 241, the registers of the *officialité* for July 30, 1545–49, and December 1552. Thanks to Professor Judith Meyer of the University of Connecticut at Waterbury for these references. In Bordeaux, the priory of La Ramé, a dependent of Fontevrault, was among the most lax and recalcitrant of the Fontevrault priories; in 1558, there was one nun left: ADM/L, H7; Beaunier-Besse, *Abbayes et prieurés de l'ancienne France,* 3:40; Eduoard, *Fontvraud,* 2:280; Toulouse: attempts to reform the prestigious Fontevrist house of Saint Catherine failed in spite of the action of the Parlement of Toulouse. In 1532, nine nuns remained: Archives Departmentales [hereafter AD] Haute Garonne, B 25, fol. 376; Xavier Courrège, "Un prieuré de Fontvristes, St. André de Longages," *Revue de Comminges* 94 (1981): 193–202. In June 1562, several nuns of the Augustinian house of Pantaléon were sentenced to be whipped and imprisoned for three years after they tried to abandon the cloister, return to the world, and marry; Joan Davies, "Persecution and Protestantism: Toulouse, 1562–75," *Historical Journal* 22 (1979): 31–51. Nîmes: the prestigious Benedictine house of Saint Sauveur was in internal chaos from the early sixteenth century, beginning with the election of an abbess that caused scandal in 1512. The bishop at the time was Briçonnet, but since he was never present the council made the issue its business; the authorities acted when it became known that the sisters wished to celebrate Protestant communion. See Chantal Beauquier, "Les évêques de Nîmes at l'abbaye Saint Sauveur de la Font," *Bulletin de l'académie de Nîmes* 50 (1971): 23–41. For Dauphiné, see Jean-Jacques Hemardinquer, "Les femmes dans la réforme en Dauphiné," *Bulletin philologique et historique du Comté des travaux historiques et scientifiques* (1959): 382–97.

44. Johann Baum, Eduard Cunitz, and Eduard Reuss, eds., *Ioannis Calvini Opera quae supersunt omni,* 59 vols. (Brunswick: C. A. Schwetske & Son, 1863–1900), 12:378; Davis, "City Women and Religious Change," pp. 82, 85; Marie Dentière, "La guerre et délivrance de la ville de Genève," in *Mémoires de la société d'histoire et d'archéologie de Genève,* ed. A. Rilliet, 20 (1881): 309–84; Jules Vuy, *Le réformateur Froment et sa première femme* (Paris, 1883); Jeanne de Jussie, *Le Levain du Calvinisme* (Chambery, 1661; reprint, Geneva, 1853), pp. 173–74; Aimé-Louis Herminjard, ed., *Correspondence des réformateurs dans la pays de langue française,* 9 vols. (Geneva, 1874), 5:295–304, 6:174; Marie Dentière, *Epistre très utile faict et composé par une femme chrestienne de Tornay, Envoyée à la Royne de Navarre soeur du Roy de France Contre les turcz, juifs, infideles faulx chrestiens, Anabaptists et Lutheriens* (Geneva, 1539); Olivia H. McIntyre, "Marie Dentière and the Reformation in Geneva" (paper presented to the American Society of Church History, Chicago, December 1985).

45. Claude Haton, *Mémoires de Claude Haton, contenent le récit des événements accomplis de 1558–1582,* ed. Félix Bourquelot, 2 vols. (Paris, 1862), 1:127.

46. C. de Bourgueville, *Les Recherches et antiquitez de la province de Neustrie et présent duché de Normandie comme des villes remarqueables d'icelle: Mais plus spéciallement de la ville et université de Caen* (Caen, 1588), pp. 162–63; David Nichols, "Social Change and Early Protestantism in France: Normandy, 1520–62," *European Studies Review* 10 (1980): 290.

47. Baum et al., *Calvini Opera,* 13:294–97.

48. *Calendar of State Papers Foreign, Elizabeth,* 1560–61, ed. J. Stevenson (London: Public Records Office, 1869), no. 735 (4), December 20, Throckmorton to Challoner; L'Abbé Edouard, *Fontevrault et ses monuments,* 3 vols. (Paris, 1873), vol. 1, pt. 2, p. 373. Ludovic Vauzelles, *Histoire du Prieuré de la Madeleine lez Orléans de l'Ordre Fontvrault avec pièces justificatives* (Orléans, 1873), p. 103, suggests that the cause of the mass departure may have been the reform of the convent spearheaded by Renée de Bourbon in 1560 or the violence committed against the convent by Calvinists after the king's departure from Orléans. Also see Poignat, *L'Abbaye de Fontvrault,* pp. 67–68.

49. Vauzelles, *Histoire du Prieuré de la Madeleine lez Orléans,* 182; Une Soeur de Boular, *Histoire de l'Ordre Fontevrault par les religieuses de Sainte Marie Fontvrault, 1100–1908,* 3 vols. (Auch, 1913).

50. André Laurenceau, "St. Loup, Orléans," *Bulletin de la société archéologique et historique d'Orléans* 45 (1973–74): 271–74; Jean Le Maire, "Le Couvent de St. Loup-lez Orléans," *Bulletin de la société archéologique et historique d'Orléans* 1 (1959–60): 146; Denis Lottin, *Recherches historiques de la ville Orléans,* 8 vols. (Orléans, 1836–45), 1:404, 405, 435; Bibliothèque Municipale, Orléans, MS 487, fol. 133 (eighteenth-century manuscript); See also MS 430, "Notes historiques."

51. N. Dursapt, "Les abbesses des Chazes," *Almanach de Brioude* (1955): 43–68, (1956): 135–66; Eugène Hagg and Émile Hagg, *La France protestant, ou vies des protestants français,* 10 vols. (Paris, 1846–58), 5:125; Schmitz, *Histoire,* 7:155.

52. Chantal Beauquier, "Les évêques de Nîmes et l'abbaye de Saint Sauveur de la Font," *Bulletin de l'académie de Nîmes* 50 (1971): 34.

53. Jules Delaborde, *Charlotte de Bourbon, Princesse d'Orange* (Paris, 1888); Yves Chaussy, Germain Guillaume, et al., *L'Abbaye Royale Nôtre Dame de Jouarre, Bibliothèque d'histoire et d'archéologie chrétiennes* (Paris: Guy Victor, 1961), chap. 5.

54. Samuel Mours, *Église Réformée de Montélimar* (Montélimar: Église Reformée, 1957), pp. 17–18, based on council registers of 1556–57.

55. Noreen Hunt, "Notes on the History of Benedictine and Cistercian Nuns in Britain," *Cistercian Studies* 8 (1973): 166, points out that the new learning of the fifteenth and sixteenth centuries seems not to have reached the English communities for women either. Gaston Duval, "La bibliothèque de l'abbaye de Montmartre," extract of the *Bulletin du Vieux Montmartre* 27 (1896); A. Dutilleux and J. Depoin, *Inventaire de N.D. Royale de Montbuisson lez Pontoise (1463–1738),* vol. 1 of *Recueil des anciens inventaires* (1896). Louis Paris, *St. Pierre d'Avenay,* 2 vols. (Paris, 1879), 2:455–92, lists 423 volumes of *histoire ecclésiastique,* 88 other books of history and piety, and 150 more "old French books never read." A comparison of libraries in male houses is striking. J. Jenny, "Propos de la réforme de Chezal-Benoît: Quelques aspects de la vie intellectuelle des abbayes de cette congrégation d'après des livres anciens de la bibliothèque de Bourges," *Cahiers d'archéologique et d'histoire du Berry,* vol. 6, which contains *Actes du 40ième Congrès de la Fédération des Sociétés Centres,* no. 62 (September 1980), pp. 114–20.

56. Beaunier and Besse, *Abbayes et prieuriés de l'ancienne France, Archives de la France monastique,* in *Revue Mabillon* 16.263, p. 196.

57. Charles Duplessis d'Argentré, *Collectio judicorum de novis erroribus . . .* , 3 vol. in folio (Paris: A. Caìlleau, 1728–36), 2:132–33.

58. Sister Claude Scholastica de Bectroz, abbess of Saint Honorat, Tarasçon, was admired by many, including Hillarion de la Coste and Ludovico Domenichi, for her knowledge of Latin and her ability to write eloquently—especially her poetry, which they described as "in the manner of Sappho." Marguerite de Navarre visited her because of her reputation for learning, and there were several other learned nuns at Saint Honorat. See Hillarion de Coste, *Les Eloges et les vies des reynes des princesses et des dames illustres en piété, en courage et en doctrine qui ont fleury de nostre temps et du temps de nos pères,* 2 vols. (Paris, 1647), 2:755–60; Ludovico Domenichi, *La Nobilità delle donne, di M. Lodovico Domenichi* (Venice, 1549).

59. Alfred Barbier, *Soeur de Brantôme religieuse de l'Abbaye de Saint Croix* (Poitiers, 1893).

60. AN, XIA 4972, December 28, 1558; XIA 8375, fols. 129r–133v, January 31, 1560; XIA 1604, November 28, 1562.

61. AN, XIA 8375, fols. 129r–133v.

62. AN, XIA 1615, fols. 6v–7r.

63. AD Haute Garonne, "Tournelle" 85, fol. 171, June 1562; Joan Davies, "Persecution and Protestantism," 48.

64. AN, XIA 1635, fol. 44v, February 26, 1572–73.

65. AN, XIA 1625, fol. 134, January 8, 1569–70; LeBeuf, *Histoire de la ville,* 5:399–404.

66. There is the example of a nun of Montivilliers who took advantage of the destruction of her convent to escape with only the clothes on her back and return to her family in Paris. See Beatrice Hibbard Beach, "A Nun of Montivilliers," *Cistercian Studies* 98 (1987): 339–50. Beach has found the notarial records reflecting the concern of the nun's parents for her financial protection and the protection of the family patrimony.

67. *Histoire du monastère de Prouillé par une religieuse Prouillé* (1898); Edibert de Teule, *Annales du prieuré de N.D. de Prouillé* (Carcasonne, 1902).

68. Eduard Maigner, "Notice historique sur l'abbaye des Ayés de l'ordre de Cîteaux," *Bulletin de l'académie delphinale* 2 (1866): 424–59.

69. Charles de Bourgueville, *Les recherches et antiquitez de la province de Neustrie à présente de la Normandie* (Caen, 1588), p. 162.

70. AN, XIA 4949, fols. 131v–133v, May 23, 1552; N. Weiss, *La Chambre Ardente* (Paris, 1889), p. 374. The *procès* of 1552 seems to have originated as early as 1547 and may be tied to suspicions of her heresy. The complaint, a litany of accusations of laxity against Renée, the other nun, and a servant, has a familiar ring when examined beside complaints against other convents. La Ramé, also a Fontrevault dependency near Bordeaux, had only one nun enjoying its fruits in 1558; ADM/L, H 7; Edouard, *Fontvraud,* 2:280.

71. Louis Audiat [Dom Boudet], "Histoire de l'abbaye de N.D. de Saintes hors les murs de la ville de Saintes," *Archives historiques de la Saintonge et de l'Aunis* 12 (1884): 294.

72. Pierre de Bourdeille, seigneur de Brantôme, *Vie des dames gallantes* (Paris: Garnier et frères, n.d.), p. 276. Madame Usèz was the sister of Françoise de Clermont-Tallart, a *politique* at Catherine's court. See also Brantôme, *Oeuvres complètes,* ed. L. Lalanne, 11 vols. (Paris, 1864–81), 7:396.

73. For other sources of empowerment of women, see Barbara B. Diefendorf, "Widowhood and Remarriage in Sixteenth-Century Paris," *Journal of Family History* 6 (1982): 379–95; Kristen B. Neuschel, "A Cannon in the House: Noble Women and Noblemen in Early Modern France," a forthcoming article which the author kindly shared with me for interpretations of other powerful sixteenth-century French women.

74. Francis Rapp, "L'Observance et la réformation en Alsace (1522–1560)," *Revue de l'église de France* 65 (1979): 41–54.

75. Merry E. Wiesner, "Religion as a Source of Public Authority for Women"; Wiesner, *Women and Gender in Early Modern Europe* (Cambridge: Cambridge University Press, 1993).

76. Perry, *Gender and Disorder,* pp. 75ff.

Barbara B. Diefendorf

An Age of Gold? Parisian Women, the Holy League, and the Roots of Catholic Renewal

In later life, Barbe Acarie, one of the founding figures of the Catholic Reformation in France, was wont to reminisce about her experiences in Paris during the six-year period when the city, having rebelled against its king, was dominated by the ultra-Catholic coalition of the Holy League. Referring specifically to the spring and summer of 1590, when the royal army of Henry of Navarre held Paris under siege, she called this period "an Age of Gold, when people didn't think about eating or drinking but only about turning to God." "She had never been happier," she recalled, "or felt more contentment."[1]

Most people recalled the siege in very different terms. Memoirist Pierre de l'Estoile described a horrifying descent into famine and fear—a time when bones from the city's cemeteries were ground into flour to stretch the insufficient grain, when the poor ate the raw flesh of dead dogs they found in the streets or chewed on the hides of mules and donkeys that had been sold for meat. L'Estoile even claimed that two or three days before the siege was lifted soldiers in the city, crazy with hunger, began to chase after little children in the streets and slaughtered and ate three of them. "This cruel and barbarous act was committed within the walls of Paris," he added, "such was the wrath of God that had descended upon us."[2]

If we believe l'Estoile, as the siege progressed, people could think of little *except* food and how to appease their starving bellies. In contrast to Acarie, who saw the mortification of the flesh induced by the conditions of scarcity as a spiritually rewarding by-product of the city's isolation, l'Estoile saw the deprivations produced by the siege as brutalizing and profane. He strongly condemned the "preachers of famine, [who preached] as if religion consisted of dying of hunger," and memorably captured the twisted value system he attributed to the League's leaders in a horrifying phrase from the captain of the Bastille about how he would eat his only child rather than give in out of sheer necessity.[3]

It is easy to empathize with l'Estoile and recoil from the view of the league expressed by Acarie. How could a time of cruel deprivation be viewed as an age of gold? Conditioned as we are by the ultimate success of Henry of Navarre's drive to establish himself as the legitimate king of France, we find it hard not to condemn out of hand the motives and policies of the League's leaders. We see no nobility in suffering that appears to have been wrongfully and even foolishly self-imposed, and we mistrust the Leaguers' argument that they were acting in the necessary defense of the holy church. Our memories crowded with images of injustices perpetrated even in our own century by religious and ideological quarrels, we are justifiably suspicious of any claim to act in defense of a single and unified truth. We want to debunk such a claim as false—a hypocritical cover for baser political motives—or, if we can be convinced that it is true, to dismiss it as invalid. If we can label proponents of the League as political usurpers and religious fanatics, they will, we believe, forfeit any further claim to our attention. And yet such a view, by foreclosing the possibility of understanding what the proponents of the League thought they were trying to achieve, also closes off the possibility of understanding some of the long-term consequences of the League.

Recent scholarship, in particular Robert Descimon's *Qui étaient les Seize?*, has helped to place the political motives of ardent Leaguers into a more benign frame of reference by recognizing in them a fierce attachment to traditional civic values.[4] At the same time, Denis Crouzet's *Les guerriers de Dieu* has done much to illuminate the frenetic religiosity of the period.[5] The important connections between the religious fervor of the League and the Catholic renewal that occurred in its wake, however, remain to be explored. Denis Richet alluded to the continuity between the two movements when he concluded an article on the processions of the League by saying that "if the political League ended in failure, the League of the devout was to survive, victorious or at least tolerated, throughout the seventeenth century."[6] It is the emergence of the *ligue des dévots*—or rather the *ligue des dévotes,* since it is the women in particular who interest me here—that I will address in this essay.

Richet concluded another article with the observation that the role played by women in the Counter-Reformation was comparable to the one they had played in the Calvinist Reformation fifty years earlier.[7] Since Nancy Roelker has contributed so much to our understanding of the role of women in the spread of Calvinism in France, it seems only fitting to dedicate to her memory this attempt to delineate some part of the role that women played in propagating a reformed Catholicism half a century later.[8]

On an individual level, at least, much more has been written about the women who took part in the Catholic Reformation than about the Calvinist noblewomen that Roelker studied. In order to keep this essay to a manageable size, however, I examine only the beginnings of the Catholic Reformation in Paris, and particularly its connections with the spirituality of the League. I focus on the women known to have been closely associated with the founding of the first reformed women's religious order in Paris, the Discalced Carmelites of Saint Teresa of Avila. I look not just at those women who became nuns when the order was founded in 1604, however—the youngest of these were just girls when the League was vanquished from Paris ten years earlier—but also at those noblewomen who lent financial and political support to the order's foundation. Many of these women can be shown to have played an unexpectedly important role in League affairs. As we shall see, however, other early supporters of the Carmelites were on the opposing side in the quarrels of the League. They were members of *politique* families loyal to the crown, and as such, suffered persecution if they remained in Paris during the troubles. These women did not see the League as a golden age, any more than Pierre de l'Estoile, also a *politique,* was inclined to do. The connection between League spirituality and Catholic renewal was thus not a simple and unilinear one; the processions of the League were not the only path to the cloisters of reformed Catholicism. We must look instead for more subtle commonalities of behavior and belief shared by the women who sided with the League and those who sided against it.

Women in the Paris League

Even casual readers of Pierre de l'Estoile's memoirs will have noticed that the women of the Guise family were very active in their support of the Holy League. Catherine de Clèves, the widow of Henri, duc de Guise, spent most of the period of the League in Paris, where she served as a symbol and rallying point for the rebellion. When she gave birth to Henri's son six weeks after his assassination, for example, the baby was brought from the Hôtel de Guise to the church of Saint-Jean-en-Grève, adjoining the Hôtel de Ville, in an elaborate procession in which the city's militia took part holding lighted torches. The baby was held at the baptismal font by "la Ville de Paris" (presumably in the person of the city's *prévôt des marchands*), and an elaborate reception was held at the Hôtel de Ville to celebrate the event.[9]

Anne d'Este, duchesse de Nemours (the widow by her first marriage of

François, duc de Guise, and mother of the assassinated Henri, duc de Guise, and his brother, the cardinal de Guise), played an even more prominent role in League politics. Arrested at the same time that her sons were assassinated by order of the king in December 1588, she was released the following month and moved into Paris for the duration of the troubles.[10] While her second son, Charles, duc de Mayenne, officially assumed leadership of the ultra-Catholic faction on his brother's death, the duchesse de Nemours played an important part in financing the League, popularizing its policies within Paris, and transmitting information about the situation in Paris to Mayenne when, as was often the case, his military operations required him to leave the capital.[11] Judging from the frequency with which she was consulted by the radical leaders of the League, the Seize, she also had considerable authority to make policy decisions in Mayenne's absence.[12]

But it was Catherine de Guise, duchesse de Montpensier, the daughter of Anne d'Este and sister of the duke and cardinal assassinated at Blois, who was the most audacious supporter of the Holy Union among the Guise women. Known to be secretly pensioning the most radical preachers in Paris, she encouraged inflammatory preaching and malicious pamphleteering against both Henry III and his successor, Henry of Navarre.[13] According to l'Estoile, just four days before he was assassinated on August 1, 1589, Henry III sent an envoy to Madame de Montpensier to tell her that he was well aware that she was the one "who was sustaining and supporting the people of Paris in their rebellion; but that if he ever succeeded in retaking the city, as he hoped shortly to do, he would have her burned alive."[14] "Fire is for sodomites like [Henry III], and not for the likes of me," she boldly retorted, alluding to vicious rumors about his sexual proclivities that she had herself helped to spread. "In any event, he could be sure that she would do her best to prevent him from entering the city."[15] On learning of the king's death, she and her mother climbed into their carriage and paraded through the streets of Paris crying out, "Good news, my friends! Good news! The tyrant is dead!" By l'Estoile's report, Madame de Nemours even climbed the steps to the high altar at the Cordeliers' church and "harangued the people about the death of the tyrant."[16]

L'Estoile characterized this act as displaying "a great immodesty and female impotence, that she should continue to gnaw on one who was dead."[17] L'Estoile's disapproval reflects not only his *politique* sentiments but also the misogyny typical of his age. For Madame de Nemours to speak publicly, and from the altar of a church, was to his mind both unseemly and pointless. Using an image that suggested a dog chewing on a bone ("mordre encore sur un mort"), he criticized her for displaying in public a satisfaction that, as a woman, she should have kept private. At the same time, unwilling to admit that this public harangue might have stirred a popular response, l'Estoile dismissed it—because it came from a woman—as a display of powerlessness. The sexual slurs evident in anti-League pamphlets and graffiti directed against the Guise women, in particular Madame de Montpensier, also show a strongly misogynistic strain. Whether caricatured on a wall as a naked woman being mounted by a mule bearing the name of the papal legate or satirized in a mock confession as having "thought to make a great sacrifice to God by offering up her private parts to advance the affairs of the League," Madame de Montpensier was belittled by the League's opponents, who sought to reduce her contributions to the cause to the offering of sexual favors.[18]

Important noblewomen were not alone in being disparaged by sexual innuendo and accusations of an unfeminine meddling in the public realm; the contributions of less prominent women to the League were treated in the same terms—or, more often, they were ignored entirely. This makes it difficult to reconstruct the role that such women played. Take Madame de Sainte-Beuve, a cousin of Barbe Acarie and, along with her, a founder of the Ursuline order in Paris. L'Estoile, referring to her as "la Sainte Veuve," suggested that she took part in the processions of the League more out of coquetry than piety. He described her, "covered only in a fine linen [shift], with a deep vee at the throat," allowing herself to be flirted with and led by the elbow through the church of Saint-Jean-en-Grève by the Chevalier d'Aumale, one of the more rakish members of the house of Lorraine, "to the great scandal of the truly devout people who took part in good faith in these processions."[19] He also contrasted her unfavorably with the well-bred wives of magistrates imprisoned in the Bastille for their suspected royalist sympathies during the spring of 1589. While the latter fasted during the Lenten season, he noted, "la Sainte Veuve" gave banquets and magnificent parties for the aristocracy of the league and openly mocked the *politique* wives (many of whom must have been her kinswomen) by saying that she took "a singular pleasure in seeing these mud-encrusted ladies go to the Bastille to mend the breeches of their husbands."[20]

Only a copy of a letter written by Sainte-Beuve's stepbrother, Antoine

Hennequin d'Assy, a president in parlement and a committed Leaguer, shows the more serious role that this rich young widow played in helping to raise money to finance the League. Writing to the duc de Mayenne in March 1589, the day after League forces suffered a crushing defeat at Senlis, Hennequin appealed to Mayenne to return to Paris to reassure the populace by his presence. He warned him that the propaganda efforts of the duchesse de Montpensier, Mayenne's sister, had lost credibility with the new defeat and that it was becoming more and more difficult to raise money for the cause. "My sister, Madame de Sainte-Beuve, is seeking to borrow money everywhere for this most pressing affair," he wrote, "but she cannot find any, because they say that she is already sufficiently and even too greatly indebted for your sake."[21]

Sainte-Beuve was not the only wealthy *parisienne* who helped raise money for the League. Her cousin Barbe Acarie seems to have been more deeply involved than previous historians have acknowledged in the attempts of her husband, Pierre Acarie, to provide funds for the wars of the League. Both husband and wife mortgaged their properties heavily to contribute funds to the cause.[22] Moreover, Barbe Acarie seems to have assisted her husband in the financial arrangements he negotiated with the Paris Chartreux, who lent their name to cover large sums of money borrowed to pay for the wars of the league.[23] Because of legal conventions that obscured the participation of married women in financial affairs by putting all transactions under the name and authority of the husband, it is impossible to determine exactly Barbe Acarie's role as a money raiser for the league. Whatever role she played in this regard can, however, be viewed as an extension of her domestic role and responsibilities.[24] The same is true of her role after the League's defeat, when she acted to repair the family's finances and secure the return of properties confiscated because of her husband's involvement with the Seize. In both cases she acted on her husband's behalf and as his agent. There can be no question, however, that she wholeheartedly supported the League, and her other activities on behalf of the Catholic Union give us a better view of her temperament and initiative.

The testimony given during her beatification proceedings gives ample evidence of the enthusiasm with which Barbe Acarie took part in the public displays of piety encouraged by the League, aided poorer neighbors in surviving the deprivations brought on by the siege, and nursed wounded soldiers brought in from the League's battles. As my initial quotation about the siege being "an Age of Gold" suggests, she experienced—or at least remembered—the five months during which Paris was held captive by the army of Henry IV as a period of spiritual exaltation. Along with other women from her parish, she was an ardent participant in the many religious processions sponsored by the League and fervently prayed that these marks of popular devotion might "appease the wrath of God and avert the great misfortunes with which the state was menaced."[25] Religious fervor and pragmatism combined in the Christian charity she offered her neighbors. She did more than most women of her station to help the poor survive the famine brought on by the siege. Learning that, like most wealthy people, her mother-in-law, Marguerite Lottin, was hiding the family's store of grain so that it would not be confiscated and redistributed to aid the poor, Acarie threatened to give the secret away if Lottin did not voluntarily yield up a generous portion to give to those who were dying of starvation.[26] In addition, wishing to share in the common suffering, she set aside as much as possible of her own portions of bread and traded it for the inferior ersatz bread that was being distributed to the poor.[27]

Most important, however, was the service she provided in helping to care for wounded soldiers and the poor. After the defeat of the League army at Senlis in May 1589, thousands of wounded soldiers were brought into Paris, even though the city's hospitals were poorly equipped to care for them. Barbe Acarie was one of the first to volunteer to help. She is said to have gone daily to the nearby hospital of Saint-Gervais to bring the patients nourishing broths and healing unguents that she made herself. She also helped clean their wounds and change their bandages. In addition to assisting the soldiers with their physical ailments, she had a spiritual mission to those who were dying. Crucifix in hand, she brought them words of comfort, urged them to make a final confession, and helped them through the terrors of death. According to André Du Val, she developed quite a reputation among the wounded soldiers, and a great many asked to have her at their side when they died.[28]

Several witnesses pointed out that it was not easy for this good bourgeoise to conquer the repugnance she initially experienced on entering the dirty and chaotic hospital, where the sick and wounded were crowded several to a bed. She had to force herself to remove the soldiers' filthy bandages and clean their putrid sores, and yet she not only persisted in her efforts but went on after this crisis was past to help tend poor patients in the Hôtel

Dieu.[29] The marquise de Maignelay credited Acarie with having been the first woman of her station to undertake this sort of charitable work in Paris—work that was later systematized and extended by Louise de Marillac and Vincent de Paul with the organization of the Dames de Charité. In fact, the practice had its roots in hospital visits begun a generation earlier. In 1578, Acarie's kinswoman Renée de Nicolay, the widow of a president in the Chambre de Comptes (and the mother of Madame de Sainte-Beuve), was asked by the supervisors of the Hôtel Dieu to help organize the visits that Parisian ladies wished to make to the hospital.[30] It is not certain that this initiative was pursued, though there is evidence that Acarie's devout aunt, Marie du Drac (also a kinswoman of Renée de Nicolay), began to visit Paris hospitals at about this time.[31] According to Acarie's eldest daughter, moreover, Acarie did not go to the Hôpital Saint-Gervais alone but rather went in the company of her devout mother-in-law, Marguerite Lottin.[32] It is probable that other devout ladies were beginning to do the same thing. Those not actually tending patients in Paris hospitals were collecting linens and other donations to serve the Hôtel Dieu in this time of crisis.[33] If Acarie was not the very first well-born *parisienne* to volunteer her time and service in Paris hospitals, she served as a model for others who followed her in this work. For my purposes, however, the most important thing about Acarie's charitable work is its connection with the particular spiritual and emotional climate engendered by the League. What became a classic form of charitable service for upper-middle-class women began as both a religious exercise and a way of helping out during a crisis.

Women, Reformed Piety, and the Experience of the League

The extreme circumstances of the League years, and particularly of the siege of 1590, provided unusual opportunities for women to play a public role in religion and politics, which in this case were identical. Thus it is not a surprise that women like Barbe Acarie should have found the period liberating—a golden age—much as do participants in revolutions or great demonstrations, even when the outcome is failure. At the same time, the events of the period generated enormous physical and psychological tensions. With League preachers calling out daily the need for atonement, might not these tensions have found one outlet in mystic rapture?

In the case of Barbe Acarie, for example, it is clear that the charitable and managerial activities in which she took part were accompanied by a deepening and interiorizing of her spirituality. Her first mystical trance, in which she lost consciousness for hours while praying in a chapel of her parish church of Saint-Gervais, appears to have taken place in the summer of 1590—just about the time the siege of Paris was lifted. During the next two years, such mystical experiences occurred with increasing frequency, and in 1593 she is said to have received invisible stigmata.[34] Except for one report that she fell into a trance while taking part in a procession with women of her parish, these spiritual experiences cannot be connected in any direct fashion with the events of the League. A much more explicit relationship is evident in the spiritual autobiography of Marie de la Trinité (Sévin), one of the first French Carmelites.

Written years later at the command of her confessor, the autobiography nevertheless conveys forcefully the heady atmosphere of apocalyptic piety that dominated in Paris during the initial stages of the League. The daughter of a president in the Cour des Aides, Marie Sévin was just seventeen when the League tightened its control over Paris in 1589. Swept up in the common enthusiasm, Sévin modified her behavior dramatically in response to the demand for penitence that thundered down from the pulpits of the League. She described her sentiments in 1589 as follows:

Along with most of the Catholics then in Paris, I tried to do what I could to appease heaven's wrath, which appeared openly in the disorders of the war than began in 1589. In a dream I saw France all in flames, and then I saw that fire put out. . . . During this time, I abandoned all that was worldly; I sold some jewels that I had in order to give the money to the poor; I dressed very modestly. I resolved to become a nun, but circumstances didn't allow me to put this into execution as yet. I did all the penitential acts that I could, and in these exercises the Lord gave me more strength than nature could possibly have done. I didn't find anything difficult. The example of a God who has endured so much for me gave me a continual and very fervent desire to suffer for his glory, even though I believed that I was infinitely unworthy. It seemed to me that I didn't want to ask to suffer, but rather that I offered myself entirely. My heart, penetrated with a pure love for Jesus Christ, seemed to yearn for martyrdom.[35]

The exaltation Sévin experienced at this time comes through with particular force in her repeated insistence on her wish for martyrdom. Transfixed by the apparent threat that the war posed to the Catholic faith and detesting the very notion of a heretic king, she felt within herself a powerful urge "to appear before the kings, the magistrates, and the people, and to speak out in their presence for the defense of Jesus Christ and his church." Recklessly confident that even the harshest measures could not dissuade her from making her stand, she was convinced that "God would make [her] worthy of dying to attest to his glory, because he formed in [her] this vehement desire for martyrdom."[36]

Marie Sévin did not speak out publicly on behalf of the League—at least there is no record that she did. If she had, she would doubtless, like Madame de Nemours, have been taunted for her unfeminine lack of decorum. It is worth noting, however, that she did defy the usual limits on female behavior by insisting that her family leave her behind in Paris when they took refuge in the royalist city of Tours. Sévin's family did not share her enthusiasm for the League and remained loyal to the crown. Like many other families from the Parisian magistracy, they became alarmed by the growing persecution of individuals perceived to be insufficiently supportive of the Seize and decided to flee to safer ground. Marie, however, refused to accompany them. She insisted that if she were forced to leave she would speak out so forcefully against heresy that she would soon be martyred for her faith. "My resolution surprised them," she recounted, "and, fearing that it would cause me to speak out too freely on this subject, they decided to leave me alone with some servants in the house."[37]

By Sévin's account, the powerful desire to devote herself to God alone lasted for "the four or five years that the troubles of war lasted in France."[38] Regarding as providential the unexpected liberty provided by her family's absence, she gave herself over entirely to devotional exercises and interrupted her newfound solitude only to go to church for mass or sermons or to take part in religious processions. She took communion frequently—daily when possible, but at least four or five times a week—and felt a particular bond with the "sacred humanity of Jesus Christ." In receiving the Eucharist, she recounted that she had no sensation of the material accidents of the bread but rather experienced an inexplicable pulse of joy and spiritual satisfaction. Elsewhere she compared the force of the divine love that embraced her to "an impetuous wind and a devouring fire." "I was entirely occupied with God," she recorded, "and belonged more to him than to myself. Nothing touched me so much as his glory and the salvation of souls."[39]

In time, however, Sévin's spiritual satisfaction began to fade. Although her autobiography provides few indications of a parallel dissatisfaction with the politics of the League, it is clear that the two were not unrelated. The period of spiritual aridity that she experienced as a growing distance from God—a cooling of his love and privation of his grace—is linked in her text to the winding down of the political crisis as the king began to speak of conversion. When her mother and sister came to Paris to urge her once again to join them in Tours, she accompanied them without fuss. Once in Tours, she discovered that the royalists—"those who followed the court"—were indeed good Catholics, and she was consoled to learn that there was "much piety and devotion" among these people that she previously had scorned.[40]

Marie Sévin recorded these experiences years later, at a time when she was ending a long career distinguished by both her admirable personal piety and the administrative skills she displayed as the founding prioress of half a dozen Carmelite monasteries. There can be little doubt, however, that the spiritual awakening she experienced at the time of the League contributed in no small measure to her determination several years later to escape from the worldly pleasures of Parisian society into the quiet cloisters of a reformed religious order where, through penitence and prayer, she might once again seek the inexplicable joys of total union with God.

Women Opposed to the League

On first consideration, the lives of Parisian women who opposed the League appear very different from the lives of women who supported the League with their attendance at sermons, participation in processions, and charitable services.[41] To the extent that the sources reveal them at all, female opponents of the League in Paris endured constant worry, privation, and harassment—sometimes outright persecution—at the hands of the Seize and their supporters. Often left behind to represent the family (that is to say, to protect the family's property from confiscation or outright pillage) when their husbands sought refuge in royalist cities, they not only had to endure the same hardships as all Parisians isolated in a city under siege, they also had to cope with public animosity that was vented in the streets and in shops, at city hall, and even in their parish churches. They were subjected to punitive taxation, summary confiscations, and even on occasion arrested and held for ransom on trumped-up charges.[42]

Among the women associated with the establishment of the Carmelites in France, the most dramatic story that has come to my attention concerning a victim of the league is that of Catherine d'Orléans, damoiselle de Longueville, the princess in whose name and by whose generosity the Carmelite order was officially founded in France. Along with her mother, the dowager duchesse de Longueville, her sister-in-law, Catherine de Gonzague de Nevers (the young duchesse de Longueville), and her younger sisters Marguerite and Eléonore, Catherine de Longueville was held prisoner in the town of Amiens for more than three years beginning in December 1588. Having traveled to Amiens for the formal entry of the young duc de Longueville, recently named governor of the province of Picardy, the women and the duke's younger brother, the comte de Saint-Pol, stayed on there to celebrate the Christmas holidays while the duke went off to visit his new province. Word of the deaths of the duke and the cardinal de Guise and the arrest of their nearest allies reached Amiens the day after Christmas, and the townspeople, inflamed by a sermon preached on behalf of the assassinated Guises, insisted on holding the Longueville women and the comte de Saint-Pol as hostages against the liberty of those arrested at Blois.[43] City officials and members of the bourgeoisie invited to attend the city's deliberations decided that they would swap their hostages for no less a person than Charles de Guise, the young son of the martyred duke and the new figurehead of the Guisard movement, and they clung to this decision in the face of every attempt on the part of the Paris Seize or League nobles to arrange other exchanges.[44]

Because of their high social standing, the Longueville women were imprisoned in a private house and not the city jails. For several months they were allowed to go outside during the daytime, but fear that they would escape caused the conditions of their captivity to be progressively restricted.[45] The comte de Saint-Pol was separated from them, but the others were allowed to remain together, at least until October 1589, when, following an attempted escape by the dowager duchesse de Longueville, they were rigorously separated and prevented from seeing one another.[46]

It is not clear why the duchess's daughters and daughter-in-law did not try to escape along with her. Presumably they thought it was too risky for all to attempt to leave at once. All four young women were in late adolescence or their early twenties, and they appear to have been in good health. Whatever their reasons for staying behind, surely they were crushed to learn of the humiliating conditions under which the duchess was returned to Amiens after her capture in a nearby small town. People came from near and far to scream insults, throw filth, and dance around the cart in which she was carried. One of the men who had helped her to escape and was returned with her was promptly beaten to death in the city streets; the other was rescued just short of death and imprisoned. According to one account of these events, the duchess herself was threatened with sword thrusts and forced to take the barrel of a loaded pistol into her mouth before the authorities rescued her from the cart. She fell into a serious illness shortly after her return, but still her daughters and daughter-in-law were kept from her.[47]

The women experienced other difficulties as well during their imprisonment. The city's records are filled with discussions of forced loans and ransoms that might be extracted from them. Possible exchanges of prisoners were repeatedly suggested, but after each discussion the city decided simply to guard its prizes still more carefully and to swap them only for the young duc de Guise and (a condition apparently added sometime in March 1589) his cousin, the duc d'Elbeuf.[48] For reasons of security, the duchess's entourage was repeatedly cut back, and the prisoners' communications with the outside world were strictly limited. Guards were replaced often so that the women would not have the opportunity to suborn them.[49] Time passed, and freedom appeared no closer.

By August 1591, the city's bad faith was evident. Despite a letter from the duc de Guise announcing his own liberty and asking that the Longueville women be freed in return, no such action was taken. Rather, the city insisted that the women were to be retained until the duc d'Elbeuf was liberated. Several days later the city added a new condition: the women were to be traded against *both* Elbeuf and the vicomte de Tavannes, and they were to pay a ransom to aid in freeing Elbeuf.[50] Once again negotiations dragged on.[51] Changes in the political scene made Amiens officials even more reluctant to give up their captives. In November 1591, Henry IV was marching toward Amiens with his army, and possession of these important noblewomen was thought to offer a possible means of dissuading Henry from an all-out attack.[52] On January 21, 1592, the city proposed holding the women until the siege of Rouen was successfully completed.[53]

By this time even Mayenne, who was at Amiens with other Catholic leaders, had lost patience. That same afternoon, he summoned the mayor to the bishop's palace and told him in no uncertain terms that he intended to take the Longueville women with him when he left Amiens the following morning. The city's attempt at remonstrances was cut off. City representatives were informed that the women had agreed to pay an indemnity against the freedom of Elbeuf and Tavannes, and the matter was—at last—taken out of the city's hands.[54]

Although we know little of Catherine de Longueville's thoughts during this ordeal, or even how she passed her long days of captivity, there is reason to believe that her imprisonment contributed to the cultivation of the piety that had already caused her to reject all suitors and insist that she wanted no husband but Jesus Christ. Certainly, all of the Longueville women were extremely upset by the fact that Amiens officials repeatedly refused them permission to attend mass. The original motive seems to have been fear that they would attempt to escape, but soon two other motives were added. The first was to extort from the duchess a letter begging for the release of the duc de Guise.[55] Second, and more important, city authorities contended that the women, like other royalists, had been excommunicated for belonging to "the party of the tyrant."[56] They were told that they would need the permission of the bishop before they could attend mass, but this permission was not granted. Even a letter from the duc de Mayenne could not change the city's policy.[57] In May 1590, Mayenne requested for the second time that the Longueville women be allowed to attend mass. This time he promised that, in exchange, he would arrange the same privilege for the duc de Guise. This was a bargain the city could understand, and for two weeks the women, under heavy guard, were allowed out for mass.[58] After much pleading and with elaborate security arrangements, the women were permitted to hear mass again on All Saints' Day and yet again on Saint Catherine's Day.[59] There is no indication that they were allowed out after this, though they remained in captivity for more than a year.

It is hard for us to appreciate how wounding this denial would have been to a pious early modern Catholic like Catherine de Longueville, who was in all likelihood used to hearing mass daily. To be denied access to the most familiar and comforting ritual of her faith, to be denied access to the Eucharist, these would have been the greatest hardships of her captivity. And adding insult to injury was the city's insistence that, along with the other women in the family, Catherine was excommunicate—cast out from the holy Catholic church and from the salvation that it promised. Even if Catherine refused to accept this judgment, to be classed with the heretics and virulently scorned by her fellow Catholics cannot have been an easy burden to bear.

Certainly it was not for Marie Tudert, another of the women later associated with the Carmelites for whom the League was demonstrably not an age of gold. The wife of Jean Séguier d'Autry, *lieutenant civil* of the *prévôté* of Paris (and after 1613 the Carmelite Sister Marie de Jésus-Christ), Marie Tudert was but twenty-two when the League seized control of Paris. Tudert had married into a family that was piously Catholic but also loyal to the crown. With the exception of one brother-in-law, the men in the family were forced to leave Paris for the duration of the League.[60] Tudert, her widowed mother-in-law, Louise Boudet, and several sisters-in-law remained alone with the family's young children. Like other women from royalist families, they were shunned by old friends, harassed by city officials, and forced to endure a number of indignities. Louise Boudet, for example, appeared before the *prévôt des marchands* in April 1589 to complain that the captain of her quarter had taken a gold chain that belonged to her.[61] She had a more serious quarrel with the city two years later. When her oldest grandson died in her arms of the plague in September 1591, city officials rushed to the house to seize the possessions of the dead lad on the ground that his mother (his nearest relative and consequently his heir) belonged to "the contrary party," and the properties were consequently forfeit.[62]

But worst of all, the women of the Séguier family heard themselves repeatedly denounced from the pulpit of their parish church of Saint-André-des-Arts. According to Pierre de l'Estoile, Christophe Aubry, the Leaguer curé of Saint-André, explicitly denounced "la lieutenante-civile" (Marie Tudert) as a *politique* on February 7, 1593.[63] In July, he denounced Louise Boudet in a way that insulted her whole family. Calling down from the pulpit that "there were ladies in Paris, and in his very parish, who pretended to be devout Catholics and yet had children at Saint-Denis and Tours [royalist cities]," he derided the women for shamelessly claiming that although "their children belonged to the party of that heretic, they yet did not cease to be good Catholics." This was a lie, the priest thundered, and all of them were damned and excommunicated.[64] On another occasion, Aubry warned the wife of President Pierre (II) Séguier that he would insult her if she dared to show up for mass; in January 1594 he again denounced Louise Boudet, this time because she advocated accepting Henry IV as king now that he had converted.[65] Again and again, Aubry—along with other Leaguer preachers in Paris—claimed that royalists and *politiques* were no better than heretics and attempted to cut them off from the Catholic community. Many of his more virulent sermons seemed to advocate violence against *politiques,* and the women had good reason to fear the local crowds. Despite the curé's unpleasantness, Marie Tudert, like other *politique* women, defiantly continued to attend mass in her parish church. Surely she intended to take what solace she could from her faith; probably she also wanted to display by her actions that—contrary to the curé's accusations—she was a faithful Catholic. Still, one might theorize that the trials of this period, and the loss of respect Tudert must have experienced for this so-called man of God, also prodded her to cultivate a more internalized and personal faith.

When Tudert entered the Carmelite convent of the Incarnation in 1613, she insisted that her greatest wish since the time of her widowhood in 1596 had been to retire from the world to dedicate herself entirely to God.[66] She claimed she had been dissuaded from making an immediate profession only by the opposition of family members who insisted that she first must raise her children, the youngest of whom was still a babe in arms. Making a vow of perennial chastity, Tudert devoted the next seventeen years to "good works: prayer, almsgiving, and visits to the poor"—the latter often in the company of her cousin Barbe Acarie.[67] Her fear of damnation is evident in a vision she had of the world all covered with traps and snares; the Lord, appearing to her, encouraged her to leave a place surrounded by so many dangers.[68] She became one of the growing number of devout women—ex-Leaguers and ex-*politiques* alike—for whom the experience of the League only intensified the conviction that the world was mired in sin and the only hope for salvation lay in retreat.

Indeed, one of the clearest signs of the spiritual impact of the wars of the League is in the tendency of women—especially widows, but also some married women—to adopt a narrowly ascetic style of living in its wake. They continued the kind of charitable work in hospitals and among the poor begun during the crisis of the siege, but they also adopted more reclusive, individualized, and penitential forms of piety. During her husband's exile after the League, Barbe Acarie cut down her meals to one a day, and that one so scanty that her friends began to fear for her health. She gave herself over to private devotions, and every evening she had her servant administer corporal discipline by scourging her.[69] Marie Sévin, briefly married in response to her parents' wishes, adopted as a young widow a life divided between pious retreat and good works. She sought to convert prostitutes to penitential reform, visited prisoners in their jail, and experienced such a great desire to aid the poor that she "wished that [her] body were cut into pieces, and each piece might serve to satisfy their hunger."[70] Sévin desire for martyrdom had returned in full force. Similar stories could be told about Charlotte de Gondi, the marquise de Maignelay, one of the Parisian noblewomen most closely associated with Acarie in her charitable works and in the founding of the Carmelites, and about other women from both *politique* and Leaguer families.[71]

We might theorize, then, that it was the trauma of the circumstances generated by the League more than the admonitions of its preachers that opened the path to the internalized spirituality of reformed Catholicism. When the League was formed, both its supporters and its *politique* opponents agreed that the disasters from which France was suffering were products of human sinfulness and signs of the wrath of God. Despite attempts by their preachers to claim the high ground of Catholic unity, the Leaguers had no monopoly on faith. Marie Tudert, Catherine de Longueville, and other opponents of the League may in fact have been prompted by the experience of having their Catholic allegiance questioned or denied to turn their faith inward and seek consolation in personal communion with God sooner than were those who, like Acarie or Sévin, joined wholeheartedly in the demonstrative and collective piety of the League. For the latter, the acts of penitential piety advocated by League preachers must have seemed, for a time at least, to offer a means of appeasing God's wrath. Even for the most idealistic, however, the vision of the League as an "Age of Gold" had to fade before the realization that atoning for human sinfulness was not to be accomplished through mass attendance at sermons and torchlight processions but rather required individual penitence, prolonged introspection, and a humble search for union with God. And so both ex-Leaguers and ex-*politiques* came to see in the ascetic cloisters of the reformed religious orders that utopian place where "people didn't think about eating or drinking but only about turning to God."

Such orders did not exist yet in France—at least not for women—and had to be created. But that is another story; the wish had to precede the reality, and it was during the League years that this wish was implanted.

Notes

1. The quotation is from the testimony of Sister Marie du Saint-Sacrement (Valence de Marillac) in the proceedings for the beatification of Sister Marie de l'Incarnation (Barbe Acarie): Archives du Carmel de Pontoise [hereafter ACP],

Procès apostolique, fol. 644r. Similar statements occur in the testimony of André Du Val, fol. 322v; Françoise de Jésus (de Fleury), fol. 339v; Marie de Jésus (de Breauté), fol. 619v; and other witnesses. I thank the Carmelites of Pontoise for graciously making this and other precious manuscripts available to me.

2. *Journal de l'Estoile pour le règne de Henri IV,* ed. Louis-Raymond Lefèvre, vol. 1: *1589–1600* (Paris: Gallimard, 1948), p. 70. See also the *Brief traité des misères de la Ville de Paris,* in *Archives curieuses de l'histoire de France depuis Louis XI jusqu'à Louis XVIII,* L. Cimber [pseud. Louis Lafaist] and Félix Danjou, eds., ser. 1, vol. 13 (Paris, 1837), pp. 271–85, especially pp. 281–82. For a Catholic perspective on the siege, see Pierre Corneio, *Bref discours et veritable des choses plus notables arrivees au siege memorable de la renommee ville de Paris* (Paris, 1590), as reprinted in Cimber and Danjou, *Archives curieuses,* ser. 1, 13:227–70.

3. L'Estoile, *Journal de l'Estoile pour le règne de Henri IV,* p. 68.

4. Robert Descimon, *Qui étaient les Seize? Mythes et réalités de la Ligue parisienne (1585–1594),* vol. 34 of *Paris et Île-de-France: Mémoires* (Paris: Hachette, 1983). For a contrasting view, see Elie Barnavi, *Le parti de Dieu: Étude sociale et politique des chefs de la Ligue parisienne, 1585–1594* (Louvain: Nauwelaerts, 1980).

5. Denis Crouzet, *Les Guerriers de Dieu: La violence au temps des troubles de religion, vers 1525–vers 1610,* 2 vols. (Seyssel: Champ Vallon, 1990).

6. Denis Richet, "Politique et religion: Les processions à Paris en 1589," in *La France d'Ancien Régime: Études réunies en l'honneur de Pierre Goubert,* 2 vols. (Toulouse: Privat, 1984), 2:623–32, republished in Denis Richet, *De la Réforme à la Révolution: Études sur la France moderne* (Paris: Aubier, 1991), pp. 69–82; the quotation is from page 81.

7. Denis Richet, "La Contre-Réforme catholique en France dans la première moitié du XVIIe siècle," in his *De la Réforme à la Révolution,* ibid., p. 93.

8. Nancy Roelker, "The Appeal of Calvinism to French Noblewomen in the Sixteenth Century," *Journal of Interdisciplinary History* 2 (1972): 391–418; and Roelker, "The Role of Noblewomen in the French Reformation," *Archive for Reformation History* 63 (1972): 169–95.

9. Pierre de l'Estoile, *Mémoires-Journaux,* ed. G. Brunet, 12 vols. (Paris, 1875–96), 3:246 (February 7, 1589).

10. Ibid., 3:200, 246: According to l'Estoile, she arrived in Paris on February 10, 1589.

11. The role that the duchesse de Nemours and other Guise women played in the League is the subject of a brief article by Eliane Viennot entitled "Des 'femmes d'État' au XVIe siècle: Les princesses de la Ligue et l'écriture de l'histoire," in *Femmes et pouvoirs sous l'ancien régime,* ed. Danielle Hasse-Dubosc and Eliane Viennot (Paris: Rivages, 1991), pp. 77–97. The subject deserves a more detailed and analytical treatment.

12. See, for example, l'Estoile, *Journal pour le règne de Henri IV,* 1:139 (November 20, 1591), p. 140 (November 21 and 22, 1591), p. 142 (November 25, 1591), p. 193 (November 3, 1592), p. 260 (May 31, 1593), p. 316 (September 3, 1593), and p. 338 (December 28, 1593); see also Corneio, *Bret discours,* pp. 242, 259.

13. See, for example, l'Estoile, *Mémoires-Journaux,* 3:53–54 (July 9, 1587), p. 66 (September 1587), p. 242 (January 26, 1589), and p. 276 (late April 1589); l'Estoile, *Journal pour le règne de Henri IV,* 1:52–53 (June 1590).

14. L'Estoile, *Mémoires-Journaux,* 3:302 (July 27, 1589).

15. Ibid.

16. L'Estoile, *Journal pour le règne de Henri IV,* 1:19 (August 2, 1589).

17. Ibid.

18. Ibid., 1:72 (describing a painting on a wall in the faubourg Saint Germain); l'Estoile, *Mémoires-Journaux,* 3:164 (citing the pamphlet "Le Miserere mei Deus"); see also ibid., 3:97 (citing the "Manifeste des dames de la court").

19. L'Estoile, *Mémoires-Journaux,* 3:248 (February 1589).

20. Ibid., 3:259 (March 18, 1589). A very similar account of Sainte-Beuve's behavior appears in the *politique* pamphlet entitled *Conseil salutaire d'un bon François aux Parisiens: Contenant les impostures & monopoles des faux predicateurs, avec un discours veritable des actes plus memorables de la Ligue depuis la journee des Barricades* (n.p., 1590), pp. 97–98.

21. L'Estoile, *Mémoires-Journaux,* 3:291–93 (citing "Lettre du Président Dassi à Monsr. le Duc de Maienne" dated May 18, 1589). Madeleine Luillier, the widow of Claude Le Roux, sieur de Sainte-Beuve, was the youngest daughter of Jean Luillier de Boulancourt and his second wife, Renée Nicolay. Antoine Hennequin d'Assy was Renée Nicolay's eldest son by her first husband, Dreux Hennequin. This letter was not mentioned by Sainte-Beuve's biographer, H. de Leymont, in *Madame de Sainte-Beuve et les Ursulines de Paris (1562–1630): Étude sur l'éducation des femmes en France au XVIIe siècle,* 2d ed. (Lyons: Librairie et Imprimerie Vitte et Perrussel, n.d.).

22. ACP, Procès apostolique, Jeanne de Jésus (Séguier), fol. 822r. According to the testimony of Nicolas Pinette de Charmoy (fol. 486r), who knew the Acaries at least from 1593, Pierre Acarie lost more than thirty thousand écus on account of the League.

23. André Du Val, *La vie admirable de la bienheureuse soeur Marie de l'Incarnation* (Paris, 1893), reproducing with a new introduction the edition of Paris, 1621), p. 85, on her acquaintance with Dom Beaucousin, the vicar of the Chartreux. The fact that Pierre Acarie spent his exile after the League with the Chartreux of Bourg-fontaine suggests that the connection with the Chartreux began during this period. See also Bibliothèque Nationale [hereafter BN], Manuscrits français [hereafter MS fr.] 3996: "Deliberations, arrests, actes & memoires tirez des registres du Parlement, de ce qui se passa à Paris durant la Ligue," vol. 1: 1588–1594, fols. 195–202.

24. According to Marguerite de Gondi, marquise de Maignelay, Pierre Acarie, "having recognized [his wife's] abilities depended [on] her for the management of all his affairs and did not meddle at all in them" (ACP, Procès apostolique, fol. 403). See also the testimony of Michel de Marillac about how she handled accounts of kinfolk for whom Pierre Acarie was named guardian (ACP, Procès apostolique, fols. 803v–804r). Obviously, beatification proceedings must be used with caution, since testimony for them was gathered with the explicit purpose of demonstrating the subject's sanctity. As with other forms of legal records, the historian using these

records must consider such questions as internal consistency, plausibility, and correspondence with other testimony in judging the credibility of different witnesses and the events they narrate. Often the best evidence comes from the descriptions of everyday events or mundane occurrences, for which exaggeration or outright invention served no purpose.

25. ACP, Procès apostolique, Marguerite de Gondi, marquise de Maignelay, fol. 619v. See also Du Val, *Marie de l'Incarnation,* p. 24; and, more generally on League processions, Richet, "Les processions à Paris."

26. ACP, Procès apostolique, testimony of Agnès de Jésus (de Lyon), fol. 9r; and Françoise de Jésus (de Fleury), fol. 339v.

27. Ibid., Marie de Jésus (de Breauté), fols. 619v–620r.

28. Du Val, *Marie de l'Incarnation,* p. 68. See also ACP, Procès apostolique, testimony of Marie de St. Joseph (Nicole Fournier), fol. 112v; Michel de Marillac, fol. 781; Marguerite de Gondi, fol. 396v; Marie de Jésus (Séguier), fol. 553; and Marie de Jésus (Acarie), fol. 516r.

29. Ibid. See especially testimony of Marie de Jésus (Séguier), fol. 553.

30. Archives de l'Assistance publique, Fonds de l'Hôtel Dieu, liasse 1438, "Registre pour les années 1574–1578," fols. 611–12.

31. François Estienne, *Oraison funebre, faicte sur le trespas de noble & vertueuse Damoiselle Marie Dudrac* (Paris, 1590), fol. 37v.

32. ACP, Procès apostolique, Marie de Jésus (Acarie), fol. 516r.

33. BN, MS fr. 3996: "Deliberations . . . des registres du Parlement," fol. 143.

34. I am following here the chronology set out by Acarie's most recent biographer, Bruno de Jésus-Marie, O.C.D., *La belle Acarie: Bienheureuse Marie de l'Incarnation* (Paris: Desclée de Brouwer, 1942), pp. 48 n, 125–27.

35. Marie de la Trinité [Sévin du Coudray], *Une glorieuse fille de Sainte Thérèse d'Avila: "Mère Sainte," fondatrice du Carmel d'Auch, 1570–1656: Vie et écrits,* ed. M. d'Aignan du Sendat (Paris: P. Lethielleux, 1930), p. 31. The autobiographical writings themselves have disappeared, but the biography based on them by M. d'Aignan du Sendat, vicar general of Auch, is simply a recopying and assemblage of first-person statements. Abandoned in 1669 (thirteen years after the death of Marie de la Trinité), probably because the compiler had gone blind, the biography was not published until 1930. I am grateful to Cynthia Cupples for first calling it to my attention.

36. Ibid., p. 32.

37. Ibid.

38. Ibid., p. 35.

39. Ibid., pp. 32–35.

40. Ibid., p. 36.

41. Scholars cannot always be sure of a woman's own political opinions, and I am including as opponents of the League women who were considered to be *politiques* because their husbands had joined the royalist camp, even if their own anti-League sentiments were not documented.

42. Documents illustrating all of these practices can be found in Archives Nationales [hereafter AN], H² 1882² and 1882³, cartons containing miscellaneous papers regarding the administration of Paris between 1591 and 1593. See also Z¹ʰ 91: Sentences du Bureau de la Ville de Paris for January–June 1591.

43. Département de la Somme, Ville d'Amiens, *Inventaire sommaire des archives communales antérieures à 1790,* vol. 3: *Série BB (39 à 323),* ed. George Durand (Amiens, 1897), pp. 148–49: proceedings of the Bureau de la Ville for December 26 and 27, 1588.

44. Ibid., p. 161: letters of March 4 and 6, 1589.

45. See, for example, ibid., p. 164: discussion of April 27, 1589, concerning the fear that the women will escape.

46. Ibid., p. 157: deliberations of January 30, 1589. See also the *Discours veritable sur l'inique emprisonnement & detention de mes-Dames les Duchesses & Damoiselles de Longue-ville, & de Monseigneur le Comte de sainct Pol par ceux de l'Union* (n.p., 1590), pp. 151–53. The presumed author of this tract is Louis de Gonzague, duc de Nevers, the father of the young duchesse de Longueville.

47. *Discours veritable,* pp. 141–53. See also Amiens, *Inventaire sommaire,* 3:184–85: meetings of September 30, and October 1 and 6, 1589.

48. See, for example, Amiens, *Inventaire sommaire,* 3:166–67, 171–71: meetings of May 6, 10, and 17; pp. 181–83: meetings of July 29 and September 1, 4, and 23, 1589.

49. Ibid., pp. 196–97, 203: proceedings of February 26 and June 18, 1590.

50. Ibid., p. 216: letter of August 31 and proceedings of September 3, 1591.

51. Ibid., pp. 217–18: September 5, 10, 12, 16, and 17, 1591.

52. Ibid., pp. 219–20: November 11 and 22, 1591.

53. Ibid., p. 222: January 21, 1592.

54. Ibid.

55. Ibid., p. 172: meetings of June 19 and 21, 1589.

56. Ibid., p. 177: discussions of July 13, 1589.

57. Ibid., p. 194: letter of January 18, 1590.

58. Ibid., p. 201: proceedings of May 17, 18, and 22, 1590.

59. Ibid., pp. 208–9: October 29 and November 21, 1590.

60. Jean Séguier, the most outspokenly royalist among the men in the family, was replaced as *lieutenant civil* in February 1589. His brothers Antoine, *avocat général* in the Parlement of Paris, and Pierre, a president of parlement, followed him into exile. See Denis Richet, "Une famille de robe: Les Séguier avant le chancelier," in his *De la Réforme à la Révolution,* pp. 238–48. The month of Jean Séguier's replacement is supplied by Descimon, *Qui étaient les Seize?,* p. 127.

61. AN, Z¹ʰ 86: Registre des sentences du Bureau de la Ville (April 14, 1589).

62. AN, H² 1882²: September 17, 1591: order from the *prévôt des marchands.*

63. L'Estoile, *Journal pour le règne de Henri IV,* p. 220.

64. Ibid., p. 279.

65. Ibid., pp. 321, 360.

66. AN, Y156, fol. 26: Donation by Marie Tudert (Marie de Jésus-Christ) to the Carmelite monastery of the Incarnation (December 27, 1614).

67. *Chroniques des Carmélites,* 1:536–37.

68. Ibid., p. 537.

69. Du Val, *Marie de l'Incarnation,* pp. 80–83.

70. Marie de la Trinité, *Mère Sainte,* p. 51. This image of the body as food recalls the practices of medieval female saints discussed in Caroline Walker Bynum, *Holy Feast and Holy Fast: The Religious Significance of Food to Medieval Women* (Berkeley: University of California Press, 1987).

71. Marc de Bauduen, *La vie admirable de tres-haute, tres-puissante, tres-illustre et tres-vertueuse Dame Charlote Marguerite de Gondy, Marquise de Magnelais* (Paris, 1666), especially pp. 124–40.

Denis Crouzet *(Translated by Michael Wolfe)*

A Woman and the Devil: Possession and Exorcism in Sixteenth-Century France

The explosion of Catholic violence in the early 1560s and the accompanying defeat of the Huguenot insurrection in the first civil war decisively blunted the initial appeal of French Calvinism, which until then had spread quite rapidly. Even so, beneath the political struggle lay other indicators of the mounting Catholic counteroffensive against heresy. Among these was the "triumphant victory by God's body over the evil spirit Beelzebub" achieved in Laon in 1566, an incident of capital importance both for its propaganda value and for the crises of mimetic possession it inspired.[1]

In regions like Laon, where eschatological fervor ran high, resistance to the Evangelical religion during the peace that followed the Edict of Amboise took the form of a ritualized combat between the Holy Spirit and Satan. This held true both in Nicole de Vervins's demonic possession and in the ensuing exorcism that authorities performed to demonstrate the diabolical nature of Calvinism. The elaborately staged struggle launched against the Devil by the mystical body of Christ—or *Corpus mysticum*—left deep impressions on the 150,000 or so people who witnessed the proceedings, according to Jean Boulaese (see Appendix). One of these was Florimond de Raemond, who saw in the possessed woman's fits reason enough to abjure Protestantism, writing later that "since my sheer existence, now miraculously saved, stands in our century as proof enough against the heretics' blindness, I will relate what I know about the miracle I saw which pulled me from the jaws of heresy. . . . She was so tormented that one could hear her bones crack, her teeth gnash as she lost all semblance of human form during her bizarre writhings."[2]

In examining these events, I will try to explain not simply what happened to Nicole de Vervins, but also the impact her case had on people who were anxiously awaiting a sign from God that might signal a return to religious unity. But first a word about the woman whose body served as a battleground in this eschatological struggle between the Devil and Christ. Nicole Obry was born on Maundy Thursday in 1549, the daughter of a penurious butcher. Her strange visions began shortly after All Saints' Day 1565, some three months after her marriage to a tailor named Loys Pierret.[3] This liturgical context informed the young woman's experience from the outset. Significantly, November 3, a day dedicated to Saint Hubert, marks a time of the year when hopeful souls await deliverance from purgatory by God. Believers can assist worthy souls by praying for them to be released from this restless condition. As she recited the *De profundis* on the tomb of her grandfather, Joachim Willot, Nicole Obry saw a ghost covered with a white cloth who seemed to resemble her dearly departed grandfather. The apparition apparently spoke to her and followed her a short while before entering her—an act that rendered her so violently ill that it was necessary to give her last rites.[4]

Whenever the ghost reappeared, a feeling of suffocation overcame Nicole; it was as if a huge stone choked her to the point where she could neither stir nor speak, "overwhelming her with a sense of heaviness, burdening her every part." After going to confession on Wednesday, November 7, Nicole Obry again saw her grandfather's ghost, only this time his face was uncovered; she immediately fell into a stupor during which the specter, surrounded by horrible sights, called to her. He urgently demanded that the living intervene to free him from purgatory, where he was wracked by "great misery and confusion" because he had died suddenly, without giving auricular confession. Speaking through Nicole, he stated that masses, prayers, and pilgrimages, as well as alms and memorial candles, if duly performed, would enable his soul to achieve eternal peace—a release that would be signaled during mass on November 19 in the form of a dove. Two days later, the men in her family made a pilgrimage to Notre-Dame de Liesse, Sainte-Restitute, and Saint-Guillian, followed telepathically by the possessed woman, who at several points described their journey to the sanctuaries as seen in her visions.

When the pilgrims returned on Monday, November 19, to attend the holy service planned for the dead grandfather, an irrepressible force suddenly seized Nicole Obry, threw her to the ground, knocked her head against the wall, and then dragged her underneath her father's bed, where the maid found her "as stiff as a board." The ghost then demanded that the pilgrims set out again, this time for Saint James of Compostella, one of the shrines he had named on November 7, but which Nicole had omitted to repeat. When the family tried to trick the ghost by having three travelers pretend to take the road to Galicia, the dead grandfather threatened to twist Nicole's arms and legs in reprisal.

Nicole's possession entered a new stage when the priest of Vervins decided to perform an exorcism. Using Nicole as a medium, the ghost explained that he had failed to fulfill his own vow to go to Saint James of Compostella if God healed his ill wife. During the days that followed, Nicole's body resisted every attempt by the priest to cast out the malign spirit; indeed, those efforts only seemed to make matters worse, since they "often left her as hard as a stone, so much so that her limbs could not be bent, nor could she regain her ability to hear and speak. Instead, all she did was bang her head against the wall and table, and occasionally try to fling herself into the fire."[5] The possessed woman simply stared wide-eyed at the bystanders who witnessed these strange events. When her grandfather spoke through her, her lips opened no wider than "a small nut," though a swelling in her throat was evident. Moreover, as a physical mark of the indwelling spirit, her body became so heavy that it took several men to carry her.

On Monday, November 26, answering a request that Robert de Coucy, co-seigneur of Vervins, archdeacon of Laon, and abbot of Foigny, had sent earlier to the cathedral dean of Laon, there arrived in town a Jacobin friar named Pierre de la Motte, who the next day immediately set about performing incantations in the Obry household.[6] In the liturgical calendar, November 26 is the day when the church honors the memory of the martyred bishop Saint Peter, who condemned the fourth-century Arian heresy and to whom Christ appeared one night carrying a torn robe which symbolized the divisions brought to the church by heretics. This timing made the next day's first avowal all the more significant. Before the possessed woman fell unconscious to the ground, the Jacobin friar forced the spirit to say that he was a demon, not the deceased grandfather's guardian angel as he had earlier pretended; the spirit's unwillingness to say anything more merely validated this avowal. Yet the end of this deception only made the possessed woman's condition even more piteous, especially on the last day of the month—a day dedicated to the apostle Saint Andrew. The demon then appeared to her in the guise of a hideous black man with huge long teeth and withered hands, who sometimes shut her up in the stable or carried her up through the chimney to the top floor of the house.

With its malefic nature now revealed, the possession now became largely shaped by the powerful liturgical observances mobilized against the demon.

Once clerical intervention on behalf of the victim began, the demon's behavior became worse and worse: on December 2, the first Sunday of Advent, while "the priest in his sermon prayed for her," Nicole Obry was tormented so furiously that her husband had to call to passers-by for help.[7] From December 3, every day after mass, for eight to ten straight hours, the exorcisms in the baptismal canon were performed as a means to reinforce the effects of the holy Host taken by Nicole at communion in the morning. Identifying himself as Beelzebub, the demon then set about disfiguring the young woman's body in an attempt to nullify the power of the risen Christ and the hope for salvation he represented to the children of Zion.

In the church calendar Advent inaugurates a time of hopeful anticipation of the *adventus*, a waiting period during which believers prepare to welcome their Savior. This holy celebration recalls those among God's chosen who lived during the days of the first covenant. It was therefore not happenstance that the demon was particularly busy on the first Sunday after Advent. On that day, the priest reads from Scripture the passage that most evokes the messianic arrival of Christ as well as his eventual return: "Scientes que hora est jam nos de somno surgere . . . nunc enim propior est nostra salus. Dies autem appropinquavit."[8] Nicole's possession therefore held significance for believers as they prepared for the Last Judgment, when the just would be rewarded with paradise while demons would drag evildoers down to the burning fires of Hell. Indeed, Nicole Obry often declared the Last Judgment to be at hand as she described the impending struggle between Saint Gabriel, who, "trumpeting from the four corners of the earth," would deliver the world from evil and Satan. Her dreadful experience at the hands of the demon, whose master was the strutting image of Hell itself, only underscored the role of human sinfulness at a time when everyone was urged to begin atonement.

After the feast day of Saint Nicholas on Thursday, December 6, and Our Lady's Conception on Friday, December 7, a large crowd gathered in the church of Vervins. Inside, from a specially erected platform on which Nicole Obry had been placed, the demon challenged the Huguenot ministers, whom he called his minions. The exorcism ceremony thus involved the faithful in an eschatological appeal, as they were asked to help to deliver the demoniac woman by singing the *Veni Creator spiritus* to the Holy Spirit. The view of the possessed woman thus inspired a sort of collective expiation during which each believer examined his conscience and prayed for the speedy coming of the Lord. The exorcists molded their dealings with Nicole Obry according to the liturgical vigil performed during Advent, when the congregation ritually invokes the Word whilst awaiting the Incarnation. They also held a crucifix before the possessed woman and traced the sign of the cross on her body with sprinkled holy water.

December 9 was the second Sunday after Advent, a day on which each believer must strive to serve God with a clear conscience to prepare the way for the Lord's return. On this day, the possessed woman transcended herself. The fuming demon bellowed and roared like a wild beast whenever a paper containing his name was burned or incantations were performed commanding him to quit the poor woman's body in the name of the Trinity. Satan's grip over her tightened at precisely the moment she hoped to achieve purification, thus showing even more strongly than before an image of the world lost to God. Whenever the consecrated Host was elevated, Nicole's stomach and throat swelled and her hideous face grimaced "with frighteningly horrible cries thundered so loudly by the devil that they could be heard far away."[9] After fainting, the possessed woman would slowly regain consciousness, confess to the priest, then recount terrifying visions of black-robed men who tried to stab her with swords, or of black catlike creatures as large as sheep that attempted to bite, scratch, and strangle her. She even said that sulphur-smelling fires shot into her eyes and mouth, nearly suffocating her.[10] She became the actual site of an eschatological battle of the End Times.

It was at this point that the Huguenots were openly implicated by Nicole Obry, who called them out by name, only to hear the devil boast that he had already won them over. When a Calvinist minister came on the scene, the devil personally recognized him as one of his minions, asking facetiously whether "one demon could chase away another. . . . He mooed like a cow whenever the minister read Marot's Psalms, asking him 'Do you think you can scare me away with these pleasant songs that I helped to compose? I will do nothing of the sort for you, because I am your master.' "[11]

Henceforth, Nicole Obry became more than just a possessed woman. In her words and disfigurements could be read the tragedy of religious division brought about by Satan's seduction of so many souls. She exemplified the Devil's power over those who had banished themselves from the mystical body of the church. She reflected the imperfection of those who had exchanged God for the Lord of Darkness and his hosts of demons. This perhaps explains why her tortured experience began two days after All Saints' Day, which ushers in the eschatological vigil for God's Kingdom, and culminated later on the first Sunday after Advent, when, between the Epistle and Gospel readings at the mass announcing Christ's Second Coming, the *Dies irae* was sung.

By way of elaboration, the demon now vouchsafed how all of Nicole's troubles had actually begun four years earlier, on July 26, 1561, a day dedicated to Saint Anne as well as a principal feast day for Vervins. It was a time when the kingdom of France nearly fell prey to the seductive ideas of the so-called Reformed religion—a coincidence that rendered Nicole's possession a symbolic event in recent history. Further investigation suggested that she had become possessed as a result of a blasphemy uttered years before by her mother. It had occurred after Nicole and her younger sister, Isabelle, had gone to a dance, Isabelle wearing an amber rosary given to her by her mother. Apparently, a woman there stole the rosary, which so angered Nicole's mother that she invited the devil to take one of her daughters.[12] "Not long afterward, great devil that I am, I came to take what the mother had promised me," Beelzebub later explained. The subsequent possession in Vervins thus becomes a case typical of cultures open to belief in fantastical punishment. The *Exempla* of Caesarius of Heisterbach, for instance, defines the appearance of the Devil as a punishment for human vice; and the phrase uttered by Nicole Obry's mother nearly repeated verbatim the angry words husbands often spit at their wives when they told them "to go to the Devil," whereupon the Devil would enter the woman's body through her ear.[13]

The long latency period between the onset of the possession and its actual manifestation provided time for sin to take hold in the young woman. During one of the exchanges with the exorcists, for example, the Devil admitted having encouraged his victim to steal money from her grandfather, while on other occasions he pushed her to take table linen, a candlestick, money from her parents' purse, and food. Beelzebub used illness to prevent Nicole from observing Lent, thus maintaining her sinful nature. Her recent marriage had also furthered the Devil's project by letting her taste carnal pleasure.

The symbolic significance of Nicole's possession was more than a personal matter, for just as she fell under Satan's spell, so too did a growing number of believers refuse God by embracing the diabolical heresy of Calvinism. Saint Anne's Day 1561 came right after the promulgation of the Edict of July, which, although it forbade all Calvinist meetings, also prohibited any violence against the Huguenots—a measure that implied tacit recognition. In other quarters, as in Artus Désiré's pamphlets and the sermons of François Le Picart, the Huguenots were denounced as blasphemers because they distorted the Holy Word as traditionally taught by the church, twisting it to justify the carnal passions they indulged after their services. From this perspective, Nicole de Vervins's experience served as an allegory about a people seduced by evil and thus deaf to God's wishes. The woman's body thus represented the body of the faithful encompassing all Christians. Her possession not only punished her for her sins, but also the faults of human society stemming from the Fall of Man, to the point where, according to the system of resemblances seen by Jean Boulaese, Nicole foreshadowed the End Times during which humankind would suffer "God's terrible swift sword of justice."[14] She thus stood as a reminder of the impending Last Judgment.

From December 15 to 20, the demonic power gripping Nicole continued to fulfill these symbolic perceptions, contrasting the Devil's works with those of Christ. Whereas Jesus restored sight to the blind, made cripples walk, healed lepers, gave speech to the mute, and raised the dead, the Devil drained away the young woman's life, rendering her insensate and immobile. Death seemed to triumph precisely when God's people should commemorate the coming of his only Son, sent to redeem their sins. Whenever the priest held the Holy Sacrament before Nicole, a moment of great ritual intensity during the Mass, she would suddenly lose all bodily control and fall down senseless. This state rendered her unable to receive the divine solace that the priest offered. "Her bones cracked as if broken by a staff . . . while frogs seemingly croaked in her stomach."[15] Openly contesting Christ's power, the Devil threw Nicole into a state of unconsciousness which symbolized the mortal consequences of Original Sin before the Redeemer's sacrifice on Calvary.

A crucial transition in this struggle against evil began on December 20, when the exorcist touched the woman with a crucifix, then placed on her lips the holy Host, which alone could release her from Beelzebub's grasp. Later, on Christmas Day, all the people of Vervins gathered together to take communion to honor the Savior's birth. Yet a perceptible growth in the demon's power had also occurred, given the excruciating pains that wracked Nicole. These tortures, Beelzebub explained to the churchmen and to their God, stemmed from the fact that "however much you strengthen yourselves against me, so I redouble my efforts against you." Nevertheless, the demon's presence briefly retreated once the priest touched her face with a crucifix, after which Nicole, though greatly weakened, seemed to revive. These spells of lucidity did not last long, however, as she soon after became lethargic and subject to terrible tortures. Indeed, on the very day when the Light of Heaven was supposed to dispel the night, promising a new life and covenant, demonic reinforcements arrived, twenty-nine in all, three of whom—Cerberus, Astaroth, and Legion—commanded the dreaded legions of darkness.[16]

The ritual encounter between God and Satan continued to adhere closely to the script provided by the liturgical calendar. A week later, for example, on the morning of Tuesday, January 1, the day when Christ's redemptive mission commenced with his circumcision—itself a symbol of the deliverance promised by baptism—La Motte, "inspired by the Almighty," placed the Blessed Sacrament on the poor woman's lips. A miracle occurred, for at that instant Nicole Obry came to her senses and opened her mouth to take in the bread of life. In the eyes of Catholics, the possession thus signified in miniature the history of the church, of a people gripped by sin and death whose only hope lay in the Messiah. To display this message of salvation and truth, Nicole Obry was permanently moved into the church of Vervins itself.

Significantly, on the next day, Epiphany, the feast of Christ the King-Messiah, a time when all believers hope one day to find their names in the Book of Life, the bishop of Laon, Jean de Bours, arrived in Vervins, and he proceeded the next day to assist in the exorcism.[17] The effects of the miracle induced by the Blessed Sacrament two days before continued; now, the demon could paralyze only Nicole's right leg and left arm. By January 19, however, Satan had forcefully returned, refusing to leave her unless she (and he) were brought to Notre-Dame de Liesse.[18] Two months had elapsed so far since the onset of this drama.

On Tuesday, January 22, the day dedicated to Saint Vincent, the deacon whose faith, despite many tortures, remained unbroken, Nicole Obry went to Liesse, helped by a young boy dressed in white. The next day found her in the sanctuary devoted to Our Lady, where after mass and a sermon by the Jacobin friar, she was placed before the holy image of the Mother of God. Carrying a crucifix and a holy wafer, La Motte summoned forth the demons, ordering them to quit the body "of this poor unfortunate."[19] No sooner were

these words uttered than the possessed woman leaped out before the congregation, turning her grossly disfigured and swollen face from side to side,
her reddened throat bulging. As the Blessed Sacrament approached her, "the
afflicted woman curled up so that her toes touched her head, her stomach
strangely distended as if pregnant, her face contorted in all sorts of bizarre
shapes."[20]

When the exorcist came to give her communion, she fell to the ground in
a senseless stupor. Yet no sooner did she receive the Host than she suddenly
regained consciousness.[21] An uproar thereupon ensued while loosened slate
fell from the church roof. Some twenty-six demons fled Nicole's body, vanquished by Christ's presence in the wafer. But the battle was not over. The
Prince of Darkness tightened his grip over the woman, who came to resemble a martyr. Her torments returned toward vespers as strongly as ever, as La
Motte renewed his efforts. Beelzebub swore that it would take the bishop of
Laon himself to evict him from the woman.

The next day, Thursday, January 24, in Pierrepont, the exorcism rites
resumed in the village church, this time with the abbot of Saint-Vincent de
Laon, Canon Boilleau, presiding.[22] When confronted with the Blessed Sacrament, the demon Legion—whom Jesus had once chased out of a possessed
man—finally deserted Nicole.[23] Beelzebub, however, reiterated his promise
not to leave Nicole unless confronted in person by Jean de Bours, bishop of
Laon.[24] That evening, therefore, the exorcists decided that they had no
choice but to take Nicole to Laon.

The possession thus became a matter to be dealt with by the upper
echelons of the church hierarchy. On January 25, the day of the conversion of
Saint Paul, evil persecutor of the faithful until his sudden, blinding encounter with Christ on the road to Damascus, a fifteen-day struggle against Satan
began. After she arrived in Laon, the ecclesiastical authorities had Nicole
Obry taken into the cathedral and placed before the main altar, where a
sermon and mass for the Holy Spirit then took place before the exorcism
rites began. The bishop summoned forth the demon after Nicole had flown
into a rage during the Elevation of the Host, and then fell motionless to the
ground. Yet when the bishop placed the Blessed Sacrament to her lips, she
again revived and made the sign of the cross, despite paralysis in her left
arm. To enhance this wondrous sight, a platform was erected inside the
church, upon which the consecrated Host's triumph over the Devil could be
watched by the growing crowd of onlookers.

The Huguenots, who considered Nicole's illness a natural one and a proof of papist superstition, convinced the bishop to allow her to be interrogated and to undergo a medical examination to ascertain whether she faked her symptoms. After pins had been stuck under the fingernails of her lifeless left arm, Nicole became frenzied, then unconscious, with barely a pulse.[25] Nothing the doctors did, be they Catholic or Huguenot, could elicit a response from her. Their powerlessness wondrously reflected in the people's imagination the woeful inadequacy of human means to treat the evil gripping the young woman. Her deathlike condition was divinely ordained and symbolized human sinfulness, which could be treated only by the Blessed Sacrament. Further proof that she was possessed occurred when Canon Marin Pelletier, witnessed by several Huguenots, recited the *Confiteor* and *Ave Salus,* prostrated himself, and put the Eucharist to her lips.[26] In response, she lifted her head, opened her eyes, and made the sign of the cross. "*Videte, Videte miraculum,*" he declared to those who beheld this miracle. Despite this prodigy, the Huguenots pressed the marshal of Montmorency to intercede. On Sunday, January 27, as if in response to these demands, Astaroth flew out of the possessed woman, breaking a church window in the process.

As related by Jean Boulaese, events thereafter tended to confirm that a miracle had indeed occurred. On January 28, a large crowd saw Nicole lash out at Jean Carlier, a Huguenot doctor, using her once paralyzed left arm, which became suddenly overpowering. Then "she walked on the bed with her feet, her head twisted around backwards, her stomach bloated, her arms waving wildly in the air."[27] Carlier tried to force medicine down her open mouth, only to see a black beast creep out of it, a sort of large fly which "people declared to be Beelzebub himself." A priest then gave Nicole the Blessed Sacrament, after which—as before—she slowly regained her senses and thanked God by making the sign of the cross. Two Huguenots who witnessed this event are said to have cried out, "I now believe it, because I have seen it. Never again will I be a Huguenot." After this verification of demonic possession, another large platform for liturgical observances was built in the cathedral choir and placed under the protection of the Virgin Mary.

Day after day, from dawn until dusk into early February, exorcism followed exorcism, each ceremonially linked to a series of solemn processions. Every morning before Nicole Obry arose from bed, the bishop and priests confessed and prayed together until the young woman awoke and prepared to confess herself and recite the book of hours. "Yet no sooner did she step out of bed than the devil seized her, making her jump into the air, kicking off her stockings and shoes, her dripping tongue all twisted."[28] She became so heavy that it took eight to ten young men to carry her through town, behind the procession of clergy, into the cathedral, which overflowed with the faithful and curious onlookers. Inside the cathedral, the procession made three circuits. During the first, the demon mocked the crowd, whistling and singing "salacious ditties," even throwing the boys' choir off-key. On the second round, he gnashed his teeth, cried out, and spit in the faces of the men carrying Nicole, trying at times to bite and scratch them. During the final circuit, the demoniac woman became so violent that several members of the audience had to assist the porters. After the sermon by the Cordelier friar, Favier, she was placed on the platform, which was topped by a dais.

While the bishop said mass and consecrated the host, Nicole "constantly writhed and shook, turning her head this way and that, her mouth so agape that her tongue spilled out over her chin."[29] Sometimes she addressed individuals in the audience, mentioning to them their particular misdeeds; sometimes she made lewd gestures; but more often she simply mocked the Catholics with derisory words customarily used by Calvinists when attacking members of the traditional church, screaming "Fie, you filthy papist toads, you who eat that pasty repast."[30] During the Gospel reading, she lowered her head, her eyes closed and her teeth gnashing. When the bishop made the sign of the cross on her forehead, she recoiled and spat as the holy water touched her face, crying out, "This water is dirty," much as a Protestant would.

The drama heightened when the bishop actually began to call forth the demon. Beelzebub averred how, with the help of other demons, he had taken possession of the young woman to fulfill a divine plan to punish people for their sins, especially "to show that I am Satan, something my Huguenots don't believe, and to make the same religion."[31] The bishop's ritual interrogation thus elicited from Satan a spectacular sort of public confession which shed light on recent events. On the one hand, the incarnation of the Devil now stood revealed as a sign of divine punishment sent to fight the evil which, according to prophesy in the Apocalypse, had seduced people in all nations; on the other hand, Nicole's possession represented a call by God for repentance and a restoration of religious unity. These revelations became even more detailed during the ensuing exorcism. The Devil stated, for example, that French Huguenots were his servants; actually, in the very town of Laon, quite recently, he had encouraged local Huguenots to boil a consecrated wafer, then feed it to dogs.[32] Despite prayers, however, the rites of exorcism seemed only to incite more violent expressions of evil in Nicole; indeed, the devil within her screamed so loudly that it seemed as if several voices came out of her throat at once.

Crucifix in hand, the bishop again offered the Blessed Sacrament to Nicole and cursed the demon: "Oh evil Beelzebub, mortal enemy of GOD, behold the precious body of our Savior and Lord JESUS-CHRIST." Still the demon refused to leave the poor woman, who stuck out a long red-and-black tongue while rolling her wide eyes "like an enraged bull." This physical resistance to the body of Christ rendered her human frame—especially her swollen, ugly face—a reflection of the monstrosity within her. At times, she "crumpled into a pile with her head bent over to her feet, so tightly it was impossible to pry her apart; yet all of a sudden she might break free of those holding her down, jumping up in the air more than six feet."[33]

The demoniac thus embodied the infernal beast within her; the demon's sheer exuberance lent credence to the belief in the cross—the same cross that Huguenots had helped to desecrate and tear down throughout the kingdom in recent years. Her unhuman nature came forth in various animal forms and strange colors as her moods swung wildly:

Bones cracked as she grew in size, which caused various parts of her body—her stomach, throat, head, and eyes—to become horribly misshaped. Hideous wrinkles covered her face, which took on the mottled look of an Indian rooster's crest, spotted with red, black, blue, gray, green, and yellow, not unlike the skin of a toad, lizard, or snake. Like a reptile's, her huge red tongue darted in and out of her mouth, which was a black spot no wider than a *liard,* occasionally changing color as it slipped over her chin or up to her ears, where it then wrapped around her head. Her voice sounded like the deep bellowing of an enraged bull, her mouth expanding beyond all measure . . . her eyes suddenly set back so far they became very small, only then to bug out from her head like the eyes of a large bull . . . bloodshot, they burned and sparkled like a lighted candle or the eyes of a cat in the dark . . . as they rolled and turned in her head. With such horrible, ugly grimaces, she argued in tormented gruntings to the wonderment of all present.[34]

The image of the inferno thus became manifest to everyone who witnessed these events. Her awful screams and deformity, as well as her noxious odor, transformed the body of Nicole Obry into an antechamber of Hell itself, a place where the Devil would torment the body and soul of every sinner who fell into his power. Suddenly, the Devil appeared to try a different gambit against the mystical body of Christ. After the bishop held the Blessed Sacrament before Nicole, she curled up and fell to the floor, blind, mute, and deaf. A man carried her to the assembled throng, some of whom touched her to see if she was as stiff as she looked. The bishop then commanded everyone present to kneel in prayer before the main altar, and together to implore God's forgiveness.

While the faithful prayed intensely, the bishop again placed the Host to Nicole's lips. She quickly regained consciousness, now radiating a graceful beauty. She appeared healthy both in body and mind, as she gave thanks to "God, my Father and Creator."[35] It seemed that, this time, the exorcism had worked. She thereafter left the church and walked through the streets amidst a rapt crowd and the joyous peals of the town bells.

These exorcism ceremonies require closer scrutiny in terms of what they represented. They not only involved the clergy of Laon and the demoniac woman; actually and in its imagination, the entire town was collectively involved each day in seeking God's intervention. The exorcism thus announced and achieved a wider reconciliation between God and his errant people, who could still find salvation despite the ruses and fallacies of the heretics. According to Jean Boulaese, after Nicole Obry arose each morning, all the believers in the town supposedly sang the *Veni Creator spiritus* and the *Ave maris stella* accompanied by "collection and the aspersion of holy water." Then came the procession, which in effect made the faithful the actors of God's miracle, since it underscored the need for them to express their desire for atonement and repentance.

This collective involvement could be seen during mass, when every Catholic humbly prayed before the Blessed Sacrament and then, when bidden by the priest, sang the hymns and canticles celebrating the miraculous effects of the Eucharist. After mass, the crowd followed Nicole Obry outside the church, though the clergy remained behind to hear confession and conduct prayers to the sound of sacred music. God's people therefore fully participated in a ritual whose success hinged on God's love and human supplication. The ritual also seemed to proclaim that if humankind returned to God, peace and forgiveness would come to them, and the punishment resulting from the sectarian divisions would end.

As early as Sunday, January 27, the day commemorating Christ's healing of a leper and a lame man from Capernaum, a first victory was achieved when the demon Astaroth was put to flight. On Saturday morning, February 2, a day dedicated to the purification of Our Lady, who brought the light to all nations, Cerberus, the guardian demon of darkness, fled through a church window when confronted with the Blessed Sacrament. Only Beelzebub held out now against God, and so strongly that several persons suggested it might be necessary to take the poor woman to the archbishop of Rheims or maybe even to the pope.[36]

The crucial day was Friday, February 8, the day of the twenty-first exorcism ceremony. Witnessing the events of this day were the town's judicial officers, doctors, and other notables, as well as the faithful, who had tried to advance God's victory over Satan by fasting, confessing, and taking communion.[37] After the usual procession, prayers, sermon, and mass, the demoniac woman became still more agitated and swollen than usual, the devil inside her now more hideous than ever. She impugned the succor offered by the Gospels, prayers, and the elevation of the cross. Beelzebub amused himself by blowing out a blessed candle placed in front of the image of the crucified Christ, his songs, laughter, and whistles provocatively showing his lack of fear. Suddenly, Nicole Obry fainted, a puff of black smoke escaping from her mouth. Many thought this signaled the Devil's retreat before the Blessed Sacrament, which gave the poor woman solace when it touched her lips. Yet it was obvious that the demon hung on, since Nicole's left arm remained paralyzed, and the exorcism ceremony therefore resumed later that afternoon.

At last the exorcist seemed on the verge of overpowering the evil spirit holding the poor woman. Standing at the altar, the bishop of Laon offered up the Blessed Sacrament, summoning the demon to leave Nicole now in the name of the Savior's precious body. Beelzebub faltered before the full apostolic authority represented by the bishop; he even regretted that he had to quit the woman's body so soon.[38] The exorcist then brought closer the Blessed Sacrament, which as always caused tremors in Nicole's body as the infernal power within her quaked.

The bishop exhorted Beelzebub to flee the possessed woman and return to his tormented existence in deepest Hell. "At that moment, there came out of the woman's mouth a long black tongue, her rolling eyes all red and white, her long face as scarlet as blood."[39] For a second time the bishop elevated the Corpus Christi. Although fifteen men tried to hold her down,

Nicole Obry jumped more than six feet into the air, her body rippling under the struggle raging within her so that "she no longer resembled a human being, but rather the living form of the great Satan himself."[40]

The exorcism thus revealed the abiding power of God, triumphantly demonstrating that in the priest resided the same power by which Christ had exorcised the demoniac at Gerasa and healed the Canaanite.[41] Over and above the duel between a minister of God and the spirit of darkness was the wider struggle of the one true church—its doctrines as well as its ecclesiastical organization—against the doubts sown by the Huguenots. When the bishop lowered the Blessed Sacrament, the demoniac became somewhat less agitated as horrified spectators looked on, their fear increasing palpably when a loud noise suddenly erupted. At this dramatic moment, the bishop urged the audience to remain calm, and then proceeded to the third decisive admonition. "Stay calm, my friends," he said, "for here is the precious body of our lord JESUS CHRIST, come to help us. Kneel in prayer to GOD."[42] It was three o'clock in the afternoon when the congregation began to pray according to the bishop's instruction.

Nicole Obry now became abruptly freed from her agony when she lifted her left arm as smoke and fire shot forth toward onlookers. Even though it was a clear day, two claps of thunder were distinctly heard. A fog hung about the cathedral towers and provided cover for Beelzebub's escape. Nicole Obry knelt to pray to God, her tear-stained face turned toward the joyful crowd. The cantors intoned *Te deum laudamus,* bells rang, and a procession went out into the streets. Public rejoicing at her long-awaited deliverance was also a triumphant celebration of the Savior's real presence in the Eucharist, leading some to exclaim: "Oh my GOD, what a great miracle. Who could not believe now that the sacrament really contains our LORD JESUS CHRIST?" Cursing the day they had left the true faith, some Huguenots now recognized in these unnatural events the validity of the Mass.[43] The confrontation between the bishop and the Devil had thus been a dogmatic dispute from which God's ordained minister had emerged the winner.

It was too much to expect the woman's ordeal to be completely over, however. Another cycle began, lasting thirty-eight days, according to Jean Boulaese. Despite Beelzebub's disappearance, over the next week Nicole Obry fell sick every morning during the novena, while masses and processions took place. From Sunday, February 10, she had syncopes and could not be revived by natural means. "Nearly dead, she was carried to the church, where she eventually regained consciousness after procession, mass, and at the very moment of communion."[44] Her life seemed to depend on receiving the Blessed Sacrament daily.

After having upheld the doctrine of transubstantiation, the focus of the possession's story shifted to the duty of fasting. On Shrove Tuesday, February 26, when the bishop of Laon returned from a journey to Paris, he found that again, Nicole Obry could not move. About two o'clock, after drinking some milk with several female companions, she had fallen into "a trance which lasted until the next day, when she was brought to the church, where she regained her composure." Ash Wednesday, the day when remorseful believers, through fasting and abstinence, resolve to combat sin by practicing mortification and penance, ushered in a new theme. Nicole Obry's experience thus represented both a form of healing and a challenge to the heretics who refused to fast during Lent. On Saturday, March 2, after praying to God, the afflicted woman asked permission to hear for three straight days the masses celebrated by the bishop and to take communion from his hands. The next day, which was the first Sunday of Lent, found her as sick as ever. Four days later, on March 7, after attending mass, she began to recover, and she did not appear thin and weak, though she had not eaten much for days. Her mortification thus coincided with the time when Christ combatted sin and Satan's power over the sick, sinners, and demoniacs. By her example, she led the way to the paschal mystery wherein God sends his saving grace to the elect. No longer a victim of Satan, she had become one of God's protected, a living example of Lent's meaning as a time of healing and renewal.

Meanwhile, the Huguenots in Laon had persuaded the marshal of Montmorency's lieutenant, La Chapelle des Ursins, to send Nicole Obry back to Vervins. On Monday, March 18, began the third stage of her miraculous experience, the ecstasy. Her journey home further illustrated God's undeniable marvels, against which man is impotent. When her affliction returned, it clearly seemed a product of the Huguenots' drive to expel her from Laon. When she stopped at the abbey of Saulvoir, she collapsed into a fit that lasted until Tuesday morning, when she seemed close to death. Only during the mass did she come back to life, when her sight returned as the priest said the *Confiteor,* her breath during the Gospel reading, and, finally, the ability to speak at the consecration and elevation of the Host.[45] She related how during the preceding fifteen or so hours of near death, "she had been alone and happy, speaking with God." Her illness had thus changed its sense and become a sign of grace that testified to her pure heart. No longer a demoniac, she was now truly an ecstatic possessed by God, an innocent chased out of Laon much as Christ had been hounded out of the synagogue in Nazareth by the Pharisees. She thereupon took communion, knowing that only the Body of Christ could protect her now.

One indicator of Nicole Obry's newfound sanctity was her refusal to eat any food. She swooned every time she attempted to swallow a spoonful of soup, and could be revived only by the Body of Christ. She could eat nothing but the Blessed Sacrament; it was as if her life, now freed from the Devil's grip, could be sustained only by Christ's real presence. Only the Son of God could look after her as she remained suspended between death and redemption, a beneficiary of the sacrifice he had made to liberate her from the Prince of Darkness.

Thanks to the intervention of the abbess of Saulvoir, Jacqueline de Châtillon, and Canon Despinois, Nicole Obry was able to return to Laon, where for the first time in many days she began again to eat normally and to enjoy life. She took part daily in the prayers at the church of Our Lady, giving thanks to God and the Virgin Mary. Her stay in town this time, which signified God's blessing to Laon, lasted from March 19 to April 2, when the Huguenots again forced her to leave. History seemed to repeat itself as God punished the city for rejecting the path of salvation represented by the presence of Nicole Obry. Four miles outside Laon, she again lapsed into a blind and mute stupor. That evening, in the town of Marle, she briefly recovered when given the Host, but lost consciousness when she tried to sip some broth. This pattern of behavior continued during the days that followed: only the Blessed Sacrament could resuscitate the young woman. No sooner did she arrive in Vervins on Wednesday, April 3, than her companions, fearful of her fragile health, decided to return immediately to Laon, the place of her miraculous cure—the place where, once freed from Satan, she had publicly demonstrated God's desire to see his people cleansed of idolatry.

On their return to this new Jerusalem, the traveling party that carried her litter passed through Pierrepont on April 4, and arrived in Liesse on Friday the fifth. It had been seventy-two hours since she had eaten anything. She was brought to the basilica and placed, unconscious, before an image of the Virgin Mary. There the same scenario as before recurred as the mysterious

power of the Eucharist revived her once again. Echoing the liturgical meaning of the holy week, Nicole Obry's experience recalled the Jews' rejection of
the Redeemer. She and her companions finally made their solemn entry into
Laon on Palm Sunday, her return in effect representing the return of Christ,
thereby affirming that the Kingdom of Heaven was open to all who believed
in the Eucharist's real presence. On the evening of the seventh, in a cart
covered with white linen, she arrived in Vaux-les-Laon, where she was refused lodging. Hovering near death, she was instead taken to the main altar
of the church. Again the miracle of the Blessed Sacrament restored her.
Several of her companions immediately demanded that she be allowed to
return to Laon, since it was only there that she was able to eat and drink
normally, to walk and speak. And just as some people from Jerusalem had
assembled to meet Christ, "a large group of clergy" from Laon came forth to
greet her.[46] Nevertheless, she was prohibited—on pain of death—from entering the town. Finding the gate of Saint Georges locked, she cried, "Ah!
Jesus? Won't you take pity on me?" Chosen by God to defend the Eucharist
against Calvinist errors, she seemed condemned to pass her remaining days
outside Laon, doomed to starve to death, a victim of the Huguenots' blind
hatred. These trials caused by the heretics only reinforced her sense of divine
mission as she replayed the Savior's last days. Her suffering at the hands of
impious men merged with the tribulations of Christ, himself also a victim of
slanderous plots.

At this point, the story of Nicole de Vervins seems to come to an end with
two encounters. The first was one final effort to fulfill the miraculous triumph of the Eucharist. This climactic episode took place at La Fère on
April 6 in the presence of her family, the priests who had escorted her, and
the prince de Condé. The main objective was to convince the Huguenot
prince to permit Nicole's Christ-like entry into Laon the next day. Again,
the mimicking of persecution by God's enemies is amplified: lying unconscious in a nearby apothecary's home, the young woman was visited by
gentlemen and servants from the prince's suite. They began to prick her
with needles, to scream into her ears, and to threaten to whip her, but she
did not stir. Her husband, her mother, and the carter who had driven her to
Laon were interrogated, as well, but to no avail.

On Palm Sunday, the day when Christ and his apostles entered Jerusalem,
thus announcing the sure entry of all Christians into the Kingdom of
Heaven, an unexpected turn of events occurred that miraculously signaled

Christ's imminent victory through the Host. It was learned toward midnight that, after five days without food, the afflicted woman had finally eaten some chervil soup. Although the Huguenots immediately saw this as proof of her deception, Jean Boulaese saw in this breakthrough proof of God's mercy and power, deciding that "Our Savior and Lord Jesus Christ, showing He wishes only the conversion of sinners, not their death . . . actually used Nicole's relatives to bring her before the prince de Condé. And though they had only tried to obtain permission for her to return to Laon, God that night suddenly restored the poor woman's health and enabled her to eat food. After all, how could she render testimony of God's power without such an intercession?"[47]

As a result, the meeting with the prince de Condé quickly became a theological disputation during which Canon Despinois, one of Nicole's most ardent supporters, declared a miracle to have occurred through the transubstantiation of ordinary bread. Then it was the mother's turn to speak with the prince, who offered one hundred écus—as well as threats—if she admitted that all of her daughter's actions had been a ruse. On Monday, April 8, after Despinois again refused to repudiate Nicole, the prince de Condé finally met with the young woman herself and questioned her. According to Boulaese, she related the story of her possession, emphasizing in particular the fact that she had gone nearly six entire days without eating. Condé brought in the Calvinist minister Jean de l'Espine, who explained to Nicole that if Satan had indeed left her, it was not due to a piece of bread but rather to God's power alone. When asked about this by the prince, she admitted that this explanation sounded plausible, whereupon she was sent back to her lodgings. A debate then ensued between the minister and Despinois, which ended on Tuesday when the canon had to sign an affidavit, though he could not keep a copy of it, before he was allowed to return to Laon. Nicole's mother was released, and Nicole and her husband were sent to Anisy. According to Boulaese's account, they were promised great wealth if they abandoned their religion. On Wednesday, April 10, the couple, though threatened with death or imprisonment, adamantly refused to bow to the prince's pressures, though they were daily subjected to Calvinist sermons in which ministers tried to make them apostates.

The paschal miracle was thus hindered, and Canon Despinois returned to Laon only to find the Huguenots openly declaring that Nicole's ecstatic experiences had all been a trick, as his signed affidavit attested. On Easter

Sunday, April 14, Despinois went to Anisy, where he attended a sermon by the Calvinist minister Parocelis and saw Nicole Obry seated beside the prince de Condé. Thus, the long, agonizing Passion of the young woman had failed to be realized as it should have been. But for the Huguenots' meddling, her return from the dead would have demonstrated to all the miraculous redemptive power of the resurrected Christ.

Having succeeded in upsetting this Catholic scenario, the prince de Condé decided on Monday, April 19, to transfer Nicole Obry to Ribemont to await trial. There she was imprisoned for thirty-nine days, until June 6, when a royal writ arrived ordering her release. The writ, dated June 1, had been obtained by Nicole's father, Pierre Obry, who had filed an appeal with the crown on behalf of his daughter on May 22.

Another important meeting took place on Tuesday, August 27, when Charles IX came to Laon. The details of the miracle were recounted to the king, who then ordered the dean of the chapter to write its history, likely because these unusual circumstances typified a reign which François de Belleforest later described as "full of marvels."[48] On Friday, August 30, the king took up residence in the château of Marchais, situated near the church of Notre Dame in Liesse, where he met with Nicole Obry and her family.

A decade later, in 1577, the possessed woman of Vervins reappeared during the first week of Lent. Now a mother with three children, she suddenly again became blind, and doctors could do nothing for her. She undertook a pilgrimage to Amiens where, on Sunday, May 19, she recovered her sight after contact with relics of Saint John the Baptist and communion at the saint's shrine. After the novena ended that day in Amiens, Nicole Obry was never again mentioned in contemporary accounts.[49]

The story of Nicole Obry's possession, in the mid-1560s' system of representations, became in effect an allegory of the past and present history of humankind. Her descent into diabolic mania exemplified the Fall of Man as well as the current loss of some of God's people to the Prince of Darkness. Once begun, the rites of exorcism introduced a soteriological element which, after intense struggle, saw the young woman's body become sanctified by the grace of Christ's sacrifice.[50] The possession thus served to exalt Christ's real presence in the Blessed Sacrament, thereby upholding Catholic doctrine against its enemies. Through wonderment it taught the need to restore confessional unity, and thus hope.[51] As this drama was played out, first in Vervins and then in Laon, before the huge enthusiastic crowds that came to see the exorcism ceremonies, a palpable sense of anxiety could be detected among those who believed that religious toleration only brought God's wrath down on his people. The Eucharist's victory over Satan encouraged extreme violence by urging true penitents to become sacrificial offerings like Christ.

The origins of the later "spirit of the Catholic League" perhaps can be found in these ramifications of the little-known story of Nicole Obry. In her was apparently defined a path of salvation that began with acknowledging sin and seeking repentance, then proceeded to penance and communion, and finally culminated in mystical ecstasy. In her could be found a path of salvation which could restore the covenant and thus reunite all good Catholics—a dream the Holy League tried to realize at the end of the century.[52]

Appendix

Jean Boulaese's role in this affair raises a number of questions. Little is known of the man called "Boulaese the presbyter," who claimed to be a "pauper" of the Collège de Montaigu. He was probably born in 1530 at Aroul au Perche-Gouël in the diocese of Chartres. He received a master of arts degree in 1551 and was ordained in 1565. The next year he was in Picardy, where he no doubt encountered Canon Despinois, from whom he first heard of the Vervins affair. This sparked Boulaese's interest to pursue the matter and perhaps explains his attendance at Charles IX's visit to Laon and his knowledge of the king's meeting with the possessed woman. In May 1567, he went to Spain hoping to present to Philip II his small yet widely circulated book, *Le miracle de Laon en lannoys representé au vif,* printed in Cambrai. The next year Boulaese became a regent professor of Hebrew at the Collège de Montaigu. In 1571 he went to Rome to present to Pope Pius V a more complete manuscript version of his original 1567 book on the Vervins affair, which included numerous other eyewitness accounts about Nicole Obry. He eventually returned to France via Avignon, where he met George d'Armagnac, to whom the book is dedicated. In 1571, during his absence, Boulaese was elected head of the Collège de Montaigu; his accession to this post was overturned, however, as a result of internal disputes in the college that dragged on interminably. Seven years later, Boulaese finally won the post, whereupon he set out to reinstate in their entirety the pedagogical and religious precepts of Standonck, only to be dismissed in 1579. He sought protection not only from George d'Armagnac, but also from Christofle de Thou and René de Birague, to whom he had dedicated the *Tabula chronographica ex collatione temporum hebraeorum* in 1575. See A. H. Chaubard's introduction to *Le miracle de Laon en lannoys, representé au vif et escript en latin, Francoys, Italien, Espaignol et Allemant* (Cambrai, 1955) for more on this episode. Boulaese was reputedly an admirer of the Jesuits. His odyssey from Laon to Paris, then to Spain and Rome, must be understood in light of his relationship as a disciple of Guillaume Postel, who also after 1566 wrote about the miracle at Laon in *De Summopere* (see Irena Backus, *Guillaume Postel et Jean Boulaese, De Summopere et Le Miracle de Laon* [Geneva: Droz, 1995]). This explains why he wished to see the vision outlined in the *Concordia mundi* realized through the eucharistic experience of Nicole d'Obry—an experience he hoped would convert the world by reestablishing its unity in the veneration of Christ's holy body. Further study of Postel's prophetic works will certainly shed light on Boulaese's reasons for publishing in 1578 *Le Manuel de l'Admirable victoire du Corps de Dieu sur l'Esprit maling de Beelzebub obtenue à Laon 1566. Au salut de tous. Par le commandement de noz benictz Pere les Papes Pie V. et Gregoire XIII, à présent.*

Notes

1. I thank Father Henri Moreau for reading this essay and offering his valuable advice, and also Professor Alfred Soman.

2. Florimond de Raemond, *L'histoire de la naissance, progrez et decadence de l'heresie de ce siècle* (Rouen, 1618), p. 204.

3. An anonymous letter dated February 6, 1566, edited by Champfleury, indicates that the initial appearance of the ghost occurred on All Saints' Day; see *Bulletin de la Société historique et archéologique de Soissons* 3 (1850): 191–96.

4. Jean Boulaese, "priest, professor of the Old Testament, poor friar attached to the College of Montagu," *Le Manuel de l'Admirable victoire du Corps de Dieu sur l'Esprit, maling de Beelzebub obtenue à Laon 1566. Au salut de tous. Par le commandement de noz benictz Peres les Papes Pie V. et Gregoire XIII, à présent* (Paris, 1578), Bibliothèque Nationale [hereafter BN], Lk⁷ 3416, pp. 47–50. An earlier edition had been published by Denys du Val in 1575, BN, Lk⁷ 3415. Also useful is the book by Abbot Jean Roger, *Histoire de Nicole de Vervins d'après les historiens contemporains et témoins oculaires ou le triomphe du Saint Sacrement sur le démon à Laon en 1566* (Paris, 1863); and Isabelle Brun, *La possession diabolique aux XVI–XVIIe siècles: Le cas de Nicole de*

Vervins (1565–1566) (Master's thesis, University of Lyons 3, 1992). The latter drew my attention to the liturgical significance of the possession and ensuing exorcisms.

5. Boulaese, *Le Manuel,* pp. 54–55.

6. See the *Manuale seu officiarum sacerdotum* (Paris, 1538), printed for the diocese of Laon, fol. 2: "Adiutorium nostrum in nomini domini. Qui fecit celum et terram. Sit nomen domini benedictum. . . . Exorciso te creatura per deum + divum / per deum + verum / per deum + sanctum." If the priest stopped at the baptismal exorcism, it was because he lacked special authorization from his bishop to proceed further.

7. Boulaese, *Le Manuel,* p. 71.

8. *Missale ad consuetudinem insignis ecclesie Remensis . . .* (Simon Vostre, 1505), fol. 1. The *Dies irae* made up the prose portion of the Mass.

9. Boulaese, *Le Manuel,* pp. 79–80.

10. Ibid., p. 96.

11. Ibid., p. 102.

12. Ibid., pp. 83–84.

13. Muriel Laharie, *La folie au Moyen Age: XIe–XIIIe siècle* (Paris: Léopard d'Or, 1991), p. 28.

14. Boulaese, *Le Manuel,* dedication to Henry III, n.p.

15. Ibid., pp. 74, 94.

16. Ibid., p. 100.

17. This day was the feast day for Saint Geneviève, a saint whose miracles help reduce the weight of sinners' faults.

18. Boulaese, *Le Manuel,* p. 111.

19. Ibid., pp. 116–20.

20. Ibid., p. 121.

21. Ibid., p. 116.

22. Boilleau, who followed Nicole Obry's experiences closely, later headed the Catholic Holy League faction that took over Laon in 1589. Charles Despinois also participated in those events. See Antoine Richart, *Mémoires sur la Ligue dans la Laonnais* (Laon, 1869).

23. See Nicolas Jovet, *Le Triomfe du S. Sacrement sur le démon: Extrait de l'originel manuscrit qui est dans le Trésor du chapître Notre-Dame de Laon* (Laon, 1682), pp. 49–58.

24. Boulaese, *Le Manuel,* p. 130.

25. Another example of demonic possession manifested mainly in the left side of the body occurred in the case of Maria Pizarro. See Jean-Pierre Tardieu, *Le nouveau David et la réforme au Pérou: L'affaire Maria Pizarro-Francisco de la Cruz, 1571–1596* (Bordeaux: Maison des pays ibériques, 1992), pp. 30–32.

26. Boulaese, *Le Manuel,* pp. 142–47.

27. Ibid., pp. 149–50, 302–5.

28. Ibid., p. 160.

29. Ibid., p. 166.

30. Ibid., p. 171.

31. Ibid., pp. 363–65.

32. Ibid., p. 175.

33. Ibid., p. 185.

34. Ibid., p. 187.

35. Ibid., p. 333.

36. Ibid., pp. 420–21.

37. The letter dated February 8, 1566, cited above in note 3, stated that the miracle occurred after a huge procession during which the Corpus Christi was carried "in great majesty."

38. Boulaese, *Le Manuel,* p. 212.

39. Ibid., p. 457.

40. Ibid., p. 213.

41. See D. Clabaine, *Le combat exorciste de l'Église* (Paris: Flammarion, 1987), p. 86.

42. Boulaese, *Le Manuel,* p. 217.

43. Ibid., p. 192.

44. Ibid., p. 225.

45. Ibid., pp. 512–16.

46. As related in O. Douen, *Essai historique sur les églises réformées du département de l'Aisne* (Paris, 1860), pp. 21–27.

47. Boulaese, *Le Manuel,* p. 548.

48. As a result, the cathedral chapter decided on October 7 to pay for a written account of the "Vervins woman who was thankfully delivered from Satan." See Edmond Fleury, *Cinquante ans de l'histoire du chapitre de Laon: Procès-verbaux et délibérations du 22 juin 1541 au 15 juillet 1594* (Laon and Paris, n.d.), p. 29.

49. It is worth noting that this later miracle in 1577 occurred shortly after the formation of the League of Péronne, over which Henry III proclaimed himself the head on December 2, 1576, following the Estates-General's call to reestablish religious unity in the kingdom. The Sixth War of Religion thereafter began, in which Nicole de Vervins perhaps tried to participate mystically. Interestingly, Soissons saw a number of exorcisms performed in 1582, as reported in *Cinq histoires admirables, esquelles est monstré comme miraculeusement par la vertu et puissance du S. Sacrement de l'Autel, a esté chassé Beelzebub Prince des diables, avec plusieurs autres Demons, qui se disoient estre ses subjects, hors du corps de quatre diverses personnes. Et le tout advenu en ceste present année 1582, en la ville et Dioce de Soissons. Recueillies des actes d'un Notaire Royal, et du Greffiers, et mises par ordre tres-fidelment, par D. Charles Soissons, au bourg saint Vast* (Paris, 1582). The bishop of Soissons was none other than Charles de Roucy, a close associate of the Guises, as probably was Bishop Jean de Bours. Was it a coincidence that the fourth case of possession related from Soissons concerned a woman named Marguerite Obry, aged twenty years or so, daughter of a vine grower named Paul Obry, who lived in the village of Villers-Saint-Paul near Clermont-en-Beauvais? This possession began early in 1577. The connection between ultra-

Catholic ideals and demonic possession recurred later with a certain Françoise Fontaine, sometime between 1591 and 1593. See *Procès verbal fait pour délivrer une fille possédé par le malin esprit à Louviers, publié d'après le manuscrit original et inédit de la Bibliothèque Nationale par Armand Bénet,* intro. B. de Morny (Paris, 1883). This case of possession began in Paris during the League, when Françoise Fontaine "suddenly saw appear before her one Sunday a person returned from the grave, a shroud covering his head." The apparition repeated very closely the words that had been spoken to Nicole Obry by her dead grandfather. "I am your uncle, François Cotté, formerly of the rue Saint Denis. It is I who torments you each night, because I suffer for not having fulfilled two vows that I made while alive. The first was to go Notre Dame de Vertu to hear mass; the other was to travel to Saint Laurent in the faubourg Saint-Denis" (p. 83). The account of the 1565–66 possession conceivably served as a model for two other cases that occurred near Laon in 1567, one at Brunhamel, the other at Bruyères. Significantly, until the city's later capture by royalists, Laon annually held a solemn procession commemorating Nicole de Vervins's deliverance from Satan in 1566. See Fleury, *Cinquante ans,* p. 306.

50. Fittingly enough, Boulaese closed his huge account of the possession with a retelling of Christ's life and resurrection, separately published as *L'Abrégée histoire du grand miracle par nostre Sauveur et Seigneur JESUS CHRIST en la sainte Hostie du Sacrement de l'Autel, faict à Laon 1566, Escrite et augmentée avec sa carte représentant le pays iceux dit* (Thomas Belot: Paris, 1573). BN, Lk⁷ 3414. The work was dedicated to Cardinal d'Armagnac and published by order of Popes Pius V and Gregory XIII.

51. This notion has been treated by anthropologists, usually in a social context, when discussing possession. See Aissa Ouitis, *Possession, magie et prophétie en Algérie, Essai* (Paris: Arcantère, 1984); and France Schott-Billmann, *Corps et possession: Le vécu corporel des possédés face à la rationalité occidentale* (Paris: Gauthier-Villars, 1977).

52. On the relationship between possession and shamanism, as well as that between sickness and sacrality, see Joan M. Lewis, *Les religions d'Extase: Étude anthro- pologique de la possession et du chamanisme* (London, 1971; French translation, pub- lished in Paris: Presses Universitaires de France, 1977).

Richard M. Golden

Satan in Europe: The Geography of Witch Hunts

In 1927 Montague Summers, an English erudite who specialized in Restoration drama as well as the occult, published *The Geography of Witchcraft*. In it, he construed contemporary accounts of witchcraft across different regions as evidence of Satan's claw gripped over Europe. He showed no interest in the topics I will consider in this essay, such as differences in law, the number of persons executed, and the gender of those accused. For, unlike historians today who study the manifestly impossible crime of diabolical witchcraft, Summers believed that Satan existed and exists, and that witches signed pacts with the Evil One; traveled to sabbats[1] to pay homage to Satan and to indulge in sexual promiscuity, cannibalism, and other loathsome behavior; and, finally, caused evil with the ultimate goal of destroying Christendom. As Summers so chillingly declared, "it is far better to believe too much than too little."[2]

Summers was a historical mountebank who used original sources and did good research, but his gullibility was exceeded only by his faith. Except for his translations of demonological treatises, his contribution to the study of the witch hunts is nil. Recent serious discussion of the geography of witch hunting began with Hugh Trevor-Roper's article "The European Witch-Craze of the Sixteenth and Seventeenth Centuries,"[3] which argues that conflict between Protestants and Catholics was the major impetus in witch hunting; Protestants looked for Catholic witches, and vice versa. Later research has shown Trevor-Roper to be wrong—while religious zeal could serve as a powerful motivator, persecution often occurred where there was no confessional conflict, where magistrate and victim shared the same religion. Trevor-Roper is correct, however, in identifying Germany, Scotland, Switzerland, Franche-Comté, Lorraine, Alsace, some parts of northern Italy, and territories north and south of the Pyrenees as regions of very active witch hunting, but he virtually ignored Scandinavia, save for Sweden, and thought that in eastern Europe only Poland persecuted witches to any extent.

Major works published in the 1990s have begun to treat the geography of witch hunting in a more systematic manner. Brian P. Levack's "The Geography of Witchcraft," contained in his synthesis, *The Witch-Hunt in*

Early Modern Europe, presents a first-rate analysis.[4] In the present essay, I added Denmark, Iceland, and Scandinavia to the areas—Germany,[5] Switzerland, Franche-Comté, Lorraine, Scotland, and Poland—that Levack identified as marked by severe witch hunting, while I judge the French to have been less active in hunting witches. Also, as a measure of witch hunting, I stress even more than he the ratio of victims to the population size rather than simply the number executed.[6] Levack ascribed the vitality of witch hunting to the nature and strength of witch beliefs, the system of criminal procedure, the degree of central judicial control, and religious zeal.[7] But the same methods of criminal procedure sometimes produced dissimilar levels of witch hunting. Despite the *Constitutio Criminalis Carolina* (popularly known simply as the *Carolina*), which in 1532 legislated criminal procedure applicable throughout the Holy Roman Empire, very different rates of execution for witchcraft prevailed across Germany. While torture was necessary for intensive witch hunting, some areas of the Holy Roman Empire that practiced torture according to the *Carolina* did not see much witch hunting. In fact, the limits imposed on the use of torture in areas subject to inquisitorial legal procedure (the Roman-Canon law of proof) made those regions at times much more similar in the handling of witchcraft cases to areas of Europe that possessed other legal procedures than Levack supposed.[8] Torture alone, then, was not sufficient to secure convictions.

Religious ardor, like torture, was a necessary ingredient in the witch-hunting brew, but it did not inexorably lead to prosecution either. Christian enthusiasm was a precondition for the hunt, but some areas of fervent religiosity—such as France, Ireland, Spain, Italy, and Portugal—normally avoided large numbers of witch trials. Broader economic and social structures certainly affected the witch hunts. Central governments, too, could curtail witch hunting, as happened in France; or promote the search for witches, as in Lorraine and Scotland. As important as Levack's work is, it still underestimates the prominent role of individuals in fomenting witch hunting. I will argue here that the decision to find witches was often not institutional, but individual and communal. Witch hunting was above all a local matter promoted by diligent men, usually judge-hunters, who took advantage of various legal systems and local conditions to determine the severity (or absence) of witch hunting in many areas.

Political and religious biases have plagued the study of the European witch hunts. Enlightenment thinkers in the eighteenth century, for example, castigated clerical superstition as the primary cause of the witch hunts; in nineteenth-century Germany, Protestant writers blamed Catholicism for the witch hunts, while Catholic historians condemned Protestantism. In the late nineteenth and early twentieth centuries, liberal rationalism accused religion in general—a view especially prevalent in universities in the United States, where scholars waging battle against religious fundamentalists found ammunition in the dogmatism, intolerance, and obscurantism that these historians highlighted in the witch hunts of the sixteenth and seventeenth centuries.[9] Some writers have even wrongly likened the tragic deaths of the thousands of accused witches to the Holocaust.[10] Feminists see in the witch hunts a brutal confirmation of the West's long-standing tradition of misogyny, rightly emphasizing that 80 to 85 percent of the victims were women.[11] Anne Llewellyn Barstow, for example, expanded Levack's treatment of the geography of witch hunting, but in the process concentrated excessively on gender. Barstow massaged the data to depict witch hunting as little more than woman hunting.

These slanted perspectives have often led to gross exaggerations of the number killed in the witch hunts in order to emphasize their horror. Compounding this problem is the fact that the historical reconstruction of the witch hunts will never be complete, given the paucity of documentation. Lacking the rigorous methodology of historical demographers, historians have had to guess at the total number of the victims of the witch hunts. Witch hunting's episodic character prevents a confident extrapolation even from the numbers we do possess. Furthermore, sixteenth- and seventeenth-century record keepers loosely used such terms as "many witches" or rounded off the numbers.[12] As a result, the numbers range from conservative estimates, accepted by most scholars, of some 100,000 (or fewer) killed to the ludicrous claim of 9 million (see table 1).

An updated geographical overview of the witch hunts across Europe will help to rectify these discrepancies by showing how the nature of witchcraft persecution and prosecution varied from one part of Europe to another. It will also show some examples of powerful men who, by dint of their zealous ambition and ability, shaped the geography of European witchcraft prosecution. Let us begin the tour in the "heartland of the witchcraze" and slowly work our way to the European periphery.[13]

There is no doubt that witch hunting was most virulent in Germany, the center of the Holy Roman Empire. Because the entire region is so amorphous—there were more than three hundred states in Germany—it has not been studied thoroughly. Estimates of the number of witches killed in Germany vary widely, reasonably between 15,000 and 20,000, but possibly as high as 50,000.[14] In fact, owing to the difficulty of making an accurate estimate, most historians of witchcraft simply omit an overall number. But it is safe to say that almost 50 percent of all witchcraft executions in Europe occurred in Germany.[15] Specific evidence for many regions is plentiful. In southwest Germany, there were 3,229 executions between 1561 and 1670.[16] The archbishop-elector of Trier managed a witch hunt that resulted in 368 burnings from 1587 to 1593. In eight years, the prince bishop of Würzburg executed 900 people, while 133 alleged witches were dispatched in one day in 1589 on the lands of the convent of Quedlinburg.[17] The diocese of Bamberg tried 1,010 witches between 1595 and 1610, while its bishop, Johann Georg II Fuchs von Dornheim, known as the "Witch-Bishop," had approximately 600 burned in the decade after 1623.[18] Bavaria had between 1,000 and 2,000 victims.[19] Examples can be multiplied, but the overall picture is clear. Witch hunting in Germany was a nasty business, though local exceptions prevent any stark generalization.[20]

Courts in Germany freely tortured witches, whose accusations under torture resulted in the arrest of numerous other suspects, thereby sparking chain-reaction panics. The normal stereotype of the witch as a quarrelsome, unmarried old woman broke down when accused witches implicated people—usually women—from other social groups. In this, perhaps the most misogynistic period in Western history, woman hating was virulent in Germany, where 80 to 90 percent of the accused witches were women.[21] Germany was the home of the most infamous witchcraft treatise, *The Hammer of Witches* (1487), which linked witchcraft to women's carnality and spiritual deficiencies. Roman law, reintroduced in the sixteenth century, made the state rather than individual accusers responsible for proving the crime of witchcraft. Roman law's provision for expert consultation brought into the courts learned university professors who firmly believed in the reality of Satan, sabbats, and witches' attempts to defeat Christendom. Finally, without supervision from a centralized state judiciary, petty judges throughout Germany could proceed with little hindrance. Germany may have been the only area in Europe where, in some trials, at least, magistrates had *all* the accused executed.

Other areas of the Holy Roman Empire also saw witch-hunting epidemics. Between 1580 and 1630, about three thousand witches were burned in Lorraine (an enormous number, for a population of some 400,000);[22] with

Table 1. Historians' Estimations of the Total Number of
Accused Witches Killed

Estimated Number Killed	Source
9,000,000	Andrea Dworkin, "What Were Those Witches Really Brewing?," *MS*, 2 (April 1974): 52.
1,000,000s	Silvia Bovenshen, "The Contemporary Witch, the Historical Witch and the Witch Myth: The Witch Subject of the Appropriation of Nature and the Domination of Nature," *New German Critique* 15 (1978): 106.
1,000,000	Wolfgang Krämer, *Kurtrierische Hexenprozesse im 16, und 17, Jahrhundert* (Munich: Scharl, 1959), p. 105; Rosemary Reuther, "The Persecution of Witches: A Case of Sexism and Ageism?" *Christianity and Crisis* 34 (December 23, 1974): 294; Lyle Steadman, "The Killing of Witches," *Oceania* 56.2 (1985): 107.
500,000	Robert E. Turner and Charles Edgley, "From Witchcraft to Drugcraft: Biochemistry as Mythology," *Social Science Journal* 20 (October 1983): 1; Gunner Heinsohn and Otto Steiger, "The Elimination of Medieval Birth Control and the Witch Trials of Modern Times," *International Journal of Women's Studies* 5 (1982): 208.
200,000–500,000	Nachman Ben-Yehuda, "The European Witch Craze of the 14th to 17th Centuries: A Sociologist's Perspective," *American Journal of Sociology* 86 (1980): 1 and "The European Witch Craze: Still a Sociologist's Perspective," *American Journal of Sociology* 88 (1983): 1276.
200,000	G. R. Quaiffe, *Godly Zeal and Furious Rage: The Witch in Early Modern Europe* (New York: St. Martin's Press, 1987), p. 79.
100,000s	Richard A. Horsley, "Who Were the Witches? The Social Roles of the Accused in the European Witch Trials," *Journal of Interdisciplinary History* 9. 4 (1979): 694.
<100,000	E. William Monter, "The Pedestal and the Stake: Courtly Love and Witchcraft," in *Becoming Visible: Women in European History*, ed. Renate Bridenthal and Claudia Koontz (Boston: Houghton Mifflin, 1977), p. 130.
100,000 maximum	Geoffrey Scarre, *Witchcraft and Magic in 16th and 17th Century Europe* (Atlantic Highlands, N.J.: Humanities Press International, 1987), p. 19; Anne Llewellyn Barstow, *Witchcraze: A New History of the European Witch Hunts* (San Francisco: HarperCollins Publishers, 1994), pp. 10, 23.

Table 1. *Continued*

Estimated Number Killed	Source
<50,000–200,000	Allison C. Coudert, "The Myth of the Improved Status of Protestant Women: The Case of the Witchcraze," in *The Politics of Gender in Early Modern Europe*, ed. Jean R. Brink, Allison P. Coudert, and Maryanne C. Horowitz (Kirksville, Mo.: Sixteenth Century Journal Publishers, 1989), p. 61.
60,000	Brian P. Levack, *The Witch-Hunt in Early Modern Europe*, 2d ed. (London: Longman, 1995), 25.

the approval of the duke and the support of the population, the magistrate Nicolas Remy was responsible for sentencing almost two thousand witches to death, 2 percent or more of those executed for witchcraft in all of Europe. This number graphically shows the decisive role of individual judge-hunters. Labeled the "scourge of witches" and the Torquemada of Lorraine, Remy worked assiduously from 1576 to 1606 to ferret out those whom he believed intended to turn Christendom topsy-turvy and work with Satan to prevent the Second Coming. Remy's enthusiastic witch hunting was successful not only because he was able to use his offices efficiently, but because Lorraine at the time witnessed epidemics, poor harvests, and increased social tensions.[23] Periodic warfare encouraged the government and populace to search for human (or inhuman) causes of the depredations. Counter-Reformation religious enthusiasm in Lorraine also found an outlet in the chase for witches. Remy himself rose from lieutenant-general of the *bailliage* of the Vosges (a post his maternal uncle had previously occupied) to a seat on the ducal court (*échevinat; tribunal des échevins*) at Nancy, to the duke's *conseil privé,* and to the highest judicial office in Lorraine, *procureur-général.* As *procureur-général,* Remy toured all the *bailliages* in Lorraine, burning witches in the villages he passed through.[24] Remy was merciless in his treatment of accused witches. "Who is there," he wrote, "who does not know that neither sex nor age is regarded by the law as any excuse for its infringement, and that no offence can be condoned on the score of human weakness? . . . Woe to those who would palliate the odium of so horrible a crime, and would diminish its punishment on the pleas of fear, age, sex, imprudence, and the like, which no sane man would dare to consider as grounds for mercy in less abominable crimes!"[25] Well educated in the law, an erudite (he cited upward of eleven hundred proper names, in addition to those of the witches, in his *Demonolatry*), Remy represented well the energetic zeal of the Counter-Reformation and was honored for his achievements during his distinguished career.[26] Consequently, Remy himself was a principal reason why the number of executed witches in Lorraine was remarkably high.

There were 1,500 known executions in Austria, but the actual number must be two or three times higher. The same multipliers are also valid for the 1,000 recorded executions in Bohemia.[27] The Southern Netherlands (now Belgium) saw at least 250 executions, while the Northern Netherlands, which secured its independence in 1648, witnessed only 150. This mild prosecution in what became the United Provinces of the Netherlands was certainly not typical of regions of the Holy Roman Empire. Indeed, the period of witch hunting ceased amazingly early in the northern provinces of the Netherlands (the last witch in Holland was executed in 1591 or 1592), thus making the intensity of witch persecution for the sixteenth century there comparable to some non-Germanic areas of Europe.[28] Luxembourg had 358 known executions in the sixteenth and seventeenth centuries, with repression in the German lands of the duchy exceeding those in the western Walloon parts.[29]

Switzerland had somewhere between six and ten thousand executions,[30] although witch hunting varied considerably from canton to canton. The most intense area of witch hunting in Switzerland and perhaps in Protestant Europe was the Pays de Vaud, whose death sentences magistrates in Bern reviewed. Between 1581 and 1620, the Pays de Vaud saw 970 burned (c. 66 percent female).[31] Witch hunts in the Jura region straddling the Franco-Swiss frontier, like those in Germany, used torture as recommended in the *Carolina* to compel suspects to name accomplices seen at the sabbat. Trials in the Jura proceeded only after the accusation of *maleficia,* or evil deeds, as did English, Scandinavian, and Russian trials. Simply to be a witch was not enough; a suspect must have worked evil. Like France, the Jura saw many cases of demonic possession. Jura witchcraft was unusual in that nearly all villages in certain areas saw witch trials, and in the high proportion of male witches—almost 40 percent.[32]

France experienced the most witch trials during the late Middle Ages, but thereafter relinquished its leading role to Germany.[33] Despite numerous cases of demonic possession from the 1560s into the early eighteenth century, some of the most celebrated involving nubile nuns and lecherous priests, the everyday situation in France was relatively tame. Witchcraft and witch hunts were rural phenomena largely limited to the north, northeast, southwest, Normandy, and a north-south spine running from Lorraine to the Alps over to Languedoc.[34] According to Robert Muchembled, French witch hunting involved the cooperation of the absolutist government and the Counter-Reformation church, which in tandem hoped to strengthen local obedience by further Christianizing peasant communities and thereby integrating them more fully into the fabric of state and church. Authorities sought to repress popular culture, which they saw as "superstitious," by principally singling out as witches marginalized females, whose persecution stood as an object lesson for other villagers.[35] Moreover, by the early 1600s, the magistrates of the Parlement of Paris, a sovereign court with jurisdiction over more than half the kingdom, stopped the witchcraft trials in opposition to the wishes of local judges and clerics. The parlement worked diligently to correct the excesses of local courts by looking for evidence of *maleficia,* not devil worship, and upholding the death sentences of only 103 of the 1,272 cases it heard on appeal.[36] There may have been 250 to 350 other local executions, both legal and illegal, in its area of jurisdiction.[37] The *parlementaires'* strong religious beliefs,[38] as seen in the Wars of Religion and in the early Catholic Reformation, thus undermine any facile connection between religious zeal and witch hunting in early modern Europe.

Information on the number of witches killed in areas under the jurisdiction of the regional parlements as well as trials in court of first instances throughout France is generally lacking.[39] It is nevertheless likely that only some five hundred witches were executed in the country—a number that may rise to several thousand if lynchings (about which little is known) are counted.[40] As Europe's most populous state, with some nineteen million people in 1600, France simply did not experience intense witch hunting, especially when compared with Germany, which had a population of sixteen million. Despite the celebrated trials involving demonic possession—Madeleine Demandols and Louis Gaufridy at Aix; Jeanne des Anges and Urbain Grandier at Loudun (known in the English-speaking world through Aldous Huxley's novel *The Devils of Loudun,* and Ken Russell's 1972 film *The Devils*); Madeleine Bavant, Mathurin Picard, and Thomas Bouillé at Louviers; and Catherine Cadière and Jean-Baptiste Girard, also at Aix[41]—and despite France being home to more demonologists (learned theoreticians of diabolism) than anywhere else,[42] France was not a particularly dangerous place for women alleged to have entered into the satanic pact.

One great exception to this relatively mild situation in France occurred in the early seventeenth century when Henry IV named Pierre de Lancre, a councillor in the Parlement of Bordeaux, to head a commission charged with investigating witchcraft in Labourd, one of the three Basque provinces in France. Despite its annexation in 1451, Labourd had not been assimilated into the dominant French culture. De Lancre's xenophobia readily identified witchcraft there as a "conspiracy of foreigners."[43] Henry IV was skeptical about demonic intervention and doubtless aimed to bypass local institutions in order to increase the crown's control in Labourd.[44] For their part, de Lancre and Jean d'Espagnet, the other member of the commission, saw Labourd as a savage land filled with inconstancy, duplicity, cruelty, sloth, and depravity—characteristics they identified with the Spanish—and fertile ground for sabbats.[45] Witchcraft prosecution in de Lancre's hands became a means to enforce government centralization, to delineate the cultural frontier with Spain, and to rid France of the minions of the Prince of Darkness. De Lancre believed the entire Basque population, save for a few families, to be infected with witchcraft,[46] a new religion that Satan had created to draw people into apostasy and idolatry and thus forfeit the grace of God.[47] Although some historians declare that he condemned six hundred witches to the stake,[48] the number is probably between thirty and fifty,[49] still a significant proportion of those executed for witchcraft in early modern France. Acting with the approval of the crown, de Lancre, like Remy, demonstrated what an active witch-hunting magistrate could accomplish in a region. That such intense witch hunting was atypical in France argues for the decisive conjunction between the local presence of witch beliefs among the populace and a judge committed to stamping out demonological witchcraft.

The regions south of France were usually spared the ravages of mass witch hunts, thanks primarily to the inquisitions in Spain, Portugal, and Italy. As in France, but earlier, there had been witch hunts in the Pyrenees and Basque areas of Spain in the early 1500s and again in 1575–77, but executions of witches nearly ceased after that. In fact, in the kingdom of Aragon witchcraft became a "forgotten crime" between 1550 and 1600, when the Aragonese Inquisition displayed only one witch among two thousand prisoners at autos-da-fé.[50] Europe's largest witchcraft trial—in reality, the greatest in history—occurred in the Basque provinces of northern Spain, where five thousand were accused from 1609 to 1611. News of trials north of the Pyrenees had swept into Spain, where sermons alarmed congregations about the dangers of witchcraft and an epidemic of dreams confirmed the existence of sabbats. Forced confessions solidified the witch panic. In 1609–10, the Logroño Inquisition proceeded against thirty-one of the accused, reconciling twenty to the church (although eight had died before the trial had ended) and burning eleven (actually, five of these had died during the trial, so the court could only consign their bones and coffins to the flames).[51] Fortunately, skepticism about witchcraft had made inroads in Spain. Alonso de Salazar Frias, one of the three judges of the local inquisitorial tribunal, stated that "there were neither witches nor bewitched until they were talked and written about."[52] The *suprema,* the supreme council of the tribunal of the Spanish Inquisition, had already in 1538 advised against believing everything in *The Hammer of Witches.* In 1614, accepting the opinions of Salazar rather than those of the other two inquisitors who had functioned on the local tribunal with him, the *suprema* returned to its skeptical position of the sixteenth century by ordering the suspension of the Basque witch trials.[53] Salazar's unflagging determination to prevent burnings has made him a hero to some historians.[54] While Remy and de Lancre burned witches in areas where a populace allowed them to join demonology to local witchcraft beliefs, Salazar had to quell trials in which elite conceptions of diabolism had already grafted on to widespread witchcraft beliefs among the populace. His success also indicates the decisive effect on witch hunting that a single individual could have. Unfortunately, a few years later, itinerant witch finders, the first being one Tarragó, spurred local communities in Catalonia to hang almost a hundred witches without involvement by the Inquisition.[55] Spain thus had individuals able to instigate as well as impede witch hunting.

For the Spanish Inquisition, witchcraft was a form of superstition, not a diabolical threat to displace Christian society. While Spain had witchcraft trials long after other European states had ceased prosecution—the last Spanish trial was in 1791—the Inquisition was not so bloodthirsty as its reputation. Of fifty thousand people tried between 1540 and 1700, the execution rate was approximately 1.6 percent.[56] This hardly fits the image of Spanish cruelty perpetuated by the infamous "Black Legend" of English and Protestant propaganda.[57] As in Italy, the Inquisition in Spain did not persecute witches to the degree that secular courts in northern Europe did. Fewer than three hundred witches were killed in Spain. *Conversos* were another story altogether, and their presence may have made extensive witch hunting unnecessary.

No great witch hunts occurred in Portugal, despite a widespread belief there in the satanic myth. The Portuguese Inquisition (1536–1821) had only one witch executed, and civil courts sentenced only five witches to be burned. Out of 11,743 trials, only 291 (2.5 percent) concerned witchcraft, sorcery, clairvoyance, or superstition. Just as in Spain, the inquisitors knew full well the demonological theories elaborated in the north, but evinced an early skepticism. Instead of witches, the Portuguese concentrated on the New Christians, recent converts from Judaism, who made up more than 80 percent of those tried in the seventeenth and eighteenth centuries. As with other European countries, Portugal was filled with agents of magic— "cunning men" and "wise women"—who tended both sick livestock and humans with their supernatural powers. There were also sorcerers who specialized in problems involving love.[58] Curiously, Portuguese cunning men derived their powers from innate qualities while sorcerers learned their techniques. This dichotomy between birth and training was typical in the African distinction between witchcraft and sorcery, but was generally absent from Europe.[59] Perhaps Portuguese exploration down the African coast in the fifteenth century had led to the importation of these African beliefs.

"In Italy," David Gentilcore argued, "in contrast to northern Europe, a witch-craze as such only took place in some alpine and subalpine areas, even though women suspected of witchcraft were tried throughout the peninsula and in Sicily."[60] The Roman Inquisition enforced safeguards, protected the rights of the defendant, and did not permit arbitrary rulings. Established in 1542 with jurisdiction throughout Italy, the Roman Inquisition between 1550 and 1700 tried at least 50,000 cases, most of which did not deal with witchcraft at all.[61] In fact, where the Roman Inquisition held sway, legal skepticism emerged early in the seventeenth century, paralleling a like development in the Parlement of Paris. All this occurred at the same time that northern regions were burning many witches.[62] Popular histories aside, the Roman Inquisition "was not a drumhead court, a chamber of horrors, or a judicial labyrinth from which escape was impossible."[63] No massive witch hunting took place in Italy. For instance, Venice avoided panic, even though witchcraft beliefs there were similar to those elsewhere in Europe. The Inquisition in Venice, in fact, sought to reintegrate the accused into the bosom of the holy mother church. Nor was there the northern European concern for physical punishment. Furthermore, the Inquisition in Venice followed strict procedural guidelines that spared the city witch hunts.[64] Executions of witches in Milan between 1580 and 1630 did not reach fifteen. In Sicily, surviving records of the Inquisition indicate 3,188 cases tried between 1547 and 1701, with twenty-five burnings for heresy; but not one of those executions was of a witch.[65] In all, Italians killed approximately two hundred witches.

Witchcraft was endemic in England, where there were as many cunning men and wise women as country curates. Nevertheless, perhaps only five hundred, and certainly not more than one thousand, witches were executed.[66] Most of the executions occurred during the Elizabethan period, save for a major episode of witch hunting during the Puritan Revolution, when the breakdown of central authority allowed one witch hunter to cause the deaths of one hundred to two hundred alleged witches.[67] Only during that grim episode did Continental ideas about night flying, the sabbat, and the satanic pact make their way into England. The imposition of diabolical theories and the massive campaign against witches in southeastern England was the work of Matthew Hopkins, the notorious "Witch-Finder General." His charisma, combined with the disorder of the civil war and the religiosity of the population, resulted in the most substantial witch hunts in English history. The opportunity was there, and Hopkins seized it. Witch seeking allowed Hopkins, son of the vicar of Great Wenham in Suffolk, to rise to prominence, though there is no evidence to suggest that he was anything but sincere in his search for witches in league with Satan.[68]

For the most part, English witchcraft was about *maleficia*, not about the devil. Torture was illegal in English common law, where accusatory procedures and trial by jury prevailed. For these reasons, England avoided the mass trials characteristic of central Europe. Hopkins succeeded in getting witches to confess to making pacts with the devil and performing evil deeds because he manipulated the legal system. He walked the accused until lack of sleep compelled them to disclose links to Satan, and pricked them to uncover evidence of the devil's mark (which the devil hid from detection, perhaps under the eyebrows, lips, or armpits, and "even in the secret parts and seate") and the witch's mark (a protuberance that demonic imps sucked).[69] Finally, because water rejected the innocent, Hopkins used the swimming test to determine the guilt of the accused. Courts had swum only two witches in seventeenth-century England before the Witch-Finder General resorted to this ordeal. Accordingly, Hopkins was able to combine seldom-used English legal procedures with Continental demonology to create an unprecedented witch hunt in England.

England's neighbor to the north was not so fortunate. With a much smaller population, Scotland endured 1,337 executions (with a margin of error of some 300).[70] Roman law, inquisitorial procedure, and torture held sway in Scotland. Under torture, witches in Scotland named accomplices, and mass panics resulted. Whereas control of witchcraft trials in England was customarily at the local level, in Scotland the central organs of government oversaw witchcraft trials and used them to create national unity.[71] Calvinist theology, which stressed God's punishment of sin with misfortune, created an environment in which witchcraft could stand as a surrogate and quite appealing explanation for misfortune. The Calvinist emphasis on a covenant with God easily led to the notion of an inverse covenant, or pact with Satan. Most Scottish witches were female (80 percent), rural, poor, and middle aged or older.[72] Scotland had the singular distinction of having a king (James VI) initiate witch hunting. James was in large part responsible for the introduction of Continental demonology into Scotland and for the mass trials in 1590 and 1591 of the so-called North Berwick witches, when more than one hundred people were accused of diabolical witchcraft and the attempted assassination of the monarch himself. James attended interrogations and interfered with the court's procedures.[73] In 1597, he published his *Daemonologie,* the only treatise on the science of witchcraft written by a monarch. Though unoriginal, the book acquainted Scots with the Continental demonologists' ideas of the witches' sabbat and the demonic pact. James wrote the book "to resolve the doubting harts of many; both that the assaults of Sathan are most certainly practized, and that the instrumentes thereof, merits most severely to be punished."[74] Though Scottish witchcraft was undeniably a complex phenomenon, James's influence on witch hunting in Scotland is indisputable.[75] By contrast, between 1324 and 1711, only eight recorded witchcraft trials took place in Ireland—all, except for the first, involving only Protestants. Perhaps Ireland's distance from the centers of the great witch conflagrations, the unbridgeable distance separating the Anglo-Irish Protestant minority from the Irish Catholic majority, and the absence of demonological writings explain the scarcity of witch hunting.[76] Or perhaps recourse to fairies as an explanation for personal misfortune made witches redundant.[77]

Iceland, tied to Scandinavia culturally and by Norwegian and, later, Danish rule (since 1380), had 120 witch trials from 1604 to 1720. Twenty-two witches were burned (between 1625 and 1685), only one a woman. The Icelandic term for *witch* itself was masculine. While there were "wise men" in Iceland, there were no "wise women," for knowledge was a male prerogative. Men, sometimes well-to-do ones, were therefore open to the charge of witchcraft. As was the case with other Scandinavian countries and England, accusations against witches involved *maleficia,* not the satanic pact. No witches' sabbat was mentioned in Icelandic trials; as in England, the witch was a solitary figure. It was only with the introduction of the Reformation in the seventeenth century that Continental demonological ideas and *The Hammer of Witches* became known. The Reformation regarded traditional patterns of behavior as heretical, part of Satan's dominion. Imposed from above, the Reformation and its attendant demonological belief structure made the situation in Iceland analogous to that in Scotland and the north of France, where new religions—Calvinism in Scotland and a reinvigorated Catholicism in France—reinterpreted local customs as witchcraft. In proportion to the population (fifty thousand), the incidence of witchcraft in Iceland was significant indeed.[78]

Denmark, like England, France, and Spain, was a relatively developed state whose central organs of government could counterbalance the desires of local courts to employ sabbat denunciations to bring in more accused witches.[79] The Copenhagen Articles of 1547 directed that no statement from a dishonest person (a category that included witches and sorcerers) could lead to the conviction of another person and that torture could be employed only after the final sentence. In 1576, appeals from lower courts were made automatic. Malefice rather than the demonic pact characterized Danish witchcraft.[80] Nevertheless, Lutheran—as was all Scandinavia—Denmark was fertile ground for witch hunting, with two thousand cases and somewhat less than one thousand victims.[81] These numbers were higher than those of any other Scandinavian country, and Denmark ended witch hunting earlier.[82] At the high point of witch persecution in Denmark, 90 percent of the accused were women, a number nearly equal to the highest figure (92 percent) in Essex, England.[83]

From the fourteenth century to the early nineteenth century, Norway and Denmark formed one kingdom. Danes staffed the Norwegian courts and political administration. As in Denmark, witchcraft as a crime meant *male-*

ficium, although the Lutheran clergy, educated in Germany and Denmark, preached far and wide about Satan, his pact, and the sabbat, and so joined demonology to popular fears of malefice. Norwegian trials (nearly all occurring between 1570 and 1700) probably totaled 1,400, and executions 350, for an execution rate of 25 percent—roughly one-half of Denmark's rate.[84] In light of Norway's scattered and small population (440,000 in 1650), the number of trials was extremely high. Unlike the situation in Denmark, courts applied torture early in the criminal process. Eighty percent of the accused were women, a fact that puts Norway in the European mainstream, as does the time of the cessation of witch trials, about 1670.[85] A specialty of Norwegian and to a lesser extent of Danish witchcraft was bewitching of ships,[86] a type of malefice of singular importance in the introduction of witchcraft to Scotland, when, returning home in 1590 with his Danish bride, King James VI encountered a storm, which was blamed subsequently on the North Berwick witches.

Sweden is another case where the introduction of learned demonology drastically altered witchcraft trials. Since the fourteenth century, Swedish law had viewed witchcraft as the performance of malefice, but in the early decades of the seventeenth century erudite ideas of the sabbat found ready acceptance and seemed to validate folk ideas of night flying and the existence of Blakulla (Blue Hill), a place where witches gathered (originally thought to be a desolate rock island in the Baltic, but referring later to any nearby hill or mountain). Although forbidden by law, torture came to be applied regularly in cases involving witchcraft. Countering these changes that intensified witch hunting, the Royal Court of Appeal, set up in 1614 in Stockholm, reviewed all death sentences decreed in local courts, save for those involving obviously clear cases. Following the pattern in other states where capital sentences were referred to a national court, the number of executions through the 1650s in Sweden was low, apparently less than one hundred.[87]

By the next decade, the situation had changed. A 1664 ordinance responded to the clerical and lay elite's desire to acculturate the rural population to stricter moral and religious behavior, for the elite viewed witchcraft as a threat to the social order rather than as a conflict between individuals. The stage was set for a mass panic in upper Dalarna (in south-central Sweden, next to Lake Siljan) beginning in 1668. A total of 279 people were tried: 210 adults and 69 children. As in Salem, Massachusetts, and Logroño, northern Spain, children played a major role, though Sweden was unique in having children as paid professional witch hunters. Swedish law forbade children below the age of fifteen to act as witnesses in court, but during the panic courts ignored this provision and the Royal Court of Appeal acquiesced. Some of the child witnesses were executed. Approximately 90 percent of those executed were women. Unlike most areas of Europe, including neighboring Norway as well as England (the benchmark for many historians of witchcraft), the accused were not the isolated poor living on the margins of rural society, but stable members of the community. Another unusual feature of the Swedish witch panic is that those accused who confessed could be spared, whereas those who persisted in denying their apostasy—and thus remained in the devil's clutches—were executed. Nowhere else in Europe, save for Italy and Iberia (where the inquisitions sought to reconcile the accused to the church), did confession mean exoneration or a mild punishment.[88] In all, there were maybe 300 victims of witch hunting in Sweden. Sweden's population hovered around 1 million, roughly equivalent to Scotland's and Switzerland's. A comparison of the executions relative to population shows Sweden's witch hunting to be about 20 percent as severe as Scotland's and 5 percent as bad as Switzerland's. However, Swedish witch hunting was almost twice as acute as that in the Southern Netherlands (250 executions in a population of 1.6 million) and three times as brutal as in the Northern Netherlands.

In the sixteenth and seventeenth centuries, Finland was an eastern province of Sweden, but Finnish witch hunts had their own momentum. In a population that by the early eighteenth century numbered only between 300,000 and 400,000,[89] about one thousand persons were accused of witchcraft, and perhaps more than one hundred of them received death sentences.[90] The most singular feature of Finnish witchcraft is that the stereotypical sorcerer was male, although in charges of diabolical witchcraft the proportion of women accused was higher. Thus in the sixteenth century 60 percent of the accused and 75 percent of those found guilty were men; by the 1670s, 59 percent of the accused and nearly 64 percent of the guilty were women. A major factor in the dissemination of demonology was the founding of a university, the Turku Academy. As in Germany and Sweden, professors were significant in spreading the new ideas about satanic witchcraft. Unlike Sweden, there were no mass trials in Finland, courts did not order formal torture, and *maleficium* was the most important factor in conviction.

On the other hand, the Swedish myth of Blakulla was present, and in some Finnish trials children were witnesses.[91]

Sweden brought witch hunting to Estonia with its conquest in the late sixteenth and early seventeenth centuries. Although law had linked witchcraft to heresy since the fourteenth century and had stipulated burning as the penalty, there is no record of the execution of a witch in Estonia before the sixteenth century. The overwhelming majority of trials occurred in the seventeenth century, with the last in 1725. There were 205 known indictments, and sixty-five death sentences. Men constituted 57 percent of the accused, and 47 percent of those known to have been executed. Estonia shared with Finland and Iceland the prominence of the male witch. The typical Estonian witch was an older, married peasant man. Although German influence and the Swedish presence spread ideas of demonology, witchcraft for the Estonian peasantry meant above all the performance of malice and/or poisoning. Even when judges introduced diabolism, there was rarely any indication of night flying to the sabbat or the pact with the devil. Belief in werewolves and in the transmutation of people into bears was extensive, however. The Swedish importation of witch hunting went hand in hand with the imposition of serfdom and the implementation of Lutheranism among a peasantry still clinging to pre-Christian rituals that the Swedes considered to be idolatrous and superstitious. The acculturation model of witch hunting applies to Estonia.[92]

Not until the sixteenth century did Poland see witchcraft trials based on the demonic pact. They began in cities where the majority of the population was German or where there were strong commercial ties with Germany. In the seventeenth and eighteenth centuries, however, 81 percent of the trials were in villages. Poland fit the European pattern with witch hunting being largely a rural phenomenon, but was atypical in that witch hunting was most severe in the early eighteenth century, long after witch hunts had disappeared elsewhere on the Continent. The kingdom of Poland, which included Lithuania and the Ukraine, was enormous in the mid-seventeenth century, before rapidly diminishing in size and then disappearing completely by 1795 owing to her predatory neighbors. Bohdan Baranowski estimated that 10,000 accused witches were burned to death or died under torture in the area of present-day Poland, with probably another 5,000 to 10,000 lynchings. This figuring of extralegal justice as accounting for an additional 50 to 60 percent of those killed has important implications for any estimate of the total number of alleged witches slain in Europe. If such factors were applied throughout the Continent, 100,000 could well become a minimal estimate. Displaying German influence, the Polish courts employed torture to force confessions; there was little chance of escaping a guilty verdict.[93] Witch hunting was more relentless in Poland than anywhere else in eastern Europe. Nevertheless, Baranowski's numbers are unrealistic because Poland had few, if any, mass trials, the nobility were not involved, and the clergy condemned the ferocity of the persecutions. Trials were for the most part individual and peasant-driven, and as such could not have resulted in large numbers of executions.[94] Additionally, eastern Poland, farther away from German influence, compares with Russia in its lack of witch hunts. An estimate of 5,000 witches killed in Poland is reasonable.

Just as in Poland, the peak period of witch hunting in Hungary occurred in the eighteenth century. The Habsburg Empress Maria Theresa initiated steps in 1756 to end the persecution of witches, and the government prohibited witch burning in 1768. Between 1520 and 1777 (the date of the last execution), there were more than eight hundred death sentences. During this period, the northwest constituted the kingdom of Hungary, which the Habsburgs ruled, while the principality of Transylvania remained autonomous. The Turks controlled approximately one-third of Hungary from 1541 to 1686, but evinced no interest in pursuing witches. Nonetheless, there were probably numerous lynchings there.[95] More than 90 percent of those tried and condemned to death were women, placing Hungary among those European states with the dubious distinction of having the most thoroughly sex-linked prosecution of witches. Much of the witch hunting in Hungary may have been due to the Austrian influence. Notions of diabolic witchcraft appeared first in territories on the western border and in areas with a large German-speaking population. Hungary accepted the Austrian penal code in 1696, and Austrian and German soldiers acted as accusers, if not as witch finders. Secular courts handled witchcraft cases. In this, Hungary fit the European pattern: where secular jurisdictions presided, the persecution of witches could be moderate or severe, but where ecclesiastical courts tried Satan's servants, witch hunting invariably was limited. Hungary's different religions played their parts as well: Lutherans, Catholics, and Calvinists started persecutions and imported foreign witch beliefs. In these ways, belated cultural influences go far toward explaining the late zenith of witch hunting in Hungary, as in Poland.[96] To be sure, Hungary

Table 2. Numbers of Witches Killed versus Regional Population

Country	Number Killed	Population in 1600, in millions
Austria and Bohemia	5,000–7,500	4.3
Denmark	1,000–	0.58
England and Wales	500–1,000	4.4
Estonia	65	0.06
Finland	100+	0.3–0.4
France	500	19.0
Franche-Comté	300	0.4
German Territories	15,000–20,000	16.0
Hungary	800+	3.0–3.5
Iceland	22	0.05
Ireland	8	1.4
Italy	200	13.1
Lorraine	3,000	0.4
Luxembourg	350+	0.25
Northern Netherlands	150	1.5
Norway	350+	0.44
Poland	5,000	3.4
Portugal	6	1.1
Russia	200+	12.0
Scotland	1,337+	0.8
Southern Netherlands	250	1.6
Spain	200–300	6.6–8.1
Sweden	300	1.0
Switzerland	6,000–10,000	1.0
Total	40,638–52,738	92.68–94.78

possessed popular notions of witchcraft—shamanism—and cunning folk were as plentiful as in England,[97] but it was the imposition of learned demonology that made large-scale persecution of witches possible, and also welcomed by the populace.

Witch hunting in Russia did not approach the levels of persecution characteristic of the West. Russia was unusual in having more male than female witches. In seventeenth-century Muscovy, for example, 70 percent of the witches were men.[98] While the tsar's civil courts matched Western ones in their cruelty, the restraint shown by the Russian Orthodox church meant that the number of witch trials was not great. The Russian people and the authorities certainly feared witches, but the fact that the church neither saw witchcraft as heresy nor elaborated a demonology meant that the persecution of alleged witches was not intense. The "people's courts," lynch justice, claimed many victims.[99] In 1977, Russell Zguta lamented that scholars had ignored Muscovite Russia during the era of witch hunting. His complaint can be echoed today. Zguta himself identified some major trials in the seventeenth century but declined to offer an educated guess as to the numbers executed. Two hundred executions would, I think, be an acceptable estimate for Russia.[100]

It should now be clear that the exact number of victims will never be known. Documents have disappeared; in some areas, trial records may have been destroyed along with the witch. Yet it is possible to offer several conclusions on the geography of the witch hunts. Witch hunting was an intensely local affair, a fact that makes any categorization of national patterns of witch hunting and macroestimates of executed witches nebulous to impossible. Many scholars have offered sundry estimates, but they are only conjectures. The estimates listed in table 2 mask the tremendous local variations that so characterized the witch hunts. Even so, such global figures of numbers killed, when seen as percentages of the total population, offer at least a crude measure of the intensity of witch hunting.

What have we learned from our tour of Europe? We knew already that *all* societies have practiced and do practice witchcraft, defined as the attempt to use magic—the supernatural—to influence the natural world. In this sense, witchcraft is sorcery and might include cursing, potions, foretelling the future, and faith healing. However, diabolical witchcraft was characteristic only of Europe (and the Western Hemisphere, a neo-Europe), for this witchcraft was a Christian heresy, a revolt against God and godly society. Persecution for diabolical witchcraft climaxed during the sixteenth and seventeenth centuries, and, in a few regions, in the early eighteenth century. The overwhelming majority of those accused, tried, convicted, and punished for consorting with the devil were women, victims of heightened misogyny.

The great European witch hunts took different forms and varied in magnitude throughout Europe, from Iceland to the Urals, from Scandinavia to Iberia. The learned science of demonology was virtually omnipresent, disseminated especially through universities and courts, but it had very different impacts in different regions. The strength of local beliefs, the legal system, the religion, the political structure of the state, and the social and economic contexts determined acceptance of or resistance to demonology. Patterns in individual states varied widely, and local conditions determined the extent of witch persecution.[101] The English southeast, the German southwest and the northern duchy of Mecklenburg, the lowlands of Scotland, the Basque region in Spain, Switzerland, Lorraine, Franche-Comté, the outlying provinces of France, Dalarna in Sweden, western and central Poland, and the western coast of Finland endured intensive witch hunting.[102] Considering deaths of witches in relation to the aggregate population shows Iceland and Norway to be regions of extreme witch hunting as well. Nevertheless, these groupings are tentative, for the high proportion of victims to population in many areas may simply reflect uncritical scholarship, as had been the case for France until recently. Russia, Ireland, Poland, Portugal, Hungary, and Transylvania especially need further research.

The witch hunting activities of such men as Nicolas Remy, Pierre de Lancre, and Matthew Hopkins at the local level remind us that using the state as a unit to plot the geography of witch hunts has limited benefits. The duke of Lorraine's support for Remy and the king of France's for de Lancre illustrate conclusively that centralized state control could either promote or inhibit witch hunting. The witch-hunting activity of King James VI of Scotland likewise argues that the analytical model that ties state centralization to limitations of witch hunting must be discarded,[103] even though there are numerous examples of central control working to constrain persecutions, such as in Spain and in areas of France where the Parlement of Paris could override local courts. Witch hunters were often the "triggers" that initiated witch trials.[104] As a rule, massive witch hunting occurred where tinhorn rulers and judges could vent their fears unimpeded by higher jurisdictions, no matter what the degree of governmental centralization was. Historians' emphasis on social-economic conditions, religious and legal developments, and political structures has obscured the pivotal influence of individuals, whose appearance and crusading energies cannot easily be explained by reference to the evolution of a society. Such an observation does not call for a return to a nineteenth-century historiographical emphasis on "great" men, but it does challenge the tendency to factor out elite individuals when weighing the causes for witch trials.[105] In truth, only when numerous microhistories of individual localities and witch hunts are completed will we be able to map the geography of witch hunting with any accuracy.

Generally, the intensity of witch hunting decreased with the distance from the core regions of central Europe, Iceland being one anomaly. France also was an exception, perhaps the most surprising one. France is the great example of an area close to Germany able to resist its misogynistic imperialism. Witch hunting in the Middle Ages meant that France had its own traditions of persecution and so resisted German ones. Unlike the situation in Germany, the Parlement of Paris applied torture moderately, and its judges early on evinced skepticism about demonological theory and charges against witches.[106] Rural areas in Europe saw most of the witch trials, though some towns also endured witch panics.[107] The courts of the Catholic Inquisition were milder in their treatment of witches than northern and Protestant secular courts, although Catholic courts (in Lorraine and Germany, for example) could be bestial, and Scandinavian courts could be relatively lenient.[108] Orthodox Christianity was even less fervent in hunting witches than its denominational rivals. And, of course, the Muslim Balkans escaped the witch hunts. Our ignorance of the exact number of witches killed does not argue for the insignificance of the witch hunts or the futility of comprehending the disparate nature of its geography. The witch hunts provide entrée to the most misogynistic epoch in the history of Western civilization, two centuries that saw sincere men war against the socially indigestible, while the geography of European witchcraft points to profound societal distinctions throughout the Continent as well as avenues of cultural and intellectual dissemination. This was an age that abhorred tolerance and viewed the persecution of certain groups—women, homosexuals, Gypsies, Jews, different Christians, vagabonds—as a duty. It was not the best of times, but nearly the worst.

Notes

I thank David Nichols, Denis Paz, and Michael Wolfe for their suggestions and help. I am especially grateful to Lawrence Estaville, whose invitation to give a talk as part of a lecture series on geography and history led me to this topic; and to Mack Holt, whose careful reading of this essay reshaped my approach. More preferable and accurate than *witch-craze* is the term *era of witch-hunts* because it encompasses the episodic and sporadic nature of the hunts for alleged witches in early modern Europe.

1. Europeans also applied the word *synagogue* to these gatherings of witches, thus reflecting their animus toward Jews. See Joshua Trachtenberg, *The Devil and the*

Jews: The Medieval Conception of the Jew and Its Relation to Modern Anti-Semitism (New Haven: Yale University Press, 1943), pp. 210, 214–15; Russell Hope Robbins, *The Encyclopedia of Witchcraft and Demonology* (New York: Crown, 1959), pp. 414–24; Carlo Ginzburg, *Ecstasies: Deciphering the Witches' Sabbath* (New York: Random House, 1991).

2. Montague Summers, Introduction to *Demoniality,* by Ludovico Maria Sinistrari (New York: Benjamin Blom, 1972), p. xliii.

3. In H. R. Trevor-Roper, *The European Witch-Craze of the Sixteenth and Seventeenth Centuries and Other Essays* (New York: Harper & Row, 1969), pp. 90–192.

4. Brian P. Levack, *The Witch-Hunt in Early Modern Europe,* 2d ed. (London: Longman, 1995).

5. I refer to Germany, nonexistent as a political unit, because of the Holy Roman Empire's changing geography and because many areas of the empire were sovereign in all but name. Because European witch hunting endured in different degrees in diverse parts of Europe from the fifteenth to the eighteenth centuries, the use of omnibus political or geographical terms can obscure the situation.

6. Levack noted the possibility of using such a ratio in a more recent work, "The Great Witch-Hunt," in *Handbook of European History, 1400–1600: Late Middle Ages, Renaissance and Reformation,* ed. Thomas A. Brady, Jr., Heiko A. Oberman, and James D. Tracy (Leiden: E. J. Brill, 1995), p. 617, which lead him to acknowledge a higher intensity of witch hunting in Scotland.

7. Levack, *The Witch-Hunt in Early Modern Europe,* pp. 231–32.

8. I thank Mack Holt, who indicated this to me. On the *Carolina,* see John Langbein, *Prosecuting Crime in the Renaissance: England, France, Germany* (Cambridge: Harvard University Press, 1974), pp. 129ff. On restraints on the application of torture, see Langbein, *Torture and the Law of Proof: Europe and England in the Ancien Régime* (Chicago: University of Chicago Press, 1976), chap. 1.

9. On the historiography, see Leland L. Estes, "Incarnations of Evil: Changing Perspectives of the European Witch Craze," *Clio* 13.2 (1984): 133–47.

10. Anne Llewellyn Barstow, *Witchcraze: A New History of the European Witch Hunts* (San Francisco: HarperCollins, 1994), p. 69. For a contrary view, see Jean-Michel Sallmann, "Witches," in *Renaissance and Enlightenment Paradoxes,* ed. Natalie Zemon Davis and Arlette Farge, vol. 3 of *A History of Women in the West,* ed. Georges Duby and Michelle Perrot (Cambridge: Harvard University Press, 1993), p. 451.

11. Adding up the specific figures in Barstow's lists (culled from historians' local studies) gives 76 percent female for those accused and 83 percent for those executed (*Witchcraze,* pp. 179–81).

12. Christina Larner, *Enemies of God: The Witch-Hunt in Scotland* (Baltimore: The Johns Hopkins University Press, 1981), pp. 15–16.

13. H. C. Erik Midelfort, "Heartland of the Witchcraze: Central and Northern Europe," *History Today* 31 (February 1981): 27–31.

14. For the lower estimate, see Wolfgang Behringer, " 'Erhob sich das ganze Land zu ihrer Ausrottung': Hexenprozesse und Hexenverfolgungen in Europa," in

Hexenwelten: Magie und Imagination vom 16.–20. Jahrhundert, ed. Richard van Dül-
men (Frankfurt: Fischer Taschenbuch Verlag, 1987), p. 165. For higher estimates,
see Robbins, *Encyclopedia,* p. 215; Rosemary Ellen Guiley, *The Encyclopedia of Witches
and Witchcraft* (New York: Facts on File, 1989), p. 369. Gerhard Schormann sensi-
bly suggested between 30,000 and 100,000 accused, in *Hexenprozess in Deutschland*
(Göttingen: Vandenhoeck & Ruprecht, 1981), 71. The number killed was far less,
though execution rates in Germany generally exceeded those elsewhere in Europe.
The lower figure of those accused, 30,000, derives from the dossiers a special unit
(*Hexen-Sonderkommando*) of the SS collected, under Henrich Himmler's directions,
that detail early modern German witch trials. The papers, however, sometimes
contain more than one witch's name; hence the figure of 30,000 is far too low.
Wolfgang Krämer gives a ludicrous estimate of 500,000 victims for the German-
speaking lands (*Kurtrierische Hexenprozesse im 16. und 17. Jahrhundert* [Munich:
Scharl, 1959], p. 105), exceeded only by William J. Bossenbrook's guess of 1
million killed in Germany between 1575 and 1700, in *The German Mind* (Detroit:
Wayne State University Press, 1961), p. 198.

15. Joseph Klaits, *Servants of Satan: The Age of the Witch Hunts* (Bloomington:
Indiana University Press, 1985), p. 138; and E. William Monter, *Witchcraft in
France and Switzerland: The Borderlands during the Reformation* (Ithaca: Cornell Uni-
versity Press, 1976), p. 191.

16. H. C. Erik Midelfort, *Witch Hunting in Southwestern Germany, 1562–1684:
The Social and Intellectual Foundations* (Stanford: Stanford University Press, 1972),
p. 32.

17. Midelfort, "Heartland of the Witchcraze," p. 28.

18. Hans Sebold, "Nazi Ideology Redefining Deviants: Witches, Himmler's
Witch-Trial Survey, and the Case of the Bishop of Bamberg," *Deviant Behavior* 10
(1989): 260, 264–65.

19. Schormann, *Hexenprozess in Deutschland,* p. 66.

20. For the low incidence of witchcraft executions in Augsburg, for example, see
Lyndal Roper, "Magic and the Theology of the Body: Exorcism in Sixteenth-
Century Augsburg," in *No Gods Except Me: Orthodoxy and Religious Practice in Europe,
1200–1600,* ed. Charles Zika (Parkville, Victoria, Australia: University of Melbourne, History Department, 1991), p. 93.

21. Localities in Germany—and throughout Europe—sometimes varied greatly
in the sex ratio of the accusers, the accused, and those tried and convicted. On
the Saar region (1575–1634), where 80 percent of the accusers were men but
130 of the 157 men tried were executed, see Eva von Labouvie, "Männer in Hexenprozess: Zur Sozialanthropologie eines männlichen' Verständnisses von Magie
und Hexerei," *Geschichte und Gesellschaft* 16.1 (1990): 66, 69. In the prince-
bishopric of Bamberg only 28 percent of the cases involved males; see Sebald, "Nazi
Ideology."

22. Robin Briggs, *Communities of Belief: Cultural and Social Tensions in Early
Modern France* (Oxford: Oxford University Press, 1989), pp. 67, 83.

23. On conditions in Lorraine, see Guy Cabourdin, *Terres et hommes en Lorraine,* 2 vols. (Nancy: Presses Universitaires de Nancy, 1984).

24. Charles Pfister, "Nicolas Remy et la sorcellerie en Lorraine à la fin du XVI siècle," *Revue historique* 93.3 (1907): 234.

25. Nicolas Remy, *Demonolatry,* trans. E. A. Ashwin, ed. Montague Summers (Secaucus, N.J.: University Books, 1974), pp. 184, 188.

26. Lucien Dintzer, "Nicolas Remy, le Torquemada Lorrain," *Le Pays Lorrain* (22 July 1930): 402, 404.

27. R. J. W. Evans, *The Making of the Habsburg Monarchy, 1550–1700* (Oxford: Oxford University Press, 1979), p. 417. Edmund Kern explained how a Lutheran witch hunter operated in a region where the Habsburg government was attempting to reintroduce Catholicism, thus underscoring the paramount importance of a dedicated individual who had the power to bring accused witches to justice, in "Confessional Identity and Magic in the Late Sixteenth Century: Jakob Bithner and Witchcraft in Styria," *Sixteenth Century Journal* 25.2 (1994): 323–40.

28. Marijke Gijswijt-Hofstra, "Six Centuries of Witchcraft in the Netherlands: Themes, Outlines, and Interpretations," in *Witchcraft in the Netherlands from the Fourteenth to the Twentieth Century,* ed. Marijke Gijswijt-Hofstra and Willem Frijhoff (Rotterdam: Universitaire Pers Rotterdam, 1991), pp. 27–30.

29. Marie-Sylvie Dupont-Bouchat, "La répression de la sorcellerie dans le duché de Luxembourg aux XVIe et XVIIe siècles," in *Prophètes et sorciers dans les Pays-Bas XVIe–XVIIe siècles,* ed. Dupont-Bouchat, Willem Frijhoff, and Robert Muchembled (Paris: Hachette, 1978), pp. 127, 138.

30. Behringer, "Erhob sich das ganze Land," pp. 161–63. Behringer believes that Guido Bader's figure of 5,417 executions (*Die Hexenprozesse in der Schweiz* [Affoltern: Buchdruckerei Dr. J. Weiss, 1945], p. 219) should be raised, perhaps to a five-digit number.

31. Peter Kamber, "La chasse aux sorciers et aux sorcières dans le pays de Vaud. Aspects quantitatifs (1581–1620)," *Revue historique vaudoise* 90 (1982): 22–23; E. William Monter, *Ritual, Myth and Magic in Early Modern Europe* (Athens: Ohio University Press, 1983), pp. 47–48.

32. Monter, *Witchcraft in France and Switzerland,* pp. 194–95.

33. E. William Monter, "French and Italian Witchcraft," *History Today* 30 (November 1980): 31; Monter, *Ritual, Myth and Magic,* p. 87.

34. Robert Muchembled, *Sorcières, justice et société aux 16e et 17e siècles* (Paris: Editions Imago, 1987), p. 10.

35. See in particular his "Lay Judges and the Acculturation of the Masses (France and the Southern Low Countries, Sixteenth to Eighteenth Centuries)," in *Religion and Society in Early Modern Europe, 1500–1800,* ed. Kaspar von Greyerz (London: George Allen & Unwin, 1984), pp. 56–65; and *Les Temps des supplices: De l'obéissance sous les rois absolus, XVe–XVIIIe siècle* (Paris: Armand Colin, 1992), pp. 129–85. For a critique, see Jean Wirth, "Against the Acculturation Thesis," in Greyerz, *Religion and Society in Early Modern Europe,* pp. 66–78; and Briggs, *Communities of Belief,* pp. 53–57.

36. Alfred Soman, "Decriminalizing Witchcraft: Does the French Experience Furnish a European Model?" *Criminal Justice History* 10 (1989): 5. In addition, Soman noted nearly six hundred other cases in the jurisdiction of the Parlement of Paris that are known only indirectly; see "La Décriminalisation de la sorcellerie en France" *Histoire, économie, société* 4.2 (1985): 181. Soman discussed sources and research techniques in other articles in his *Sorcellerie et justice criminelle: Le Parlement de Paris (16e–18e siècles)* (Aldershot, England: Variorum, 1992).

37. Soman's figures, cited by Briggs, *Communities of Belief*, p. 10.

38. See Nancy Roelker, *"One King, One Faith": The Parlement of Paris and the Reformations of the Sixteenth Century* (Berkeley: University of California Press, 1996).

39. Briggs, *Communities of Belief*, p. 10. In fact, so great is the problem with sources that many scholars discussing specifically French witchcraft do not even venture an estimate. See Monter, "French and Italian Witchcraft," pp. 31–35; Muchembled, *Sorcières, justice et société*; and Nicole Jacques-Chaquin, "Sorcellerie, sorciers," in *Dictionnaire du Grand Siècle*, ed. François Bluche (Paris: Fayard, 1990), pp. 1459–60.

40. William Monter suggests five hundred (personal conversation, January 1995); Soman, "Witch Lynching at Juneville," *Natural History* 95.10 (October 1986): 6–15, 108. For Europe as a whole, see Richard A. Horsley, "Further Reflections on Witchcraft and European Folk Religion," *History of Religions* 19 (August 1979): 91.

41. Robert Mandrou, *Magistrats et sorciers en France au XVII siècle: Une analyse de psychologie historique* (Paris: Plon, 1968), pp. 197–261; on Cadiere and Girard, see B. Robert Kreiser, "The Devils of Toulon: Demonic Possession and Religious Politics in Eighteenth-Century Provence," in *Church, State, and Society under the Bourbon Kings of France*, ed. Richard M. Golden (Lawrence, Kans.: Coronado Press, 1982), pp. 173–221.

42. See Sophie Houdard, *Les sciences du diable: Quatre discours sur la sorcellerie* (Paris: Editions du Cerf, 1992); and Nicole Jacques-Chaquin, "Représentations du corps sorcier à l'âge classique," *Revue des sciences humaines* 49.198 (1985): 51–68.

43. Nicole Jacques-Chaquin, "Demoniac Conspiracy," in *Changing Conceptions of Conspiracy*, ed. Carl F. Graumann and Serge Moscovici (New York: Springer Verlag, 1987), p. 77.

44. D. P. Walker, *Unclean Spirits: Possession and Exorcism in France and England in the Late Sixteenth and Seventeenth Centuries* (Philadelphia: University of Pennsylvania Press, 1981), pp. 36–37, 40; Sarah Ferber, "The Demonic Possession of Marthe Brossier, France 1598–1600," in *No Gods Except Me: Orthodoxy and Religious Practice in Europe, 1200–1600*, ed. George Zika (Parkville, Victoria, Australia: University of Melbourne, History Department, 1991), p. 59.

45. Houdard, *Les sciences du diable*, pp. 162ff. See also Gerhild Scholz Williams, *Defining Dominion: The Discourses of Magic and Witchcraft in Early Modern France and Germany* (Ann Arbor: University of Michigan Press, 1995), pp. 89–119.

46. Pierre de Lancre, *Tableau de l'Inconstance des mauvais anges et démons. Où il est*

amplement traicté des Sorciers, et de la Sorcellerie. Livre tres-utile et necessaire non seulement aux Iuges, mais à tous ceux qui vivent sous les loix Chrestiennes. Avec un discours contenant la Procedure faite par les Inquisiteurs d'Espagne et de Navarre, à 53. Magiciens, Apostats, Iuifs et Sorciers, en la ville de Logrogne en Castille, le 9. Novembre 1610. En laquelle on voit combien l'exercice de la Iustice en France, est plus iuridiquement traicté, et avec de plus belles formes qu'en tous autres Empires, Royaumes, Republiques et Estats. Par Pierre de Lancre, Conseiller du Roy au Parlement de Bordeaux. Maleficos non patrieris vivere. Exod. 22. Revue, corrigé, et augmenté de plusieurs nouvelles observations, Arrests, et autres choses notables. (Paris, 1613), p. 38.

47. Pierre de Lancre, *L'Incredulité et mescreance du sortilege plainement convaincue. Où il est amplement et curieusement traicté, de la verité ou Illusion du Sortilege, de la Fascination, de l'Attouchement, du Scopelisme, de la Divination, se la Ligature ou Liaison Magique, des Apparitions: Et d'une infinitié d'autres rares et nouveaux subjects. Par de L'Ancre conceiller du Roy en son Conseil d'Estat* (Paris, 1622), p. 401.

48. E.g., Charles Alva Hoyt, *Witchcraft* (Carbondale: Southern Illinois University Press, 1981), p. 64; Robbins, *Encyclopedia,* p. 298; and Guiley, *Encyclopedia of Witches,* p. 193. Henry Charles Lea casts doubt on this total; see *Materials toward a History of Witchcraft,* ed. Arthur Charles Howland, 3 vols. (Philadelphia: University of Pennsylvania Press, 1939), 3:1294; Briggs traced the myth of the six hundred to a 1695 pamphlet, in *Communities of Belief,* p. 11. Jean Palou estimated five hundred in *La Sorcellerie* (Paris: PUF, 1957), p. 65.

49. Nicole Jacques-Chaquin, introduction to *Tableau de l'inconstance des mauvais anges et démons,* by Pierre de Lancre (Paris: Aubier, 1982), p. 11; Briggs, *Communities of Belief,* p. 11.

50. Gustav Henningsen, *The Witches' Advocate: Basque Witchcraft and the Spanish Inquisition (1609–1614)* (Reno: University of Nevada Press, 1980), p. 22; E. William Monter, *Frontiers of Heresy: The Spanish Inquisition from the Basque Lands to Sicily* (Cambridge: Cambridge University Press, 1990), pp. 267–69.

51. Gustav Henningsen, "The Papers of Alonso de Salazar Frias. A Spanish Witchcraft Polemic, 1610–14," *Temenos* 5 (1969): 86.

52. Cited in Henningsen, *The Witches' Advocate,* p. ix.

53. Gustav Henningsen, "The Greatest Witch-Trial of All: Navarre, 1609–14," *History Today* 30 (November 1980): 36–39.

54. Henningsen, *The Witches' Advocate,* pp. 386–88.

55. Monter, *Frontiers of Heresy,* p. 274.

56. Monter, *Ritual, Myth and Magic,* p. 69.

57. See Henry Kamen, *Inquisition and Society in Spain in the Sixteenth and Seventeenth Centuries* (Bloomington: Indiana University Press, 1985); Kamen, "500 years of the Spanish Inquisition," *History Today* 31 (February 1981): 37–41; Edward Peters, *Inquisition* (New York: Free Press, 1988); Monter, *Frontiers of Heresy,* p. 74.

58. Francisco Bethencourt, "Portugal: A Scrupulous Inquisition," in *Early Modern European Witchcraft: Centres and Peripheries,* ed. Bengt Ankarloo and Gustav Henningsen (Oxford: Oxford University Press, 1990), pp. 403–22.

59. The classic study outlining this distinction is Edwards Evans-Pritchard, *Witchcraft, Oracles and Magic among the Azande* (Oxford: Oxford University Press, 1937).

60. David Gentilcore, *From Bishop to Witch: The System of the Sacred in Early Modern Terra d'Otranto* (Manchester: Manchester University Press, 1992), p. 12.

61. Monter, *Ritual, Myth and Magic,* p. 64.

62. John Tedeschi, "Inquisitorial Law and the Witch," in *Early Modern European Witchcraft: Centres and Peripheries,* ed. B. Ankarloo and G. Henningsen (Oxford: Oxford University Press, 1990), pp. 83–118.

63. Tedeschi, "Preliminary Observations on Writing a History of the Roman Inquisition," in *Continuity and Discontinuity in Church History,* ed. F. F. Church and T. George (Leiden: E. J. Brill, 1979), p. 242. On the relative mildness of the various Italian inquisitions, see E. William Monter and John Tedeschi, "Towards a Statistical Profile of the Italian Inquisitions, 16th to 18th Centuries," in *The Inquisition in Early Modern Europe: Studies on Sources and Methods,* ed. Gustav Henningsen and John Tedeschi (DeKalb: Northern Illinois University Press, 1986), pp. 130–57.

64. Ruth Martin, *Witchcraft and the Inquisition in Venice, 1550–1600* (London: Basil Blackwell, 1989), pp. 253–55.

65. Gustav Henningsen, " 'The Ladies from Outside': An Archaic Pattern of the Witches' Sabbath," in *Early Modern European Witchcraft: Centres and Peripheries,* ed. B. Ankarloo and Henningsen (Oxford: Oxford University Press, 1990), pp. 193–94.

66. Larner, *Enemies of God,* p. 65; Christina Larner, "Witch Beliefs and Witch-Hunting in England and Scotland," *History Today* 31 (February 1981): 33, gives five hundred as a ceiling. Other historians have set the total at less than one thousand, beginning with C. L'Estrange Ewen in *Witch Hunting and Witch Trials* (London: F. Muller, 1929), p. 112; and, more recently, Robbins, *Encyclopedia,* p. 164; Keith Thomas, *Religion and the Decline of Magic* (New York: Charles Scribner's Sons, 1971), p. 450; Marianne Hester, *Lewd Women and Wicked Witches: A Study of the Dynamics of Male Domination* (London: Routledge, 1992), p. 128.

67. For a challenge to this chronology, see Janet A. Thompson, *Wives, Widows, Witches and Bitches: Women in Seventeenth-Century Devon* (New York: Peter Lang, 1993), pp. 101–2. Local studies continue to confront regional and national generalizations, demonstrating that a micro approach to witch hunting is optimal, though unrealizable.

68. See J. O. Jones, "Matthew Hopkins—Witchfinder," in *The Lives of Twelve Bad Men,* ed. Thomas Secombe (London, 1894), pp. 55–66; Richard Deacon, *Matthew Hopkins: Witch Finder General* (London: F. Muller, 1976). In *The Discovery of Witches* (London, 1647), Hopkins denied that he had hunted witches for profit.

69. Richard Bernard, *A Guide to Grand-Jury Men* (London, 1627), p. 112.

70. Larner, *Enemies of God,* p. 63.

71. Larner, "Witch Beliefs and Witch-Hunting in England and Scotland," p. 36.

72. Larner, *Enemies of God,* pp. 89, 91, 200–201.

73. See the first written account of Scottish witchcraft in the anonymous *Newes from Scotland. Declaring the Damnable life and Death of Doctor Fian, a notable Sorcerer, who was burned at Edenborough January last* (Edinburgh, 1591).

74. James VI, *Daemonologie* (Edinburgh, 1597), p. ix.

75. Christina Larner, "James VI and I and Witchcraft," in *The Reign of James VI and I*, ed. Alan G. R. Smith (New York: St. Martin's Press, 1973), pp. 74–90. See also Deborah Willis, *Malevolent Nurture: Witch-Hunting and Maternal Power in Early Modern England* (Ithaca: Cornell University Press, 1995), pp. 123–58.

76. Robbins, *Encyclopedia*, p. 275.

77. G. R. Quaiffe, *Godly Zeal and Furious Rage: The Witch in Early Modern Europe* (New York: St. Martin's Press, 1987), p. 47.

78. Kirsten Hastrup, "Iceland: Sorcerers and Paganism," in *Early Modern European Witchcraft: Centres and Peripheries* (Oxford: Oxford University Press, 1990), ed. B. Ankarloo and G. Henningsen, pp. 383–401. Barstow failed to consider this point for any locale except Scotland (*Witchcraze*, pp. 58, 76–77). A comparison of the intensity of witch hunting throughout Europe necessitates attention to population. For example, if France, with its population of nineteen million in 1600, had the same degree of witch hunting as did Iceland, approximately 8,360 witches would have been killed; for England the number would be 1,936, almost four times the number actually executed.

79. Soman, "Decriminalizing Witchcraft," p. 14.

80. Jens Christian V. Johansen, "Denmark: The Sociology of Accusations," in *Early Modern European Witchcraft: Centres and Peripheries,* ed. B. Ankarloo and G. Henningsen (Oxford: Oxford University Press, 1990), pp. 340–41.

81. Gustav Henningsen, "Witchcraft in Denmark," *Folklore* 93.2 (1982): 135.

82. E. William Monter, "Scandinavian Witchcraft in Anglo-American Perspective," in *Early Modern European Witchcraft: Centres and Peripheries,* ed. B. Ankarloo and G. Henningsen (Oxford: Oxford University Press, 1990), p. 427.

83. Henningsen, "Witchcraft in Denmark," p. 135; A. D. J. Macfarlane, *Witchcraft in Tudor and Stuart England* (London: Routledge & Kegan Paul, 1970), p. 160. On Danish misogyny, see Inga Dahlsgard, "Witch-Hunts and Absolutism in Ancient Denmark," *Cultures* 8.4 (1982): 32–40.

84. Hans Eyvind Naess, "Norway: The Criminological Context," in *Early Modern European Witchcraft: Centres and Peripheries,* ed. B. Ankarloo and G. Henningsen (Oxford: Oxford University Press, 1990), pp. 371–72.

85. Ibid., pp. 378–79.

86. Monter, "Scandinavian Witchcraft," pp. 427–28.

87. Bengt Ankarloo, "Sweden: The Mass Burnings (1668–1676)," in *Early Modern European Witchcraft: Centres and Peripheries,* ed. B. Ankarloo and G. Henningsen (Oxford: Oxford University Press, 1990), pp 285–86, 288–91.

88. Ibid., pp. 292–317; Birgitta Lagerlöf-Génetay, *De svenska häxprocessernas utbrottsskede 1668–1671. Bakgrund i Övre Dalarna. Social och eckesiastik kontext* (Stockholm: Almquist & Wiskell International, 1990), pp. 211–23 (English summary).

89. Eino Jutikkala and Kauko Pirinen, *A History of Finland* (New York: Praeger, 1962), p. 131.

90. For exact known numbers, see Antero Heikkinen and Timo Kervinen, "Finland: The Male Domination," in *Early Modern European Witchcraft: Centres and Peripheries,* ed. B. Ankarloo and G. Henningsen (Oxford: Oxford University Press, 1990), pp. 319–21.

91. Ibid., pp. 322–24, 329–30, 336–37; Antero Heikkinen, *Paholaisen Liittolaiset Noita-ja magakäsityksiä ja-oikeudenkäyntejä Suomessa 1600-luvun jälkipuolella (n. 1640–1712),* Historiallisia tutkimuksia, 78 (Helsinki, 1969), pp. 374–94 (English summary).

92. Mala Madar, "Estonia I: Werewolves and Poisoners," and Juhan Kahk, "Estonia II: The Crusade against Idolatry," in *Early Modern European Witchcraft: Centres and Peripheries,* ed. B. Ankarloo and G. Henningsen (Oxford: Oxford University Press, 1990), respectively, pp. 257–72 and pp. 273–84.

93. Bohdan Baranowski, *Procesy Czarnowic w Polsce w XVII i XVIII wieku* (Lodz: Zaklad im. Ossolinskich we Wrocladiu, 1952), pp. 178–81 (French summary).

94. Interestingly, Von Janusz Tazbir stated that these factors prevented a high number of witches from being killed, but then accepted Baranowski's estimates ("Hexenprozesse in Polen," *Archiv für Reformationgeschichte* 71 [1980]: 281, 296–99). Behringer believes the number of executions ran to several thousand (see "Erhob sich das ganze Land," p. 155).

95. Gabor Klaniczay, "Hungary: The Accusations and the Universe of Popular Magic," in *Early Modern European Witchcraft: Centres and Peripheries,* ed. B. Ankarloo and G. Henningsen (Oxford: Oxford University Press, 1990), pp. 220–21, 223. Transylvania, Moldavia, and Wallachia have not yet been systematically studied. See Henry Charles Lea, *Materials toward a History of Witchcraft,* pp. 1259ff.

96. Klaniczay, "Hungary," pp. 222, 226–30; András Iklódy, "A magyarországi boszorkányüldözés történeti alakulása," *Ethnographia* 93 (1982): 298 (English summary).

97. Tekla Dömötör, "The Cunning Folk in English and Hungarian Witch Trials," in *Folklore Studies in the Twentieth Century: Proceedings of the Centenary of the Folklore Society,* ed. Venetia J. Newell (Woodbridge: Rowman and Littlefield, 1980), pp. 183–87. On shamanism in Hungary, see Klaniczay, "Hungary," pp. 244–55; and Gabor Klaniczay, *The Uses of Supernatural Power: The Transformation of Popular Religion in Medieval and Early-Modern Europe* (Princeton: Princeton University Press, 1989), pp. 129–50.

98. Valerie A. Kivelson, "Through the Prism of Witchcraft: Gender and Social Change in Seventeenth-Century Muscovy," in *Russia's Women: Accommodation, Resistance, Transformation,* ed. Barbara Evans Clements, Barbara Alpern Engel, and Christine D. Worobec (Berkeley: University of California Press, 1991), p. 75.

99. Zoltán Kovács, "Die Hexen in Russland," *Acta Ethnographica Academiae Scientarium Hungaricae* 22 (1973): 73.

100. Russell Zguta, "Was There a Witch Craze in Muscovite Russia?" *Southern Folklore Quarterly* 41 (1977): 119–28.

101. A point Joseph Klaits emphasized nicely in demonstrating that local conditions, not Louis XIV's absolutist state, bear responsibility for the decline of witch hunting in Alsace; see "Witchcraft Trials and Absolute Monarchy in Alsace," in *Church, State, and Society under the Bourbon Kings of France,* ed. Richard M. Golden (Lawrence, Kans.: Coronado Press, 1982), pp. 163–64.

102. Brian Levack stressed the unevenness of witch hunting within European states in *Witchcraft in Continental Europe: Local and Regional Studies,* ed. Levack vol. 5 of *Witchcraft, Magic and Demonology,* 12 vols. (New York: Garland, 1992), pp. ix–x.

103. The fact that Europe became a "persecuting society" in the Middle Ages precisely when rulers commenced to strengthen their dominions should lead historians to question a facile equation between strength at the center and impediments against persecution. On the development of persecution, see R. I. Moore, *The Formation of a Persecuting Society: Power and Deviance in Western Europe, 950–1250* (Oxford: Basil Blackwell, 1987), which argues that in the eleventh and twelfth centuries, "persecution became habitual. . . . [D]eliberate and socially sanctioned violence began to be directed, *through established governmental, judicial and social institutions,* against groups of people defined by general characteristics" (p. 5). On the other hand, the unfolding of religious toleration speaks to influence from the top down and from the center to the periphery. Toleration as anathema—even its historical linguistic meaning connotes the bearing or suffering of something evil— was so deeply ingrained in Christian civilization that only gradual state intervention could force a resistant population to abide those who embraced unconventional beliefs.

104. Marijke Gijswijt-Hofstra, "The European Witchcraft Debate and the Dutch Variant," *Social History* 15 (January 1990): 187.

105. Hilde De Ridder-Symoens pointed out that human qualities, such as sadism, religious zealotry, misuse of power, corruption, and psychopathy, could determine local panics; see "Intellectual and Political Backgrounds of the Witch-Craze in Europe," in *La Sorcellerie dans les Pays-Bas sous l'ancien régime: Aspects juridiques, institutionnels et sociaux,* ed. Sylvie Dupont-Bouchat (Belgium, Kortrijk-Heule: UGA, 1987), p. 57.

106. Alfred Soman, "Les procès de sorcellerie au parlement de Paris (1565– 1640)," *Annales: Économies, sociétés, civilisations* 22 (1977): 804; Soman, "The Parlement of Paris and the Great Witch Hunt (1565–1640)," *Sixteenth Century Journal* 9.2 (1978): 44.

107. The Northern and Southern Netherlands, the German regions, and Switzerland experienced witch hunting (see Gijswijt-Hofstra, "The European Witchcraft Debate and the Dutch Variant," 192; Monter, *Witchcraft in France and Switzerland*). Of course, the rural location of witch hunts reflected where most people lived. For example, 85 percent of Danish witch trials took place in the countryside, home to between 80 and 90 percent of Denmark's population (Jens Christian V. Johansen, "Witchcraft in Elsinore 1625–1626," *Mentalities* 3 [1985]: 1).

108. Yves Castan noted clearly the link between governmental power in large states and the ability to moderate witch hunting and, concurrently, the tendency of strong ecclesiastical organizations (the inquisitions) to militate against an aggressive pursuit of witches; see *Magie et sorcellerie à l'époque moderne* (Paris: Albin Michel, 1979), pp. 19, 50.

Alfred Soman

Anatomy of an Infanticide Trial: The Case of Marie-Jeanne Bartonnet (1742)

Infanticide, one of the fundamental taboos of Christian civilization, played an astonishingly large role in French criminal justice under the Old Regime. Research in the archives of the Parlement of Paris (the high court of appeal for a population of eight to twelve million: half of France) indicates that from the sixteenth century to the eighteenth, approximately 1,500 women—and only a handful of men—were executed for the crime of child murder. At the height of the "infanticide craze" (roughly 1565–1690) this single crime accounted for two-thirds of all women condemned to death at common law. Its share of *all* death sentences pronounced by the parlement was never less than 18 percent and rose as high as 34 percent—in other words, one hanging in three.[1]

If the magnitude of the "infanticide craze" is surprising, no less so is the definition of the crime that sent so many Frenchwomen to the scaffold. We are not talking about a broad range of crimes involving the killing of young children; nor about accidental or fraudulent deaths of infants at the hands of their nurses, wicked stepmothers, or brutal stepfathers; nor the taking of abortive brews and potions in order to terminate pregnancies; nor even the murder by its parents of an unwanted baby—malformed, or who could not be fed, or who was, to their regret and disappointment, a girl. All these offenses were matters of deep concern to neighbors and to the authorities, but since most were not susceptible of legal proof, they never came to court, except, occasionally, as crimes peripheral to some other charge. The abandonment of newborn babies in public places was also a major problem, punished with varying degrees of severity though never by hanging, even when the child died from exposure; a mother who left her infant in a basket outside a church or hospital was obviously not guilty of premeditated murder. Homicides of stepchildren are not altogether absent from the archives, but among the hundreds of infanticide (and abandonment) trials I have examined, in not a single case did the prosecution or the defense suggest that the motive for the crime was Malthusian—infanticide as a primitive form of contraception—or sexist (when a female baby was concerned). Infanticide undoubtedly occurred for such reasons; so, too, the murder of disfigured infants; and yet no such cases seem to have been prosecuted.

The crime designated "infanticide" (*homicide de son enfant*) was uniformly of one type (which either excluded or absorbed all other forms of child murder): a woman conceived a child illegitimately, concealed her pregnancy, gave birth in secret, and then killed her baby or deliberately let it die in a desperate attempt to suppress the evidence of her shame and dishonor. In a sample of 291 cases (in fourteen years between 1569 and 1608), the accused was usually unmarried (63 percent), and most often a domestic servant; 13 percent were married women whose husbands were absent; and 18 percent were young widows. The women invariably claimed that their babies were stillborn or had died of natural causes. In nine trials out of ten, the mother was the sole defendant. Accomplices were rare, the father of the victim being far less commonly accused than its maternal grandmother. Witchcraft, contrary to a widespread misconception, was an issue never even raised.[2]

This narrow definition of the crime can be traced back to the fourteenth- and fifteenth-century letters of remission studied by Y.-B. Brissaud, where it was already the sole type of infanticide to be found in the archives of the royal chancellery. Then, in the aftermath of the Hundred Years' War and consequent on the increasing centralization of French justice, child murder—together with all capital crimes except certain homicides—ceased to be remissible; like other common-law offenses it came within the competence of the sovereign courts, namely the parlements.[3]

Not until the 1530s, however, do the archives of the Parlement of Paris begin to reflect its new role as appellate court for definitive sentences rendered throughout its jurisdiction by subalternate courts. The new style of record keeping, introduced tentatively in 1535 and permanently in 1539, enables researchers to observe the parlement's jurisprudence with respect to infanticide on the eve of Henry II's famous edict on the subject in February 1556/57. The problem confronting the courts was that the crime was extremely difficult to prove unless the judges resorted to torture, whereas French justice, in an effort to enhance its public image, was in the process of eliminating torture from routine judicial procedure. The confession rate under ritual application of physical pain had already fallen to less than 10 percent and was to decline further to a mere 2 percent by 1620.[4]

The reduction in the violence of torture was not primarily for humanitarian reasons, although there are clear signs, as early as the mid-sixteenth century, of a definite squeamishness regarding pain and physical mutilation.[5] Far more important was the aim to make judicial procedure what the French today would call "transparent," that is to say, clear and aboveboard. The goal of the high magistracy was to utilize common-law criminal justice as a showcase for the monarchy. The excellence of criminal justice in France—the only country in Europe where all sentences (except temporary banishment) were automatically appealed, and the accused was present *in person* when his or her case was reviewed by the highest judges in the land—would redound to the credit of the king as a perfect incarnation of *le roi justicier* (the king as judge).

In the interests of judicial transparency, a scrupulous policy of attenuated torture was given priority, and so the attack on the "wave" of child murders that seemed to threaten the foundations of society took the form of a redefinition of the evidentiary rules, making infanticide the first and only "special case" (*crimen exceptum*) in French law. Thenceforth, in the case of a dead infant, a concealed pregnancy and a clandestine delivery were no longer mere presumptions of guilt; the royal edict of February 1557 declared them to be conclusive proof of guilt, and torture was discontinued in infanticide trials.

The edict begins with a short preamble on the importance of baptism and Christian burial, and deplores infanticide, which effectively deprives a newborn child of these two sacraments.

When they appear before our judges, women accused of this crime say they were ashamed to reveal their fault [namely, an illegitimate conception] and that their babies were stillborn. In the absence of any proof of these statements, the judges are of two minds: some opt for the death penalty; others for torture, in order to learn from these women's mouths whether the fruit of their wombs was indeed alive or dead at birth. But because they do not confess under torture, they are released from prison, free to commit the same offense again. We therefore decree that, for the future, any woman who shall be duly convicted of having concealed both her pregnancy and her confinement, without having declared either one or the other, and without sufficient witness to one or the other, and in particular shall not be able to produce evidence of the life or death of her child as it came forth from her womb, and afterward it shall be found that the child was deprived of the holy sacrament of baptism and of public Christian burial, such a woman shall henceforth be considered to have murdered her child and shall be put to death.[6]

The edict remained in force until it was repealed in 1791. Although the statute did not specifically make such a provision, it soon became obligatory for every parish priest in the realm to read the text from his pulpit at regular intervals—once a month or once every three months—so that ignorance of the law could not be claimed as an excuse. Unlike the long series of ineffective legislation against dueling, the single promulgation in 1557 was sufficient. A woman who destroyed her baby to save her honor was guilty of a compound offense: "killing a child conceived in crime."[7] She was the epitome of the "bad girl," enveloped in an unholy nimbus of sexual profligacy, venereal disease, blatant social ambitions, blackmail, and stolen linen—a stand-in, if you will, for all the criminals right-minded people dreaded and could not punish. By "right-minded people" I mean, of course, the huge portion of the population believing itself to be law-abiding and respectful of the values of honor, property, and the social hierarchy. As the future would show, the French judiciary (from parlements down to village courts) was satisfied with its new infanticide law. Indeed, the satisfaction must have extended to the vast majority of the king's subjects (all those "right-minded people"), for, in a state without a police force, criminal justice could hardly have been imposed from above on an unwilling population.[8]

Within ten years of its enactment, the edict produced the desired effect. As the conviction rate on appeal suddenly rose to more than 60 percent, courts of the first instance were increasingly ready to assume the expense of a formal trial. The number of infanticide appellants more than tripled, and the annual number of hangings rose from two or three to ten or twelve—a level maintained with few fluctuations until 1680, when a decline in the conviction rate brought about a gradual reduction in the number of accused women.

Although the text of the law remained unaltered, its interpretation underwent two important modifications, both related to developments in forensic medicine. Starting in 1619, the Parlement of Paris refrained from pronouncing a sentence of death unless the autopsy performed on the infant cadaver indicated that the baby had met a violent end. Sixty years later, around 1680, the "lung test" made it possible to distinguish between live births and stillbirths. Simultaneously, the whole society was making a major investment in foundling hospitals, a program conceived specifically as a deterrent to infanticide.

After 1680, the crime of child murder entered a long, slow phase of decriminalization. By the middle of the eighteenth century, hangings were back down to two a year, and the number of accused women was declining rapidly, soon to reach its lowest level since before the edict. The great "infanticide craze" was virtually ended; but for more than one hundred years (ca. 1565–1690) infanticide trials—not witchcraft trials—had constituted the major *legal* outlet for the misogynistic feelings so prevalent in early modern society. From 1565 to 1625, the Parlement of Paris pronounced the death penalty on a total of 57 women for the crime of witchcraft, and 625 women for the crime of infanticide—eleven times as many!

This unsuspected disproportion is revealed by patient sifting of the criminal archives, and yet the questions it raises reach far beyond the sphere of justice. Social historians will need to reexamine their sources in an effort to account for these incontrovertible statistics. In order to assist them in their task, I propose here to analyze in detail a single infanticide trial, hoping thereby to avoid many of the mistaken hypotheses, stemming from an inadequate understanding of the judicial institution, offered to explain the witchcraft phenomenon in terms of misogyny and repression of popular superstition.[9]

The case of Marie-Jeanne Bartonnet dates from 1742, when the "infanticide craze" was all but over. Nevertheless, despite the fact that it was one of the last of the great wave of trials for child murder, the Bartonnet case is typical in all important respects. The following analysis is intended to provide a circumstantial example of French judicial procedure under the Old Regime (as distinguished from abstract descriptions based on legislation and jurists' commentaries, which are so often misleading).[10] In addition, I attempt to show at each step of the way how procedure is reflected in the surviving documents, thus furnishing a much-needed practical guide to the criminal archives of the Parlement and the Châtelet of Paris.[11]

In August 1742, Marie-Jeanne Bartonnet, twenty-one years of age, arrived in Paris, ostensibly to find work as a domestic servant. Her only contacts in the capital were Claude Le Queux, a thirty-four-year-old water carrier whom she had known in her childhood in her native province of Brie, and his spinster sister Marie, eight years his senior, who was casually employed doing odd domestic chores. The brother and sister occupied a one-room rented apartment on the fifth and top floor of a house on the rue de Soly (today the rue d'Argout) a few steps to the east of the Place des Victoires with its equestrian statue of Louis XIV. Marie-Jeanne moved in with them temporarily and supported herself as a seamstress.

She was almost seven months pregnant. She may have hoped that, in the anonymity of the city, far from the watchful eyes of her village, she could manage her lying-in without disgrace. Her condition may not have been apparent. Claude and Marie Le Queux later declared they had noticed nothing, even as her time of confinement drew nigh. The voluminous skirts and petticoats of the period would have hidden her swollen belly, except, perhaps, from the vigilance of the proprietors of the building, the dancing master Jean-Claude Pâris (aged forty) and his wife, Marie-Marguerite Lescuyer (thirty-four), who were concerned to protect the good reputation of their house. In any event, that is what they deposed *after* the fact.[12]

A little after ten o'clock on the night of Monday, October 22, Marie-Jeanne rose from the bed she shared with Marie Le Queux, complaining of stomach cramps, and went down one flight to the privy on the fourth floor, where her loud groaning soon set up such a clamor that she aroused the entire house.[13] The proprietress subsequently testified to the following:

The 22nd of the month, between ten and eleven in the evening, the witness, hearing someone groaning, went out into the stairwell and asked what the racket was all about. A woman neighbor replied that it was Marie-Jeanne in the toilet, suffering from colic. Since she suspected the girl was pregnant, she went back into her apartment and told her husband, M. Pâris, that he should go up and get that girl out of the toilet. [The dancing master evidently said it was her job, not his.] She returned to the stairs and, as the groaning continued, she went up to the toilet and found the said Bartonnet on the seat, having a difficult bowel movement, so she claimed. Seeing some drops of blood on the tile floor, she [the witness] made her get up from the seat, and the said Bartonnet immediately lost a lot of blood and asked for towels. The witness led her upstairs to the room where she lived with the Le Queux.

To all appearances, Marie-Jeanne had just had a miscarriage—or worse! A midwife was sent for—Marguerite-Angélique Berthet, known as the *dame* Destouches, sixty years old, who lived nearby on the rue Montmartre. According to her testimony, "she mounted the stairs to the fifth floor where she found a girl or a woman seated on a chair, her feet bathed in blood, to whom she announced, 'I have come to deliver you.' The said woman replied, 'It's done.'" By now, the proprietress and the midwife both suspected that Marie-Jeanne had given birth and had dropped the baby down into the cesspool. The midwife asked "who had advised her to do such a thing and [said] that it was a hanging offense. The girl answered that no one had advised her, and that the midwife had saved her life—which words she accompanied with a meaningful look." The toilet was choked with blood and, although no baby was found, M. Pâris—"unwilling," said his wife, "that this crime go unpunished"—went out to find a sergeant of the watch, who took him round to the nearest officer of justice, François Merlin, in the Place des Victoires. In fact, M. Pâris had no alternative; in light of the scandal attending the discovery of the crime, had he not gone to the authorities he would have been an accessory after the fact. It was then about one in the morning. Commissioner Merlin, awakened, no doubt, from a sound sleep, took down M. Pâris's statement in the form of a *procès-verbal.* Then, as nothing more could be done at so late an hour, they all went back to their respective beds.

In the morning the wheels of justice were set in motion. The *procès-verbal* was communicated to the king's attorney at the Châtelet, who requested (as always, in writing) the judge of the criminal bench (*lieutenant criminel*) to issue two warrants: the first, to have the septic tank opened to search for the baby; the second, for the arrest of Marie-Jeanne Bartonnet.[14] Both mother and child were to be examined medically.

Authorization was quickly obtained, and at two o'clock the same afternoon Commissioner Merlin was back at the scene of the crime, accompanied by a deputy royal attorney, a journeyman cesspool cleaner and his apprentice son, and four policemen. Two of the latter arrested Marie-Jeanne and had her carried in a sedan chair to the prison of the Grand Châtelet, where she was bedded down in the infirmary.[15] The other two policemen were needed to keep order among the small crowd of spectators who had gathered to watch the opening of the tank, despite the overpowering stench.[16] The young apprentice waded into the mess and, near the mouth of the conduit, fished out "the cadaver of a male infant newborn, with contusions on several parts of its body." A soldier took the dead baby to the morgue, where, the following day, an autopsy was performed by a physician, two surgeons, and two licensed midwives. They reported finding "a cadaver of a newborn male with a large contusion on its head in the middle portion of the coronal. On opening the said contusion, we found signs of considerable hemorrhaging on the pericranium and a dent in the skull made by a blunt instrument, or a fall, or by other means. After opening the said cadaver and performing the necessary experiments [to ascertain whether the lungs had breathed],[17] we concluded that the child was alive at birth and died, in our opinion, as the result of a fall, or of blows received on the head."

Meanwhile, on the previous day, immediately on her arrival at the prison infirmary, the same medical team had visited Marie-Jeanne Bartonnet. They declared: "We found her in bed complaining of colic cramps. Having examined her private parts, we found the vulva very open. From it oozed a milky discharge streaked with blood and containing some membranous bits of placenta. We also observed that her breasts were swollen, and we drew forth some milk. For these reasons we conclude that the said Marie-Jeanne Bartonnet has recently given birth." At five o'clock the same afternoon, Marie-Jeanne underwent her first interrogation, based on the information contained in Merlin's *procès-verbal*. The examining magistrate was a counselor of the Châtelet.

The suspect gave her name and age and said she was from Brie, but refused to specify the village. Her silence is understandable. However much or little she comprehended of what was in store for her, she was certainly overcome with shame and moved by a natural desire to spare her family and friends the painful knowledge of her disgrace. In addition, if she was protecting someone, that someone might be an accomplice. Her tone of voice, her facial expression, and her general demeanor may have given some indication of her motivations, but the magistrate did not press the point, neither then nor later, in the second interrogation. He could easily have discovered the name of the village from Claude Le Queux. If he did, the detail was not important enough to be inserted into the trial documents.[18] In all other respects, Marie-Jeanne's line of defense was the best possible one she could have adopted in the circumstances.

The following is a verbatim translation of the Bartonnet interrogation, except that I have rendered the dialogue back into the first and second person instead of the monotonous third person employed in the legal transcript—which was never intended to reproduce the exact words, but rather to express them in conventional language, which was far more stilted and formulaic, no doubt, than the actual dialogue.[19] My comments on various aspects of the exchange have been relegated to notes.

Q. How long have you been in this city and why did you come here?

A. I came here two months ago to find work in domestic service.

Q. Why did you seclude yourself in the room rented by Claude Le Queux?

A. Because he is from my part of the country.

Q. Is it not true that the real reason for your coming to Paris is that, knowing yourself to be pregnant, you thought you would be better able to conceal your pregnancy and destroy your child?

A. I did not even know I was pregnant.

Q. You know very well you had sexual intercourse with a man, and therefore you knew the risk you ran of becoming pregnant.

A. I believe I had intercourse with a man, but I don't know who he is or where he lives.[20]

Q. How long ago did you have intercourse with a man?

A. I think it was about ten or eleven months ago.[21]

Q. Why, when you knew you were pregnant, did you not stay in your part of the country and confide in one of your relatives, who would have helped you in your travail without creating any scandal, and taken charge of your child?

A. I never knew I was pregnant.

Q. Yesterday, at ten o'clock in the evening, did you not go to the toilet on the fourth floor of the house where you live?

A. Yes, although I do not remember what time it was.

Q. Did you not go to the toilet when your labor pains were such that you knew you were about to give birth, in order to be able to throw your baby into the cesspool?

A. When I felt the pains I thought it was colic or an attack of diarrhea.

Q. Is it not true that, in the toilet, the baby fell onto the floor, and that you picked it up and threw it into the cesspool?

A. No.

Q. Tell us how your baby was born and if it did not happen that, when you were sitting on the toilet, the child fell down [directly] into the cesspool.

A. I don't know how it happened. I thought it was diarrhea.

Q. You are not telling the truth. You must have known, from the great quantity of blood on the seat and on the floor, that you were having a baby.

A. I saw blood but nothing else, and I couldn't tell where the blood was coming from.

Q. Did you not take drugs in order to make yourself abort?

A. No.[22]

Q. Were you in your ninth month?

A. I have no idea.

Q. Is it not true that, while you were giving birth, your screams aroused the neighbors, among them the wife of M. Pâris who lives in the same house, and when she asked you what was the matter, you replied you had an attack of colic?

A. Yes, but I did not cry out.[23]

Q. Is it not true that Mme Pâris [*la femme* Pâris], out of concern for your condition, sent for a midwife who, having examined you, concluded that you had just given birth?

A. No. She did not examine me.

Q. We show you this foetus [*sic*] of a boy apparently newborn and full term. Do you recognize it? Tell the court if it is not the same as the one you bore and threw into the cesspool.

A. I do not recognize it. I never saw it before, and I did not throw it into the cesspool.

Q. Did not the said Le Queux, with whom you lodged, know that you were pregnant? And did he not conspire with you to destroy your baby?

A. No.

Q. Have you ever had a child before?

A. Never.

Q. Have you ever been arrested before?

A. No.

Q. Will you accept the testimony of the witnesses?

A. Yes, if they tell the truth.[24]

The above was read back to the accused, who persisted in her replies and declared that she did not know how to write or sign her name.

Many a criminal trial—when the charges were insubstantial and/or there was little evidence to connect the accused with the offense committed—terminated at this point. But there was a prima facie case against Marie-Jeanne Bartonnet under the edict of 1557. She had declared her pregnancy to no one; there was no witness to her delivery; her baby had been found and it had died unbaptized.[25] Still, the case against her was not proved until the depositions of the witnesses were taken down in writing—a procedural step common to both civil and criminal suits.

With the completion of the first interrogation, the initial warrants issued by the judge were exhausted. New authorization was needed, and the following morning, Wednesday, October 24, the *lieutenant criminel* granted the request of the king's attorney to proceed by *information*.[26] In the course of the same day, Commissioner Merlin collected the depositions of eleven witnesses. Six of them had but marginal importance—the two policemen who arrested Marie-Jeanne, the other two who observed the opening of the septic tank, plus two neighbors present at that malodorous event. The material witnesses were five in number and are already familiar to us: Monsieur Pâris and his wife, Claude Le Queux and his sister Marie, and the midwife.[27]

In my narrative of the dramatic events of Monday night I have anticipated most of their pertinent testimony, and there is little to add. The witnesses concurred on all the essentials. M. Pâris and Marie Le Queux confirmed the midwife's account of Marie-Jeanne's confession: "I have come to deliver you"; "it's done [*c'est fait*]"—although the second half of the midwife's version of her dialogue with the accused was not supported, no one else having heard the girl try to suborn the witness or seen her "meaningful look." All the other inhabitants of the house, we may be sure, had formed a crowd at the top of the stairs, but none of them was subpoenaed.

At ten o'clock the next morning, October 25, Marie-Jeanne, still in the prison infirmary, underwent her second interrogation (based on the *information*) and again refused to name her native village.

Q. Are your father and mother alive? Where do they live?

A. I have neither father nor mother. Where they lived is my own business.

Q. Where did you live before coming to Paris?

A. I lived with honest folk, and it's none of your business.

Q. Is it not true that, Monday evening, you were in bed with Marie Le Queux, and got up at about ten o'clock complaining of colic, and went down to the toilet where you remained more than a quarter of an hour, groaning incessantly?

A. I having nothing to say.

Q. You must answer the question, otherwise your trial will be conducted according to the rules governing voluntary mutes, and you will no longer be allowed to reply.
No answer.

Q. We warn you for the second time to answer the question, otherwise [etc.]
No answer.

Q. We warn you for the third time [etc.]
No answer.[28]

Q. Is it not true that, knowing from your labor pains you were about to give birth, you got up from bed with Marie Le Queux in order to have your baby in the toilet and throw it into the cesspool?

A. I have nothing to say.

Q. You must tell us in what manner you gave birth. Was it that, on entering the toilet, the baby fell and you picked it up to throw it into the cesspool? Or did it happen that, while you were on the seat, the baby fell by itself into the cesspool?

A. I have nothing to say.

Q. Is it not true that Mme Pâris went up to the toilet, drawn thither by your groans and screams, and found you sitting on the seat? That she asked you what was the matter, and you replied you were having a difficult bowel movement?

A. You don't need me to tell you.

Q. Is it not true that Mme Pâris saw drops of blood on the floor? And when she got you up from the seat, you immediately lost a lot of blood and asked for towels?

A. I did not ask for towels.

Q. Is it not true that Mme Pâris fetched a midwife who thought you were yet to give birth and who tried to examine you? And when she said she had come to deliver you, you answered that it was done, and that the baby was in the toilet?

A. That is not true.

Q. Who is the father of the baby? and when did you have intercourse with him?

No answer.

Q. When you gave birth, were you in the ninth month of your pregnancy? And did you not take drugs to induce labor?

No answer.

Q. Did the man with whom you had intercourse advise you to come to Paris the better to hide your condition and destroy your child?[29] Was Claude Le Queux, with whom you lived, not informed of your pregnancy, and did he not plan with you to kill your baby?

A. No one has the right to say that.

Q. Do you not know that the commissioner had the cesspool opened, and in it was found the baby we showed you in your first interrogation?

A. I know nothing about all that.

Q. Will you accept the testimony of the witnesses?

A. Yes, if they tell the truth.

The above was read back to the accused [etc.]

Thus far, except for the imprisonment of the accused, the trial has been no different from a civil suit. The next step in the proceedings was the distinguishing mark of a criminal prosecution—the Continental equivalent of cross-examination of the witnesses. Since the reintroduction of written procedure in the twelfth and thirteenth centuries, the verification of the witnesses' testimony was accomplished by confronting the accused with each deponent successively. Originating in a sedentary society where everyone knew everyone else's private business, where good relations and long-standing animosities among neighbors were matters of public concern, confrontations were a logical and often efficacious method of unmasking calumny and subornation. The accused was not allowed access to legal counsel because experience had shown that this only opened the door to chicanery and intimidation of the witnesses. Instead, the judge himself fulfilled the role of counsel and guaranteed the rights of the defendant.[30] Once again, written authorization was necessary to proceed, thereby fixing the responsibility in cases where it could later be claimed that the prosecution was extortionate.[31]

First, the witnesses were summoned to repeat their testimony (*récolement*). They could add to it, subtract from it, and make any other changes without incurring charges of perjury. The second, final version was binding. Claude Le Queux was the only witness who made a significant change in his testimony in the course of this particular *récolement,* adopting his sister's version of what had passed between Marie-Jeanne and the midwife.[32]

Then came the "confrontation."[33] The accused was led into the presence of each witness, ignorant (in principle) of the nature of the testimony against her, other than what she had surmised by common sense and from the questions asked at her interrogation. This was her chance to disqualify the witness for personal reasons, and it had to be done *before* she heard the deposition. A witness could be impeached on grounds of inferior social position, immoral life, or a previous criminal record; or if he or she was a "mortal enemy" of the accused or had ties of blood, marriage, or dependence with a person known to be inimical. The rights of the accused were carefully explained to her, and she was given an opportunity to prove her assertions by witnesses or by documents.

The procedure of confrontation was hedged about with a great many stringent regulations, which are spelled out in detail in the criminal code of 1670.[34] More important than the precise nature of the safeguards is the determination with which the parlement insisted they be followed to the letter, in an effort to prevent the king's justice from being used as an instrument for settling private scores—which took priority over every other consideration. Among the 185 infanticide cases I located by sampling (1681–1787), 5 were remanded because the *récolements* and confrontations had been improperly performed; in 2 other cases the entire procedure was declared null and void. In 1697, for example, Jeanne Barbouze and her accomplice/lover appealed a sentence (death for her, banishment for him) passed by a judge in the Auvergne. The Parlement of Paris invalidated the confrontations and sent both appellants back to the nearest royal judge, at Aurillac, for the procedure to be redone correctly. The entire cost of this additional round-trip journey to the remotest corner of the jurisdiction was borne personally by the first judge. The bill for transporting two criminals back and forth must have come to more than the price of 150 cows—a lesson the judge would not forget in a hurry.[35] Thus the parlement obliged the local magistrates to act themselves as attorneys for the defense.

Alas for Marie-Jeanne Bartonnet. She was unable (or perhaps unwilling) to impeach the witnesses, many of whom she did not know at all. The midwife she had never seen before the fatal night. On the other hand, her relations with Claude and Marie Le Queux, and their relations with the landlords of the building, seem to have been left out of the investigation. Witnesses in criminal trials usually took great care to conceal such matters, confining their testimony to a strict minimum; and the magistrates most often allowed them to have their way (for coercion of witnesses would presumably have made them even more wary of testifying in future cases). We have already seen that Claude Le Queux was not required to specify Marie-Jeanne's native village; nor was he examined concerning his past relations with the accused and how it had been arranged that she come to live with him. In a similar vein, the trial documents are silent concerning the "woman neighbor" mentioned in the landlady's deposition. How did she know that the noise coming from the fourth-floor toilet was being made by Marie-Jeanne and that she was suffering from colic? It is important to realize that the written records of all criminal trials are riddled with mysterious silences and cannot be expected to tell the whole story.[36]

The confrontation proceeded in the following manner: for each witness, after the formalities of mutual recognition and impeachment had been accomplished, the deposition was read out and confirmed under oath by the witness. Then the accused was given the opportunity to dispute it. Marie-Jeanne, no longer so surly as she had been at her second interrogation, stuck doggedly to her story: "she didn't know she was pregnant"; "she felt pains which she thought were colic and went to the toilet to relieve herself, believing that nature would take its usual course"; the childbirth "was mere chance [*hasard*] and an accident." She objected strongly to the midwife's testimony, and her words have a ring of plausibility.

"I have come to deliver you," Mme Destouches had greeted her breath-lessly after climbing five flights of stairs. To which she had muttered, "C'est fait." Three other witnesses reported this initial exchange. But it was not necessarily self-incriminating. The thing that was "done" or "over" was most likely her terrifying ordeal in the toilet. At any rate, her words could not be construed unambiguously as a confession. The alleged attempt to suborn the midwife was likewise unauthenticated, for it took *two* witnesses to prove a fact. What is significant is that Mme Destouches seems to have *anticipated* a confession. As the full horror of the situation dawned on her and she found herself face-to-face with an act of legendary iniquity, she expected the evil truth to come tumbling out the unfortunate girl's mouth, or to dart out of her eyes. According to the tenets of early modern psychology, truth was a vital force struggling to free itself from the trammels of the flesh.[37] By 1742, when Marie-Jeanne stood trial, this attitude was fast disappearing among intellectuals, but its hold on the populace was still tenacious. Thus Mme Destouches, like many a witness, saw what she expected to see.

The evidence against Marie-Jeanne Bartonnet was not conclusive. The prosecution had failed to prove the confession she had allegedly made on the night she gave birth. Without such proof, the crucial deposition was the testimony of the wife of M. Pâris. She alone had discovered Marie-Jeanne in the toilet. It was she, therefore, who could testify to the clandestine delivery. And it was she who was the key witness to the concealed pregnancy, for she was the logical person to whom Marie-Jeanne should have declared her condition. The *déclaration de grossesse* required by the edict did not necessitate a formal statement to a priest or a judicial officer; it could be made to anyone of responsible social position (as distinct from a poor nobody like Marie Le Queux). The other witnesses indirectly corroborated the evidence given by the landlord's wife, and the remainder of the proof was furnished by the meticulous procedure observed in the opening of the cesspool, plus the medical examinations of Marie-Jeanne and her dead baby. When Marie-Jeanne was unable to challenge the testimony of her landlady, her doom was sealed.

After the confrontations on November 6, the Bartonnet dossier, now complete, was transmitted to the king's attorney at the Châtelet. On November 19, he wrote his *conclusions*. *Conclusions* never weighed the evidence (which was left to the appreciation of the judges); they presented a simple, chronological inventory of the procedural steps of the trial, followed in this case by the attorney's recommendation of the death penalty. "In the name of the king, I ask that Marie-Jeanne Bartonnet be declared duly charged with and convicted of concealing her pregnancy, of hiding her delivery, and of destroying her child, and, for reparation, that she be hanged." On November 27 there was a final interrogation in plenary session,[38] and the court voted for capital punishment, adding to the royal attorney's conclusions that her body be left hanging from the gallows for twenty-four hours and then be taken to rot on the gibbet at Montfaucon.

All criminal sentences (except those prescribing temporary banishment) were automatically appealed to the parlement; and so, the day following her sentencing, Marie-Jeanne was transferred from the Grand Châtelet, across the Pont au Change, to the Conciergerie on the Île de la Cité.[39] The guard who conducted her carried with him a complete copy of her trial papers sewn and sealed into a little burlap sack, which he deposited with the clerk of the parlement. The case was quickly assigned to one of the counselors of the court—M. Joly de Fleury—who prepared his report and may have interviewed the prisoner informally.[40] As an appellant from a death sentence, Marie-Jeanne had routinely been consigned to one of the women's dungeons. If her trial had dragged on, she might, at the discretion of the court, have been moved upstairs to the relative freedom of one of the airier cells around the courtyard, where criminals and debtors mingled promiscuously. She was in the Conciergerie for only nine days, however, so it is unlikely that she changed cells.[41]

The counselor's report was read to the criminal chamber in an afternoon session; the magistrates studied the case, and the next morning the appellant was introduced into the courtroom and seated on the traditional *sellette* (a low wooden stool), where she was interrogated by the president of the chamber, M. Lamoignon.[42] Marie-Jeanne's final interrogation took place on December 5, exactly one week after she appealed. This time she gave her age as twenty-two, one year more than she had admitted to when first questioned in the infirmary of the Grand Châtelet.

There is a major difference between this interrogation and the preceding ones. The dialogue was continuous, without pauses to allow the clerk of the court to record more than a small portion of what transpired. Of all that was said, only the following survives in the clerk's notebook:[43]

Q. Did she give birth in the toilet in M. Pâris's house?

A. She went to the toilet, but does not know whether she gave birth.

Q. How many months was she pregnant when she gave birth?

A. Has no idea.

Q. Who is the man responsible?

A. His name is Nicolas.

Unfortunately, in all but a small minority of the many hundreds of infanticide trials I have tabulated, we can get no more particulars of the crime than those provided by this sort of scrappy note taking—sometimes more detailed (especially in the sixteenth and early seventeenth centuries), sometimes even less so.

Marie-Jeanne was dismissed from the courtroom, and the magistrates put the case to a vote. Until 1555, the votes were inscribed in the notebooks immediately following the interrogations; after that date they were jotted down on slips of paper; a few are still found inserted between the pages of various registers, but the vast majority are irretrievably lost. The first judge to express his opinion was the counselor who had reported the case, then, in reverse order of seniority, the other ten or twelve counselors present, and, last, the president—a prudent measure to neutralize his preponderant influence. In case of a tie, the lesser punishment prevailed; a majority of two or more was required for the death penalty.

Notwithstanding her clearly established guilt under the terms of the edict, Marie-Jeanne was given the benefit of the doubt. There was no proof that she had willfully destroyed her child; its injuries might have been inflicted by its fall down the drainpipe, and that fall could conceivably have been accidental. Unlike the subordinate courts, which were enjoined to "follow the rigor of the law," the Parlement of Paris was an authorized dispenser of the king's grace and was empowered to spare her life.[44] In accordance with a jurisprudential principle established in 1619, the parlement therefore condemned her not to death, but to *omnia citra mortem* (everything except death).[45] In the sixteenth century that Latin phrase designated public whipping on three separate days (with a rope around the neck), then perpetual banishment from the kingdom of France and confiscation of property.[46] By 1600, the second and third floggings had been eliminated, and maximum banishment was reduced in the seventeenth century to extend no further than the limits of the parlement's jurisdiction. Meanwhile, however, branding with a hot iron came into increasing favor. Originally intended for thieves as a substitute for cutting off an ear, by the late seventeenth century it was applied to a broad range of crimes, providing a means to identify recidivists.

On December 7, two days after the parlement voted and a little more than six weeks after the commencement of her trial, Marie-Jeanne was sent back to the Grand Châtelet to be flogged at the "usual crossroads," branded on both shoulders with a fleur-de-lis, and banished forever from the jurisdiction of the Parlement of Paris. The sentence was executed on December 14.[47] All her worldly goods were confiscated and she was fined two hundred livres, a sum earmarked to cover the costs of her trial whether or not she could pay it.

The parlement never explained its reasons for convictions or for granting clemency. In the decision, the magistrates closed ranks and presented a façade of unanimity to the world. The judgment itself stood as the sole public commentary on the evidence and on the person of the criminal. In infanticide trials, however, the simplification of the evidentiary rules (defined by the edict of 1557) and the resulting standardization of prosecutions make it possible to hypothesize why the court decided as it did. Marie-Jeanne may have been a consummate actress, but it seems more likely that she was what she appeared to be: a country girl so naïve that she could have a baby in fifteen minutes and afterward deny it had happened. Her obstinate refusal to confess surely explains her escape from the gallows.

As for the father of the baby, he was neither prosecuted nor summoned to the parlement to be admonished. Although in cases of homicide, theft, and witchcraft, the courts took a lively interest in suspected accomplices, in trials for infanticide the seducer was not regarded in this light. That her lover's name was Nicolas seems to have been extracted from Marie-Jeanne as an act of submission to the court rather than for any practical value it might represent. Even if Nicolas had in fact advised her to go to Paris and hide her condition in Claude Le Queux's tiny apartment, there was no way on earth to prove it—any more than it could have been proved that her benefactors in the capital had willfully shut their eyes to her protuberant belly. The definition of infanticide tended to concentrate attention on the mother as protagonist and keep the spotlight focused on her. Fewer than one infanticide appellant in ten entered the Conciergerie in company with an accomplice.

There is a strange epilogue to the "great infanticide craze." As the rate of prosecution declined and as the number of babies abandoned in foundling hospitals soared to unprecedented heights, the image of the infanticidal mother as a "bad girl" was completely reversed. The pendulum of public sympathy swung in the other direction, and she became a *victim*—seduced and abandoned by a man who was himself beguiled by the Devil. By 1775, the Sturm und Drang school of German literature had transformed her into the heroine of a new genre of sentimental tragedy. Gretchen in part 1 of Goethe's *Faust* (1808), Effie Deans in Sir Walter Scott's *The Heart of Mid-Lothian* (1818), and, especially, Hettie Sorrel in George Eliot's *Adam Bede* (1859) are all, in a sense, spiritual kin of Marie-Jeanne Bartonnet.

Notes

To Elizabeth A. R. Brown and to Sarah Ferber, who gave me much sound advice during the writing of this article, I offer my heartfelt thanks.

1. A discussion of the sources and research techniques employed in this essay may be found in A. Soman, *Sorcellerie et justice criminelle: Le Parlement de Paris (16ᵉ–18ᵉ siècles)* (Aldershot, England: Variorum, 1992); see also my article "Sorcellerie, justice criminelle et société dans la France moderne," *Histoire, économie et société* 12 (1993): 177–217; statistics on infanticide trials are presented on pp. 205–7. The following pioneering studies were particularly suggestive: R. W. Malcomson, "Infanticide in the Eighteenth Century," in *Crime in England, 1550–1800,* ed. J. S. Cockburn (London: Methuen, 1977), pp. 187–209; P. C. Hoffer and N. E. H. Hull, *Murdering Mothers: Infanticide in England and New England, 1558–1803* (New York: New York University Press, 1981); Keith Wrightson, "Infanticide in European History," *Criminal Justice History* 3 (1982): 1–20.

2. Charlatans and "magicians" were sometimes accused of selling abortive potions, but the evidence was always inconclusive. The very definition of infanticide eliminated any suspicion of witchcraft, although it was conceivable that a witch could murder her infant. The widow Colette Douffière is the only woman to have been convicted of both crimes; see her *arrêt* in Archives Nationales (hereafter AN), X²ᴮ 149, February 10, 1587.

3. Y.-B. Brissaud, "L'infanticide à la fin du Moyen Age, ses motivations psychologiques et sa répression," *Revue historique de droit français et étranger* 50 (1972): 229–56; Claude Gauvard, *"De grâce especial": Crime, État et société en France à la fin du Moyen Age* (Paris: Publications de la Sorbonne, 1991), pp. 65, 75, 656–59. In France, the "common law" (*droit commun*) was applicable to the domiciled population; vagabonds and recidivists were tried summarily (and without appeal) by the constabulary (*maréchaussée*).

4. On torture, see Soman, "La justice criminelle au XVIᵉ–XVIIᵉ siècles: Le Parlement de Paris et les sièges subalternes" in *Sorcellerie et justice criminelle,* article

VII, pp. 38–49, originally published in the *Actes du 107e Congrès national des Sociétés savantes (Brest, 1982), Section de philologie et d'histoire jusqu'à 1610,* 2 vols. (Paris: Bibliothèque Nationale, 1984), 1:15–52.

5. Ibid., pp. 37–38.

6. F.-A. Isambert et al., eds., *Recueil général des anciennes lois françaises,* 29 vols. (Paris, 1821–33), 13:471–73 (my abridged translation; the full text deserves a close perusal). Cf. the edict of the Holy Roman Emperor, Charles V, *Constitutio criminalis carolina* (1532), arts. 35–36; and the English law of 1624 (21 James I, c. 27). In *The Heart of Mid-Lothian* (1818), Sir Walter Scott gave a remarkably clear analysis of the Scottish statute of 1690 (note 8 and chap. 22, Everyman's Library edition, pp. 544–45, 237). The French law was similar to the Scottish, except for the fact that, in France, unless a cadaver was discovered, there was no *corpus delicti.*

7. "D'avoir tué ce qu'elle avait fait naître avec crime," (Esprit Fléchier, *Mémoires sur les Grands-Jours d'Auvergne, {1665},* ed. Yves-Marie Bercé [Paris: Mercure de France, 1984], p. 157). Cf. an English commentary of 1680: "Lewd whores, who having committed one sin, to avoid their shame . . . privately destroy the infant" (Zachary Babington, *Advice to Grand Jurors,* p. 174, cited in J. M. Beattie, *Crime and the Courts in England: 1660–1800* [Princeton: Princeton University Press, 1986], pp. 113–14). Cf. John Bunyan (also in 1680): "the murder of the babe begotten on the defiled bed" (cited by Malcomson, "Infanticide in the Eighteenth Century," p. 189).

8. In the absence of a police force with investigative powers, no proceedings could be instituted without the full and voluntary cooperation of neighbors—open cooperation, for in France, anonymous denunciations were not admissible at law (Ordonnance of January 1560/61, art. 73, in Isambert, *Recueil* 14:83). On the behavior of the neighbors in two cases of infanticide, see "Le témoignage maquillé," in Soman, *Sorcellerie et justice criminelle,* article XI.

9. Cf. A. Soman, "Decriminalizing Witchcraft: Does the French Experience Furnish a European Model?" *Criminal Justice History* 10 (1989): 1–22 (reprinted in *Sorcellerie et justice criminelle,* article XV).

10. In addition to my article cited above in note 8, Elisabeth Labrousse and I have published two essays containing detailed analyses of criminal procedure: "La querelle de l'antimoine: Guy Patin sur la sellette," *Histoire, économie et société* 5 (1986): 31–45; and "Un bûcher pour un judaïsant: Jean Fonanier (1621)," *Dix-septième siècle* 39 (1987): 113–32. Both are reprinted in my *Sorcellerie et justice criminelle,* article IX and X.

11. For the Bartonnet trial, the written procedures are preserved in AN, Y 10095, November 27, 1742: sentence pronounced by the criminal judge of the city of Paris at the Châtelet; attached to it, a fair copy of her dossier, similar in every respect to the file sent to the parlement when she appealed. The *minutes* (original rough drafts bearing the magistrates' and witnesses' actual signatures) of the two *procès-verbaux* of October 23, the *information* of October 24, and the supplement to the latter (October 27) are located among the papers of Commissioner François

Merlin, in bundle Y 12929. If needed in the course of the appeal, the parlement could send for them (this happened in the case of Marie Mallet from Montluçon in the Bourbonnais: Paris, Archives de la Préfecture de Police [hereafter APP], A^B 120, fol. 77, June 13, 1770). Subsequent documents are cited below in notes 15, 31, 39, 40, 43, 45, and 47. Additional examples of complete written trials are relatively easy to find, thanks to the prison ledgers (APP, series A^B). Since the name of the local court is legibly inscribed in the left-hand column, all that is necessary is to identify an infanticide appeal originating in a tribunal whose archives are extant—for instance, the Châtelet of Paris (for the eighteenth century) or the seigneurial jurisdiction of the faubourg Saint-Germain-des-Prés (for the seventeenth). The date of the sentence permits the researcher to proceed directly to the documents in the archives of the lower court; the date of the *arrêt* provides easy access to the appeal procedures in the archives of the parlement. The same method (or the manuscript inventory: AN, X 60–69) may be used to find eighteenth-century examples in provincial archives.

12. The owners or chief tenants of an eighteenth-century Paris house generally occupied the lower floor(s) immediately over the shop on the street level. Their tenants, the urban proletariat, lived above them. The case I am considering is typical in that none of the three occupants of the room on the top floor could read, write, or so much as sign his or her name, whereas their landlords were literate.

13. Eighteenth-century toilets were very much like modern ones, except for the absence of running water; a jug and a brush were handy for rinsing the bowl. There were normally two *cabinets* in a Paris house, one for the upper floors, one for the lower. They consisted of a closet in which the main conduit, 21 centimeters (8¼ inches) in caliber, was joined by an upward-slanting branch pipe of the same diameter ending in a funnel-shaped *lunette* with a removable seat. The vertical conduit descended directly to a subterranean septic tank, emptied periodically by a professional cleaner of cesspools (*vidangeur*). I am obliged to Pierre-Denis Boudriot for this information. For the general background, see his article "Essai sur l'ordure en milieu urbain à l'époque pré-industrielle," *Histoire, économie et société* 5 (1986): 515–28.

14. The best study of criminal procedure at the Châtelet is the unpublished doctoral dissertation (*troisième cycle*) by Alexandre Mericskay, "Le Châtelet et la répression de la criminalité à Paris en 1770" (Université de Paris-IV, 1984).

15. Her entry into prison is recorded in APP, A^B 196 (unfoliated), October 23. The Grand Châtelet records go back to 1669 (A^B 136).

16. Note that the policemen were present not to conduct the investigation but to maintain order. In the seventeenth century, before the establishment of an urban police force, the role of the policemen was filled by the judicial officers themselves and by the more prominent neighbors. See the infanticide trial of Barbe Pichancourt at Saint-Germain des-Prés (AN, Z² 3433, February 18, 1621).

17. The medical report on Anne Huyard's baby (AN, Y 10040, sentence of April 24, 1731) furnishes a description of this procedure: "Having opened the said

cadaver we found the lungs well inflated and, having detached a piece of lung, we dropped it in water. It floated. We therefore concluded that the said infant was born alive." Regarding this experiment (*la docimasie pulmonaire*), see Marie-Claude Phan, "Les déclarations de grossesse en France (XVIe–XVIIIe siècles)," *Revue d'histoire moderne et contemporaine* 22 (1975): 66–88, at p. 83.

18. Another infanticide appellant, "a woman named Jeanne who refused to give her last name," was booked into the Conciergerie on September 25, 1682 (APP, A^B 67, fol. 21r); she kept her name secret throughout the appeal proceedings (AN, X^2A 1046 and X^2A 406, October 14, 1682), although she risked recognition when she was sent back to Guéret to be executed. Cf. the interrogation of Marie Hanault, who assumed her aged mother had died of grief and shame (AN, Y 10020, March 20, 1703).

19. The exact words of the accused are occasionally found in *procès-verbaux* of torture, where they are written in italic script. Even then, however, regional dialects and Occitan (a different language altogether, spoken in the South) are given in Parisian French.

20. Notice that the answer goes beyond the question. It would be an error to assume that Marie-Jeanne volunteered the second part of her reply, which is manifestly her response to a question so obvious that the clerk did not bother to record it. Once aware of this stylistic device, the reader quickly learns to punctuate the text with missing questions. When the accused spontaneously offered a piece of information, the examining magistrate usually noted the circumstance ("dit de soi" or "ajoute de soi"); this happened three times in the interrogation of Anne Huyard (see above, note 17).

21. Ingenuous or astute? It all depends on *how* she said it.

22. Up to this point, the interrogation has been restricted to the material contained in Merlin's *procès-verbal,* in which there is no mention of abortion. The question is gratuitous. It occurs routinely in most trials involving sexual misconduct and reflects the concern of the magistracy about abortive practices, which could not be prosecuted at law because they could not be proved.

23. The witnesses, in fact, did not testify that she screamed (*crier*) but that she groaned (*se plaindre*). Marie-Jeanne insisted on the distinction, thereby providing another insight into her character.

24. Had she not added this proviso, Marie-Jeanne would have thrown her case away. She would have conceded the truth of whatever had been, or might still be, said against her. A flat rejection of the witnesses, without giving any reason, produced a poor impression on the court. She answered correctly, as most criminals did. Either the correct response was common knowledge, or the examining magistrate had advised her how to avoid trapping herself, or both.

25. In the case of Catherine Bachevillier, no baby was found when the privy was searched, and she was released with a simple admonition. Since connivance was suspected in the Bachevillier affair, ten months passed before her second interrogation (AN, X^2A 1066, May 20, 1702; X^2A 1067, March 20, 1703).

26. The term in French has a meaning quite different from its use in English law (*OED,* 5th definition). To each witness in turn, the investigating officer read the initial complaint or denunciation and asked what he or she knew about it. The resulting answers were, of course, guided by further questions whose omission from the documents creates a false impression of spontaneous, uninterrupted speeches by the deponents. Sometimes the questions were tailored in advance for each witness: five such individualized lists can be found in the sorcery trial of the village priest Nicolas Du Douyt at the *officialité* (bishop's court) of Paris (AN, Z$^{1-0}$ 111, October 6, 1621). See also an *information* dated October 16, 1654, in the archives of Saint-Germain-des-Prés (AN, Z^2 3515): it contains but two depositions, and they are formulated in almost identical terms (I am grateful to Bruno Isbled for this reference).

27. Commissioner Merlin neglected to take the depositions of the *vidangeur* (cesspool cleaner) and his apprentice. This oversight was corrected on Saturday, October 27. The young man added a detail not explicit in the medical report—to wit, that the infant's flesh showed no signs of decomposition.

28. Technically, after the third admonition, any silence could be interpreted as assent. Like many threats, this one does not seem to have been carried out. There was probably a pause in the proceedings and a certain amount of unrecorded dialogue before the interrogation was resumed.

29. The complicity of the baby's father is the object of another question regularly asked in most infanticide trials. See above, note 22.

30. See A. Soman, "La justice criminelle," in *Sorcellerie et justice criminelle,* article VII, pp. 49–50; see note 24, above. Cf. Louis Bernard Mer, "La procédure criminelle au XVIIIe siècle: L'enseignement des archives bretonnes," *Revue historique* 274 (1985): 9–42 (pp. 25–27).

31. The written authorization is at the end of the second interrogation and is also marked by a new entry in the ledger of the Grand Châtelet (APP, A^B 196, November 5, 1742).

32. "La sage femme arrivée, lad. Bartonnet lui dit que l'affaire était faite et qu'elle n'avait plus besoin d'elle."

33. All this was done on Tuesday, November 6, two weeks after the commission of the crime. The delay may have resulted from Marie-Jeanne's slow convalescence, her refusal to confess, or the fact that most magistrates were on vacation in late October and early November, the slowest period of the judicial year (corresponding to the harvest and hunting seasons).

34. Title XV (Isambert, *Recueil* 18:400–403). On this as on most other points, the code contains no innovations; it merely gathers together for the first time, and arranges in rational order, the rules established in scattered legislation since the late fifteenth century. See the full text of the lively confrontations in Guy Patin's trial in 1653 in Labroussse and Soman, "La querelle de l'antimoine," pp. 39–42. For an unpublished example in which the accused demolished the case for the prosecution, see the confrontations of Nicolas Du Douyt, cited above, note 26 (AN, Z$^{1-0}$ 111, October 5, 1621; Z$^{1-0}$ 112A, February 1, 1622).

35. APP, A^B 76, fol. 152; two months later the appellants were readmitted into the Conciergerie (fol. 196v); she was ultimately whipped, branded, and banished for nine years; he was admonished. Cf. ibid., fol. 117r: Georgette Delabrosse was sent back to Mâcon (not quite so expensive) and eventually declared insane. See also the case of Marie Hanault (1703), in Soman, "Le témoignage maquillé," pp. 100–101.

36. Cf. Natalie Zemon Davis, *Fiction in the Archives: Pardon Tales and Their Tellers in Sixteenth-Century France* (Stanford: Stanford University Press, 1987), p. 44.

37. I have analyzed diplomatic dispatches and the pamphlet literature of the late sixteenth and early seventeenth centuries to elucidate this attitude with respect to truth and evil in speech and writing; see A. Soman, "Press, Pulpit and Censorship in France before Richelieu," *Proceedings of the American Philosophical Society* 120 (1976): 439–63, pp. 457ff.

38. The record of this *interrogatoire sur la sellette* is usually missing from the eighteenth-century files of the Châtelet, although it is found in the seventeenth-century dossiers of Saint-Germain-des-Prés.

39. APP, A^B 105, fol. 193v.

40. AN, X^{2A} 1301, December 1, 1742. When he took possession of the file, the *conseiller-rapporteur* signed the register; his name was crossed out when he returned it. Beginning in 1560, the movements of the file were carefully recorded in another series of registers (AN, X^{2A} 1201 *et seq.*). Unfortunately, there is a gap between 1717 and 1749.

41. Relocation from a dungeon to a *chambre* was not recorded in the prison ledgers. The sanitary conditions in the Conciergerie must have been exemplary. Although it could hold more than two hundred inmates, there were very few deaths or transfers to the hospital.

42. The mechanics of appeal procedure are revealed in the private diary of President Nicolas de Bellièvre. See Labrousse and Soman, "Un bûcher pour un judaïsant."

43. AN, X^{2A} 1107, December 5, 1742. By the mid-eighteenth century, the clerks no longer scribbled in shorthand as they had done earlier; the handwriting had become almost copperplate, with a corresponding loss of detail in the record.

44. In a 1698 case, the criminal court of Crépy-en-Valois condemned Françoise Brault not to death but to flogging, branding, and nine years of banishment. Although the high court endorsed this sentence to the letter, it nevertheless administered a mild rebuke to the local judge for having exceeded his authority: "Enjoint de juger à l'avenir les femmes et filles qui seront convaincues d'avoir celé leurs grossesses suivant la rigueur de l'ordonnance du roi Henri Second" (APP, A^B 77, fol. 111r). I found two other similar injunctions in infanticide cases (AN, X^{2A} 542, July 12, 1707, Françoise Lambert; X^{2A} 570, May 27, 1712, Marie Sollays). In neither did the parlement condemn the appellant to death. For a comparable precept in a poisoning trial, see X^{2A} 554, December 5, 1709, Marie Boucault; the sentence of the lower court had prescribed whipping and banishment; in this case the parlement ordered her to be hanged. The parlement differed from the lower

courts; it was not bound by legislation or by the traditional rules governing legal proof. Its judgments were based on conviction "beyond a reasonable doubt" (in early modern French: *les vray-semblables;* in modern French: *l'intime conviction*). See "Récit particular et veritable du procès criminel de monsieur le mareschal de Biron," written in 1602 by the king's attorney general, Jacques de la Guesle (Bibliothèque Nationale de France, MS français 23972), published in Philippe de Canaye, *Lettres et ambassade,* 3 vols. in-fol. (Paris, 1635–36), where it is inserted at the end of vol. 1 or 2, separate pagination, pp. 56–57.

45. *Arrêt* of December 5, 1742: the *minute* is in carton AN, X^{2B} 1991, and the text transcribed into the register AN, X^{2A} 734. In both documents her name is spelled "Martonnet," as if, until then, she had been suffering from a headcold.

46. It also included, where applicable, *amende honorable* (public penance and the recantation of a verbal offense). *Amende honorable* was extremely rare in infanticide cases.

47. See APP, A^{B} 196, December 7, 1742 (her return to the Grand Châtelet).

III

Identities

in Flux

Donald R. Kelley

New World, Old Historiography

At the end of Cervantes's great novel, Quixote's chronicler, Cid Hamete, reveals the calling of the historian. "For me alone Don Quixote was born and I for him. His was the power of action, mine of writing." This might well be the confession of the historiographers of the New World from Peter Martyr and Oviedo down to William Hickling Prescott and Samuel Eliot Morrison. In 1849, after finishing his histories of Ferdinand and Isabella and the conquests of Mexico and Peru, Prescott was tempted to retire from his literary efforts, which he had carried on under extraordinary physical handicaps, but in the end he found he could not give up his enterprise, and so he devoted himself anew to his volumes of Philip II of Spain. "Now Muse of History," he confided to his diary, "nevermore will I forsake thy altar—yet I shall have but little incense to offer."[1] Prescott was only one in a long line of sacrificers at this altar, *conquistadores* of the histories of Spain and New Spain, who followed the deeds of the sword with those of the pen—if not, as Lord Acton preferred to say, with the sponge—and with whatever literary incense they might possess.

I, too, bring small incense, and what I have I bring only to the secondary enterprise of Clio, which is the history of history. The interplay and tension between tradition and innovation and the ancient topos of novelty, which have been characteristic of the art of history since its Herodotean origins, were intensified by the cultural shock of the discoveries and the need to assimilate them to the conventions of Western historiography. What I want to discuss is how the discoveries and the formation of New Spain have been accommodated to—and yet at the same time have acted to modernize and to universalize—the old tradition of Eurocentric and Euromorphic historical writing.

The discovery of the New World was not unexpected on a certain level of European consciousness and expectation, and there had been numerous suggestions heralding some such revelation from the land of the setting sun and the mysterious antipodes. "Let us seek those who dwell under another sun, on the other side of the world," Walter of Châtillon had written in the twelfth century, "lest our glory should fade and our courage miss a chance to shine; this way an immortal song will be our reward."[2] Dante also (in words placed in the mouth of Ulysses) envisioned a "world that has no people,"[3] while Francesco Petrarch sang of

> The daylight hastening with winged tips
> Perchance to gladden the expectant eyes
> Of far-off nations in a world remote.[4]

In 1487 the Florentine poet Pulci offered a more specific prediction:

> Men shall descry another hemisphere. . . .
> At our Antiopodes are cities, states,
> And thronged Empires, ne'er divined of yore.
> But see, the Sun speeds on his western path
> To glad the nations with expected light.[5]

This muffled chorus of "prophetic voices" speaking of an antipodean world echoed some of the anticipations Columbus himself shared and which he combined with other perceptions of the reality of the encounter.

From the first news of the Columbian expedition, beginning with the admiral's own letter (a précis of his journal) published just after returning from his first voyage in the summer of 1493, the historians took over from the poets (although Columbus's first letter was rendered into Italian verse); and they never spared hyperbole in their estimates of the discovery.[6] It was propitious—some contemporaries would say providential—that the event coincided with the take-off period of the new art of printing and its employment for the dissemination of "news." Indeed it was the Columbian revelation, together with the Ottoman threat and the invasion of Italy by the French in 1494, that supplied the incentives for the beginnings of modern European journalism in a recognizable form. And then, as always, the news called at least as much for rhetorical virtuosity as for concern for the facts, and prodigies as well as sober ethnographic description were featured in the pamphlets issuing from the presses of the 1490s.[7]

"The most memorable, honorable, and advantageous enterprise that ever succeeded in Spain was the discovery of the western Indies, which are with reason called the 'new world,' a marvelous event which after so many centuries has been reserved for this age,"[8] wrote Juan de Mariana, greatest of Spanish humanist historians, at the end of the sixteenth century, in words that express—though certainly not for the first time—the challenge that the discovery has posed to writers across four centuries of historiographical exploration. In the 1520s Peter Martyr, the Columbus of New World historiography, admitted to a "joyous mental excitement" and told Pope Clement VII, "The vastness of the subject I am treating requires Ciceronian inspiration."[9] Such was the question faced by Prescott and his predecessors: how could historians do justice to what Francesco López de Gómara called the greatest event since the creation of the world ("la mayor cosa después de la creación del mundo")—excepting, for Christian peoples, the Incarnation?[10]

The resources of European historiography were barely up to the task. European historical writing at the turn of the sixteenth century was a mixture of the old and the new.[11] Medieval chronicles and universal histories competed with narratives in the new humanist manner, the critical study of antiquities with the rehearsal of old mythical traditions, and the new art of printing easily accommodated both.[12] The classical theory and practice of history had indeed been restored and modernized by Italian scholars such as Leonardo Bruni and Flavio Biondo and carried on by certain Hispanized Italians ("italos españolizados," Sánchez Alonso called them).[13] Spanish celebrators of the "art of history" such as Juan Luis Vives, Sebastian Fox-Morcillo, and Luis Cabrera de Córdoba continued the humanist quest for an authentic and complete history ("legítima y perfecta historia").[14]

Yet older medieval assumptions, values, and expectations persisted. Providential visions were easily assimilated to the attitudes and aspirations of Renaissance scholarship, and national histories looked back not only to Livy but also to Eusebius as a model for celebrating the story of a chosen people. "It is well to learn the course of history from the beginning of the world or of a people continuously right through their course to the latest times," wrote Vives, who, in his humanist-style praise of the *ars historica,* invoked the names of Paulus Orosius and Paulus Diaconus as well Bruni and Biondo.[15]

This conflation of the old and the new is well illustrated in the history of the Indies written by Bartolomé de Las Casas in his declining years. Las Casas defined history in the famous Ciceronian formula—"testigo de los tiempos, maestra de la vida, vida de la memoria, luz de la verdad y de la antigüedad mensajera"—and emphasized the importance of eyewitness testimony over the secondary fabrications of armchair historians ("por mis ojos he visto").[16] This old argument was taken from Thucydides, confirmed by Isidore of

Seville's etymology deriving *historia* from the term meaning "to see," and illustrated with reference to canon law requirements of documentary authenticity; and it was given concrete reinforcement by Las Casas's personal experiences in New Spain from 1502 to 1566. At the same time, and on a more speculative level, this elderly Dominican friar set the great story of the Conquest within the framework of the Augustinian and Orosian visions of history—that is, as both "the true education of the human race" (anticipating the formula of Lessing) and an account of "the desires and punishments of sinful men." Though a proud Spaniard, Las Casas wrote in the spirit not only of national expansion but also of Christian universalism—of the "living God" (here citing the apostles Barnabas and Paul) "who in times past suffered all nations to walk in their own ways."[17]

It is through the ancient topos of novelty that the history of the Americas has been written for five centuries. The ancients were palpably ignorant about much of the natural and social worlds: and—as every universal historian of the New World found it necessary to demonstrate at length—Augustine and the other Christian Fathers were wrong on the question of the antipodes.[18] There were repeated efforts to interpret the behavior of the Amerindians in terms of ancient conceptions of "barbarism," employing especially Tacitus's descriptions of the customs of the ancient Germans (which were becoming popular after the rediscovery of Tacitus's *Germania* in the fifteenth century);[19] but finally, in the vast literature of discovery, the judgments of novelty prevailed among both admirers and critics of the inhabitants of the New World.

I have referred to humanism as if it was an improvement on medieval conceptions of history; yet there is a confusion between tradition and innovation. For humanist scholars, while they applied the tools of philology to discredit ancient myths and medieval anachronisms, fell into their own kinds of credulity and thus created, or revived from ancient sources, their own historiographical fictions (some of which we continue to share). The extreme example, noted by Jean Bodin in the sixteenth century, was the boast of some nations that they were descended from the gods.[20] Modern historians may have dropped that ancient conceit, but it has not prevented them from justifying national exceptionalism on the hardly more defensible grounds of imputed social and constitutional antiquity and racial superiority.

In the mainstream of European historiography the discovery—*il inventio, la descubrimiento, la découverte, die Entdeckung*—of the New World was directly assimilated to, and indeed made the cynosure of, the epic story of the Spanish monarchies. The discovery crowned a millennium-long tradition of imperial claims and mythology enhanced most recently by the glorious Reconquista and the surrender of Granada, which Columbus himself had witnessed; and it has been a matter of intense national pride, involving not only the territorial pretensions of particular European states but also their claims to priority in the discovery. For contemporaries more impressed with individual heroism than government sponsorship, this earthshaking and earth-circling event was an Italian achievement exploited by the Spanish. According to the French humanist Louis Le Roy, celebrating the novelties of his age in 1575, "The enterprise was begun by Cristoforo Colombo the Genoese, and by Amerigo Vespucci the Florentine, a person of excellent understanding and fine judgment who deserves no less praise than the famous Hercules; then it was continued by the Castilians, rivals for the same honor and eager for gain, who by great courage and incomparable endurance have continued to make other discoveries."[21] Most historians accorded priority to the Spanish. According to Peter Martyr, himself an Italian, Ferdinand and Isabella were the true initiators of the undertaking.

The telling of the story of the New World was, of course, taken up by Protestants as well as Catholics, and with very much the same sense of a mission that was, as the Huguenot Jean de Léry put it, "holy and truly heroic."[22] Underneath this conventional awe Léry displayed a curiosity and a range of human sentiment—"between disapproval and delight," wrote his translator—that opened his eyes to behavior rivaling the prodigies reported by Pliny and other ancients. In fact, Léry was horrified by the actions of the turncoat (as he believed) Villegagnon, who allegedly had several Huguenots drowned "because of their adherence to the Gospel"; and his account was inserted in his friend Jean Crespin's martyrology.[23] Léry himself had barely escaped such martyrdom in France during the massacres of Saint Bartholomew, and he had suffered terribly during the siege of Sancerre in 1573, which he endured with François Hotman and other followers of Coligny. None of this measured up to his experiences in the New World, however. Eschewing the "painted lie of fine language," Léry hoped his unadorned narrative would do justice both to the truth and to the fantastic character of his experiences.

The history of the Americas has always posed an extraordinary literary challenge to historians. In the later seventeenth century Antonio de Solis published a "monument of national enterprise" (as Prescott called it) that confronted this problem. There were three great actions, wrote Solis in this enormously popular work—those of Columbus, Cortés, and Pizarro—and it was very hard to reduce these to, or blend them into, a single narrative; and so, in order to preserve continuity and drama, he decided on a threefold structure.[24] This was also the solution of Prescott, who conceived a love-hate relationship with the work. Though Solis himself claimed "to draw the truth, pure and unmix'd [from] the very soul of history," Prescott found the book "well tinctured with the bigotry—superstition of his countrymen of the 17th cent[ur]y."[25] To Prescott, Solis was an "unshrinking apologist . . . [for] national aggrandizement." Yet, if Prescott despised the moral judgments of Solis, he could not help being captivated by the power of the work—to the extent, indeed, that he resolved not to read it again in order to avoid imitating it too closely. "Viewed as a work of art," he wrote, the history of Solis "perhaps claims precedence over every other." Nor could Prescott avoid casting his own narrative as a dramatic struggle between winners and losers.

This trajectory of imperial advance has remained central to the story of the discoveries, and, of course, it has been reinforced by that formative and sustaining myth of modern historiography: the modern belief in Progress. The idea of Progress again illustrates the curious collaboration of medieval and modern conceptualizations, being in effect the offspring of the marriage between two offshoots of Western Platonism: the Augustinian conception of history as a pilgrimage toward enlightenment, and Renaissance ideals of human learning. The notion—or rather the rhetorical topos—of the superiority of Moderns over Ancients, publicized by humanist rhetoric and documented by reports of new inventions and discoveries, produced a secular eschatology of Progress and Perfectibility and derivative claims to Modernity. Humanist scholars like Christophe Milieu and Louis Le Roy celebrated this theme with reference to geographical and scholarly explorations a generation before Bacon employed it in his own *Advancement of Learning*.[26]

The ideology of Progress originally found (and sometimes still finds) its legitimacy in a theory of providential history, even as it found (and often still finds) its confirmation in new factors of political expansion and material gain—the Renaissance version of modernization theory. Here again medieval conceptualizations joined humanist rhetoric in expressing a modern, or modernized, myth. One perennial theme, celebrated by poets, lawyers, and theologians as well as historians, was the idea of a "translation of empire" (*translatio imperii*) from the Medes, Persians, and Greeks to the Romans, and (via Charlemagne) to the "Holy Roman Empire of the German Nation," as it was called in the fifteenth century. The rationale of this succession of world empires was again providential, on the biblical grounds that "God transfers kingdoms from one people to another because of injustice, injuries, blasphemies, and other evils."[27]

In the age of Columbus the last of the Four World Monarchies seemed to have devolved finally on the German nation. Yet for at least two centuries the national monarchs of France and Spain had laid claim to imperial status—that is, had claimed to be, according to the famous canonist formula, "emperor in his kingdom" (*rex imperator in regno suo*) and thereby to possess the honors, privileges, preeminences, and divine authority of the ancient caesars. French and Spanish jurists denied the pretensions of the German emperor to be "lord of the world" (*dominus mundi*) on the grounds that many parts of the Western world, especially the kingdoms of France and Spain, had never been under Roman dominion. It is worth noting that these were precisely the allegations made (and the authorities cited) by the sixteenth-century jurist Francesco Vitoria, though he applied it to the anti-imperialist thesis denying the rights of *dominium* of Christian conquerors over "barbarians," who likewise had never been subject to Rome, papal or imperial.[28]

The Spanish imperial tradition was long in the making and can be traced back to the time when, according to the old proverb, "Spain gave many emperors to Rome."[29] The idea of a unified kingdom of Spain (Hispania) underlying the several crowns of Castile, León, Navarre, and so on, was reflected in historical as well as legal sources, especially from the time of Alfonso el Sabio. The *Prima Crónica general de España* commissioned by Alfonso expressed the "moral unity of Spain," which was personified in the image of "Blessed Lady Spain" and which José Antonio Maravall has discerned beneath the surface of Iberian particularism. From the thirteenth century, what Maravall called the "rich Alfonsine tradition" of historiography was further enriched by the incorporation of a Visigothic mythology and by the claim, shared by other European monarchs, that the Spanish king was *rex imperator in regno suo.* According to the Romanoid *Siete Partidas,* the Spanish king—*rex hispaniorum* or *totius Hispaniae Rex*—had the same authority in the temporal sphere as the Roman emperor: "Quanto en lo temporale, bien asi como el emperador en su imperio."[30] Long before the joint reign of Ferdinand and Isabella, then, there were notions of union and aspirations to empire. Of course these national and imperial ideals were enhanced both by the crusading impulse against Islam leading to the Reconquista and by the impulse to exploration leading to the Columbian Conquest.

Historians of the New World took up and adapted these old themes. Oviedo continued to represent the "empire" of Charles V as a descendant of the Roman *imperium,* although the voyage of Magellan three years after his election had opened even grander vistas; and Thomas Campanella's vision of a Spanish empire still had associations with the old Translation theory.[31] Nor did humanists like Mariana seriously alter this plot, derived from the tradition of vernacular chronicles that had dominated Spanish historiography since the thirteenth century. By the fifteenth century, however, the notion of "empire" was acquiring more mundane and territorial connotations based on imputations not of God's disfavor but of his favor. As Nicolai Rubinstein has shown, politics Italian style increasingly shifted the idea of *imperio* from its original legalistic and Ghibelline associations with the German empire to a more realistic—indeed Machiavellian—acknowledgment of political and military expansion. For reasons both old and new, then, this imperial dominion was radically redefined in the context of the new realities and power configurations of the early modern period.

Columbus, too, the forefather of New World historiography, had something of the old as well as the new spirit. His deeds were forward looking, but his thoughts were often drawn back to medieval myth. The book culture he brought to his efforts was prophetic and looked not backward to history but rather forward to its "climax"—as indeed befits the legends that have accumulated around him and have made him a human metaphor for the act of discovery. For Columbus, the Holy Spirit worked in the ignorant as well as the learned. In his *Book of Prophecies,* which he sent to Ferdinand and Isabella in 1502, he wrote of being "made the messenger from the new heaven and the new earth of which Our Lord spoke through the mouths of Saint John the Baptist in the *Apocalypse* and of Isaiah." According to the Romantic historian Edgar Quinet, who quoted this work in the mid-nineteenth century, Columbus transcended the rubrics of medieval and modern, possessing as he did "the soul of Joan of Arc and the soul of Galileo" and, for his superhuman foresight and deeds, should be admitted to the great canon of Western prophets—Dante, Joachim of Fiore, Saint Francis,

Michelangelo, Savonarola, Campanella, and the great figures of the French Revolution.[32]

To these should be added the archetypal figure of Adam, who began the naming process, without which stories could never be told, or history written. This naming process—political onomastics, it might be called—was the linguistic face of empire building and no less hegemonic in its effects, language being, as the humanist Antonio de Nebrija told Queen Isabella, "the tool of empire." Columbus's own account emphasized the act of taking possession ("he tomado posesion") whether by law or by force ("tomó posesion . . . en forma de derecho" or "hallé tomé por fuerça" are repeated phrases in his letters) and then of naming these possessions ("puse nombre" or "puse nombre nuevo").[33] These themes were repeated even more aggressively by later explorers, whose assignments were more carefully defined for the benefit of a greedy home government. They were carried over, too—often with literary, religious, or ideological euphemisms and embellishments—into later, more derivative narratives.

A nice illustration of the mixture of violence, legalism, and piety of the foundational actions making up the story of the discoveries can be seen in Cortés's famous victory near the Tabasco River (named, of course, by the Spanish) on the island of Cozumel. Four times (witnessed by the royal notary) Cortés tried to tell the Indians he did not want war (only agreement to his terms), but "it was the determined will of the Indians to resist."[34] The battle itself, described by Bernal Díaz, had been sealed with the miraculous appearance of San Iago, or perhaps San Pedro, to which the Indians also testified (though not Díaz); and this victory of four hundred Spaniards over forty thousand barbarians, according to Gómara, was a clear sign of God's special favor.[35] Afterward the Tabascan Indians were represented by Gómara as begging forgiveness and making a treaty of peace before submitting to the standard process of conversion.[36] According to Cortés, they "grieved and were willing to be subjects of that prince of whom he had spoken." So Cortés left them, he reported, "loyal subjects of Your Majesties." This William Robertson translated to mean that, following normal European diplomatic convention, "they acknowledged the King of Castile as their sovereign."[37]

The papal bulls of donation had given Their Most Catholic Majesties the right to take possession over the new territories (and their inhabitants), at least as Spanish jurists interpreted the famous *Inter caeteros* of 1493; and this legal doctrine was overlaid with elaborate ceremony which no doubt impressed the conquered natives.[38] The formal act of taking possession, drawing on the ceremonial of chivalry, was equally stereotypical and, as it were, ready-made for historiographical consumption; it was performed almost as if future historians were watching—as indeed one was. "Then Cortés took possession of that land for the King, performing the act in the name of the King," wrote Díaz in his eyewitness account. "He did it in this way: he drew his sword, and, as a sign of possession, made three cuts in a large silk-cotton tree which stood in that great courtyard, and cried that if any person should raise an objection he would defend the King's right with his sword and his shield, which he held in his other hand."[39] And the soldiers cried out their approval of this right. From this time on, lawyers would dispute this right of possession and its consequences; but historians for the most part described, celebrated, and embellished the accomplishment, even when they disagreed with the best—most profitable or most just—policies for carrying on the quest for empire.

Legally as well as historiographically, then, the New World was assimilated into the legal and cultural categories of Europe and subject to its judgments. At first this was not "America" either in name or conception; it was an "imaginary space" (as Anthony Pagden and others have remarked) to be filled in by European "prejudices" and "fore-structures," which ranged from medieval lore to Aristotelian philosophy and Roman law.[40] America itself received its name only a decade after the discovery, and then under the most curious circumstances of misinformation, publicity, and cartographic fortune, through which a whole hemisphere—as it turned out—was named after a minor Florentine merchant-adventurer and publicist. ("Strange that broad America," Emerson remarked, "must wear the name of a thief.")[41] Even the dim outlines of the new continents would not be apparent for many years; and the nature of the native populations would demand centuries of study and the creation of disciplines hardly imagined by Renaissance scholars, including the new sciences of ethnography and cultural anthropology.

From the beginning, then, the *descubrimiento* seemed to transcend history. Its meaning has been sought and expressed in terms not of a vulgar Rankean, Samuel Morrisonian, or Gradgrindian quest for the facts but rather of something like Hans Blumenburg's conception of a modern "work on myth," or perhaps Edmundo O'Gorman's arguments, formulated more than forty years ago, anticipating recent intellectual fashions, such as those of

Stephen Greenblatt and other spokesmen for the New Historicism—for the "invention" rather than the "discovery" of America.[42]

This is a distinction that may have been lost on Renaissance scholars, since both ideas were encompassed and perhaps confused in a single Latin term. *Inventio* was a commonplace figuring centrally not only in humanist rhetoric and scholastic logic but also in ancient and modern myth; and it suggested founding as well as finding. In 1499 Polydore Vergil published a little encyclopedia (and contribution to the Renaissance genre of heurematography) entitled *On the Inventors of Things,* which honored not only the founders of arts and sciences but also navigators, including Neptune, the mythical creator of the *ars navigatoria,* and the merchants who came in their wake.[43] At the outset of his book Vergil remarked that such discoveries or inventors had always been ranked among the gods, though good Christians could offer them only the small incense of human praise. Among these Martyr proposed to nominate Columbus as one of the greatest—and so he has been, to the accompaniment of many national holidays, parades, festivals, and centennialism marked by scholarly conferences.

In one fundamental respect the humanist vision of history was transformed by the first encounters with the New World, and this was a new appreciation for the creative power of nature. This is illustrated by a locus classicus of the old humanist perspective, Francesco Petrarch's account of his ascent of Mount Ventoux. Recovering from his awe inspired by the grandeur of the mountain scenery, Petrarch was possessed by another thought, which turned him, as he put it, "from the contemplation of space to that of time" and then, in his Augustinian way, to various retrospective and introspective explorations. In a sense what the Columbian moment of discovery signified for humanist historians was just such a turn back from the contemplation of time to that of space. For the opening of a new hemisphere fantastically expanded the old Christian and medieval "universal history," which had been limited to the Eurocentric notion of the Four World Monarchies and the "translation of empire." The conventional "theater" of human history was enlarged beyond recognition by the outpourings of sixteenth-century travel literature. The *mundus novus* of Vespucci and the *orbis novum* of Martyr made the fabled Antipodes into a reality that was illustrated not only by spectacular maps and globes but also by the writings of geographers, topographers, and chorographers, and by those Bodin called "universal geographistorians" (*geographistorici universales*).[44]

Awareness of the antipodes gave new life to the old quarrel between Ancients and Moderns that had been reignited by humanism. The idea of empire was given an enlarged geographic base, utopian visions a new location, and historians a new dimension to explore. History was literally globalized, and ancient environmentalist and ethnographic ideas were reinstated within the expanding "new horizons" of the Renaissance.[45] As Antonio de Solis wrote, much of the so-called empire of Spain "consisted not so much in any Thing real, as in the Hope which had been conceived by several Discoveries and inroads made by some of our Captains with various Success, and more Danger than Profit."[46]

In any case the new imperial idea (transferred in effect from the Austrian line of the Habsburgs) was seized on and elaborated by all the historians of New Spain. "Amidst the storms and troubles of Italy," wrote Peter Martyr, "Spain was everyday stretching her wings over a wider sweep of empire, and extending the glory of her name to the far Antipodes." And as Gómara put it at the end of his *Historia general de las Indias,* "Never before has a king or nation occupied and subjected so much in so short a time as ours, nor has deserved what they have done by preaching the holy gospel and converting idolaters, for which our Spaniards are deserving of praise in all parts of the world."[47] In the seventeenth century a new theory of Four Monarchies was proclaimed by Lope de Vega, who instructed Philip III about the extent of his *Invicta monarchia:*

Quatro coronas tienes,
. . . en Africa y Europa
en Asia y en America triunfante.[48]

Yet there was a darker side to this picture of Hispania Triumphans. In his *History of Italy* Francesco Guicciardini noted the contradictions of the Spanish accomplishment, acknowledging the Spaniards as indeed "worthy to be celebrated with eternal praise for their skill, their industry, their resoluteness, their vigilance and their labors," yet at the same time finding them flawed by an "immoderate lust for gold and riches," which tended to discredit their missionary impulse and portended future tragedy.[49] In retrospect the world-shaking and world-shaping consequences of the *descubrimiento de las Indias* seem to reflect the duality and to recapitulate the tragic extremes of Spanish history, the glory and misery expressed in the historiographical topoi, noted by Maravall, concerning the heights and depths of Spanish experience (*de excellentia Hispaniae* and *deploratio Hispaniae*).

The tragic dualism of Spanish history reappeared in the "great debate" of the sixteenth century over the legitimacy of Spanish conquest, which divided historians and jurists alike. On one side (the minority opinion, to be sure) were "idealists" like Las Casas who stressed the natural civility, cultured communism, and lack of "commercial spirit" of the Indians; on the other side were "realists" like Oviedo—Acton's "man with the sponge"— who denounced the Indians as "dirty, lying cowards," incapable of work and thwarting Spanish policy by dying intentionally.[50] Las Casas complained that Oviedo was always "condemning the Indians and excusing the Spaniards for the decimation they brought about in the Indies."[51] For Las Casas, such opinions, which were expressed also by Herrera and Gómara, constituted a basis neither for imperial policy nor for the writing of human history. "The universal way of the soul's deliverance," Las Casas said, quoting from Augustine's *City of God* (book 2, chap. 32), was "granted by the divine passion to the nations universally."[52]

How could the new members of the "world of nations" be understood and characterized by practitioners of the old historiography? At first, only in the ethnographically impoverished but mythologically rich categories and language of European tradition. In his first report Columbus represented the natives as "virtuous savages," and as Howard Mumford Jones remarked, the "myth-making process began at once."[53] The image of the "good savage" was countered by that of the bad barbarian, and, of course, both of these ideal types could find support in classical tradition. Like the ancient Germani in the recently rediscovered work of Tacitus, the modern "barbarians" could be portrayed as either innocent and admirable or godless and abominable. Las Casas pictured them as virtuous cultivators of "natural reason," while most historians regarded them as truly children of darkness. Martyr accused the Indians of behaving like "Scythians" or credulous pagans. "You thought that ancient superstition had perished," he remarked to the cardinal of Aragon (referring to the "prophetic delirium" of an Indian priest), "but you see that such in not the case."[54]

What, then, was the original condition of the Amerindians? Were they brothers to the Christians or, as John Rastell put it, descended "from a different Adam"?[55] Were they living in a state of bestiality or in a prelapsarian paradise? The debate was never resolved, but to champions of empire it made little difference. To European observers the most fascinating trait of the Indians—aside, perhaps, from their cannibalism and an inclination to sodomy—was their nudity:

They've found in Portugal since then
And in Hispania naked men,
And sparkling gold and islands too
Whereof no mortal ever knew.[56]

This was something invariably commented on because it suggested that the Indians were in a state of nature and ready to receive the stamp of true religion and subjection to civilized rule. "For these new nations," Peter Martyr wrote, "are as a *tabula rasa;* they easily accept the beliefs of our religion and discard their barbarous and primitive rusticity after contact with our compatriots."[57]

There was, then, agreement among all parties about the need to bring the Indians into the Christian fold—into the structures of European culture and the perspective of Western history. Even in the great "battle of books" between Las Casas and Sepúlveda there was no disagreement about the need for conquest, only whether the conquest should be political or spiritual.[58] Las Casas himself regarded the conversion of the Indians—as Sepúlveda did their subjection—as the fulfillment of the old idea of universal empire. Nor, until our own century, did the moral dilemmas of imperialism and colonialism call into doubt ideas of progress and modernization; and indeed these assumptions still tend to inform historical narrative on almost every level.

In one way or another modernization theory has furnished what post-modernists regard as the "metanarrative" of Western history. To many historians the great story of discovery, conquest, and cultural (and economic) assimilation had a dramatic unity, representing as it did both the culmination of the tradition of world empire (and, for some, the world-church) and the revelation of unsuspected novelties that set off the modern age from all that preceded. By the later seventeenth century, however, the grand themes of empire and modernization seemed to have passed Spain by, her past glories being overshadowed by the mercantile successes of England and Holland. For Spain, conquest and possession did not bring the material progress achieved by other states, and the loss was felt by historians, too. It is on this note of decline that Robertson ended his *History of America,* Prescott his *History of Ferdinand and Isabella,* and Merriman his *History of the Spanish Empire,* which he dedicated to Prescott.[59] Not for these epigones of Martyr and Mariana the tracing of "decline and fall"; not for them the unhappy, inglorious, undramatic tales of the losers in the greater epic of western

European progress; not for them, even, the later stages of the genocidal tragedy described by Las Casas.

In the seventeenth century (to conclude on a somewhat hypothetical note) the symbol of Spanish character was no longer Cristobal Colón, Hernán Cortés, or even Bartolomé de Las Casas; it was Don Quixote. The age not only of the chivalrous knights but also of their modern epigones, the *conquistadores,* and of their first chroniclers, was passing. "The historical greatness of Spain lies in bygone centuries," Thomas Mann wrote, referring specifically to "that travesty of a tragedy," as he called Cervantes's great paradoxical novel, in which, Mann remarked, "[Spain] looks as into a mirror at its own *grandezza,* its idealism, its lofty impracticality, its unmarketable high-mindedness."[60] When these themes become a subject for irony and satire, however, when there are no longer knights-errant in the world, the historians depart. Or rather, they resort to nostalgia, antiquarian investigation, and their own sort of mythmaking. The armor of the *conquistadores,* like that of Quixote (as Cid Hamete tells us at the end of the novel), has been hung up as a trophy; what remains is only the telling, and the retelling, of the story.

Still, we are left with the question of how to tell it. Is it an endless debate between scholars; a chivalric romance; a grand epic of human effort and agony; a comedy of errors between alien cultures; or an appalling postclassical tragedy? Or is it all of the above? In any case it is a tale of wonder that still needs thinking—and, no doubt, writing—about.

Notes

1. *The Literary Memorabilia of William Hickling Prescott,* ed. C. Harvey Gardiner, 2 vols. (Norman: University of Oklahoma Press, 1961), 2:193. A version of this paper was delivered at the conference "Spanish Historical Writing about the New World," held at Brown University, May 6–7, 1992, to which I was invited through the good offices of Nancy Roelker.

2. Cited by Charles Singleton in his edition and translation of Dante's *Divine Comedy,* 6 vols. (Princeton: Princeton University Press, 1970), *Inferno,* Commentary, p. 467.

3. *Inferno,* chap. XXVI, p. 115.

4. *Canzoniere,* no. iv, translated by Charles Sumner in *Prophetic Voices Concerning America* (Boston, 1874), p. x.

5. Cited and translated in W. H. Prescott, *History of the Reign of Ferdinand and Isabella the Catholic,* 2 vols. (Philadelphia, 1872), 2:116.

6. B. Sánchez Alonso, *Historia de la historiografía española,* 3 vols. (Madrid: Revista de Filología Española, 1944–50); Eduard Fueter, *Geschichte der neueren Historiographie,* 3d ed. (Berlin: R. Oldenbourg, 1936); James Westfall Thompson, *A History of Historical Writing,* 2 vols. (New York: Macmillan, 1942); A. Curtis Wilson, *The Historiography of Latin America: A Guide to Historical Writing, 1500–1800* (Metuchen, N.J.: Scarecrow Press, 1975); Georges Cirot, *Mariana historien: Études sur l'historiographie espagnole* (Bordeaux: Feret et fils, 1905); Edmundo O'Gorman, *Cuatro historiadores de Indias: Siglo XVI* (Mexico: Secretaría de Educación Pública, 1972); Anthony Grafton, *New Worlds, Ancient Texts: The Power of Tradition and the Shock of Discovery* (Cambridge: Harvard University Press, 1992); and Angel Delgado-Gomez, *Spanish Historical Writing about the New World, 1493–1700* (Providence: John Carter Brown Library, 1992).

7. D. R. Kelley, *The Beginning of Ideology* (Cambridge: Cambridge University Press, 1981), p. 225.

8. Juan de Mariana, *Historia de rebus Hispaniae libri XXX,* book xxvi, chap. 3: "La empressa mas memorable, de mayor honra y provecho que jamás sucedió en España, fué el descubrimiento de las Indias Occidentales; las quales con razon por su grandeza llaman el nuevo mundo; cosa marvellosa, y que de tantos siglos estaba reservada para este edad." See Georges Cirot, *Mariana historien* (Paris, 1905).

9. *De Orbe Novo: The Eight Decades of Peter Martyr d'Anghera,* trans. F. A. MacNutt (New York: G. P. Putnam's Sons, 1912), 2:331.

10. Francisco López de Gómara, *Historia general de las Indias,* 2 vols., (Madrid: Espasa-Calpe, 1932), chap. ccxiv.

11. See D. R. Kelley, "Humanism and History," in *Renaissance Humanism: Foundations, Forms, and Legacy,* ed. Albert Rabil Jr., 3 vols. (Philadelphia: University of Pennsylvania Press, 1988), 3:236–70; and, for a selection of humanist statements about the writing of history, D. R. Kelley, *Versions of History from Antiquity to the Enlightenment* (New Haven: Yale University Press, 1991), pp. 218ff.

12. See especially C. A. Patrides, *The Grand Design of God* (London: Routledge & Kegan Paul, 1972).

13. Sánchez Alonso, *Historia,* 1:356.

14. Luis Cabrera de Córdoba, *De Historia para entenderla y escribirla* [1611] (Madrid: Instituto de Estudios Politicos, 1948), 28; and see Urbano Gonzalez de la Calle, *Sebastián Fox Morcillo: Estudio histórico-crítico de sus doctrinas* (Madrid: Asilo de Huéfanos del Salgado Corazón de Jesús, 1903).

15. Kelley, *Versions of History,* p. 257.

16. Bartolomé de las Casas, *Historia de las Indias,* ed. Agustín Millares Carlo (Mexico: Fondo de Cultural Economica, 1951), p. 8.

17. Ibid., p. 17.

18. E.g., Juan de Torquemada, *Monarquia Indiana* (Mexico: Chávez Hayhoe, 1969), p. 11.

19. D. R. Kelley, *"Tacitus Noster:* The *Germania* in the Renaissance and Reformation," in *Tacitus and the Tacitean Tradition,* ed. T. J. Luce and A. J. Woodman (Princeton: Princeton University Press, 1993), pp. 152–67.

20. Jean Bodin, *Method for the Easy Comprehension of History,* trans. Beatrice Reynolds (New York: Columbia University Press, 1945), p. 334.

21. Louis Le Roy, *Le Vicissitude ou variété des choses en l'univers* (Paris, 1575).

22. Jean de Léry, *History of a Voyage to the Land of Brazil, otherwise called America,* trans. Janet Whatley (Berkeley: University of California Press, 1990), p. xli.

23. Ibid., p. 218.

24. Antonio de Solis, *The History of the Conquest of Mexico by the Spaniards,* trans. Nathaniel Hooke (London, 1738), p. 3.

25. Prescott, *Literary Memorabilia,* 2:23.

26. Milieu, *De scribenda universitate rerum historia* (Basel, 1551), p. 183; and Le Roy, *La Vicissitude,* p. 98.

27. *Liber ecclesiastici,* 10:8.

28. Francesco Vitoria "On the American Indians," 2:1, in *Political Writings,* ed. Anthony Pagden and Jeremy Lawrance (Cambridge: Cambridge University Press, 1991), p. 253.

29. See especially José Antonio Maravall, *El Concepto de España en la edad media,* 2d ed. (Madrid: Instituto de Estudios Políticos, 1964); also Gaines Post, *Studies in Medieval Legal Thought: Public Law and the State, 1100–1322* (Princeton: Princeton University Press, 1964), pp. 482–93.

30. *Siete partidas,* 4 vols. (Barcelona, 1843–1844), 2:1.

31. See Anthony Pagden, *Spanish Imperialism and the Political Imagination* (New Haven: Yale University Press, 1990), p. 43; Pagden, *European Encounters with the New World* (New Haven: Yale University Press, 1993), p. 43; and Pagden, *Lords of All the World: Ideologies of Empire in Spain and France c. 1500–c.1800* (New Haven: Yale University Press, 1995).

32. Edgar Quinet, *Les Jésuites,* in *Oeuvres complètes,* 30 vols. (Paris: Slatkine, 1989), 2:31; and see Marjorie Reeves and Warwick Gould, *Joachim of Fiore and the Myth of the Eternal Evangel in the Nineteenth Century* (Oxford: Oxford University Press, 1987), p. 79.

33. Christopher Columbus, *The Four Voyages of Columbus,* trans. Cecil Jane (New York: Dover, 1988), "Premier viage de Colón," p. 3. See also Patricia Seed, "Taking Possession and Reading Texts: Establishing the Authority of Overseas Empires," *William and Mary Quarterly,* ser. 3, 49 (1992): 183–209.

34. Hernán Cortés, *Five Letters to the Emperor,* trans. J. Bayard Morris (New York: W. W. Norton, 1928), p. 11.

35. Bernal Díaz, *The Conquest of New Spain,* trans. J. M. Cohen (Baltimore: Penguin Books, 1963), p. 70.

36. Francisco López de Gómara, *Cortés: The Life of the Conqueror by His Secretary,* trans. Lesley Byrd Simpson (Berkeley: University of California Press, 1964), p. 47.

37. William Robertson, *The History of the Discovery and Settlement of America* (New York, 1829), p. 201.

38. See James Muldoon, *Popes, Lawyers, and Infidels* (Philadelphia: University of Pennsylvania Press, 1979), p. 137, on the *requierimiento*.

39. Díaz, *The Conquest of New Spain,* p. 71; and Patricia Seed, "Taking Possession and Reading Texts: Establishing Authority of Overseas Empires," in *Early Images of the Americans: Transfer and Invention,* ed. Jerry M. Williams and Robert E. Lewis (Tucson: University of Arizona Press, 1993), pp. 111–47.

40. In a very large literature, see especially Pagden, *The Fall of Natural Man and Spanish Imperialism* and *Lords of All the World;* also Lee Eldridge Huddleston, *Origins of the American Indian, European Concepts 1492–1725* (Austin: University of Texas Press, 1967); *First Images of America: The Impact of the New World on the Old,* ed. Fredi Chiapelli (Berkeley: University of California Press, 1976); and Grafton, *New Worlds, Ancients Texts;* also recent popular accounts such as Kirkpatrick Sale, *The Conquest of Paradise: Christopher Columbus and the Columbian Legacy* (New York: Penguin Books, 1991); Eviatar Zerubavel, *Terra Cognita: The Mental Discovery of America* (New Brunswick: Rutgers University Press, 1991); Dora Beale Polk, *The Island of California: A History of the Myth* (Spokane: Arthur H. Clark, 1991); and Karen Ordahl Kupperman, ed., *America in European Consciousness, 1493–1750* (Chapel Hill: University of North Carolina Press, 1995).

41. Ralph Waldo Emerson, *English Traits* (Boston, 1856), p. 152.

42. Edmundo O'Gorman, *The Invention of America* (Bloomington: Indiana University Press, 1961); see also Stephen Greenblatt, *Marvellous Possessions: The Wonder of the New World* (Chicago: University of Chicago Press, 1991); E. Zerubavel, *Terra Cognita;* and Kupperman, *America in European Consciousness.*

43. *De Rerum inventoribus,* 3:15; and see Brian P. Copenhaver, "The Historiography of Discovery in the Renaissance: The Sources and Composition of Polydore Vergil's *De inventoribus rerum,* I–III," *Journal of the Warburg and Courtauld Institutes* 41 (1978): 192–214.

44. Bodin, *Method,* p. 367.

45. See Geoffroy Atkinson, *Les nouveaux horizons de la Renaissance française* (Paris: Droz, 1935).

46. Solis, *The History of the Conquest of Mexico,* p. 19.

47. Gómara, *Historia general de las Indias,* chap. ccxxiv.

48. "You hold four crowns . . . in Africa and Europe, in Asia and, triumphantly, in America."

49. Francesco Guicciardini, *The History of Italy,* trans. Sidney Alexander (Princeton: Princeton University Press, 1969), p. 179.

50. Bartolomé de Las Casas, *The Tears of the Indians,* trans. John Phillips (London, 1656); and see Benjamin Keen, *The Aztec Image in Western Thought* (New Brunswick, N.J.: Rutgers University Press, 1971), p. 79.

51. Bartolomé de Las Casas, *History of the Indies,* trans. André Collard (New York: Harper & Row, 1971), p. 100.

52. Las Casas, *Historia de la Indias,* p. 15.

53. Howard Mumford Jones, *O Strange New World; American Culture: The Formative Years* (New York: Viking Press, 1952).

54. Martyr, *De Orbe Novo,* 1:174.

55. Richard H. Popkin, *Isaac Peyrère (1596–1676)* (Leiden: E. J. Brill, 1987), p. 33.

56. Sebastian Brant, *The Ship of Fools,* trans. Edwin H. Zeydel (New York: Dover, 1944), p. 22. Cf. "Premier viage de Colón," p. 7: "La gente d'esta isla y de todas las otras que he fallado y he avido noticia, andan todos desnudos." And see Richard Trexler, *Sex and Conquest: Gendered Violence, Political Order, and the European Conquest of the Americas* (Ithaca: Cornell University Press, 1995).

57. Martyr, *De Orbe Novo,* 2:189.

58. See Lewis Hanke, *All Mankind Is One* (DeKalb: Northern Illinois University Press, 1974).

59. It may be relevant to pay tribute here to my mentor, Garrett Mattingly, who was Merriman's student and protégé and who introduced me to Spanish history—a far remove but not wholly disconnected from the tradition on which I am reflecting.

60. Thomas Mann, "Voyage with Don Quixote," in *Essays of Three Decades,* trans. H. T. Lowe-Porter (New York: Alfred Knopf, 1948), p. 437.

William Bouwsma

Montaigne and the Discovery of the Ordinary

Montaigne's *Essais* were immediately popular, and his readers have ever since been attracted to various facets of this complex work. They have loved Montaigne for his intimate tone and the variety of his interests. They have appreciated his individuality and independence of mind, been cheered by his irreverence, found his skepticism bracing, and even—taking him at face value—found comfort in his fideistic piety. Many have admired his classical learning and seen in him a moralist refreshing in tone if conventional in content.[1] These characteristics of his work can be described as *extraordinary*.

There is, however, a quite different element in Montaigne's achievement that is perhaps more central to the *Essais,* and certainly of greater historical interest: his discovery and celebration of the *ordinary.* This, paradoxically, is probably even more extraordinary, in the context of the aristocratic culture of his time, than those aspects of his thought listed above. His celebration of the ordinary is historically significant because it connects him both with the humanist tradition of Renaissance Italy and with the egalitarianism of our own world that so fundamentally differentiates it from the world he inhabited. In modern culture the celebration of the ordinary has found expression in the ordinary-language philosophy associated with Ludwig Wittgenstein, the "prosaics" of Mikhail Bakhtin, and the focus of the new social history on ordinary people and everyday life, notably represented by the Annalistes.[2]

This aspect of Montaigne's concern figures prominently in what is still the most generally satisfactory study of his thought, Hugo Friedrich's *Montaigne,* first published in 1949 and recently translated into English.[3] It is "not the extraordinary," Friedrich observed, "but rather the ordinary man who appears in the *Essais* as the greatest of all wonders." Montaigne found "the proper spotlight that allows us to be astonished at *the wonder of ordinariness.*"[4] More recently the Canadian philosopher Charles Taylor emphasized the larger significance of this insight: Montaigne's "affirmation of ordinary life," Taylor pointed out, his "notion that the life of production and reproduction, of work and family, is the main locus of the good life, flies in the face of what were originally the dominant distinctions of our civilization.

For both the warrior ethic and the Platonic, ordinary life in this sense is part of the lower range, part of what contrasts with the incomparably higher." Though recognizing its biblical origins and the influence of the Reformation in promoting this position, Taylor identified Montaigne as the first major thinker fully to affirm it.[5] Disregarding the hierarchies of value in the traditional culture of his time, Montaigne deliberately turned his attention to the ordinary.

The impetus behind this shift was his revulsion, not uncommon in his time, at the falseness, the inauthenticity, of contemporary society and culture.[6] Instead of *being* themselves—that is, taking their lives seriously—too many of the human beings of his time, as Montaigne saw only too well, only *played* out their various roles in society. Indeed, he was doubtless thinking of his own career as a magistrate when he described how a man might be escorted ostentatiously "back to his door, with awe, from a public function" and how he would then drop "his part" along with his gown. But "the higher he has hoisted himself," Montaigne concluded, "the lower he falls back; inside, in his own home, everything is tumultuous and vile."[7] The unkempt household becomes a metaphor for the inner life of the public man intent on rising in the world. Montaigne's withdrawal from that world to his library in the tower room of the château on his family estate allowed him to recover his own authentic self and, in the words of Erich Auerbach, be "at home in existence" without the "fixed points of support" supplied by a traditional but artificial culture.[8]

His need for authenticity found expression in his attitude toward nature, which meant, for him, the common and ordinary aspects of life as he saw them in the lives of peasants and in the homely comparisons of Socrates, whose mouth was "full of nothing but carters, joiners, cobblers, and masons."[9] Montaigne's contempt for philosophy and philosophers (except for Socrates) was a response to the same need. Taylor has noted that the affirmation of ordinary life regularly involved "a polemical stance towards traditional views and their implied elitism."[10] Thus Montaigne was particularly hostile to the effort of philosophers to reduce the world to static generalities built up into pretentious systems of thought. "Philosophy is but sophisticated poetry," its claims mere fictions, he declared in one of his less hostile moments. Usually he was more acerbic. Sounding like Augustine, he described the most sublime inquiries of classical wisdom as no more than "the clatter of so many philosophical brains." Above all, like earlier humanists, he regarded the questions discussed by philosophers as irrelevant to the practical concerns of existence; he noted especially the inability of philosophy to comfort suffering, thereby "confessing her impotence, and sending us back not merely to ignorance . . . but to stupidity itself, to insensibility and nonexistence."[11]

He also objected to the grand conceptual schemes aimed at by philosophers on the ground that no human being can "see the whole of anything"; it was impossible, therefore, to treat any subject systematically and completely.[12] This position found expression in his rejection of the novel cosmology of Copernicus, but his objection applied equally to all the competing cosmological schemes of his time.[13] All philosophy, for Montaigne, was at once falsification of the world—morally suspect as a presumptuous effort by philosophers to present themselves and their projects as extraordinary—and essentially meaningless.

In the *Essais,* he insisted immediately on his own ordinariness. "I am myself the matter of my book," he declared in his "Epistle to the Reader," and he warned his reader, somewhat disingenuously, that it would therefore "be unreasonable to spend your leisure on so frivolous and vain a subject."[14] "I consider myself," he wrote, "one of the common sort, *except in that I consider myself so;* guilty of the commoner and humbler faults, but not of faults disavowed or excused; and I value myself only for knowing my value." He dwelt at some length on the disadvantages of worldly greatness.[15]

Though fluent in Latin, he also associated himself with the ordinary by writing the *Essais* not in the language of the cultivated, but in that of ordinary people. Earlier humanists had ridiculed the jargon of the schools for its incomprehensibility, but they continued to write mostly in Latin. By contrast, Montaigne wrote in French, even when he was most serious. He thought the "common language" appropriate, indeed "easy," for every subject except law, an exception that, given his reservations about that tangled subject, reflects rather on the law than on the language.[16] He participated fully in the Copernican revolution in language that was everywhere decentering a previously unitary linguistic and semantic universe. He might well be considered the first "ordinary language" philosopher.

He was also radically innovative in his choice of the most ordinary subjects as points of departure for his essays. Indeed, for Montaigne the notion of an "ordinary" thing was almost a contradiction in terms, since "from the most ordinary, commonplace, familiar things, if we could put them in their proper light, can be formed the greatest miracles of nature and the most wondrous examples, especially upon the subject of human actions."[17] "There is no subject so vain," he remarked elsewhere, "that it does not deserve a place in this rhapsody."[18] Any topic was for him "equally fertile": "a fly will serve my purpose."[19] He claimed to have regularly started off with "the first subject that chance offers": all things were, for Montaigne, "equally good."[20]

These views were embedded in various assumptions fundamental to his thought, notably in his holistic conception of human being. Auerbach described this as an expression of "Christian-creatural realism" because it rejected the traditional hierarchy of discrete faculties modeled on the cosmos.[21] For Montaigne, the entities that make up human being, first of all soul and body, were in fact united and inseparable. Those who insisted on dividing them were mad for wanting "to get out of themselves and escape from man." "Instead of changing into angels," he continued, "they change into beasts."[22] On the contrary, "there is nothing in us that is purely either corporeal or spiritual, and . . . we do wrong to tear apart a living man. . . . Those who want to split up our two principle parts and sequester them from each other are wrong. . . . [We] must couple and join them together again."

One implication of this position was that the body deserved more respect than it had traditionally been accorded. "The body has a great part in our being," Montaigne continued; "it holds a high rank in it."[23] By the same token the position of the mind was diminished. This had, first of all, epistemological implications. Thus Montaigne rejected the common belief in a correspondence between mind and world, its capacity to mirror nature. With Richard Rorty, and perhaps only a step from Giambattista Vico, he denied the adequacy of the generalizing intellect to comprehend nature in lofty philosophical abstractions. God's wisdom may have shaped the universe, he observed, "but we do not see its arrangement and relationship."[24] Traditional philosophy could not claim to know "the bounds and limits of God's will and the power of our mother Nature. . . . [T]here is no more notable folly than to reduce these things to the measure of our capacity and competence."[25] Reason "is so lame and so blind that there is nothing so clear and easy as to be clear enough to her; the easy and the hard are one to her; all subjects alike, and nature in general, disavow her jurisdiction and mediation." He relished the old story, though slightly modifying it, of the stargazer who, oblivious to his surroundings, fell into a well.[26]

This anthropology also had ethical implications: it meant that the mind was in no position to rule over and guide the rest of the personality. Given this view, he flatly rejected the venerable notion that to know the good is to do the good. A man, he was convinced, "sees the good and does not follow it, and sees knowledge and does not use it."[27] He was himself, he had observed, unable to control one unusually interesting area of his body; indeed, he could not even control his mind. "Memory sets before us," he wrote, "not what we choose but what it pleases." Far from ruling in lofty independence, the mind served, by rationalization, impulses arising elsewhere in the personality. Indeed, his sexual appetite was itself "less dissolute" than his reason.[28]

He minimized the value of reason on two principal counts. The first was its tendency, always presumptuous, to generalize, which flew in the face of the infinite variety of things. For Montaigne, actual things were "always dissimilar: there is no quality so universal . . . as diversity and variety." His nominalism was radical. A human being, he insisted, can experience the world only as an innumerable series of "disconnected pieces."[29]

In addition, the mind, as Montaigne saw it, did not exist in lofty isolation from the contingencies implicit in earthly existence; it shared inevitably in, its perceptions were always conditioned by, particular circumstances, notably by time and change. The world and everything in it, including human beings, were, for Montaigne, "but a perennial movement." This was a major element in his objection to the putatively timeless truths of philosophy.

He observed that he was himself constantly changing. Thus in the *Essais* he could only portray himself as he existed from moment to moment, constantly guarding against the all-too-human temptation to impose permanence or coherence on himself. "I cannot keep my subject still," he observed. "It goes along befuddled and staggering with a natural drunkenness. I take it in this condition, just as it is at the moment I give my attention to it. I do not portray being: I portray passing . . . from day to day, from minute to minute. My history needs to be adapted to the moment. I may presently change, not only by chance but also by attention." The *Essais,* then, could record only "various and changeable occurrences . . . whether I am different myself, or whether I take hold of my subjects in different circumstances and aspects. So, all in all, I may contradict myself now and then. . . . [M]y mind . . . is always in apprenticeship and on trial."[30]

This conviction was related to a historicism that led him to deny the assumption of some among his contemporaries, implied by their use of ancient terms to designate modern institutions, that these were identical and continuous with those of antiquity.[31] He knew that language too was ruled by change; Montaigne was strikingly aware of linguistic drift, that practical and messy product of ordinary experience and everyday life.[32] As a result, his affection for the classics notwithstanding, his work often suggests an awareness of the gulf between his own time and the great ancients. He thus brought to a climax the anticlassicism implicit in the Renaissance discovery of the "otherness" of antiquity. Instead of venerating their authority, he used classical authors much as Abelard had used the Fathers in *Sic et non:* they illustrated for him the diversities and contradictions produced by intellectual effort.

These dimensions of his thought virtually compelled his choice, indeed his invention, of the essay as the medium for his own reflection.[33] "Of a hundred members and faces that each thing has," he wrote of the workings of his thought, "I take one, sometimes only to lick it, sometimes to brush the surface, sometimes to pinch it to the bone," working always "without a plan and without a promise."[34] One consequence for the internal structure of the essay, as Zachary Schiffman has noted, was that, like Rabelais and probably for the same reason, Montaigne, having lost all confidence in the ontological matrix that had traditionally ordered them, could often only make *lists* of things.[35] The title of his *Essais* is an appropriate designation, as Friedrich has noted, for "miscellany-type documents."[36] Montaigne himself compared an essay, "a hodgepodge of various items," to a mixed salad.[37] Friedrich may have exaggerated in describing the *Essais* as random accumulations of unrelated items; Montaigne's protestations of artlessness were part of his art. But he was incapable, and disapproved except for aesthetic or rhetorical purposes, of ordering the contents of his mind.

But he was not, as he has commonly been regarded, a radical skeptic, if only because he knew that total skepticism would stultify both judgment and action. He attacked not belief as such, which is indispensable to human existence, but only the beliefs developed by the presumptuous and fallible intellect and expressed in an impotent academic philosophy. As Nancy Struever has argued, Montaigne sought to "mend" a "web of belief made inauthentic by a defective conception of human being." Serious ethical reflection is at the heart of the *Essais;* their essential concern is to establish a sounder foundation for human behavior than that provided by traditional culture, for in no area did its failures seem more conspicuous or more dangerous. The prescriptive moralism purveyed by philosophers, but also by unimaginative humanist pedagogues, had proved, by its results, useless. Both based ethics on external authority, when a reliable virtue depends on internalization.[38] On this point, his thought, however secular it may have been, has affinities with a major insight of contemporary religious thought.

Montaigne respected the more ordinary sources, so often scorned by intellectuals, for this kind of knowledge. He thought highly of the guidance supplied by the body and the senses, resources available to everybody: in the first place because they enable human beings to know what is pleasurable and makes for happiness.[39] Like Lorenzo Valla, Montaigne finally sided with the Epicureans against the Stoics. He also had a high regard for custom, as a distillate from the concrete and practical experience of ordinary people, as a guide for life.[40] His respect for custom and tradition was not the simple expression of an innate conservatism. It emerged out of his conviction that an authentic moral life is developed from a complex reflection on the particularities, contingencies, and ambiguities of the collective and personal encounters of ordinary life.[41]

The subject of Montaigne's *Essais,* as moral reflection, thus had to be himself. He proposed to "set forth a humble and inglorious life" because "you can tie up all moral with a common and private life just as well as with a life of richer stuff," for "each man bears the entire form of man's estate."[42] The communion with himself entailed by this project demanded absolute honesty; it required him to review all the experiences, however untidy and unflattering, and however immediately unpromising for this purpose, that might contribute to ethical insight.[43]

Traditional ethical philosophy had ignored the difficulty of its task. "Even good authors" were deficient. Thus the ancient biographers "choose one general characteristic, and go and arrange and interpret all a man's actions to fit their picture; and if they cannot twist them enough, they go and set them down to dissimulation."[44] Their blindness to the complexity and volatility of human nature, the indifference induced by their philosophical presuppositions, explained the inefficacy of their ethics.

Constantly aware of the difficulty of the human subject, Montaigne was resolved to avoid this mistake. He knew that "we are all patchwork, and so shapeless and diverse in composition that each bit, each moment, plays its own game. And there is as much difference between us and ourselves as between us and others."[45] "There are secret parts in the matters we handle," he wrote again, "which cannot be guessed, especially in human nature—mute factors that do not show, factors sometimes unknown to their possessor himself, which are brought forth and aroused by unexpected occasions."[46] He was particularly impressed by the difficulty posed for the project by the changeability of human beings. In the very first of the essays he remarked on this, presenting man as "a marvelously vain, diverse, and undulating object" on which it is hard to found any constant and uniform judgment."[47]

But his goal was not mere self-knowledge, much less another lofty theory. "We must not nail ourselves down so firmly to our humors and dispositions," he insisted. "Our principal talent is the ability to apply ourselves to various practices." Thus the ethical life that results from this introspection is practical. It consists of a constant adaptation to the changing circumstances of our lives that, indeed, finally makes a virtue of inconsistency. It also requires the maintenance at all times of a delicate balance among the diverse demands of life. "It is existing, but not living," Montaigne maintained, "to keep ourselves bound and obliged by necessity to a single course. The fairest souls are those that have the most variety and adaptability."[48] Thus Montaigne envisioned mature human existence as constant ethical practice. In Struever's formula, he exemplified "theory as practice."

Montaigne's position has social and political consequences that, flowing from his rejection of any ontological foundation for order and degree and the positive value he attributed to the ordinary, link the Renaissance to the modern world.[49] He saw no reason to believe in the superiority of the powerful and learned to ordinary folk, whether in virtue, happiness, or in intrinsic interest; indeed, he thought the opposite more likely.[50] He shared Machiavelli's distrust of utopianism, and knew too that "imaginary, artificial descriptions of a government prove ridiculous and unfit to put into practice."[51] He was also linked to Machiavelli by republican sympathies of the kind that had earlier found expression in Florentine civic humanism; for example, his preference for republican over imperial Rome. "The old Rome," he believed, had "borne men of greater worth, both for peace and for war, than that learned Rome that ruined itself."[52] He even hinted at sympathy with the assassins of Caesar.[53]

Montaigne's discovery of the ordinary was, of course, not immediately decisive. The late sixteenth and early seventeenth centuries constituted one of the most chaotic periods in European history; the disorder of the times was much on Montaigne's mind and was a major stimulus to the *Essais*. The general result of the unrest is well known. The need for order, as it so often does, left power once again in the hands of the *extraordinary* forces in society—those able, in churches and states, to impose order from above. The next stage in European history, though the significance of such labels can be exaggerated, is commonly considered in its religious aspect the age of "confessional orthodoxy," and politically the period of "early modern absolutism." The Renaissance was followed by an Old Regime whose culture was again largely respectful of classical authority, and eventually of new rational and scientific certainties of the kind that Montaigne rejected.

This deference toward authority helps to explain how Montaigne was read, and why his discovery of the ordinary went largely unnoticed by his thousands of readers. His apparent respect for the classics in his many citations from the best ancient authors made him seem reassuringly conservative, and he was long admired as a kind of modern Seneca. Under these conditions his celebration of the ordinary had no impact, for centuries, on either moral discourse or historiography. Long after Montaigne, historians mostly stuck to the doings of the extraordinary classes; indeed, they often worked for rulers, the most extraordinary people of all. The ordinary found expression chiefly among the least aristocratic groups in Europe: in Dutch painting or in English fictions that dealt, sometimes satirically, with lower-class life.

The ordinary began to reappear in the eighteenth-century novels of Defoe and Fielding, and notably in the rediscovery of the wonder of the ordinary by the romantic movement; and in the nineteenth century Balzac, Dickens, and a host of other novelists treated ordinary lives and problems seriously for a far larger reading public composed of relatively ordinary folk. The novel, indeed, was to become the primary vehicle for the depiction of the ordinary: closer to ourselves, in James Joyce's meticulous portrayal of a day in the life of Everyman and Everywoman in Dublin, or Proust's hundred-page account of a dinner party. Now, of course, we have John Updike's Rabbit; and one of the most talented among younger American novelists, Nicholson Baker, comes even closer to Montaigne. Baker's first novel consists entirely of a minute description of the lunch hour of a man who, like Montaigne, keeps lists to maintain some kind of order in his life: an hour in which the chief event is the purchase of a pair of shoelaces.[54]

But historians have been on the whole slower than painters or novelists to register impulses from the culture of their own time. Only in the last few decades have they taken any general notice of ordinary life. The most influential have been the French (chiefly social) historians of the Annales school, led by Lucien Febvre and Marc Bloch, and more recently by Fernand Braudel and Emmanuel LeRoy Ladurie.

As a historian of Renaissance culture, however, a subject of small interest to the Annalistes,[55] I cannot resist pointing out that they were anticipated in their attention to the ordinary by two classic historians of the age of the Renaissance: Jacob Burckhardt and Johann Huizinga. Burckhardt's understanding of culture was essentially anthropological: culture consisted for him of the collective attitudes, values, and behavior patterns of human beings in the past. And Huizinga, in his own time a rebel against conventional historiography, went further in the same direction. "The specific forms of the thought of an epoch," he wrote, "should not only be studied as they reveal themselves in theological and philosophical speculations, or in the conceptions of creeds, but also as they appear in *practical wisdom and everyday life.* We may even say that the true character of the spirit of an age is better revealed in its mode of regarding and expressing trivial and commonplace things than in the high manifestations of philosophy and science."[56] The peculiar responses of the senses—not only of the eye and ear but also of touch, smell, and taste—were, in his view, historically significant. The passions as well, the manner in which they were regarded and the ways they were given expression, were, for him, all a part of history, and as such solicit our attention. So were dreams, fantasies, delusions, fads, games, and symbolic structures: these were no longer too frivolous for serious study, or only errors happily transcended by a more enlightened age, but profoundly instructive reflections of the human condition. Apparently without the help of Freud, Huizinga was also aware of the erotic element in culture. Just as Montaigne pointed ahead to the importance of the ordinary in modern culture, so Burckhardt and Huizinga, writing very much in the spirit of Montaigne, pointed to its prominence in modern historiography.

Notes

1. See Donald Murdoch Frame, *Montaigne in France, 1812–1852* (New York: Columbia University Press, 1940), preface, p. vii, summarizing earlier studies of Montaigne's readership.
2. See Gary Saul Morson and Caryl Emerson, *Mikhail Bakhtin: Creation of a*

Prosaics (Stanford: Stanford University Press, 1990), which associates these various phenomena, pp. 35–36. It is remarkable, given his interest in ordinary experience, that Bakhtin seems to have ignored Montaigne.

3. Hugo Friedrich, *Montaigne,* trans. Dawn Eng (Berkeley: University of California Press, 1991).

4. Ibid., p. 144, italics added; see also pp. 18–20.

5. Charles Taylor, *Sources of the Self: The Making of the Modern Identity* (Cambridge: Harvard University Press), 1989, pp. 23, 178–84, 211–302.

6. This is the starting point of Jean Starobinski's stimulating *Montaigne en mouvement* (Paris: Gallimard, 1982); my citations of this work refer to *Montaigne in Motion,* trans. Arthur Goldhammer (Chicago: University of Chicago Press, 1985). For a profound meditation on this problem, see Lionel Trilling, *Sincerity and Authenticity* (Cambridge: Harvard University Press, 1971).

7. "Of repentance," p. 614; I cite throughout from *The Complete Works of Montaigne,* trans. Donald Frame (Stanford: Stanford University Press, 1958).

8. Erich Auerbach, *Mimesis: The Representation of Reality in Western Literature,* trans. Willard Trask (Princeton: Princeton University Press, 1953), p. 311.

9. This is the general point in "Of physiognomy," especially pp. 802–3. Montaigne is here, as he often does, making his reading serve his own purposes.

10. Taylor, *Sources of the Self,* p. 23.

11. "Apology for Raymond Sebond," pp. 379, 383, 361–66, 401.

12. "Of Democritus and Heraclitus," p. 219.

13. "Apology for Raymond Sebond," p. 429.

14. P. 2; Friedrich, *Montaigne,* pp. 224–27, notes the originality in such public discussion of himself.

15. "Of presumption," p. 481; "Of the disadvantages of greatness," pp. 699–703, emphasis added.

16. "Of experience," p. 816. On the significance of Montaigne's use of the vernacular, see Friedrich, *Montaigne,* p. 23; and the stimulating treatment in Richard Waswo, *Language and Meaning in the Renaissance* (Princeton: Princeton University Press, 1987), pp. 174–81.

17. "On experience," p. 829.

18. "Ceremony of interviews between kings," p. 32.

19. "Of presumption," p. 501.

20. "Of Democritus and Heraclitus," p. 219.

21. Auerbach, *Mimesis,* pp. 304–5.

22. "Of experience," p. 856.

23. "Of presumption," pp. 484–85.

24. "Of a monstrous child," p. 539.

25. "If is folly to measure the true and false by our own capacity," p. 132.

26. "Apology for Raymond Sebond," pp. 328, 402.

27. "Of pedantry," p. 104.

28. "Apology for Raymond Sebond," pp. 365, 425, 419.

29. "Of experience," p. 815; cf. "Of drunkenness," p. 244.

30. "Of repentance," pp. 610–11; cf. Starobinski, *Montaigne in Motion*, p. 14 and passim, on Montaigne's development of "a new concept of identity" as both changing and continuous.

31. Cf. "Of the vanity of words," p. 223; and "Of experience," p. 819.

32. Cf. Waswo, *Language and Meaning*, pp. 174–81, for Montaigne's strikingly modern view of language; and Morson and Emerson, *Bakhtin*, pp. 144–45, for linguistic drift as a product of everyday life. This does not mean that Montaigne had developed a fully modern historical consciousness. Although the *Essais* were revised and expanded over a period of twenty years, he took no interest in tracing development in his own thought; on this point compare Zachary Sayre Schiffman, *On the Threshold of Modernity: Relativism in the French Renaissance* (Baltimore: Johns Hopkins University Press, 1991), pp. 59–73.

33. Cf. Starobinski, *Montaigne in Motion*, p. 35, on this point.

34. "Of Democritus and Heraclitus," p. 219.

35. Schiffman, *On the Threshold of Modernity*, pp. 4–10, 73.

36. Friedrich, *Montaigne*, p. 340. See also pp. 349–50 on the appropriateness of the essay form for Montaigne's project.

37. "Of names," p. 201.

38. Nancy S. Struever, *Theory as Practice: Ethical Inquiry in the Renaissance* (Chicago: University of Chicago Press, 1992), pp. 182–209. This work places Montaigne in a line extending from Petrarch through Valla and Machiavelli to Vico and Gramsci. Victoria Kahn makes a similar point in *Rhetoric, Prudence and Skepticism in the Renaissance* (Ithaca: Cornell University Press, 1985), pp. 115–51.

39. "Of experience," pp. 850–51.

40. Cf. Starobinski, *Montaigne in Motion*, especially pp. 252–56.

41. The ethical principle attributed to Tolstoy by Morson and Emerson is helpful for understanding Montaigne: "the idea that real ethical decisions are made, and one's true life is lived, at everyday moments we rarely if ever notice" (*Bakhtin*, p. 23).

42. "Of repentance," p. 611.

43. Hence, as Struever observed, the large proportion of "waste" in the *Essais*, if one attempts to interpret them as an *argument* (*Theory as Practice*, pp. 200–201).

44. "Of the inconsistency of our actions," p. 239.

45. Ibid., pp. 243–44.

46. "Of repentance," p. 618.

47. "By diverse means we arrive at the same end," p. 5.

48. "Of three kinds of association," p. 621. While Starobinski and Struever agree on the necessity in this enterprise of absolute honesty, Starobinski emphasizes its importance for the consolidation of an authentic identity; Struever also gives it a historical context by presenting it as a radical extension of humanist reformism.

49. Some of these consequences are explored in David Lewis Schaefer, *The Political Philosophy of Montaigne* (Ithaca: Cornell University Press, 1990).

50. "Of the inequality that is between us," pp. 191–96.

51. On Montaigne's affinities with Machiavelli, see Marcel Tetel, "Montaigne and Machiavelli: Ethics, Politics and Humanism," *Rivista di Letterature Moderne e Comparate* 29 (1976): 165–81; and, for a subtle discussion, Struever, *Theory as Practice,* pp. 201–9. The quote is from "Of vanity," p. 730.

52. "Apology for Raymond Sebond," p. 359.

53. Cf. "Of books," pp. 300–301.

54. Nicholson Baker, *The Mezzanine* (New York: Weidenfeld & Nicolson, 1988).

55. Cf. Emmanuel LeRoy Ladurie, "L'histoire immobile," *Annales: Économies, sociétés, civilisations* 29 (1974): 673–82.

56. Johann Huizinga, *The Waning of the Middle Ages: A Study of the Forms of Life, Thought, and Art in France and the Netherlands in the XIVth and XVth Centuries,* trans. F. Hopman (London: Edward Arnold, 1924), p. 206; emphasis added. Cf. *"The Waning of the Middle Ages* Revisited," in William J. Bouwsma, *A Usable Past: Essays in European Cultural History* (Berkeley: University of California Press, 1990), pp. 325–35.

Zachary Sayre Schiffman

An Intellectual in Politics: Montaigne as Mayor of Bordeaux

❦ Book 1 of Thomas More's *Utopia* epitomizes the dilemma of the intellectual in politics, caught between abstract ideals and political realities. The bulk of book 1 consists of an extended exchange—the "Dialogue of Counsel"—between two interlocutors, "Raphael Hythlodaeus" and "Thomas More," about whether a man of learning should serve his king. The ironically named Hythlodaeus—from the Greek for "expert in trifles"—represents the ideal of the learned man. His knowledge comes not only from books but also from experience; indeed, he is introduced both as a scholar well versed in classical philosophy and as a traveler freshly returned from an extended stay in the New World. Although self-effacingly portrayed in comparison to Hythlodaeus, the figure of More is also a man of learning; he is conversant in the classics and has a clear, inquiring mind, along with a desire to make his learning useful in the world. Throughout the dialogue, More attempts unsuccessfully to convince Hythlodaeus to enter the service of his king, in order that others may benefit from his vast knowledge and experience.

The dialogue culminates after More cites Plato on the necessity of combining governance with philosophy, to which Hythlodaeus replies that the madness of warmongering is so thoroughly ingrained in kings that they would ridicule or distrust sane, responsible, pacific advice. At this point, More plays the trump card of humanism. Of course, he argues, a "scholastic" philosophy that expresses its truths inflexibly is unsuitable for rulers. But there is another kind of philosophy that adapts itself to its audience and seeks gradually to win over the will. By combining learning with this rhetorical sense of decorum, one can at the very least temper the madness of kings, doing good by minimizing evil. To this Hythlodaeus responds, "By this approach, I should accomplish nothing else than to share the madness of others as I tried to cure their lunacy"—sleep with dogs and you catch fleas. The dialogue ends on this note, a sobering comment on the humanist pretension to awaken virtue through eloquence and thereby reform the political world.[1]

The occasion for the composition of the dialogue was, of course, Thomas More's invitation to join Henry VIII's council. His decision to do so despite the outcome of the dialogue may reflect More's belief that learning with no practical application in the world really was "trifling," as Hythlodaeus's name implies. Whatever the reason for More's decision, *Utopia* (both in book 1 and as a whole) establishes More's opinion that the intellectual who adheres to the ideals of his education can have no role in a hopelessly corrupt political world, lest he himself be corrupted. Although Montaigne probably did not read *Utopia,* he could clearly see—writing some sixty years later—what More had foreseen, that humanist hopes for political reform were unrealistic. In the *Essais,* Montaigne likened the man in politics to one swept up in a crowd, deprived of his freedom of movement: He who walks in the crowd must step aside, keep his elbows in, step back or advance, even leave the straight way, according to what he encounters. He must live not so much according to himself as according to others, not according to what he proposes to himself but according to what others propose to him, according to the time, according to the men, according to the business.[2]

So much for the pretense of using rhetoric to bring others around to one's own enlightened ways. But much like More, Montaigne found himself increasingly drawn into the political world, albeit less willingly. And as this involvement grew, he would establish a role for the intellectual in politics that would transcend the impasse apparent in the "Dialogue of Counsel."

Montaigne's protestations throughout the *Essais* that he is a mere Everyman living out an obscure life in private belie the fact that he was born to, and raised for, a life of public service. Even after his so-called retirement from public life, he nonetheless continued to serve his king, both as an individual and as a magistrate. And this service ultimately earned him the trust of the most powerful figures in the realm. Although he was not one of the leading actors in the events of his day, he was always cast in major supporting roles. As the eldest son of a family that had recently graduated to the nobility, Montaigne was destined for a life of public service. His father, Pierre Eyquem, had adopted the noble profession of arms and served with the king's army in Italy until 1528; after his return, he held a succession of municipal offices in Bordeaux: *jurat* (city councilman), provost, deputy mayor, and mayor. This last office was one of considerable prestige; election to it was reserved for the nobility and required the king's approval. His father's selfless devotion to public office served as an inspiration for Montaigne, who later wrote, "There never was a more kindly and public-spirited soul" (3.10, p. 983).[3]

Montaigne's famous education, which probably culminated with some form of legal training, served as his passport into the growing royal bureaucracy. In 1554, when Montaigne was twenty-one, his family purchased for him a seat on the newly created Cour des Aides of Périgueux. The king had created the court, which would preside over regional matters, with the sole intention of selling its offices in order to pay for a recent war with the Habsburgs. His act undercut the prerogatives of the Parlement of Bordeaux, which agitated against the new court and succeeded in absorbing its jurisdiction in 1557. In return for this royal concession, however, the parlement had to accept the former magistrates of the Cour des Aides as *parlementaires.* The addition of new members to the parlement diminished the value of existing offices and diluted revenues, or *épices,* from the sale of justice. Montaigne's debut as a *parlementaire* was thus inauspicious, for the presence of the new members was deeply resented, and they were initially subjected to constant harassment.[4]

Such behavior fostered Montaigne's abiding contempt for his fellow magistrates and for the venality of justice that fueled their avarice. Early on he served as a spokesman for the newcomers when the rest of the parlement spitefully denied them certain ceremonial rights. And in 1565, when the parlement was preparing to receive Charles IX, Montaigne proposed that the councillors remonstrate with the king against the venal system. He denounced it to his colleagues, blaming the "disorder of justice" on the multitude of officers, their unsuitability for office, and their sale of justice.[5] Years later he repeated these charges in the *Essais:* "What is more barbarous to see than a nation where by lawful custom the charge of judging is sold, and judgments are paid for in ready cash, and where justice is lawfully refused to whoever has not the wherewithal to pay?" (1.23, p. 116). The reasoned contrast here between the ideal of justice and its reality is worthy of a Hythlodaeus.

Perhaps the only bright spot in his career as a *parlementaire* was Montaigne's friendship with Étienne de la Boétie, who reinforced Montaigne's tendency to approach the problems of the realm with a combination of rationalism and idealism. In his "Memoir Concerning the Edict of January 1562," La Boétie proposed an alternative to Catherine de Médicis's new policy of religious toleration.[6] Catherine had promulgated the Edict of January, granting the Huguenots freedom to worship in public, in an effort to use the Huguenot nobility to counterbalance the power of the Catholic Guises, whom she had supplanted as regent with the accession of Charles IX.

Religious considerations weighed more heavily than political ones in La Boétie's thinking about Catherine's policy, for he regarded uniformity of religion as the primary form of social cement. He believed that religious differences stemmed from abuses in the church and that the reform of these abuses would reunify the faith, obviating the need for toleration. The recent failure of the Colloquy of Poissy had demonstrated that the task of reconciliation could not be entrusted to theologians; consequently, La Boétie proposed to use *parlementaires*. He maintained that the reform of the Gallican church was a civil rather than a religious affair. With a civil institution undertaking the task of reform, Huguenots need not submit to Rome, nor Catholics to Geneva; instead, both sides could yield to the judgment of the king's parlement. Barely two months after La Boétie formulated his plan, the duke of Guise attacked a congregation of Huguenots worshipping at Vassy, thus igniting the first of the Wars of Religion in France and foreclosing, at least for the moment, all thoughts of reconciliation. Like his friend, Montaigne, too, sought a nontheological basis for the reunification of the church. Sometime before 1565—perhaps after March 1563, when the Peace of Amboise raised new hopes of reconciliation—Montaigne conceived of the idea of translating Raymond Sebond's *Natural Theology*. Sebond, a fifteenth-century Spanish theologian, had claimed that the fundamental truths of the Christian religion could be found with certainty in the natural world of God's creation instead of in Scripture, which was always subject to misinterpretation. Pierre Bunel had given a copy of the book to Montaigne's father, recommending it as an antidote to religious innovations. Although Montaigne claimed to undertake the translation at his father's behest, his embellishment of Sebond's argument makes clear his intention to provide Frenchmen with a nondogmatic basis for faith acceptable to Catholics and Huguenots alike. In a similar vein, he also modified Sebond's extravagant claims for the infallible truth of his method, thus demonstrating his distrust of all forms of dogmatism. This translation represents the spiritual counterpart to La Boétie's civil plan for religious reconciliation.[7] But Montaigne's idealistic hopes were no more realized than his friend's. While he worked on the translation, the Second War of Religion erupted; and soon after he published it, the third one began. Montaigne decided to retire from public life in 1569, while this third war still raged. Years later, he described his unsuccessful attempt to apply the ideals of his education to political life: "I once tried to employ in the service of public dealings ideas and rules for living as crude, green, and unpolished—or unpolluted—as they were born in me or derived from my education, and which I use conveniently in private matters: a scholastic and novice virtue. I found them inept and dangerous for such matters" (3.9, p. 970). The decision to retire resulted at least in part from Montaigne's political disillusionment. Like Hythlodaeus, he now considered himself unfit for public service in a corrupt world.

The major political undertaking of his early retirement further discouraged him from public life. While visiting Paris sometime between 1572 and 1578, Montaigne became involved in an attempt to reconcile Henry of Navarre and Henry, duke of Guise. The Huguenot Navarre had come to Paris in 1572 to wed the king's sister, Margaret of Valois; this celebration was intended to ratify the recently signed Peace of Saint-Germain, which concluded the Third War of Religion by according the Huguenots extensive privileges. The duke of Guise was deeply involved in the Saint Bartholomew's Day massacre, the Catholic's reaction to this impending Huguenot triumph. After the massacre, Navarre became a prisoner of the court and was forced to convert to Catholicism. In 1576, he escaped from Paris, renounced Catholicism, and joined the Huguenot armies in southern France, which were then engaged in the Fourth War of Religion. Montaigne may have acted as an intermediary between Navarre and Guise during a trip to Paris between 1572 and 1576, when they were both at court; or he may have acted as Navarre's emissary in Paris between 1577 and 1578, when Guise was at court.[8]

According to Montaigne, the attempt to reconcile the two failed because Navarre spurned Guise's overtures and, henceforth, Guise had no choice but to consider Navarre his mortal enemy. During these negotiations Montaigne was surprised to discover "that religion, which is alleged by both, is used speciously as a pretext by those who follow them; as for the rest, neither one regards it."[9] Perhaps the translator of Raymond Sebond tried to reconcile the antagonists on the basis of their religious beliefs, only to discover that his rational approach was "inept and dangerous."

Not long after Navarre's escape from Paris in 1576, Huguenots and moderate Catholics forced the humiliating Peace of Monsieur on the newly crowned Henry III. Zealous Catholics reacted to this, yet another Huguenot victory, by forming Catholic leagues that coalesced into a unified party under the leadership of the duke of Guise. With the formation of the Holy League, the king briefly renewed the war and obtained a more favorable peace agreement, the Edict of Poitiers, in 1577. Navarre's return to southern France accelerated the political disintegration of Montaigne's province of Guienne. According to the Peace of Monsieur, Navarre was appointed the royal governor of the province; but the king also appointed a belligerent Catholic, Marshal Biron, as lieutenant governor to oversee royal interests. At first, Biron contented himself with engineering bureaucratic obstructions to Navarre's authority; eventually, however, he began seizing towns throughout the province. Catherine de Médicis personally tried to restore order in 1578, when she escorted her daughter, Margaret, back to Navarre, who had left his wife behind when he escaped from Paris. Catherine and Navarre reconciled the Catholics and Huguenots in the Treaty of Nérac in February 1579. But the peace was short-lived. In November, the prince of Condé seized the town of La Fère in Normandy, and Navarre, his coreligionist, began to prepare for war. In May 1580, Navarre attacked Cahor and captured it after a bloody battle. Biron reacted vigorously, waging a bitter campaign against Navarre throughout Guienne; among other places, Catholic troops captured the strategic town of Mont-de-Marsan in September, which (as we shall see) later became an important point of contention. Meanwhile the king's army, commanded by Marshal Matignon, besieged and recaptured La Fère. This war was clearly civil rather than religious— Protestant ministers even preached against it—and neither side cared to prolong it. In November 1580, the Treaty of Fleix, which largely reaffirmed that of Nérac, ended the war.

With warfare continually sputtering and flaring in southern France, the nature of the fighting changed. Frequent skirmishes between armed bands replaced the occasional battles between armies, and the region was plagued with endemic conflict characterized by sudden assaults on villages, castles, and homes—often accompanied by the massacre of the defenders. Montaigne's remark, "I have gone to bed a thousand times in my own home, imagining that someone would betray me and slaughter me that very night," aptly sums up the prevailing state of anarchy (3.9, p. 948). During this period, Montaigne may have joined a vigilante force of local nobility.[10] Later, he served with the royal army besieging La Fère in the summer of 1580. After his friend and neighbor Philibert de Gramont was killed, Montaigne accompanied the body to Soissons, whence he embarked on a two-year sojourn in Italy.

This trip was born of Montaigne's desire to escape not only the headache of household management but also the chaos of civil war:

The other thing that invites me to these excursions is that the present moral state of our country does not please me. I could easily console myself for this corruption [as] regards the public interest . . . but not with regard to my own. I in particular suffer from it too much. For in my neighborhood we have now grown old, through the long license of these civil wars, in so riotous a form of government . . . that in truth it is a marvel that it can subsist. (3.9, p. 933)

The period of prolonged license had the effect of turning values topsy-turvy. Echoing Thucydides on the moral effects of civil strife, Montaigne wrote, "Even the qualities that are not reproachable in me, I have found useless in this age. My easygoing ways would have been thought cowardice and weakness; fidelity and conscience would have been thought squeamish and superstitious; frankness and independence, troublesome, thoughtless, and rash" (2.17, p. 629).

Montaigne apparently shared Thucydides's judgment that in this topsy-turvy world, violent brutes invariably eliminate their more intelligent opponents, who delude themselves with the notion that their superior intellect will enable them to anticipate any blows. When he embarked on his trip, Montaigne probably felt he had no recourse but to surrender the polity to its brutish elements.

He would have stayed in Italy much longer, and perhaps even traveled on to other, more exotic countries, had he not been forced to become mayor of Bordeaux. He was chosen to succeed Marshal Biron, who was concurrently mayor of the city and lieutenant governor of Guienne. As mayor, Biron had consistently denied Navarre entrance to Bordeaux, the principal city of the province over which Navarre was nominally governor. Catherine de Médicis had failed to reconcile the two men in 1578, and their mutual animosity had contributed to the outbreak of war in 1580. Although Biron's vigorous campaign forced Navarre to negotiate at Fleix in November 1580, the marshal was sacrificed in order to maintain the peace he had helped to win. He was forced to retire to his estates in April 1581, thus vacating both the lieutenant governorship and the mayoralty.[11]

During the peace negotiations at Fleix, Navarre probably insisted that the mayoralty be separated from the lieutenant governorship, permitting a more equitable balance of power in the province. Marshal Matignon, who had just recaptured La Fère, was chosen to replace Biron as lieutenant governor; and the marquis of Trans, who hosted the negotiations, probably suggested Montaigne for the municipal office. Trans was Montaigne's neighbor and patron, having previously sponsored him for the Order of Saint Michel. Both Navarre and his queen, Margaret, approved of this suggestion. Navarre had trusted Montaigne as an intermediary in the unsuccessful negotiations with Guise in Paris and had named Montaigne a gentleman of his chamber in 1577. Margaret had liked Montaigne's translation of Sebond's *Natural Theology* and had asked him to compose what became the "Apology for Raymond Sebond." Finally, both Henry III and Catherine de Médicis approved of the appointment, for Montaigne's loyalty to the crown was well known and had been reaffirmed by his recent service at the siege of La Fère.[12]

Biron's term as mayor officially expired in August 1581. The marshal schemed for reelection, but the *jurats* of Bordeaux unanimously chose Montaigne, the king's man. Montaigne learned of his election during his stay at the baths of La Villa in September and immediately declined the honor. But more letters awaited him when he arrived in Rome in October, and friends in Rome probably advised him to accept the position. Despite this pressure, he tarried in Rome for another two weeks before reluctantly starting homeward, where he arrived on November 30. Meanwhile the king, thinking Montaigne was still in Rome, politely ordered him by letter to return immediately, adding that he would be "greatly displeased" should Montaigne refuse the position.[13]

Fortunately for Montaigne, the mayoralty was by now largely a ceremonial office. After a violent tax revolt in 1548, the king had reorganized the municipal government, making it more amenable to his will. The mayor's tenure in office was reduced from an indefinite period to a two-year term; and, although the *jurats* ostensibly retained the right to elect the mayor, they really only ratified the king's choice. Furthermore, after Biron's double appointment as mayor and lieutenant governor of the province, the mayoralty had virtually ceased to exist. By the time Montaigne assumed the office, the mayor's duties were reduced to presiding over the *jurade* (which could function perfectly well without him) and representing the city on diplomatic missions and formal occasions.[14]

The reestablishment of an independent mayoralty may have stirred thoughts of a renaissance of municipal authority. Montaigne's father had once been a selfless, conscientious mayor, and the *jurats* probably expected the same energetic leadership from Montaigne. But when he first addressed them, he explicitly stated that he would not follow his father's example: "I added very clearly that I should be very sorry if anything whatsoever were to weigh so heavily on my will as their affairs and their city had formerly done on his" (3.10, pp. 982–83). During his first term in office, Montaigne often remained at his estate, communicating with the *jurats* by letter. He wanted to remain aloof from public office, fulfilling only its minimum requirements.[15]

Montaigne's ability to sustain his aloofness ended soon after his reelection to the mayoralty on August 1, 1583. Only a few days later, Henry III provoked a major crisis by expelling Margaret of Valoise from Paris. He had invited his sister to join the court in 1582, hoping that Henry of Navarre would accompany his wife, thus facilitating the reassertion of royal authority in the south. Navarre's refusal to follow Margaret was only one of a succession of political disappointments, and her presence in Paris quickly became an embarrassment. In frustration, the king summarily expelled her from the city on August 8, 1583. When he learned of the insult, Henry of Navarre demanded a royal apology before he would receive his wife.[16]

Navarre sought to use the incident as a means of gaining political concessions from the king. In particular, he wanted the return of Mont-de-Marsan and the renewal of the Huguenot privilege to maintain eight security towns, granted by the Peace of Monsieur in 1576.[17] Mont-de-Marsan, a town in Navarre's patrimony, had been captured by Biron in 1580 and should have reverted to Navarre according to the Treaty of Fleix. The king, however, wanted to keep this strategically located town, from which he could threaten both Navarre's capital of Nérac to the northeast and his kingdom of Béarn to the south. The Edict of Poitiers issued in 1577 limited the maintenance of the security towns to a period of six years, by which time peace was to have been restored throughout the kingdom. The Huguenot troops in the towns were to be paid by the king, who instituted a special tax on the surrounding regions for this purpose. In September 1583, the privilege to garrison the security towns expired, but Navarre refused to relinquish them, claiming that peace had not yet been established throughout the kingdom.[18] And even before the expiration date, the king had stopped paying the Huguenot troops, although he continued to collect the tax earmarked for them.

A confrontation between Navarre and Matignon, the lieutenant governor of Guienne, had been developing over these two issues during the months before Margaret's expulsion from Paris. Throughout the summer, Matignon had been ignoring Navarre's repeated requests to turn over the town and pay the garrison.[19] The king's insult now provided Navarre with an excuse to take decisive action, and on the night of November 21, 1583, his troops seized Mont-de-Marsan in a sudden assault. Matignon responded within days by encircling Nérac with garrisons and positioning himself to retake Mont-de-Marsan. Navarre, in turn, set the withdrawal of Matignon's garrisons as the price for Margaret's return to Nérac. The situation quickly became deadlocked, and civil war appeared likely.

Caught in a standoff with Matignon, Navarre sought Montaigne's support. A few days after his seizure of Mont-de-Marsan, Navarre had his trusted adviser and chief polemicist, Philippe Duplessis-Mornay, initiate a correspondence with Montaigne designed to bring the mayor of Bordeaux over to Navarre's side. As a gentleman of Navarre's chamber and a loyal servant of Henry III, Montaigne would have been a useful go-between, if not a valuable ally. Of this correspondence, only Duplessis-Mornay's half is extant in five letters, which attempt to woo Montaigne at each crucial turn of events.[20] The nature of Montaigne's response can be inferred from comments in book 3 of the *Essais*—written just after his mayoralty—that describe how he openly maintained both his affection for Navarre and his loyalty to Henry III (see 3.1, p. 772). By preserving his personal integrity, Montaigne retained his political effectiveness during this crisis, enabling him to provide valuable service as an intermediary.

Montaigne's friendship and loyalty were soon put to the test. In lieu of their back wages, Huguenot troops in the security town of Mas-de-Verdun began seizing shipping on the Garonne River, thus severing Bordeaux's vital trade with Toulouse. On December 13, Montaigne met with Navarre at Mont-de-Marsan and remonstrated with him to preserve the freedom of commerce in the province ("Letters," pp. 1378–79). Navarre, however, claimed that Matignon was responsible for paying the garrisons. He hoped to pressure Montaigne into siding with him on this issue. If he could gain the mayor's support, he could make the maintenance of the security towns a further condition for Margaret's return, thus using the threat to Bordeaux as a means of forcing Matignon's withdrawal.[21] During this meeting Montaigne corresponded with Matignon, making clear his refusal to be manipulated ("Letters," p. 1379).

Ultimately, neither side was eager to go to war over an insult to the queen of Navarre, and so an accord was eventually reached. In January 1584, Navarre received his wife without a royal apology, in return for Mont-de-Marsan and the withdrawal of Matignon's garrisons. Both sides tacitly ignored the sensitive security town issue. In April, Margaret was officially reunited with her husband, who, during her absence, had acquired a new mistress—Diane d'Andoins, widow of Montaigne's friend and neighbor Philibert de Gramont, killed at the siege of La Fère.[22]

Montaigne was responsible for the subsequent reconciliation of Navarre and Matignon. The marshal so distrusted Navarre that he refused to withdraw his garrisons until Navarre and Margaret were actually reunited; indeed, an angry Henry III had to command him to obey orders.[23] Navarre, however, was more willing to make amends. He sent Matignon a letter of friendly greeting in May 1584, using Montaigne as his messenger.[24] In December, Navarre honored Montaigne with a visit to his château, where the subject of reconciliation was discussed. Soon afterward the viscount of Turenne, who had accompanied Navarre during the visit, wrote Montaigne, "I beg you to keep a hand in this [the reconciliation], for it is well known that by your persuasion and as you press for it, this can happen."[25] Montaigne probably arranged the successful meeting between the two former adversaries in June 1585. Two years later, during the last of the civil wars, Matignon delayed joining his forces with those of the Catholic League, which were led by the duke of Joyeuse; the impatient duke went off to fight Navarre alone. Perhaps, had Navarre and Matignon not been reconciled, the marshal would have hurried to his rendezvous with the duke, and Navarre rather than Joyeuse would have fallen at Coutras.

Montaigne's involvement in high politics did not end with his mayoralty. Three days after the great Huguenot victory at Coutras in October 1587, Navarre again visited Montaigne's château, perhaps to seek his further services as intermediary with Matignon and Henry III. And three months later, Montaigne embarked on a trip to Paris bearing, at Matignon's request, messages from Navarre to Henry III. Montaigne was clearly involved in the attempt to reconcile the two kings, whose alliance might counterbalance the resurgent Catholic League and restore peace to the kingdom.[26] Indeed,

Montaigne had become quite comfortable with his role as adviser and intermediary, and, had he lived long enough, he would have gladly joined Navarre's court after the latter was crowned king of France (see 3.13, p. 1055;
and "Letters," pp. 1399–1400).

The king's insult to Margaret thus catalyzed events that ultimately forced
Montaigne back into the same political world he had previously fled. The
king violated the Treaty of Fleix by keeping Mont-de-Marsan; Navarre
violated the Edict of Poitiers by keeping his security towns. The king rashly
insulted Margaret and then refused to apologize; Navarre capitalized on the
king's blunder by playing the outraged husband, all the while cavorting
with his new mistress. And for Montaigne's eyes, Duplessis-Mornay dressed
this petty affair in the garb of virtue, justice, and honor; the king's apologists no doubt did likewise. In his previous period of political involvement,
Montaigne was discouraged to find that the ideals of his education did not
apply in a political world where parties pursued only their own advantage.
Now, he discovered a new point of orientation. Because Montaigne believed,
like Hythlodaeus, that he could not give himself to the political world
without compromising himself, he subordinated his public role to the requirements of his own nature. He articulated this new rule of political
conduct in book 3 of the *Essais,* which he began writing in the summer of
1585, after Marshal Matignon succeeded him as mayor of Bordeaux. The
very first essay of book 3, "Of the useful and the honorable," opens with an
allusion to his recent mediation between Navarre and Matignon:

In what little negotiating I have had to do between our princes, in these divisions
and subdivisions that tear our nation apart today, I have studiously avoided letting
them be mistaken about me and deceived by my outward appearance. Professional
negotiators make every effort within their power to conceal their thoughts and to
feign a moderate and conciliatory attitude. As for me, I reveal myself by my most
vigorous opinions, presented in my most personal manner—a tender and green
negotiator, who would rather fail in my mission than fail to be true to myself.
However, up to this time it has been with such good luck (for certainly fortune has
the principal share in it) that few men have passed between one party and another
with less suspicion and more favor and privacy. (Pp. 768–69)

In other words, rather than sacrificing the virtues that made him unfit for
public service, he played them up, and in so doing boldly played himself on

the public stage. This open and forthright behavior, which came most naturally to him, won the trust of both sides. Although he modestly credited his success chiefly to fortune, he nonetheless reiterated throughout book 3 a new rule of conduct for the political world, based on the principle that one should always act in accordance with one's own nature.[27]

Nowhere is this theme more apposite to politics than in the essay "Of husbanding your will" (3.10), in which Montaigne described his conduct as mayor. Here he justified his aloofness from public office by declaring that "we must lend ourselves to others and give ourselves only to ourselves": "If people have sometimes pushed me into the management of other men's affairs, I have promised to take them in hand, not in lungs and liver; to take them on my shoulders, not incorporate them into me; to be concerned over them, yes; to be impassioned over them, never."

Passion "mortgages" the soul, alienating it from itself and pledging it to others: "Men give themselves for hire. Their faculties are not for them, they are for those to whom they enslave themselves; their tenants are at home inside, not they. This common humor I do not like. We must husband the freedom of our soul and mortgage it only on the right occasions; which are in very small number, if we judge sanely" (pp. 980–81).

In an ironic twist, Montaigne argued that those who have mortgaged their souls are less effective politically than those who carefully distinguish between themselves and their public duties: "We never conduct well the thing that possesses and conducts us" (p. 985). Thus, a degree of aloofness from public office is necessary to maintain one's effectiveness as a political actor. In another ironic twist, Montaigne inverted the classical commonplace—used by More to convince Hythlodaeus to enter the king's service—that the public interest may necessarily entail personal sacrifice.[28] For he who understands "the friendship that each man owes to himself," public service entails not the need for personal sacrifice but the opportunity for personal growth: "This man, knowing exactly what he owes to himself, finds it in his part that he is to apply to himself his experience of other men and of the world, and, in order to do so, contribute to public society the duties and services within his province. He who lives not at all unto others, hardly lives unto himself" (p. 984).

In other words, one undertakes public service in order better to understand oneself. And the better one understands oneself, the more effective one is in one's dealings with others. Thus, Montaigne overturned the traditional dichotomy between public welfare and private advantage by subsuming the former under the latter, transforming politics into a reflexive activity that mirrors the self.

The admonition to follow one's own nature was not an invitation to license. According to Montaigne, the excesses of civil war are born of passions and ambitions that distract one from one's self. In this way, individuals become (as it were) "denatured," incapable of even recognizing virtue, let alone distinguishing it from vice: "Men of our time are so formed for agitation and ostentation that goodness, moderation, equability, constancy, and such quiet and obscure qualities are no longer felt" (p. 999). Montaigne avoided this pitfall by conducting his mayoralty in the modest, open manner befitting himself. Others might criticize the "natural languor" of his administration, but, he maintained, he gave as much of himself to the polity as the circumstances required, acting not for the sake of ambition but for the public good (p. 998). And he would have been capable of more vigorous action had the circumstances demanded it. But under no circumstances would he have allowed himself to be swept away by political passions. Those who are swept away become so denatured as to delude themselves into thinking that evil acts are honorable when done for the right cause.

Montaigne's new rule of conduct enabled him, as a man of learning, once again to engage in politics. But he did not regard learning as a prerequisite for effective political action. The self-knowledge that made such action possible derived from any form of "commerce" with others, direct as well as vicarious. All that was required, as Montaigne outlined in his essay "Of the art of discussion" (3.8), was that one engage with others in an open and forthright manner, conversing with them in an effort not to score points and win arguments but rather to learn about them and their world, and, in so doing, about oneself. Montaigne incorporated this notion of conversational tact, grace, and generosity of spirit into his nascent ideal of *honnêteté,* with which he described the personal integrity born of self-knowledge, an integrity that best equipped the individual for life in society. Learning was not essential for *honnêteté:* "A wellborn mind that is practiced in dealing with men makes itself thoroughly agreeable by itself" (3.3, p. 802).

Wherever he went, Montaigne always sought the company of *honnestes hommes* and *honnestes femmes.* In his experience, however, such people were rare; and in lieu of them, he took comfort in his association with books, which were constant and dependable, albeit less lively. Hence, learning still played an important role in the formation of the political actor. The substance of one's learning, however, was less important than how one processed it. Ideally, it served to provide the material on which one "essayed" oneself, testing one's judgment in an effort to discover one's own nature. And on the basis of this discovery, one could contribute to civil society the duties and services within one's province.

Montaigne's conception of learning thus differed from that of a Hythlodaeus, for whom the lifelong study of philosophy entailed the adoption of fixed moral and political principles. It also differed from that of a More, who combined Hythlodaeus's principles with rhetoric, hoping to make them more palatable to kings. For Montaigne, these kinds of learning really were "trifling" because they were not necessarily reflexive. They usually served to import foreign rules for living rather than to aid in the discovery of one's own. The true intellectual entered the political world armed not with abstract ideals and rhetorical strategies, but with a clear sense of who he was, under which he subsumed his public duty, which he performed to the best of his capacity. The intellectual, as such, thus had a role to play in politics, and especially so in an age of civil war, when the self-knowledge born of learning protected him against passion and ambition, better enabling him to serve the public good.

Four hundred years after Montaigne proposed to revise the standard of political behavior, another intellectual in politics, Vaclav Havel—dissident playwright, leader of the "Velvet Revolution," and president of Czechoslovakia—expressed similar sentiments in an address to an audience at New York University on the nature of modern politics. Despite the potential for corruption, he declared, the essence of politics is not "dirty"; corruption is a function of purely human wickedness, born of the enticements of power. And on this account, political life, at its very heart, makes the highest demands on human integrity: "It is not true that people of high principle are ill-suited for politics. The high principles have only to be accompanied by patience, consideration, a sense of measure and understanding for others. It is not true that only coldhearted, cynical, arrogant, haughty or brawling persons can succeed in politics. Such people are naturally attracted by politics. In the end, however, politeness and good manners weigh more."[29]

Havel's style of politics is rooted in reactions to the humanist ideal that eloquence can serve as the true instrument of action in the world by inspiring virtue. One aspect of More's genius was to reveal the naïveté of this ideal, positing a disjunction between learning and politics that displays a deep and abiding pessimism. And one aspect of Montaigne's genius was to overcome this disjunction, positing a redefinition of learning that displays a fundamental optimism. In a move that entirely transcends humanist discourse, Montaigne showed how learning serves not to reveal virtues and spur the will toward them but rather to reveal the self. In a diverse, complex, and often corrupt world, the self is the touchstone for all action, ultimately engendering not solipsistic indulgence but respect for others. Learning thus informs a style of political behavior characterized by "patience, consideration, a sense of measure and understanding for others," a style in which "politeness and good manners weigh more" than cynicism and bullying.

Notes

1. Thomas More, *Utopia,* ed. Edward Surtz, S.J. (New Haven: Yale University Press, 1964), pp. 49–50.

2. Michel de Montaigne, *Essais,* in *Oeuvres complètes de Montaigne,* ed. Albert Thibaudet and Maurice Rat, Bibliothèque de la Pléïade (Paris: Gallimard, 1962), book 3, chap. 9, p. 970. Subsequent references to the *Essais* are listed in the text, citing book, chapter, and page number (e.g., 3.9, p. 970). All translations are from *The Complete Works of Montaigne,* trans. Donald M. Frame (Stanford: Stanford University Press, 1958).

3. On Montaigne's family, see Théophile Malvezin, *Michel de Montaigne: Son origine, sa famille* (Bordeaux, 1875); Donald M. Frame, *Montaigne: A Biography* (New York: Harcourt, Brace & World, 1965); and Roger Trinquet, *La jeunesse de Montaigne* (Paris: A. G. Nizet, 1972).

4. On the Cour des Aides and its absorption by the Parlement of Bordeaux, see Simone Quet, "La Cour des Aides de Guyenne: Ses rapports avec le parlement de Bordeaux," *Revue historique de Bordeaux* 32 (1939): 97–111; C.-B.-F. Boscheron des Portes, *Histoire du parlement de Bordeaux,* 2 vols. (Bordeaux: Charles Lefebvre, 1877), 1:103–11; and Frame, *Montaigne: A Biography,* pp. 46–51.

5. For this incident, see F. Hauchecorne, "Une intervention ignorée de Montaigne au Parlement de Bordeaux," *Bibliothèque d'humanisme et renaissance* 9 (1947): 164–68.

6. For the text of this work, see Paul Bonnefon, "Une oeuvre inconnue de La Boétie: Le Mémoire sur l'édict de janvier 1562," *Revue d'histoire littéraire de la France* 24 (1917): 1–33, 307–19.

7. This relationship between the two works is suggested in Fortunat Strowski,

Montaigne: Sa vie publique et privée (Paris: Éditions de la Nouvelle revue critique, 1938), pp. 95–96.

8. For the dating of these negotiations, see Frame, *Montaigne: A Biography,* p. 140 (which favors the earlier dates); and David Maskell, "Montaigne médiateur entre Navarre et Guise," *Bibliothèque d'humanisme et renaissance* 41 (1979): 541–53 (which favors the later dates). I am not entirely convinced by Maskell's ingenious argument, which may give too much weight to reports of friendship between Navarre and Guise during the former's captivity in Paris.

9. Montaigne related this event to Jacques-Auguste de Thou in 1588. See de Thou's account, quoted in Frame, *Montaigne: A Biography,* pp. 140–41.

10. Strowski, *Montaigne: sa vie publique et privée,* pp. 176–77.

11. Sidney H. Ehrman and J. W. Thompson, eds., *The Letters and Documents of Armand de Gontaut, Baron de Biron, Marshal of France (1524–1592),* 2 vols. (Berkeley: University of California Press, 1936), 2:644–45.

12. On Montaigne's election, see Frame, *Montaigne: A Biography,* p. 244; Paul Courteault, "Montaigne maire de Bordeaux," *IVe Centenaire de la naissance de Montaigne, 1533–1933* (Bordeaux: Delmas, 1933), pp. 73–75; Alexandre Nicolas, *Les belles amies de Montaigne* (Paris: Dumas, 1950), pp. 135–45.

13. Frame, *Montaigne: A Biography,* pp. 223–24.

14. For a history of the mayoralty, see Camille Jullian, *Histoire de Bordeaux* (Bordeaux, 1895), pp. 175–79, 336–46, 378–82; Courteault, "Montaigne maire," pp. 80–82, 91–92; Frame, *Montaigne: A Biography,* p. 227. For a description of the municipal government, see H. Barckhausen's introduction to the *Archives municipales de Bordeaux,* vol. 2, *Livre des privilèges* (Bordeaux, 1878).

15. See Montaigne, "Lettres," in *Oeuvres complètes,* pp. 1372, 1382–83; subsequent references are cited in the text as "Letters."

16. For accounts of this incident, see Jean H. Mariéjol, *A Daughter of the Medici: The Romantic Story of Margaret of Valois,* trans. John Peile (New York: Harper, 1929), pp. 135–54; Philippe Duplessis-Mornay, *Mémoires et correspondance,* 12 vols. (Paris: Treuttel et Würtz, 1824–25), 2:365–66, 369; G. Baguenault de Puchesse, "Le renvoi par Henri III de Marguerite de Valois," *Revue des questions historiques* 70 (1901): 389–409; Zachary S. Schiffman, "Montaigne and the Problem of Machiavellism," *Journal of Medieval and Renaissance Studies* 2 (1982): 247–48.

17. The security town issue became more complex with each peace treaty, for some of the towns were captured and others were substituted for them. Furthermore, the Treaty of Nérac established fourteen additional security towns to be maintained for six months—predictably, they were not relinquished by the Huguenots, and their disposition became associated with that of the original eight towns. For the texts of the various treaties, see Eugène Haag and Émile Haag, *La France protestante,* 10 vols. (Paris, 1846–58), 10:127–41, 142–56, 159–67, 171–78; see also Jean H. Mariéjol, *Catherine de Médicis,* 2d ed. (Paris: Hachette, 1920), pp. 317–18.

18. Duplessis-Mornay, *Mémoires,* 2:358–62.

19. See Henri IV, *Recueil des lettres missives,* ed. M. Berger de Xivery, 9 vols. (Paris: Imprimerie Royale et Imprimerie Nationale, 1843–76), 1:518, 525, 565–67, 577–78; Schiffman, "Montaigne and Machiavellism," p. 248.

20. Duplessis-Mornay, *Mémoires,* 2:382–83, 385–87; 393–94, 401–2, 518–19; for the proper dating and analysis of this correspondence, see Schiffman, "Montaigne and Machiavellism," pp. 248–49.

21. For Navarre's scheming in this matter, see his letter of December 17, 1583, to the *jurats* of Bordeaux, in Courteault, "Montaigne maire," pp. 104–5. In it he mentioned discussing the security town issue with the king's emissary, Bellièvre, who had been sent specifically to negotiate Margaret's return to Nérac. On Navarre's attempts to join these two issues, also see Mariéjol, *Daughter of the Medici,* p. 152.

22. On the reconciliation, see Duplessis-Mornay, *Mémoires,* 2:518–19; Henri IV, *Lettres,* 1:624–27; Mariéjol, *Daughter of the Medici,* pp. 153–53. On Diane d'Andoins, see Raymond Ritter, *Une dame de chevalerie: Corisande d'Andoins,* new ed. (Paris: Albin Michel, 1959), especially chap. 8, which recounts her friendship with Montaigne.

23. Duplessis-Mornay, *Mémoires,* 2:555; Catherine de Médicis, *Lettres de Catherine de Médicis,* ed. Baguenault de Puchesse, 10 vols. (Paris, 1899), 8:176.

24. Henri IV, *Lettres,* 1:661.

25. J.-F. Payen, *Nouveaux documents inédits ou peu connus sur Montaigne* (Paris, 1858), pp. 49–50.

26. On Montaigne's further services as intermediary, see Frame, *Montaigne: A Biography,* pp. 269–76; Donald M. Frame, "New Light on Montaigne's Trip to Paris in 1588," *Romantic Review* 51 (1960): 161–81; Garrett Mattingly, *The Armada* (Boston: Houghton Mifflin, 1959), pp. 159–62.

27. On this general theme, see Schiffman, "Montaigne and Machiavellism," pp. 251–58.

28. More, *Utopia,* pp. 16–17.

29. Excerpts from this address are printed in the *New York Times,* Sunday, July 26, 1992, sec. 4, p. 7.

Silvia Shannon

Villegagnon, Polyphemus, and Cain of America: Religion and Polemics in the French New World

In 1555, Nicolas Durand de Villegagnon, under the sponsorship of King Henry II of France, set sail with a contingent of men to establish a colony in Brazil. Villegagnon countenanced the presence of men sympathetic to the Reform and eventually welcomed two pastors sent by Calvin from Geneva in 1557. Whether this meant that the colony was intended to provide a Protestant refuge is open to debate, because a few months later Villegagnon turned on the two Calvinist pastors and their twelve brethren, first with verbal reprimands and then with expulsion from the colony. When five of the Calvinists returned, he executed three of them. In 1560, taking advantage of Villegagnon's temporary return to France, the Portuguese seized Fort Coligny. Villegagnon remained in France, where he eventually became a partisan of the Guises and the Catholic cause in the French Wars of Religion.

This failed colony merits our attention because events there foreshadowed the larger struggle looming between Catholics and Calvinists. In the Fort Coligny episode one recognizes the same fluidity of the "reform" in the mid-1550s, the eventual failure of religious coexistence due to the hardening of the confessional lines, and the emerging linkage between Calvinism and sedition that would occur later in France on the eve of the Wars of Religion. Villegagnon was attacked by a number of Calvinist writers for his actions in Brazil. Pierre Richer, one of the two pastors sent by Geneva to Brazil, described Villegagnon as a "cyclopean monster without the eye" and told how "this execrable Polyphemus" disturbed his "peaceful existence."[1] Jean de Léry, in his *Histoire d'un voyage,* described Villegagnon as the first to shed the blood of God's children in the discovered lands, thus making him "the Cain of America."[2] The choices of Polyphemus, the host who devoured his guests, and Cain, the man who killed his own brother, as descriptors of Villegagnon reveal the Calvinists' hatred of him. From their perspective, he was a monster who enticed the Calvinists to come to a place of refuge, only to betray them. This episode in Franco-Brazilian history remains a puzzle, in part because Villegagnon's colony in Rio de Janeiro, Brazil, is so often characterized as a Protestant refuge. But was this true? If it was, then Villegagnon probably deserved the opprobrium heaped on him by Richer and others. This essay will reexamine Villegagnon and his role in Brazil by showing that the colony was intended as a military outpost, not a Protestant refuge. The tragedy of the events in Brazil arose not from Villegagnon's perfidy but from the Calvinists' misplaced hope to make it a refuge.

The French colony in Brazil has long been shrouded in mystery. At its inception, Henry II wanted the whole enterprise kept secret to avert possible hostilities with Spain and Portugal. Receipts of provisions bought by Villegagnon in Rouen in 1555 refer to the expedition as a "secret voyage . . . by the order of the king."[3] When Villegagnon received the funds for the trip, the royal order did not explain the purpose of the disbursement.[4] Despite all this secrecy, there was clear royal approval for the venture. The primary source of funding was the crown, which gave Villegagnon two ships and ten thousand francs for the initial voyage. Royal prisons in Paris and Rouen were scoured for manpower for the enterprise. In 1556, Villegagnon's nephew, Bois Le Comte, received crown funds for three more ships with arms and men for a second expedition. It was on this trip that the Calvinist delegation from Geneva traveled. Royal support was regularly solicited and received throughout the lifetime of the colony, though never generously enough for Villegagnon. Even so, it continued as late as August 13, 1560, as seen in an order by the Parlement of Paris to release prisoners for the trip.[5] Such visible royal support was not matched by a clear explanation of the colony's purpose other than that it was an outpost in Brazil. Some people assigned a religious purpose to the enterprise, although the Spanish and the Portuguese had no doubts about the commercial and military nature of the colony.

The view of the colony as a refuge arose from seeing the events in Brazil through the prism of the French Wars of Religion. Most of the eyewitness accounts of the colony were published during the height of the Wars of Religion. A large gap of time passed between the events in Brazil and the publication of the well-known accounts of Jean de Léry, a Calvinist, and André Thevet, a Catholic. Their writings are colored not only by their confessional differences but also by their deep animosity toward each other. With the exception of Thevet's the major accounts reflect a Calvinist perspective that invariably perceived the colony as a refuge.[6] Calvinist authors were more interested in retelling their own or their brethrens' confrontations with Villegagnon as a way to discuss their election than in recording the daily events of the colony. The events that took place in Brazil thus entered into the martyrologies published by members of the Reformed church during the French Wars of Religion.[7] Some accounts even depicted Villegagnon as an inhuman monster that the followers of the true Gospel had to overcome.[8] The *Bref recueil de l'affliction et dispersion de l'Église des fidèles au pays du Brésil* explicitly states that the story of the martyrdom is being told to comfort and inspire "all the faithful be they in France or in Flanders or elsewhere." Martyrologies have no interest in recounting events that might distract from the impact of the martyrdom. For example, in the *Bref recueil* the narrative moves from the arrival of the men in Brazil in 1557 to the martyrdom of the three men "for the Truth of the Gospel" in 1558 with no explanation of the intervening events.[9]

Discontinuities in the primary sources also skew our understanding of the events. Existing accounts cover the period from Villegagnon's departure in July 1555 to February 1556.[10] A significant gap, however, exists between February 1556 and March 1557, when the two pastors, Pierre Richer and Guillaume Chartier, and the twelve other men from Geneva finally arrived. The only accounts of the period thereafter, until their departure in early 1558, are Calvinist ones that have little to say about the colony because the Calvinists lived with the Tupinamba Indians from late 1557 to 1558 after being expelled from Fort Coligny by Villegagnon.[11] Almost no sources describe the ensuing period from 1558 to the collapse of the colony in 1560. These lacunae perhaps explain why the Calvinists' experiences, though limited in time, tend to overshadow the colony's longer existence. Yet despite these distortions it is still possible to reevaluate Villegagnon's activities in Brazil by placing him in the context of the period immediately preceding the French Wars of Religion.

Born in Provins, Nicolas Durand, the future sieur de Villegagnon, came from a family whose members rose to lesser noble rank through service in the royal law courts.[12] Nicolas attended the University of Paris, where he became well versed in theology, Latin, Greek, and the classics. His strong training in theology eventually found expression in the long theological tracts he later published.[13] Following his family's tradition, he began a career in the Parisian law courts, where he might even have met Calvin.[14] In 1535 he abandoned his law career for a military one. He became a *chevalier* of Malta and went off to fight the Turks in Algiers with Charles V.[15] Injured in battle, he recuperated in Italy in the household of his patron, Guillaume du Bellay. In the 1540s, Villegagnon established close links with the houses of Lorraine and Montmorency, rising to the position of vice admiral of Bretagne. In 1554 he quarreled over military matters with the governor of Brest, Jérôme de Carne, after which he decided to embark on a bold adventure by leading a colonial enterprise to Brazil. There is evidence to suggest that Villegagnon had already been to Brazil.[16]

Whether or not Villegagnon had been there before, an expedition to Brazil was not an unnatural one for a Frenchman. French traders had been in Brazil since 1509. Fifty Brazilian "savages" had even performed in front of King Henry II and Catherine de Médicis during the royal *entrée* to Rouen in 1550.[17] A small number of Frenchmen lived among the Tupinamba, mortal enemies of the Portuguese, in the area that would eventually be known as Rio de Janeiro. What was novel about Villegagnon's trip was not its destination but its royal sponsorship for a settlement. Villegagnon received command of the naval expedition and of the colony itself, both of which represented great opportunities for a man of the lesser nobility. How Villegagnon gained the support of Henry II is unclear. Writers then and now give Gaspard de Coligny credit for the idea of a French colony in Brazil. Coligny's role also makes it easy to ascribe a religious motive to the colony's foundation. Already in the sixteenth century, Protestants argued that Villegagnon only feigned a desire to provide asylum for them in order to convince Coligny to help him gain Henry II's ear. Coligny then supposedly kept the colony's religious purpose a secret from the king. This version of events is told in the accounts of Jean de Léry, Marc Lescarbot, Jean Crespin, and Lancelot de la Popelinière.[18] The *Histoire ecclésiastique* (1580), for example, asserts that Coligny supported the idea of the refuge "favoring as much as he could the party of the Religion."[19]

A number of historians, taking their lead from this official Protestant version, have continued to insist that Coligny knew of the plan to make the colony a Protestant refuge in 1555. For example, de Thou wrote that even though his express purpose was to further France's name and trade, Coligny was hoping to found a refuge. In our own century, Jules Delaborde went as far as to suggest that the idea of the refuge originated with Coligny. This prevailing, though mistaken, version of the colony's purpose continues in Junko Shimizu's recent biography of Coligny, though she argued that such support did not imply conversion to the Reform. Shimizu stated that the colony was "virtually a Protestant emigration."[20] Frank Lestringant, who has written extensively on the writings of André Thevet and Jean de Léry, also accepts the notion of a Protestant refuge.[21] Brazilian historians in recent years have emphasized the commercial side of the colony but still see it as a Protestant refuge supported by Coligny.[22]

This scenario is problematic on a number of levels. First, there seems to be a merging of the emigration of July 1555, Villegagnon's first trip, and the second of 1556, when the Calvinists traveled to Brazil. The presence of a few Protestants on the first voyage was not unusual given Protestantism's appeal to individuals involved in shipping and trade. Prominent members of the crew who soon became Protestant include Villegagnon's pilot, Nicolas Barré; his old companion at arms, Thoret; and two lesser gentlemen, de Boissy and La Chapelle. Whether these men converted before or after the arrival of the Calvinists is unknown.[23] The only two extant accounts of the initial voyage, Barré's letters and Thevet's account, do not allude to a Protestant asylum. Nicolas Barré presented this trip as no different from other trips he may have taken, while Thevet, the Catholic "priest," vehemently denied this interpretation of the colony's foundation.[24]

We know that Villegagnon had considerable difficulty in recruiting individuals for the initial journey. Despite public calls for volunteers "*à la trompette*," Villegagnon apparently had to resort to royal decrees granting him prisoners from Paris and Rouen, men not known for their good character or devotion.[25] There is no evidence of an appeal for Protestant travelers before the request for the Calvinist delegation from Geneva made in 1556, well after the initial settlement was in trouble. One senses from Léry's account that the Calvinists considered themselves a minority on the ship and then on the island.[26] Thus there never was a massive emigration of Calvinists to the colony, nor did their departure end the colony, since Villegagnon continued to build the fort and to request additional troops and men for the colony. Villegagnon's letter to Guise in November 1557 significantly omits any mention of the Calvinists' departure, dwelling instead on the topic of trade.[27] Portuguese sources, more abundant than the French, stress the threat the French colony posed to Portuguese traders. Portuguese and Spanish descriptions also refer to the intense shipping schedule protected by Fort Coligny, built by Villegagnon.[28] Thus apparently the colony continued to function until the Portuguese took it by force after a twenty-day siege in March 1560.

Coligny's overt involvement in creating a Protestant refuge in 1554–55 also seems dubious. Coligny's support does not necessarily imply his conversion, and it is very hard to imagine that Coligny schemed to dupe Henry II in 1555. His position, though in the ascendant, was not sufficiently secure at that time to use Henry II's interest in foreign affairs as a means to distract him from persecution of the Protestants. Coligny was too cautious to undertake such a dangerous move unless he had already decided to favor the Protestant cause. Such a scenario would require us to push forward the dates of Coligny's conversion. Interestingly, the initial accounts of the colony by Crespin and Richer fail to mention Coligny in this regard. Only Léry's stresses Coligny's role.[29] Coligny would play a role in the later emigration of 1556, though even then it was marginal.[30]

A man of Villegagnon's social position certainly needed powerful patrons to help him obtain funding and ships from the crown. Coligny's support as admiral of France was acknowledged in Villegagnon's decision to name the fort in Rio de Janeiro after him, but Coligny was not his only patron. Villegagnon was very close to the cardinal of Lorraine and the duke of Guise. In fact, Villegagnon had accompanied Mary Stuart to France from Scotland. The support of the Guises was as important to Villegagnon as Coligny's, so much so that in 1557 Villegagnon asked the duke of Guise to lobby Henry II for funds and ships.[31] In August 1560, when the Guises certainly controlled royal policy, the crown was still willing to provide support for the colony. Villegagnon's close ties to the Guises led Léry to ascribe Villegagnon's animus toward the Calvinists to pressure from the Guises.[32] In all likelihood the Guises and Coligny simply collaborated to help a mutual client establish a French outpost in Brazil.

Villegagnon was a good choice for this adventure in early French colonialism. His joining Emperor Charles V to fight the Moors in Algiers and Malta and later the Turks in Hungary demonstrated his interest in travel and in daring feats. Villegagnon's reputation as a freelance Crusader and religious fanatic overlooks the constant encouragement he received from members of the French court, such as the constable of Montmorency, who wanted him to spy on Charles V's fortifications, weapons, and strategies.[33] His considerable expertise in the planning and construction of fortifications clearly suggests that the building of a fort was the primary purpose of the mission. The strategic placement of the settlement, first on a rock controlling entry to the River of January, and then on an island, was, as Crespin explained, "according to a promise that he made to king Henry II" to protect the numerous French merchants from Honfleur who traded with the Brazilian Indians.[34] In 1556, Simon Renard expressed concerns about the fort's ability to block Spanish trade with the Indies.[35] Villegagnon's own letter to the duke of Guise in November 1557 clearly indicates that his major goal was to build a fortification to protect French ships and merchants and to create a permanent colony.[36] To this end, Villegagnon wanted to ensure that the colony contained artisans of all occupations; some of the existing contracts indicate a stay of two to three years for the craftsmen.[37] Military considerations led Villegagnon to prohibit the transport of women to the colony, where hard labor was required and chastity was enforced. Eventually, in 1556, an exception was made and five women were allowed to come.

Villegagnon was more than just a military man sent to protect French merchants and pirates. De Thou described him as a man of great courage and noted that he was "something that is rare in his profession, well versed in Letters."[38] This cultured quality had helped Villegagnon to rise at the French court and perhaps also explains why he allowed Calvinists to come to his colony.[39] Villegagnon's exposure to humanism at the University of Paris might have been orthodox, but life in Paris in the 1520s must have exposed him to the growing calls for reform in the church. While not a humanist himself, Villegagnon could write and speak Latin and had a passing knowledge of Greek. His theological disputes with the Calvinist pastors Richer and Chartier in Brazil centered on the Bible itself, which was used as the authority. In addition, Villegagnon had brought with him a number of religious books, which he freely interpreted, as so many did at the time.[40] His close association with Guillaume du Bellay and Jean du Bellay in Italy in the 1540s must have exposed him to a very lively intellectual humanist circle. Not only French writers like Rabelais frequented their household, Greek and Eastern scholars were visitors, too. He was introduced to Renée de France and had become her client. While Villegagnon was primarily a military client and not a social equal, some of the individuals he associated with in Italy were deeply involved in humanism and the *préréforme*. At the very least he was aware of men like Jean du Bellay who opposed religious persecution while searching for a common ground on which to base the "pure Gospel."

The fluid religious scene in the 1540s and 1550s deeply affected many men and women sympathetic toward reform. A strong Catholic, Villegagnon would not have been unusual in his desire to see a more vigorous faith, based on the Gospel, established in his colony.[41] Villegagnon was probably sincere when he wrote to Calvin in 1557 stating his desire to establish the pure Gospel in the New World.[42] This did not mean he had left the Catholic fold, although it would be interpreted by the Calvinists as such. In all probability, Villegagnon simply left for Brazil as a man sympathetic to toleration and religious reform. This may explain why Coligny helped to satisfy Villegagnon's request for pastors and Protestant colonists in 1556 even though Coligny had not yet converted to the Reformed church.

Villegagnon's direct appeal to Geneva seems to have coincided with a conspiracy against him. Nicolas Barré and Villegagnon himself told of a plot that came to light in February 1556 after the ships that brought them left for home. Barré recounted that "we discovered a conspiracy by all the artisans and laborers we had brought with us and that numbered about thirty against Villegagnon and all of us that were there with him." According to Barré, the workers had despaired at the hard conditions and labor since "they had not come but for lucrative and personal profits."[43] They were incited to rebel against Villegagnon by a Norman *truchement,* or interpreter, who had been living with a native woman. Villegagnon, who had set very rigid regulations about relations between the French and the native women, had ordered the Norman either to abstain from sexual contact with the Indian woman or marry her. Barré seemed impressed with the high moral standard set by Villegagnon, who "ordered his house as an upright and God fearing man."[44] The rebellion was eventually put down, with harsh punishment for the ringleaders. Villegagnon apparently was shaken by the experience, which he attributed to a lack of morals and religion on the part of "twenty six of our mercenaries," and the conspiracy led him to fortify the settlement against the settlers themselves. To ward off further rebellion, Villegagnon "did not cease to admonish them and to turn them away from vices and to instruct them in the Christian religion, even establishing every day public prayers evening and morning: and by means of this duty and attention we passed the rest of the year in greater tranquillity."[45]

In the letter from which this quote is taken, Villegagnon not only equated morality with religious devotion, he stressed the notion that "good men" willingly perform hard labor and obey authority.[46] No direct evidence exists that the rebellion motivated Villegagnon's request to Calvin to send pastors and good men willing to work in Brazil, though some sixteenth-century contemporaries believed that this was the case.[47] The lack of an exact date for the request to Geneva renders the precise sequence of events unsure. Nonetheless, from the outset, Villegagnon believed that he did not have the kind of men needed to create a solid, God-fearing colony and military outpost. For example, a number of soldiers, laborers, and artisans abandoned ship after a storm at sea, leaving him with a handful of overpaid workers of low moral character.[48] Villegagnon's letter written to Calvin on the arrival of the Calvinists compliments the newly arrived Calvinists, who are described as "persons, from whom not only I have nothing to fear but I can trust with my life."[49] According to Léry and Crespin, Villegagnon wanted to acquire from Geneva a minister to instill morality and preach the Gospel, as well as artisans and skilled workers; he did not invite a massive and indiscriminate Protestant emigration.[50] It was the Calvinists who answered his request who saw the colony in Brazil as a possible refuge.

Later, Villegagnon vehemently denied that he had ever written such a request directly to Calvin. The fact that Villegagnon dared Calvin to produce the letter suggests that Villegagnon knew that it did not exist.[51] Since his sole existing letter to Calvin, dated March 1557, recounts all of the events since his arrival in Brazil, it would seem that the first time he wrote directly to Calvin was *after* the arrival of the Genevans. Yet he could have contacted Geneva indirectly. Official Calvinist sources are vague about how the request was made. The register of the Company of Pastors indicates that a formal request was made, but it does not name the source. Significantly, however, the two pastors sent from Geneva, Pierre Richer and Chartier, were among the first pastors to be sent out on a pastoral mission. Their mission was to tend to the religious life of the colony and to spread the Gospel to the natives.[52] With the pastors came twelve volunteers, all men with skills needed in the colony. The fact that the volunteers from Geneva had skills Villegagnon needed to replenish after the defections and losses at sea is another sign that the request had to have come from Villegagnon himself or someone very familiar with the colony's needs in France Antarctique. The *Histoire ecclésiastique* claims that Villegagnon made the request through an intermediary.[53] Geneva's decision to send its first missionary pastors to Brazil reflects the importance attached to the request, which Coligny may have facilitated but would not have imposed on Villegagnon without his prior consent.[54] Villegagnon's denial strains credulity given that the Genevan contingent, led by the Sieur du Pont, was expected by Bois Le Comte at Honfleur.[55] Henry II obviously did not initiate an expedition for heretics. More telling is that Villegagnon greeted the Genevans arriving in Brazil as brothers and granted the pastors the right to establish their ministry. Villegagnon later admitted to Catherine de Médicis that he had, in fact, allowed them to preach and conduct services.[56] Villegagnon therefore probably lied when he denied having made the request to Geneva.

In all likelihood, Villegagnon thought at first that his labor problem was solved. Unlike the mercenaries or paid laborers on the first ships, these Calvinists shared a similar code of personal morality, a willingness to work hard, and a commitment to the survival of the colony. These qualities matched Villegagnon's personal chastity and his desire to prevent immorality in the colony.[57] He entrusted the construction of the fort to men who, as Léry noted, willingly carried the earth and rocks to build what they thought was a refuge.[58] For a few months, life was tranquil on the island despite the miserable heat and arduous work schedule imposed by Villegagnon to finish the fort. Villegagnon had told Léry and the others that he wanted to establish a place where the Gospel would be pure. Problems arose, however, when the Calvinists decided to celebrate the Lord's Supper according to their understanding of the "pure Gospel." This, of course, sparked an intense discussion of the doctrine of transubstantiation, a theological dispute that touched on a very sensitive issue. As the head of the colony, Villegagnon took an interest because he considered himself responsible for the spiritual well-being of the colonists. Fancying himself a theologian, he decided to consult the Bible and the writings of the Church Fathers, and, as Léry described it, he developed his own interpretations based on his books and sources. Showing his lack of knowledge of the Reformed church, Villegagnon at first was convinced that the theological errors sprang from the pastors, not Calvin. Even if Villegagnon had met Calvin in the 1520s, the Calvin he would have remembered was probably an Erasmian humanist and not the controversial author of *The Institutes of the Christian Religion.*[59] Even by the mid-1550s, when Villegagnon left France, the French Reformed church was still somewhat disorganized and lacked trained pastors. Whatever familiarity he may have had with religious reformers in France or Italy did not prepare him for the men from Geneva. Furthermore, men like Chartier and Richer thought this new refuge in Brazil was a poor place to trim religious issues. Though physically isolated by the Atlantic, Villegagnon nevertheless found that the hardening confessional lines in France had spilled over into the colony itself.

Villegagnon suspended Calvinist services and sent Chartier back to France in June 1557 to consult with Geneva.[60] In the meantime, Villegagnon impatiently continued his theological inquiries into Richer's version of Christianity. By Pentecost, he had decided that Chartier's and Richer's version of Calvin's teachings was unacceptable to him. The major source of controversy was the Calvinists' rejection of the real presence in the Host, not Léry's uncorroborated claims that Villegagnon was influenced by letters from the Guises warning him not to endanger his position at court by allowing Calvinist worship in Brazil.[61] Even if Villegagnon received such letters, there is no doubt that he was also confronted with teachings he found unacceptable, especially about the Eucharist. The discussions that took place in Brazil between Villegagnon and Richer on this issue would be repeated between Catholics and Calvinists in a more formal setting at the Colloquy of Poissy in France a few years later, with similar consequences. Instead of drawing the two sides into a better understanding of theological issues, the efforts in Brazil and later at Poissy undermined religious toleration by accentuating the doctrinal incompatibility between Catholics and the Reformed church.[62]

Villegagnon's initial willingness to give the Calvinists freedom of worship sprang from a shared desire for a purer church and moral life, but he lost whatever sympathy he may have felt for the Reform after his confrontations with Richer. He probably never envisioned allowing two different and competing versions of Christianity in his colony. Entrusted with the ministry of the whole community, the pastors made some converts, which troubled others in the colony and eventually led Villegagnon himself to reject the Reformed church. Villegagnon's increasing disaffection with the men in his colony, whom he now considered to be lazy, probably doomed the Genevans, who, when Villegagnon banned Calvinist services, stopped working and refused to obey him. According to Léry, Du Pont "informed him [Villegagnon] that since he rejected the Gospel, we were no longer his subjects, and did not plan to be his servants any longer: and we would not carry earth and rocks to his fort."[63]

In fact, they established their own community inside the larger colony. The Genevans' insubordination forced Villegagnon to isolate them from the rest of the colony. Nineteenth-century historian Paul Gaffarel faulted Villegagnon for focusing on theological disputes instead of seeing the men from Geneva as settlers; for the sake of the colony Villegagnon should have allowed the religious issue to fade.[64] Yet Villegagnon saw the welfare of the settlement as being at stake in the theological dispute. And the Genevans wanted more than just a place to settle: they wanted a place where they would not have to compromise their faith. The issue could not be ignored; it was a visible theological difference apparent anytime the Lord's Supper was celebrated. For Villegagnon, the theological dispute held immediate implications for his authority over the colony. Like the French crown, he saw dissent as inherently subversive. Because it delayed the completion of the fort, the Genevans' labor strike represented an intolerable act in Villegagnon's eyes. This episode no doubt reminded him of the last time workers had rebelled. His tolerance for the men of the Reform thus ended when the Genevans' beliefs compromised the colony itself. From that time on, Villegagnon could not separate their behavior from their religious beliefs. Villegagnon's perceptions of the Calvinists as conspirators against authority foreshadow a later common opinion about them in France as seeking "a state within the state."

The Genevans no doubt saw Villegagnon's attitude as a betrayal. Richer had initially believed Villegagnon to be another Saint Paul.[65] Despite his explicit initial assurances of freedom of worship and even the establishment of a Genevan-style church, Villegagnon soon began to persecute the Calvinists. First he prevented them from preaching, and then he forced them to live with the Indians on the mainland until a ship could take them back to Europe in 1558.[66] Five of the men found the trip home so intolerable that they decided to turn back. After extensive interrogations, Villegagnon condemned three of them to death. Hands tied behind their backs, they were tossed off rocks into the ocean, becoming martyrs to the Reformed church as a result.

The execution of these three Calvinists—Pierre Bourdon, Mathieu Verneuil, and Jean du Bordel—is what convinced other members of the Reformed church that Villegagnon was a monster who killed out of vengeful religious animosity.[67] Yet Villegagnon's reasons for shedding Calvinist blood were not so simple. When the men returned to the colony, Villegagnon was already ill tempered. He had lost valuable workers and faced the prospect of losing the support of Coligny and even the Guises once the news reached France. A tough taskmaster, Villegagnon increasingly feared a rebellion on the part of the remaining workers, possibly led by the men who had returned. Despite a lack of evidence, his suspicious mind and his experience with the rebellion against him in 1556 probably sufficed to convince him of their treasonable intent.[68] Léry and Crespin are correct that the men were executed for their religious beliefs. In Villegagnon's mind, no clear line separated their religious views from their behavior. Léry would claim that the Calvinists had rejected using force against Villegagnon out of respect for his authority.[69]

Although the colony lasted another two years, Villegagnon later became convinced that the religious turmoil had destroyed it and never forgave the Calvinists for this. Yet it was not religious turmoil in Brazil that destroyed the colony; rather, the increasingly polarized religious situation in France had rendered support for an overseas colony a luxury the crown could not afford. To the Calvinists, then, Villegagnon deserved the epithets "Polyphemus" and "Cain of America." After all, he had violated the rules of hospitality by harming his guests, and he had turned from brother to killer. He had invited the Calvinists to the colony and allowed them to establish their church. For the Reformers, Villegagnon surpassed cruelty to become the embodiment of the evil that the godly had to overcome. The Protestant martyrologies now had their villain.

On returning to France, Villegagnon seemed more than willing to assume the role assigned to him by the Calvinist pamphlet writers who accused him of persecuting the Calvinists and committing atrocities.[70] In response, he glossed over his earlier toleration of Calvinism and fiercely attacked its tenets. In July 1560 he even offered to debate Calvin in person to prove the falsity of the Reformer's views. When that offer was rejected, Villegagnon wrote a number of theological tracts refuting the religious views of Richer and Calvin.[71] Most significant, Villegagnon several times warned Catherine de Médicis of the danger posed by Calvin's views: "These people under the pretext of religion intend the subversion of this polity and consequently the crown of your son."[72]

Villegagnon's striking transformation in 1560–61 into a virulent anti-Calvinist who denounced Calvinism as a devilish threat to the state may reflect his decision in late 1559 to side with the Catholic Guises. Opportunism was not the sole motive for this about-face, however. Villegagnon's own experience with the Calvinists in Brazil had convinced him that they would not compromise their religious views for the sake of political obedience. The arrogant independence he saw in the Calvinists sprang, he believed, from their religious views, thus making them as dangerous as the motley group of immoral workers who had originally accompanied him to Brazil. Villegagnon feared that the problems the Calvinists had caused in Brazil would recur in France if Catherine de Médicis was not careful, and by 1561 he no doubt thought he saw Catherine repeating the same mistakes he had made by treating the Huguenots in a conciliatory fashion. In light of his experience in Brazil, he could tell Catherine de Médicis that toleration of the Reformed church threatened to destroy French society as it had destroyed France Antarctique.[73]

Villegagnon's conflation of religious and political behavior was very much a characteristic of his age. His original vision to create an inclusive colony foundered on his unwillingness to accept any challenge to his authority or to the timely completion of the fort. His growing doctrinal rigidity and intolerance of dissent, while clearly shaped by his experiences in Brazil, nonetheless reflected a general shift at the time throughout France and even Europe. Thus, what happened in Brazil between 1555 and 1560 to the Calvinists and to Villegagnon was a portent of the storm that was to rage in France for the next thirty-six years.

Notes

1. Pierre Richer, *La réfutation des folles resveries, exécrables blasphèmes, erreurs et mensonges de Nicolas Durand, qui se nomme Villegagnon, divisée en deux livres* (Paris, 1561), pp. 1–3. My essay focuses on the actual sense of betrayal felt by the Calvinists as conveyed by the term *Polyphemus*. See Frank Lestringant, "Calvinistes et cannibales. Les écrits protestants sur le Brésil (1555–1560)," *Bulletin de la Société d'Histoire du Protestantisme Français* 126 (1980): 9–26, 167–92, which discusses the symbolic use of the term *Polyphemus* as describing the Catholic Villegagnon, not the cannibalistic Tupinamba.

2. Jean de Léry, *Histoire d'un voyage faite au Brésil, outrement dit Amérique* (Paris, 1578), p. 422. Janet Whatley has edited and translated Léry into English under the title of *History of a voyage to a Land known as Brazil, otherwise called America* (Berkeley: University of California Press, 1990). Good introductions to Léry can be found in Whatley's preface and in Frank Lestringant, *Le huguenot et le sauvage* (Paris: Aux Amateurs des Livres, 1990), pp. 47–81. On the use of Old Testament figures in martyrologies, see Charles H. Parker, "The French Calvinists as the Children of Israel: An Old Testament Self-Consciousness in Jean Crespin's *Histoire des Martyrs* before the Wars of Religion," *Sixteenth Century Journal* 16 (1993): 227–48.

3. Edouard Gosselin, ed., *Documents authentiques et inédits pour servir à l'histoire de la marine normande et du commerce rouennais pendant les XVIe et XVIIe siècles* (Rouen, 1876), p. 147.

4. See Claude Haton, *Mémoires de Claude Haton contenant le récit des événements accomplis de 1553 à 1582, principalement dans la Champagne et de la Brie*, 2 vols. (Paris, 1857), 1:38.

5. Gosselin, *Documents authentiques*, 149.

6. André Thevet first published an account of the voyage in his *Singularitez de la France antarctique, autrement nommée Amérique* in 1557. An unreliable source because he had left Brazil by the time the Calvinists arrived, he commented on their presence in a number of editions of his *La Cosmographie universelle d'André Thevet, cosmographe du Roy* (1575) and *Histoire d'André Thevet Angoumoisin, Cosmographe du Roy, de deux voyages par lui faits aux Indes Australes* (1587–88) during the height of the Wars of Religion. Jean de Léry's compelling first-person narrative provided the standard version incorporated into other sixteenth-century works. For example, following Léry, Jacques Auguste de Thou challenged Thevet's credibility in his *Histoire universelle de Jacques Auguste de Thou depuis 1534 jusqu'en 1607* (London, 1734), vol. 2, pt. 16, pp. 650–52. On Thevet, see Frank Lestringant, *André Thevet, Cosmographe des derniers Valois* (Geneva: Droz, 1991).

7. The domestic relevance of the pamphlets about Villegagnon published in 1560–62 and their distortion of the historical records of the colony is the subject of my "Military Outpost or Protestant Refuge? The Expedition of Villegagnon to Brazil in 1555" (paper presented at the 25th meeting of the French Colonial Historical Society in June 1995), to be published in the forthcoming *XXV Proceedings of the French Colonial Society*.

8. Léry was probably the source for the most famous account in Jean Crespin's *Histoire des martyrs persecutez et mis à mort pour la vérité de l'Évangile*, first published in 1564. For examples of the characterization of Villegagnon as inhuman, see anonymous, *L'Estrille de Nicolas Durand, dict le sieur de Villegagnon* (Paris, 1561); and anonymous, *La response aux lettres de Nicolas Durand de Villegagnon, adressées à la Royne mère du Roy* (Paris, 1561).

9. Anonymous, *Bref recueil de l'affliction et dispersion de l'Église des fidèles au pays du Brésil, partie de l'Amérique Australe où est contenu sommairement le voyage et navigation faicte par Nicolas de Villegagnon audict pays du Brésil et de ce qui en est advenu* (n.p., 1563), p. 10v.

10. Nicolas Barré, *Copie des quelques lettres sur la navigation du chevalier de Villegagnon* (Paris, 1557), in Henri Ternaux-Compans, *Archives de voyages ou collection d'anciennes relations*, 2 vols. (Paris, 1840), 1:102–16; and Thevet, *Singularitez.*

11. The two major accounts that tell of this period are Richer, *La réfutation;* and Léry, *Histoire d'un voyage.* Villegagnon left no account of the history of the colony; we only have letters in which he discussed some of the events at Fort Coligny.

12. Richer mocked Villegagnon for his pretensions of nobility and called him an "homme incognu" (*La réfutation,* p. 6). A number of Protestant pamphlets refer to him as "dict le sieur de Villegagnon."

13. Villegagnon refuted Calvin's theological views in a number of texts. See, for example, *Response par le chevalier de Villegaignon aux remonstrances faictes à la Royne mère du Roy* (Paris, 1561), which uses Richer as Villegagnon's adversary to counter Calvin's views on two hundred theological issues.

14. Despite the lack of solid evidence, most historians believe that Villegagnon and Calvin knew each other personally. Paris seems to be the likely place where they met. See Arthur Heulhard, *Villegaignon, Roi d'Amérique, (1510–1572)* (Paris, 1897), p. 4. Villegagnon alluded to an old friendship in *Propositions contentieuses entre le chevalier de Villegaignon et maître Jehan Calvin concernant la vérité de L'Euchariste* (Paris, 1561), letter 7. Heulhard's apologetic account of Villegagnon's early career, though quite complete, must be used with care. Two recent biographies of Villegagnon—Léonce Peillard, *Villegagnon, vice amiral de Bretagne, vice roi du Brésil* (Paris: Perrin, 1991); and Chermont de Brito, *Villegagnon, rei do Brasil* (Rio de Janeiro: Livraria Francisco Alves, 1985)—also attempt to lessen Villegagnon's responsibility for the events in Brazil and are generally unsympathetic to the Reform.

15. Becoming a *chevalier* of Malta boosted social mobility for a non-noble desirous of a military career in the sixteenth century; see Peillard, *Villegagnon,* pp. 21–22.

16. Claude Haton, in *Mémoires,* p. 36, stated that Villegagnon wanted to return to Brazil to Christianize the Indians.

17. Ferdinand Denis, *Une fête brésilienne, célébrée à Rouen en 1550* (Paris, 1851).

18. Léry, *Histoire d'un voyage,* pp. 2–5; Marc Lescarbot, *Histoire de la Nouvelle France, contenant les navigations, découvertes et habitations faites par les François es Indes Occidentales & Nouvelle-France sous l'avoeu & authorité de nos rois très-chrestiens, & les diverses fortunes d'iceux en l'execution des choses, depuis cent ans jusques a hui. En quoi est comprise l'histoire morale, naturale, & geographique de la dite province: avec les tables & figures d'icelle (1612),* 2 vols. (Paris, 1866), 1:136–37; *Histoire ecclésiastique des églises réformées au royaume de France,* 2 vols. (Anvers, 1580), 2:158–59; Lancelot Voisin de la Popelinière, *Les Trois Mondes du seigneur de la Popelinière* (Paris, 1582), p. 4. A slightly different version is given in Louis Maimbourg's *Histoire du Calvinisme,* 2 vols. (Paris, 1582), 2:100–105, in which Villegagnon is depicted as a man with Protestant leanings in need of a refuge first helped and then abandoned by a Calvinist Coligny when Villegagnon "reconverted" to Catholicism. Surprisingly, Jean Crespin's account omits any mention of Coligny's involvement either in 1555 or 1556. See his *Histoire des martyrs persécutez et mis à mort pour la vérité de l'Évangile* (Paris, 1609), pp. 433, 433v, 434.

19. *Histoire ecclésiastique,* 3:158.

20. For a discussion of Coligny's role, see De Thou, *Histoire universelle,* vol. 2, pt. 16, pp. 648–50; Jules Delaborde, *Gaspard de Coligny, Amiral de France,* 2 vols. (Paris, 1879), 1:144–48; Junko Shimizu, *Conflict of Loyalties: Politics and Religion in the Career of Gaspard de Coligny, Admiral of France, 1519–1572* (Geneva: Droz, 1970), p. 25.

21. This theme runs through Lestringant's *Le huguenot et le sauvage.*

22. See, for example, Sérgio Buarque de Holanda, ed., *História General da Civilizaçao Brasileira, a Epoca Colonial* (Rio de Janeiro: Bertrand Brasil, 1989), p. 148.

23. Thoret abandoned the colony for Brittany after a conflict with Villegagnon; La Chapelle and Boissy left the island and joined the Genevans when they were expelled by Villegagnon in late 1557.

24. For Barré's view of the trip, see his *First Letter,* reprinted in Ternaux-Compans, *Archives,* pp. 102–12; Thevet defended Villegagnon in his *Histoire des deux voyages,* pp. 108–10.

25. Haton, *Mémoires,* p. 38. Villegagnon was forced to visit the prisons, where he sought young men of differing professions.

26. Léry, *Histoire d'un voyage,* pp. 12–13, 22, 67. The sole Protestant source that suggests a strong presence of Protestants prior to the arrival of the Genevans is *Histoire ecclésiastique,* 3:159.

27. Letter from Villegagnon to the Duke of Guise, from Rio de Janeiro, Brazil, dated November 30, 1557, kept at the Museo da Marinha, Rio de Janeiro, Brazil; the letter is reprinted in Brito, *Villegaignon,* p. 145.

28. See Simão de Vasconcellos, *Chronica da Compañía de Jesus no Estado do Brazil* (Lisbon, 1856), pp. 137, 145–47, 316–17. Jesuits such as Manuel da Nobrega played up the Protestant presence in the fort to convince the Portuguese to seize it.

29. Léry's portrayal of Coligny as a Protestant as early as 1555, although a distortion, perhaps arose from his intense gratitude to Coligny's son, François de Châtillon, who saved his life during the 1573 siege at Sancerre and to whom his *Histoire d'un voyage* is dedicated.

30. See Shimizu, *Coligny,* p. 25. Heulhard, in his *Villegaignon,* pp. 128–29, argued that Coligny deliberately sabotaged Villegagnon's commercial colony by turning it into a refuge in 1556. Heulhard's view is inconsistent with the facts, as this essay demonstrates.

31. Letter from Villegagnon to the Duke of Guise, from Rio de Janeiro, dated November 30, 1557, p. 32; and Léry, *Histoire d'un voyage,* p. 87. In the 1580 edition of this work, Léry added the rumor that the whole enterprise was concocted by the Cardinal of Lorraine to hurt Coligny and the Calvinists; see *Histoire d'un voyage* (Paris, 1580), p. 76.

32. Heulhard, *Villegaignon,* pp. 11–34.

33. Ibid.

34. Barré, *First Letter,* pp. 102–12; Crespin, *Histoire des martyrs,* pp. 434–434v.

35. Charles Weiss, ed., *Papiers d'État du cardinal de Granvelle* (Paris, 1844), letter of Ambassador Simon Renard to the princess of Portugal, n.p. August 1556, 4:659–70.

36. Letter from Villegagnon to the Duke of Guise, from Rio de Janeiro, dated November 30, 1557.

37. *Documents authentiques,* pp. 147–49; *Bref recueil,* p. 10.

38. De Thou, *Histoire universelle,* vol. 2, pt. 16, p. 647.

39. Letter of introduction to Francis I from Langey, reprinted in Heulhard, *Villegaignon,* p. 9. Villegagnon demonstrated his impressive knowledge of Latin in his *Relation de l'expédition de Charles V contre l'Alger* (Paris, 1542).

40. Léry, *Histoire d'un voyage,* pp. 83–85.

41. Lestringant (*Thevet,* pp. 82–83) argued that Thevet formed part of this multiconfessional group. On the fluidity of the years 1555–60, see Nancy L. Roelker, "Family, Faith, *Fortuna*: The Châtillon Brothers in the French Reformation," in *Leaders of the Reformation,* ed. Richard DeMolen (Selinsgrove, Pa.: Susquehanna University Press, 1984), pp. 247–77, which makes the point that "conversion" then meant spiritual conversion, not necessarily an allegiance to a church. In France, the *préréforme* tended to be "evangelical."

42. Letter from Villegagnon to Calvin, from Rio de Janeiro, dated March 31, 1557. The best French translation of the original letter, written in Latin and kept in the Bibliothèque de Genève, is found in Peillard, *Villegagnon,* pp. 139–43. Léry, in his *Histoire d'un voyage,* provided another, less accurate translation from the Latin. For a translation into English of Léry's version of the letter, see Whatley, *History of a Voyage,* p. xlix.

43. Barré, *Second Letter,* reprinted in Ternaux-Compans, Archives, p. 113.

44. Ibid.

45. Letter from Villegagnon to Calvin, from Rio de Janeiro, dated March 31, 1557.

46. Villegagnon's attitude was recognized by the author of *Bref recueil,* pp. 4, 8v.

47. For example, see Crespin, *Histoire des martyrs,* p. 433v.

48. Barré, *First Letter,* p. 213. For the low quality of workers, see *Bref recueil,* p. 5, where it is written that "most of them were rustics, without any instruction of honesty and civility, given to many vices."

49. Letter from Villegagnon to Calvin, from Rio de Janeiro, dated March 31, 1557.

50. Léry, *Histoire d'un voyage,* pp. 5–6; Crespin, *Histoire des martyrs,* p. 433v. Crespin even said that when the Genevan craftsmen were forced to leave, Villegagnon tried to steal their tools (p. 436v).

51. *Response aux libelles d'injures publiez contre le chevalier de Villegagnon* (Paris, 1561).

52. *Registres de la Compagnie des Pasteurs de Genève au temps de Calvin,* ed. Robert Kingdon, 2 vols. (Geneva: Droz, 1962), vol. 2 states: "Tuesday, 25 August, following the letters written to this Church to send ministers to the new islands conquered by the French, M. Pierre Richier et Guillaume Charretier were selected." After 1555, assignments followed formal requests from a church needing a pastor. See Robert Kingdon, *Geneva and the Coming of the Wars of Religion in France* (Geneva: Droz, 1956), p. 31. With Thevet's departure in early 1556, no priest remained in the colony. Jean Cointat is described in the sources as *docteur* of the Sorbonne, not a member of the clergy.

53. This official Protestant source states that the function of the journey was to establish "some place that would served as a refuge to those of the religion who wish to leave to settle the country and advance the Gospel by winning the inhabitants to the knowledge of the Truth" (*Histoire ecclésiastique,* 3:159).

54. Heulhard tried to exonerate Villegagnon by placing the total "blame" for the arrival of the Genevans on Coligny (*Villegaignon,* pp. 127–28).

55. Léry described Philip de Corguilleray, sieur du Pont, who headed the Genevan delegation, as Coligny's former neighbor; see *Histoire d'un voyage,* pp. 6–7.

56. Catherine de Médicis did the same at court in 1561–62. For Villegagnon, see *Responses aux libelles,* pp. 2–4.

57. This is especially true in Léry, *Histoire d'un voyage,* pp. 82–83, defending Villegagnon from subsequent charges against him of having violated his own rule by cohabiting with "savage" women.

58. Léry, *Histoire d'un voyage,* pp. 65–66.

59. On Villegagnon's use of texts, see Léry, *Histoire d'un voyage,* pp. 83–85. On Calvin's early years, see William Bouwsma, *John Calvin, A Sixteenth Century Portrait* (Oxford: Oxford University Press, 1988).

60. In his *Responses aux libelles,* p. 4, Villegagnon claimed that he sent Chartier back with a letter to Calvin outlining "things that he found wrong in his doctrine and his people." Regrettably, this letter, which is the only letter Villegagnon admits to having written to Calvin from Brazil, is lost. On the return of Chartier, see Olivier Reverdon, *Quatorze Calvinistes chez les Topinambous* (Geneva: Droz, 1957), p. 65.

61. Léry, *Histoire d'un voyage,* pp. 76, 87–88; *Bref recueil,* pp. 25–25v.

62. On the Colloquy, see Donald Nugent, *Ecumenism in the Age of the Reformation: The Colloquy of Poissy* (Cambridge: Harvard University Press, 1974).

63. Léry, *Histoire d'un voyage,* p. 91. Villegagnon would be deeply affected by this withdrawal of political obedience, something that he would use against the Calvinists in France to show that they were seditious. On May 10, 1561, Villegagnon would write to Catherine de Médicis on the political significance of their religious views. See Villegagnon, *Lettres du chevalier de Villegagnon sur les Remonstrances faites à la Royne mère du Roy, souveraine Dame* (Paris, 1561).

64. Paul Gaffarel, *Histoire du Brésil français au seizième siècle* (Paris, 1878), pp. 254–55.

65. Léry, *Histoire d'un voyage,* p. 66.

66. La Popelinière, *Les Trois Mondes,* p. 16; Léry, *Histoire d'un voyage,* p. 379; Gaffarel, *Histoire du Brésil,* p. 271.

67. The story of the martyrdom is told in great detail in Crespin, *Histoire des martyrs.*

68. Crespin, *Histoire des martyrs,* p. 453; *Bref recueil,* p. 17. Referring to the three men, Villegagnon wrote: "after having been nourished and welcomed by me during ten months, and sent off peacefully, they returned to trouble us in our religion and to incite my people against me, while awaiting the return of their captain" (*Response aux libelles,* p. 2).

69. Léry, *Histoire d'un voyage,* p. 93. Gaffarel suggested that some threats may have been made on their departure; see *Histoire du Brésil,* p. 271.

70. These include *Remonstrance à la Royne mère du Roy par ceux qui sont persécutez pour la parole de Dieu* (Paris, 1560); *Histoire des choses mémorables survenues en la terre du Brésil depuis l'an 1555 jusqu'à l'an 1558* (Geneva, 1561), p. 70; *L'Estrille de Nicolas*

Durand; La Response aux lettres de Nicolas Durand; and Anonymous, *La réfutation des folles resveries et mensonges de Nicolas Durand* (Paris, 1562).

71. These were his *Lettres du chevalier de Villegagnon sur les Remonstrances à la mère du Roy; Propositions contentieuses entre le chevalier de Villegagnon et maître Jehan Calvin concernant la vérité de l'Euchariste; Response aux libelles d'injures publiez contre le chevalier de Villegagnon* (Paris, 1561); *Response par le chevalier de Villegagnon aux remonstrances faictes à la Royne mère du Roy.*

72. Villegagnon, *Lettres du chevalier,* n.p.

73. See Villegagnon, *Lettres du chevalier,* and *Response par le chevalier,* pp. 7–18. On Villegagnon's assertion that religious betrayal lost France Antarctique, see his *Response aux libelles.*

Mack P. Holt

Burgundians into Frenchmen: Catholic Identity in Sixteenth-Century Burgundy

One of the themes of Nancy Lyman Roelker's last book, a study of the religious attitudes of the sixteenth-century judges in the Parlement of Paris, is that the humanist and Gallican training of lawyers such as Étienne Pasquier, Jacques-Auguste de Thou, and Pierre de l'Estoile informed definitions of French identity that equated *le bon français* with *le bon catholique.* As a corollary, this means that they tended to view Huguenots as foreigners within the body politic during the Wars of Religion. This largely explains why these Gallican *parlementaires* and so many others like them vigorously protested the Edict of Nantes in 1598. Although the so-called *politiques* genuinely favored peace as essential for the survival of the state, they had never advocated religious toleration as a means to permanently settle the civil wars. At most, they were willing to accept a *temporary* period of religious coexistence, until all of France could be reunited under *une foi, un roi, une loi.* Thus, for these men French identity was distinctly Gallican and Catholic.[1]

My own study of the province of Burgundy during the Wars of Religion involves the enfolding of religious tensions into an emerging identity of Burgundians as Frenchmen—an identity that had grown out of the duchy's absorption into the French crown after the death of the last independent Valois duke of Burgundy in 1477. Just as Nancy Roelker asked it of her Parisian *parlementaires,* I thought it appropriate to ask what it meant to a Burgundian in the sixteenth century to be French. How did the confessional tensions of the civil wars affect this identity as it had taken shape since 1477? Evidence from the province of Burgundy makes it clear that Nancy Roelker's conclusions regarding the Catholic identity of sixteenth-century Parisian lawyers can also be extended to Burgundians, who defined themselves by the formula "one faith, one king, one law" at the close of the civil wars.

On January 23, 1474, Charles the Bold, the last Valois duke of Burgundy, made his "joyous entry" into Dijon, the capital of his duchy, amid a lavish display of royal ceremonial that surpassed even the ritualistic symbolism of his three predecessors. Borrowing heavily from similar municipal entries of the kings of France, the Burgundian dukes intended for all their subjects to recognize that despite the Burgundian state's young heritage, they were as important as any king or emperor in Europe. Mounted on a white stallion, Charles was decked out in full armor studded with precious stones. His kneecaps and epaulets were edged with pearls, and his breastplate was covered with rubies, diamonds, and other gemstones. Around his shoulders was draped an Italian-style silk cape embroidered with "the largest pearls." Topping it all off was a splendid gold crown encrusted with rubies, pearls, diamonds, and sapphires. The Neapolitan ambassador present at the entry noted that "to me it looked like the crown of a king. . . . Truly it was a most splendid and magnificent spectacle." Another spectator remarked that "it was the most ostentatious entry that had ever been seen." Arches depicting both Christian and mythical scenes had been constructed along the route to the ducal palace, with Hercules and Jason among the most prominent ancient heroes. Large platforms constructed along the route bore figures dressed as Old Testament prophets along with a figure dressed as Jesus Christ. Charles was escorted by a phalanx of clergymen, the knights of the Order of the Golden Fleece, a host of other Burgundian nobility, several hundred armed soldiers, as well as the mayor and municipal magistrates of Dijon. On reaching the ducal palace in the center of town, Charles delivered a rousing address which spelled out the grandiose designs of his reign, just in case the spectacle of his entry had left anyone in doubt. For too long, he noted, "the former kingdom of Burgundy had . . . been usurped by the French and made a duchy of France," a fact that should give all his subjects "cause for sorrow." He went on to outline the great war soon to take place between the house of Burgundy, aided by Charles's brother-in-law, Edward IV of England, and Louis XI of France. By renewing the alliance with England established between John the Fearless and Henry V at Agincourt, Charles planned to resurrect the kingdom of Lotharingia under the house of Burgundy, thereby reestablishing the powerful ninth-century middle kingdom and buffer state—named after Charlemagne's grandson, Lothair—that lay between France and the Empire that stretched from the North Sea to the Mediterranean. The assembled throng lustily replied with shouts of "Long live the duke!" and "Long live Burgundy!" Two days later, on January 25, in a far more somber ceremony at the high altar of the cathedral of Saint Bénigne, Charles made a second address. With the relics of the saint who had allegedly brought Christianity to Burgundy in the late second century before him, and with one hand on a manuscript copy of the Gospel of Saint John, Charles the Bold promised to protect the holy Catholic church and to uphold and respect all the traditional liberties, privileges, charters, and franchises of his subjects in return for their oath of loyalty.[2]

Three years later he was dead, lying in a ditch, his severed head impaled on a Swiss pike. Charles's ambitious scheme foundered on a battlefield near Nancy in Lorraine (the French name for Lotharingia), thus ending his bid to resurrect the house of Burgundy. His only heir was his unmarried nineteen-year-old daughter, Mary, whom many Burgundians immediately pro-claimed as their new sovereign duchess. King Louis XI of France wasted little time, and on January 12, 1477—just two days after receiving news of the Burgundian defeat at Nancy—a royal army surrounded the city of Dijon and readied its artillery. The French king sent out peace feelers by promising to uphold all Burgundian liberties and privileges in return for recognizing his authority. In Ghent, the daughter of Charles the Bold wrote to the quickly assembled estates of Burgundy to urge them to hold out and resist, claiming that "the duchy of Burgundy was never part of the domain of the French crown."[3] Above all, she appealed to their "foy de Bourgogne." When the mayor of Dijon, Étienne Berbisey, and the president of Charles the Bold's council, Jean Jouard, both recommended submission to the French king, many of the popular classes in the duchy's capital demonstrated openly in favor of "rebellion and disobedience." The decidedly unjoyous entry of the French troops into Dijon occurred nevertheless only a fortnight later on February 1, sparking in its wake an open rebellion all over the duchy and county of Burgundy. Franche-Comté was the first to rebel, organized by Jean de Chalon, prince of Orange, as the towns of Saint-Jean-de-Losne and Auxonne declared for Mary of Burgundy. By early spring the resistance had spread to the duchy itself, as Autun, Nuits, Tournus, Avallon, and the Chalonnais declared for the *foy de Bourgogne.* The presence of royal troops in Dijon itself prevented any outburst of anti-French sentiment there until June, when a four-day demonstration of support for Mary of Burgundy by artisans and wine growers turned violent. The so-called Mutemaque of June 26–29 resulted in the assassination of Jean Jouard, who had helped negotiate the submission to the king only months before. Thus it became clear to Louis XI that he would somehow have to deal with the *foy de Bourgogne.*[4]

Anyone with a knowledge of French history after 1477 knows that the preceding narrative, while unremarkable in factual outline, masks as much as it reveals about the incorporation of the duchy of Burgundy into the kingdom of France. The "joyous entry" of 1474 belies the fact that Charles the Bold had become distinctly unpopular in the duchy by 1477 on account of his political ambitions. And while there was some opposition to Louis XI initially, it quickly evaporated. The French king appeased the elites, most of whom supported the overtures of Berbisey and Jouard in Dijon, with the announcement that he would create a permanent parlement in the Burgundian capital. After Mary of Burgundy announced her engagement to Maximilian of Austria in the spring of 1477, any Burgundians still undecided quickly came to the conclusion that reintegration into the French state offered far more benefits than domination by the Habsburgs.[5] Tensions still remained between the duchy and the crown in the sixteenth century, and they became particularly acute during the Wars of Religion. Their root cause was neither provincial particularism nor difficulty in assimilating a distinctly Burgundian identity—the *foy de Bourgogne*—into a French one. Indeed, the principal problem in making Burgundians into Frenchmen during the religious wars was rather the opposite. The turbulent relationship between the duchy of Burgundy and the French crown for the century and a quarter after the death of Charles the Bold was a result of the fact that the *foy de Bourgogne* was so traditionally French.[6] When the French hold on that identity began to slip with the advent of the religious wars, many Burgundians were convinced that it was their duty to try to make Frenchmen into Burgundians.

Unlike the provinces of Brittany and Provence, both also incorporated into the French crown following the end of the Hundred Years' War, or the region of Alsace acquired by Louis XIV in the seventeenth century, the duchy of Burgundy presented no linguistic or cultural differences to encumber its assimilation following the death of Charles the Bold in 1477. And unlike these other regions, the duchy of Burgundy had enjoyed an earlier history as part of the French domain. Moreover, there was no question that the Valois dukes of Burgundy (1363–1477) considered the kings of France their suzerains and owed them homage and fealty. The Parlement of Paris routinely heard appeals from the duchy, despite the fact that the Valois dukes erected parlements of their own in Dôle and Beaune. So, there was every reason to expect a relatively smooth transition from the rule of Charles the Bold to that of Louis XI. What, then, was the *foy de Bourgogne*?

Despite, or maybe because of the fact that the duchy of Burgundy was linguistically, culturally, and politically French, the Valois dukes had made Herculean efforts to construct a distinctly Burgundian identity. There was certainly a need to unify the disparate and geographically farflung components of the Burgundian state. Through marriage and inheritance, the Valois dukes of Burgundy had constructed a large and diverse territory by the late fourteenth century, which more than doubled the size of their holdings along the Saône River in the duchy and county of Burgundy. To the north lay the counties of Artois, Flanders, Holland, Zeeland, Hainault, and Namur, as well as the duchies of Brabant and Luxembourg. These Burgundian Netherlands were separated from the duchy and county of Burgundy to the south by the independent duchy of Lorraine, where Charles the Bold lost his life in 1477 trying to seize this missing link in his territories so that he could re-create the early medieval kingdom of Lotharingia. These territories were further divided by politics and language. Whereas the counties of Artois and Flanders were legally French royal fiefs, the remaining lands formed part of the empire. Moreover, whereas the language of the French holdings and the county of Burgundy was French, the language of the remaining northern lands was Dutch or Flemish, apart from Luxembourg, where German predominated.[7] Thus, the Valois dukes had every reason to want to establish an identity of their own to create a perception of unity, even if unification was beyond their grasp.

This desire to establish a sense of unity became a necessity when their alliance with the Lancastrian kings of England resulted in the dukes' fighting against France in the Hundred Years' War. Burgundy's participation in that conflict helped to generate the sense that the Burgundian holdings formed an independent European state on a par with France and England, and the dukes had an income, an army, and a clientage network of nobles, artists, and intellectuals that could rival that of any monarch in Europe. Certain institutions created by Philip the Bold and John the Fearless early on served to integrate their many territories. There was a single chancellor and a single chancery, a single council—the Council of Burgundy—that served as a supreme law court, and a single financial organization, all created on the French model. And even if the creation in 1463 of a representative body called the States-General did not foster much unity—it did not include the duchy and county of Burgundy in the south—other institutions did.[8] Warfare necessitated the organization of an army drawn from every part of the duke's holdings. Much like the Union of Arms of Olivares in seventeenth-century Spain, the army of the Valois dukes provided some de facto integration, as the war against Ghent in 1453 and the war of the League of the Public Weal in 1465 brought together men from the diverse parts of the Burgundian state.[9] And even the overwhelming desire of Charles the Bold for a crown in the 1470s was motivated as much by a need for a symbol of unification as by personal ambition.

The most visible perception of Burgundian identity, however, was provided by the church. Burgundy had been created in the first place only by permission of the pope. Pope Urban V's dispensation in 1369 had allowed the first Valois duke, Philip the Bold, to marry Margaret of Flanders, thus uniting the Netherlands in the north with the two Burgundies in the south under a single ruler. And a firm papal alliance remained a vital part of the dukes' policies thereafter, culminating in Philip the Good's receiving from Rome virtual control of a number of politically significant bishoprics and archbishoprics within his lands: Tournai, Liège, and Utrecht among the most prominent. Based on mutual advantage, the Burgundian-papal alliance became a linchpin of European diplomacy in the fifteenth century, as the dukes reaped perquisites and ecclesiastical appointments in return for supporting papal political policies. In many ways the Burgundian dukes of the fifteenth century exercised as much control over the higher positions in the church as the kings of France did after the Pragmatic Sanction of 1438. Defense of the church and the Christian religion thus became a fundamental part of ducal policy as well as Burgundian identity.

The importance of religion to Burgundian unity is perhaps most visible in the creation of the chivalric Order of the Golden Fleece by Philip the Good in 1430, as yet another device to unify the noblemen from the many components of his state. According to the articles of its foundation, the order was created "to the end that the true Catholic Faith, the Faith of Holy Church, our Mother, as well as the peace and welfare of the realm may be defended, preserved and maintained to the glory and praise of Almighty God our Creator and Saviour, in honour of his glorious Mother, the Virgin Mary, and of our Lord." So, whatever else it represented, the *foy de Bourgogne* was joined together with the defense of Christianity and the mother church. This explains why the Burgundian dukes also sought to demonstrate ceremonially that their authority was just as sacerdotal as the sacral monarchy of France. If the subjects of the French king Charles VIII could describe him in a royal entry as the lamb of God and the prince of peace, Philip the Good benefitted from like depictions by the painter Jan van Eyck. Whether it was the transposition of ducal and sacred power in his altarpiece at Ghent, *The Adoration of the Lamb,* or the depiction of Philip's powerful chancellor, Nicolas Rolin, seated next to the Virgin and Christ child, the message was the same. The *foy de Bourgogne* subsumed loyalty to duchy and duke under loyalty to God. As already noted, when Charles the Bold made his "joyous entry" into Dijon in January 1474, he passed beneath a large platform on which stood the Lamb of God himself.[10]

As the Burgundian identity had been constructed from a French mold, it is not surprising that the subjects of the duchy proved to be as loyal to their new kings as they had been to the Valois dukes. Any lingering opposition to the reunion with France or remaining devotion to the descendants of Mary of Burgundy surely would have come to the surface during the aftermath of the Treaty of Madrid in 1525. After his disastrous defeat by the imperial forces of Charles V (Mary of Burgundy's grandson) at Pavia in 1525, Francis I was captured and forced to agree to humiliating terms of surrender in order to secure his release. What Charles wanted most of all from Francis was the duchy of Burgundy, so that he could reunite the two Burgundies once more. Though he never intended to honor it, Francis duly signed over the duchy to the emperor in the peace treaty. And while their reaction probably did not influence Francis's decision to break the treaty once he was liberated, his subjects in Burgundy voiced a nearly unanimous desire to remain a part of France. When the provincial estates of Burgundy met in Dijon in June 1526, the deputies of the Third Estate wanted the king to know that the duchy "was one of the principal jewels in the French crown" and that they would always remain the king's true subjects. They also invoked the *foy de Bourgogne* by calling Francis's attention to the first oath he had made to God "to safeguard the rights of the crown and not to alienate any territory incorporated within it." They went on to point out that the king had also sworn to God "to maintain and protect them, as the shepherd is required to look after his flock." They closed their plea to the king by declaring their intention "to live in obedience to their natural prince, which is true freedom and liberty according to God's commandment." Any memories of raising the standard of Mary of Burgundy had long since been forgotten.[11]

There was no serious dissension between the king and his Burgundian subjects, in fact, until the eve of the religious wars, when various commentators from the duchy began to display a renewed interest in safeguarding the Catholic church and the true faith. As the crown began to depart from the traditional stance of *rex christianissimus,* upholder of "one faith, one law, one king," with the recognition of the Huguenots in the various edicts of pacification in the 1560s, many Burgundians found themselves in the position of arguing that the king (and the Queen Mother, Catherine de Médicis, during the regency of Charles IX) was abandoning the very French identity that had so shaped the *foy de Bourgogne* a century earlier. As a result, defenses of Burgundian identity began to become more strident throughout the religious wars. Couched in the traditional language of particularism and provincial distance from the crown, such arguments insisted that Burgundian identity and French identity were both forged out of the *foy* of the Catholic church. Many writers went so far as to imply that if the king of France was unwilling to protect that common bond, which united all true Frenchmen, then Burgundians might have to step into the breach. Three testaments of Burgundian identity stand out among many published during the Wars of Religion: those of Jean Bégat, a judge in the Parlement of Dijon; Pierre de St.-Julien, a historian and ecclesiastical deputy to the estates of Burgundy; and Étienne Bernard, Burgundian deputy to the Estates-General of 1588 and future mayor of Dijon.[12] Together they announced that due to the crisis of heresy, assimilation of the duchy into the French crown now required making Frenchmen into Burgundians.

From the first signs of royal willingness to tolerate the new religion within the kingdom in the Edict of January 1562, reaction in the duchy was hostile at every social level.[13] When the first civil war ended in stalemate, the resulting peace edict signed at Amboise in March 1563 once again legally recognized the Huguenots' right to coexist in the kingdom. The Parlement of Dijon, like all the other sovereign courts, refused to register the edict.[14] When the estates of Burgundy approached the court to see if the *parlementaires* would join them in lobbying the king and Queen Mother against the edict, the judges quickly agreed and selected a small delegation to go to Paris. The head of this select group was Jean Bégat, former *échevin* on the Dijon city council, and now a judge in the parlement.[15] In Paris in May 1563 he presented a remonstrance to Charles IX outlining the Burgundians' complaints.[16] His humanist-influenced legal training obliged Bégat to argue from a historical perspective, and he began his appeal with the Christian emperors of Rome. He noted how Constantine and Justinian had both vowed to tolerate neither Arianism nor any other heresy in the empire, while the king's own predecessor, Clovis, after his baptism and consecration at Reims, forced the Arian Visigoths out of Gaul altogether. Bégat then pointed out to Charles IX that Saint Augustine had also underscored the duty of a prince to respect religion. "Since kings have been well apprised and instructed in the faith of God," they should dutifully exterminate any heresy or pagan sect that threatens the unity of the church. "Thus, Sire, since you are Christian and carry the title of Most Christian among all Christian kings . . . [and] you believe what the Roman church believes and know that all contrary doctrine is error . . . how can it be that you would suffer among your subjects a law so contrary and foreign that allows not only the public profession, but also the free and public exercise [of heresy], to the scandal and ruin of your own religion?"[17] Bégat's language was explicit: heresy was "contrary and foreign," that is, non-French.

Recognizing that the young Charles IX was still a minor, Bégat then moved on to a more recent predecessor, Philip Augustus, who was crowned king of France in 1180 at the age of thirteen. This young monarch acquired "his glorious name of Augustus" by his efforts to drive out those enemies of the church "who made war on the clergy and also condemned the mass and Holy Sacrament of the altar." "It seems, Sire, that your own regnal annals have provided you with evidence that, when it pleases God to give us kings of such a tender age, as you are, the church of our kingdom is likely to be afflicted and tormented by schisms and heresy. But these same annals also clearly show that it is as bad an experience for heretics as for young kings, as these kings of such tender age are the ones responsible for driving the heretics out." Bégat confirmed the point with an exaggerated account of how Simon de Montfort, at the head of a troop of 8,000 Catholics, defeated 100,000 Albigensians in battle during the reign of the twelve-year-old Louis IX. Did not the king know his duty, Bégat continued, "now that the subjects of this kingdom are divided over religion?"[18]

After a great many more historical examples, Bégat got around to underlining his main point: that the holy Catholic faith was the tie that bound the kingdom together. He used Burgundy itself as an example, noting that the people of the duchy and the county of Burgundy had continued to think of themselves as one Christian commonwealth even though France and the

Habsburgs had divided them politically nearly a century ago. And although His Majesty and the king of Spain still fought each other, the people of Burgundy remained neutral and thought of themselves as "one common people and members of one common body." The same was true of the kingdom of France, though if the king allowed the new religion to break down this common bond of Catholicism, it would lead to the ruin of the kingdom. "Religion, Sire, as Plato said, is the only sure bond of charity and peace, forging a similarity of morals and wills in one common measure."[19]

As Bégat had been dispatched to Paris to argue against the registration of the new peace edict in Burgundy, he eventually moved on to specific reasons why the new religion ought not be tolerated at all within the duchy. First of all, Burgundy formed "a perpetual frontier" along France's eastern border, guarding the kingdom from both Geneva and the empire. France had other borderlands that served to safeguard and shield the kingdom: Brittany and Normandy from the English, and Narbonne from the Spanish. These regions had natural barriers, oceans or mountains, to serve as the bulwark of defense, "but our towns in Burgundy make up your border and frontier without any natural defenses or seas or mountains, not only against one prince but against many. . . . Now this frontier, Sire, has always protected you, for nearly a hundred years, because of the loyalty of our inhabitants." Thus Bégat concluded that the safety of the kingdom of France depended on maintaining the loyalty of the Burgundians, which the king could not afford to allow religion to divide.[20]

Jean Bégat also pointed out to the king that Burgundy was unusual in that its towns held free elections to elect their mayors, and every male resident was allowed to participate, regardless of rank or estate. In Dijon, Beaune, Auxonne, Seurre, Nuits, indeed in all the principal towns except Chalon, a mayor was elected who had complete jurisdiction of the town. "When it is time to select the mayor, there is not even the humblest wine grower, who does not leave his rustic craft and goes to the polling site with tools in hand, in order to cast his opinion." If religion were to divide this process, each side wanting to elect a mayor of his own faith, "how many riots and uprisings will we see in future?"[21] Bégat was speaking from direct experience, since two years before in the capital of Dijon a Protestant candidate had entered the contest for mayor, causing quite a stir when, even though he lost, he garnered 123 of the 496 votes cast.[22] But what especially worried the Burgundian judge was the possibility that a Protestant might actually win such an election. The thought of a Huguenot as mayor was all the more galling because every newly elected mayor was customarily sworn in at the high altar of Dijon's largest parish church, where a priest held a consecrated Host before the mayor as he uttered the oath of office with one hand on the Gospels. Wouldn't this be just "illusion and mockery," Bégat chided, "seeing that the new religion teaches such oaths to be impious?"[23]

In closing, Bégat reminded Charles IX that "the two religions cannot survive if both are exercised publicly, without one ruining the other or both being ruined." His loyal subjects in Burgundy thus begged him "to favor the one your predecessors have left to you, in which you were anointed and consecrated as their king, and from which you received your most sacred and most Christian scepter." These same loyal subjects also "beg you to recall, Sire, that this territory of Burgundy, when it was restored and incorporated into the French crown after the death of Charles the Bold, King Louis XI, then on the throne, promised . . . that the inhabitants of this territory would be maintained under the crown of France in the Roman Catholic religion."[24] Bégat was thus implicitly suggesting that Burgundian loyalty was contractual and therefore revocable if Louis XI's promise was broken. What Bégat was telling the king was very clear: the Catholic religion was "the tie that binds." If the crown and people of France were bound together by this religion, then to be French was to be Catholic. Or, put another way, to be French was to have *la foy de Bourgogne*.[25]

As the religious wars raged on, other Burgundian voices echoed Bégat's sentiment. In 1581, nearly two decades after Jean Bégat's remonstrance to Charles IX and the Queen Mother, Pierre de St.-Julien, a cleric and historian from Chalon, published his *De l'origine des bourgongnons*.[26] Another six civil wars had been fought since Bégat's remonstrance, and Burgundians had resisted each of the successive edicts of pacification just as they had done in 1563. Unlike the situation in 1563, when Bégat protested the recognition of Protestantism, the Huguenots had been virtually driven out of the duchy of Burgundy by 1581.[27] Even though the growth of the new religion had been stunted since the Saint Bartholomew's Day massacres in 1572, there were many in the duchy who still worried about the confessional struggle. And rightly so, since after seven wars of religion the minority sect had not been eliminated. Each successive edict of pacification continued to recognize the Huguenots' legal existence and presence within the kingdom.

While his work focused on the origins of the two Burgundies—duchy and county—as well as the origins of the provincial estates of Burgundy, which he placed in the late Roman and early medieval period, St.-Julien also had a great deal to say about the world in which he wrote.[28]

Pierre de St.-Julien opened his seven-hundred-page history with a startling announcement of the Burgundians' right to choose their own princes. Whereas Bégat had ended his remonstrance with just a hint of a contract between king and people, St.-Julien stated it baldly in his introduction. There are few people happier than the Burgundians, he argued, because they are "perpetually free." "If some princes have ruled over them (as is certainly the case), it is because they [the Burgundian people] have chosen to accept them, rather than because they were forced to take them." St.-Julien then went on to outline Burgundy's loyalty to the Catholic church, describing Saint Bénigne's arrival in Dijon to preach the gospel around A.D. 170. But it was his own contemporaries that St.-Julien was commenting on when he said that the people of Dijon "are good Catholics [and] enemies of heresy and division," and in Beaune "the people . . . are faithful to their king, enemies of sedition, devoted to the honor of God, and affectionately embrace the union in and under the faith and obedience of the holy Catholic and apostolic church."[29] Thus, St.-Julien was apparently much more willing than Bégat to make loyalty to the crown conditional on the king's support of the true faith. In this striking way, St.-Julien stoked the fires of popular sovereignty much like the Huguenots had recently done. The *Vindiciae contra tyrannos* had been published only three years before St.-Julien's *De l'origine des bourgongnons,* which foreshadowed Catholic appeals for popular sovereignty after the death of the duke of Anjou in 1584 made Henry of Navarre the heir presumptive.[30]

St.-Julien clearly thought of the estates of Burgundy as a representative body with significant political responsibilities, and he provided this august institution with a classical heritage, claiming that Julius Caesar and modeled them on the Assembly of Gauls. As the "protectors of the property, franchises, privileges, and liberties of their homeland," the *élus* who sat in this institution "were magistrates no less inviolable and sacred than the tribunes of the Roman people." This classical underpinning buttressed his claim that the estates of Burgundy, representing the people, could even depose kings. "It is very certain," he argued, "that the Burgundians are not easily moved to change their prince, unless necessity forces them to do so."

Besides the requirement to maintain all their traditional liberties and privileges, a prince must punish those who violate "la foy publique." St.-Julien's conflation of *foy publique* with the traditional *foy de Bourgogne* becomes clear in his next statement: only those who are "unstable in religion [and] irresolute in their beliefs" would dare oppose such an ancient and worthy institution as the estates. "The estates are the most handsome trademark that Burgundians could have, and it would be better if Burgundy lost its title of first peerage in the realm of France than the use of its estates. . . . The estates are the nose on the face of the Burgundian state, from which it would be impossible to tear off without damaging the visage."[31]

St.-Julien then turned to a discussion of the device and insignia of the ancient Burgundians, a cat accompanied by the words "Everything by love, nothing by force," which presumably was how Burgundian princes governed their subjects:

The cat was the ancient symbol of the Burgundians, which signified the love of liberty, and that force held less sway over them than courage. And as the cat is more ardent in chasing rats when it is fat and well-fed than when it is thin and starving, so are Burgundians more ready to obey and serve when they are well treated by their prince than when they are annoyed, tormented, and mistreated. Besides, no people love their prince more than the French . . . under which name I include all the subjects of the crown of France.[32]

St.-Julien had no sooner pointed out that Burgundians were good Frenchmen than he abruptly changed direction by turning to consider those who had already amply proven themselves disloyal and unfaithful to the French monarchy: the Huguenots. He was especially scornful of the Protestant nobility, "who have rejected obedience to the king . . . [and] who ignore the true meaning of the Scriptures and the virtue of God." Moreover, they "have preferred to separate themselves from the union of the Roman Catholic and apostolic church, in order to follow the winds of new opinions." St.-Julien left no doubt that God was likelier to shed his grace on a people "united in the same religion" than on a divided nation.[33] After a lengthy passage describing the various heresies that divided the early church, St.-Julien rattled off a list of the principal suspects responsible for similar division in his own day: Wyclif, Hus, Luther, Melanchthon, Zwingli, Oecolampadius, and Calvin. A cleric, St.-Julien launched into the principal theological issue separating Catholics and Protestants: salvation. He especially excoriated the Swiss ministers for their vile doctrine of predestination. "It goes too far into the vault of God's secrets," he lamented, "and it opens up the way to believe that all that Jesus Christ did and suffered for us was useless and without purpose, since we could only be that which predestination has determined for us. All these distillers of subtleties and authors of contention have transformed the faith of thousands into smoke."[34] In the next thirty pages St.-Julien denounced other Protestant doctrines and practices, such as the primacy of Scripture, vernacular Bibles, the priesthood of all believers, and new interpretations of the Eucharist. At the same time, he underscored the merits of the saints and the doctrine of original sin.[35] While Jean Bégat likely shared these views, St.-Julien was deviating from their common course: that Burgundians and all true Frenchmen were loyal Catholics.

This theme was securely reestablished when the Burgundian historian turned his attention to chivalric orders. A perfect *chevalier* "would have to swear (with his hand grasping a holy relic) that he would spare neither his life nor any means at his disposal for the maintenance of the Roman Catholic religion and growth of the Christian faith, the service to his prince, [and] the defense of his homeland."[36] Although these themes were common to any number of chivalric orders, St.-Julien was clearly evoking memories of the knights of the Golden Fleece, whose founding he went on to describe. He recounted how the original twenty-four *chevaliers* who were inducted into the order by John the Good in 1430 had their names and coats-of-arms emblazoned on the walls of the Sainte-Chapelle, the duke's private chapel in the ducal palace in Dijon, which became the permanent meeting place for the order. Just as the original *chevaliers* of the Golden Fleece were created to fight the infidel Turks in the Holy Land, so new Burgundian knights must be ready to fight the infidel Huguenots at home. And despite the fact that several current knights of the order, such as William of Orange, were Protestants, St.-Julien had no doubt that the original twenty-four knights would stand firm with Burgundian Catholics to safeguard the true faith in 1581 just as they had done in 1430:

That is how the names and arms of the previously mentioned knights of the Golden Fleece came to be arranged and placed in order in the Sainte-Chapelle in Dijon. . . . Now, if Dijon were to fall to the mercy of those pernicious Huguenots (who take delight in destroying all ancient things in order to introduce their novelties, which consist only of words that begin forcefully then vanish into the wind), then at least I have recorded some memory of these celebrated figures, who are named and inscribed in the said Sainte-Chapelle in Dijon.[37]

St.-Julien further explained that many more such venerated knights were needed to safeguard the faith because "of the civil wars the rebels and disturbers of public tranquillity have waged against our kings, the sons of Henry II, against the *bonnes villes* and rural countryside of France." And what was worse, "so many people have joined this conspiracy of sectaries called Huguenots, and along with the true and ancient religion have abandoned the loyalty owed to the king and have forgotten the love of their homeland."[38] Although he did not mention it by name, St.-Julien may also have been thinking of a more recently created order, the Confraternity of the Holy Ghost founded by Gaspard de Saulx, seigneur de Tavannes, in 1567 in Dijon to serve as shock troops "for the defense and growth of the said Catholic church and faith," according to the confraternity's articles of association. Besides Dijon, Tavannes's example inspired the creation of other confraternities in Beaune, Chalon, Tournus, and Mâcon, where they proved to be an effective bulwark against heresy.[39] These were the very sort of good Christian knights to whom St.-Julien was appealing.

After lengthy diversions to discuss the founding of the towns of Autun, Mâcon, Chalon, and Tournus, Pierre de St.-Julien closed his long history by returning to his central theme of the French nation's indebtedness to Burgundy for safeguarding the true faith.[40] He thought it ironic that when the Romans founded the city of Dijon, the Burgundian capital, they named it "DIVIO, in honor of their gods." Calling it Divionensis, they then constructed there "a superb and magnificent temple."[41] What St.-Julien's sixteenth-century readers would have made of this allusion to the Burgundian capital as a "city of God" is an interesting question, especially given the fact that the author had cited Saint Augustine repeatedly over the previous six hundred pages. Saint Augustine's *City of God,* after all, was aimed against the very pagan gods for which Dijon was named. St.-Julien's point was clear, however: the Burgundian capital had been a godly city from its founding and had continued on its sacred mission to safeguard the true religion ever since. At this point, St.-Julien took perhaps his greatest liberties with the evidence, even as it was known in the late sixteenth century. In order not to undermine his argument, he insisted that the ancient tribe of Burgundians was not tainted with Arianism, as the medieval histories suggested, but was the conduit by which the true orthodox faith was transmitted to Clovis and the Franks. Although he had cited him repeatedly through the work without so much as a hint of skepticism, St.-Julien denounced Gregory of Tours for getting the early history of the Burgundians all wrong. Had Gregory not confused the Burgundians with the Goths and Vandals, "who had been notoriously polluted with the false opinions of Arius," then all successive historians would not be in such great error. To St.-Julien, the miraculous victory over the Huns, when three thousand Burgundians defeated ten thousand Huns, was a sure sign that God had been on their side. "The Burgundian faith [*la foy des Bourgognons*] was pure, sincere, and Catholic," he concluded.[42] After all, Clotild, niece of the king of Burgundy, had introduced the true faith of orthodox Christianity to Clovis in the first place, thus making *la foy de Bourgogne* responsible for bringing Christianity to France and for making its king a *rex christianissimus*.[43] Readers of St.-Julien's history during the Wars of Religion had to strive to apply the lessons of the past to the present in order again to turn a French king into a good Christian Burgundian.

To be sure, Henry III was no Clovis, as became apparent after the death of Anjou in 1584, when he eventually recognized the Protestant Henry of Navarre as his heir. The subsequent revival of the Catholic Holy League and the appropriation of monarchomach political ideology from the Huguenots helped to create the most serious crisis of the Wars of Religion. Even as Anjou lay dying in the spring of 1584, there was already talk of overturning the Salic law of succession in order to maintain the Catholic purity of the monarchy.[44] This placed Burgundian Catholics in a difficult position, as their loyalty to the French king ever since 1477 had been based on the fact that he was both the defender of the faith and their legitimate sovereign. Their loyalties were further tested in December 1588 when, with the Estates-General assembled at Blois, Henry III engineered the assassinations of Henry, duke of Guise, and his brother, the cardinal of Guise. As most Burgundians fully supported the Guise-led League—and a third Guise brother, Charles, duke of Mayenne, was the governor of Burgundy—a constitutional crisis loomed as they had to choose between the Salic law and the Catholicity of the crown. Unsurprisingly, most Leaguers opted for the latter, and the remainder of the meeting at Blois in December 1588 and January 1589 was taken up in arguing that the Catholicity of the crown ought to be recognized as just as much a part of French fundamental law as the two components long accepted by juristic writers, namely, the inalienability of the domain and the Salic law. Even though most Leaguer deputies at Blois perceived the novelty of the 1588 Edict of Union's declaration that the crown's Catholicity constituted a fundamental law, a distinct few argued that it had always been viewed as such.[45] One such deputy was Étienne Bernard, *avocat* in the Parlement of Dijon and Burgundian representative of the Third Estate.[46]

Although renowned for his oratorical skills, it was a published version of one of Bernard's speeches that exhibited his reasoning to the fullest. Over-shadowed in the chamber of the Third Estate at Blois by the Sixteen (or Seize) from the Parisian delegation, the radical and pro-Spanish faction that dominated the League in the capital, Bernard decided to publish an extended version of the address he had delivered to the estates several months after the meeting had closed. Written one month after the assassination of Henry III in August 1589, Bernard's *Advis des Estats de Bourgongne aux françois* was published in four different editions between September 1589 and January 1590.[47] Bernard began his "advice" by noting that the power and authority of kings came from God, who could transfer their crowns to others if they refused to carry out his holy wishes on earth. This is exactly what happened in August 1589, he argued, when Henry III was assassinated in Paris. After a lengthy excoriation of the dead king, Bernard moved directly to the issue at hand: the need "to band together and to come out against Henry of Bourbon, to break up his designs, and to block his usurpation of the crown."[48] He thought it a sacrilege that a relapsed heretic excommunicated by the pope should accede to the French throne. Bernard's principal justification for this argument fell back on a notion common to both Jean Bégat and Pierre de St.-Julien: to be French was to be Catholic. "Oh stupid and insensitive people, you are neither Christian nor French if you support his party and favor his cause. It is a certain maxim proven by experience that a heretic cannot and should not reign amongst Christians and Catholics." Bernard even mentioned Jean Bégat's remonstrance of 1563 to lend weight to his argument. Accepting a heretic as king, he continued, "is not to be French, because the principal foundation of the state, the richest ornament of France, the most precious jewel in its crown, the only prerogative of the royal scepter, is the Roman Catholic religion alone, in the brilliance of which France, above all other monarchies, has always shined."[49]

Bernard did not dodge the issue of the Salic law. He noted that since the time of Clovis two qualities had ensured the legitimate succession of the crown on the death of a king of France: "that the succeeding prince be nourished, instructed, and confirmed in the one and true Christian religion, without any taint of heresy whatsoever, and that otherwise he be nearest in line by the royal blood." But Bernard argued that the two requirements were not equal. "The first quality is of such greater necessity, as it emanates from God and serves a loftier and immortal end, which is the soul."[50] Thus, Bernard not only argued that the Catholicity of the crown was a part of French fundamental law, he also insisted that it took precedence over the Salic law whenever the two were in conflict. The Salic law was made by mortal and transitory men, the Salian Franks, whereas the true faith came from the divine and eternal creator. How, he then asked, could any true Frenchman accept Henry of Navarre as king, a man not only condemned by the pope and the Estates-General at Blois, but also excluded by the fundamental laws of the realm? "If you are Catholic and French, could you honestly chose as king the one whom Geneva prefers, whom England desires, whom all Protestants wish for, whom the Rochelais honor, and whom all heretics defend?"[51]

Like Pierre de St.-Julien in his history of the origins of Burgundy, Étienne Bernard evoked the memory of the knights of the Golden Fleece when he compared the nobility of France to Crusaders who had pledged their lives to defend the true faith from the infidel in the Holy Land:

Certainly, I love, praise, and respect so many of those [nobles] who hold steadfast to their honor; but we see and recognize so many others, who have forgotten their station and duty . . . and are still mounted and armed in the service of the king of Navarre, against the service of God, the true religion, and their homeland. Is this, gentlemen, how you follow the virtue of your forefathers? . . . Do you want to lose and destroy now what they so dearly accomplished and preserved in their lifetime? They have demonstrated from here to Palestine that they carried the sword for no other purpose but to spread and defend the faith, yet you curry fortune in order to ruin it.[52]

Bernard thus implied that not only was it necessary to be Catholic in order to be French, but that it was necessary to be Catholic to be noble. Wasn't it true, he asked, "that this troop of gallant knights would demand an account some day of the zeal and fervor that you owe to the church's defense?" Wasn't it a fact "that the true marks of nobility and the only path to virtue come only by aligning yourself with the foundations, advancement, and conservation of the true faith?" And wasn't it clear "that it is not necessary to recognize any other French noblemen except those who are touched with the same zeal?"[53]

Having invoked the memory of the good Christian knights of the past who devoted their lives to defending the faith, Bernard then offered his fullest and most explicit expression of Burgundian loyalty to the Christian church: the *foy de Bourgogne.* "If it ever came to pass that the rest of France wanted to accept as its king the king of Navarre, something God will never allow, then it would be necessary that Burgundy resist alone, that she hold fast, that she stand firm, that by her fortitude she stop the rot of heresy, that she drive away the current taste for these insipid opinions, and that she carefully guard the pledges and privileges of which she is honored." Burgundy had to stand alone to safeguard the true faith because Burgundy was "the first peerage of the crown and the original wet-nurse of Christian kings."[54] The last phrase, "la première nourrice des Rois Chrestiens," is a clear allusion to Clotild's role in the conversion of her husband, Clovis. In his choice of words Bernard also evoked a still more sacred image: as the Virgin Mary suckled the Christ child, so did the Burgundian princess Clotild nurse the king of the Franks to the true faith.

Like Jean Bégat and Pierre de St.-Julien before him, Étienne Bernard then recalled the particular pledge made by Louis XI a century earlier when Burgundy was reincorporated into France. Bernard insisted that if Louis had promised his Burgundian subjects anything, "it is that at the time of the reduction of the duchy, it was treated and explicitly given to us that lords, gentlemen, and all subjects would be maintained and preserved in the Roman Catholic and apostolic religion, without any future changes. And that if King Louis XI had been so much as suspected of heresy, they would have sooner killed themselves before giving in and submitting to his domination."[55] Thus, the arguments of Jean Bégat in 1563, Pierre de St.-Julien in 1581, and Étienne Bernard in 1589 had come full circle. Just as Clotild, the daughter of a Burgundian king, had been the one first responsible for making Clovis and all future Frankish kings into "Most Christian Kings," so now in the crisis caused by a heretical succession to the throne, all Burgundians had to go on fighting, alone if necessary, to make Frenchmen into Burgundians.

If the "joyous entry" of Charles the Bold in 1474 was the point of departure for this investigation of Burgundian and French identity, another "joyous entry" is necessary to conclude it. When Étienne Bernard first published his Catholic call to arms in September 1589, no one could have predicted what would actually transpire over the next five years. Even though there had been much talk of Henry of Navarre abjuring his Calvinist faith in order to reunite the kingdom under the traditional "one law, one faith, one king," many on both sides in 1589 still hoped for a military victory. France would endure much more suffering and distress during the wars of the Holy League before military stalemate, the threat of a Spanish monarch, and Navarre's good timing made reunification of the kingdom possible. Indeed, the threat of a power even more foreign than Protestantism proved to be the final straw. The militant Sixteen of Paris, who alone favored turning to the daughter of Philip II of Spain to replace the heretic Navarre at the Estates-General in the spring of 1593, proved unable to sway the rest of the league to accept a Spanish monarch. Although the Infanta Isabella Clara Eugenia was the granddaughter of Henry II and Catherine de Médicis, there was no doubt that she was the pawn of her father, Philip II. In the view of all but the Sixteen, the French monarch had to be both French and Catholic. Henry of Navarre made the going easier for moderate Leaguers and royalist *politiques* alike when he publicly announced his conversion to Catholicism in July that same year.[56]

Navarre, crowned as King Henry IV in February 1594, made his first entry into the Burgundian capital on Sunday, June 4, 1595, after a long but successful military occupation of the duchy. As one might expect from the rhetoric of Bernard, Burgundy held out until the end. The Leaguer-controlled towns considered Henry's abjuration in 1593 and his coronation in 1594 still insufficient in June 1595, because Pope Clement VIII had not yet recognized the newly Catholic king. The duke of Mayenne and many of his most zealous followers still controlled Dijon and the fortified château attached to it and vowed to fight until the bitter end. When a royal army under the command of *maréchal* Biron captured Beaune in February 1595 and then Autun in May, however, the final fall of the league in Burgundy looked inevitable. At this stage, the municipal magistrates and the leaguer rump of the Parlement of Dijon began negotiations with Biron and the king that eventually led to a settlement. Biron and the royal army entered the Burgundian capital peacefully on May 28, 1595.[57] One of those who played a major role in the negotiations between the Dijon magistrates and Biron was Perpetuo Berbisey, *conseiller* in the Parlement of Dijon and the great-grandson of Étienne Berbisey, the Dijon mayor who had welcomed both Charles the Bold and Louis IX into the capital a century earlier.[58]

When Henry IV entered the city of Dijon on June 4, 1595, he was unprepared for the welcome he received. As he entered the Porte-Saint-Pierre on the southern edge of town around ten o'clock in the morning, the king was met by the mayor, René Fleutelot, the *échevins* on the city council, and the *avocats* and judges from the parlement "with their knees on the ground and their heads bared." After delivering a harangue of loyalty, devotion, and obedience to the king, the mayor and *échevins* rose to their feet and kissed the king's leg. A procession of clerics from the various churches and orders of the town then escorted Henry up the hill to the Sainte-Chapelle. The streets were packed with people, and shouts of "Vive le Roi!" filled the air. In the former ducal chapel before the altar, Henry heard mass, kissed the cross, and swore to maintain and safeguard the Roman Catholic and apostolic religion, in which he hoped to live and die. "And all the people were so overjoyed and happy to see His Majesty," according to the records of the city council, "that the streets were completely filled and every window was packed, with everyone shouting in great voice, 'Vive le Roi!' Those who felt the luckiest were those men, women, and children who were able to approach His Majesty to embrace and kiss his leg."[59]

It would be foolish to suggest that *la foy de Bourgogne* was responsible for Henry's abjuration of Protestantism or his eventual success in reuniting the kingdom. Moreover, as presented in this essay, that *foy* was a product of elite culture based on a chivalric heritage, and unlikely to appeal to the popular classes. I have argued elsewhere, however, that a similar Catholic identity rooted in the duchy's wine industry was also a component of Burgundian popular culture.[60] Yet even if Burgundy did become the heart of the resistance under the League because of Mayenne's governorship, the same sentiments of devotion to Catholicism were widely felt elsewhere throughout the realm. This only underscores, however, the deepseated ties that the duchy of Burgundy had forged with France in 1477. Assimilation of the duchy into the French crown proved to be successful and unproblematic. The provincial resistance during the Wars of Religion was thus not a question of Burgundian identity struggling for survival in the face of being swallowed up by the gigantic French lily. The problem for most Burgundians was that French identity kept edging farther and farther away from its own Catholic moorings as Protestantism, politics, and military failure held the crown hostage. For those in Dijon in June 1595 who witnessed Henry IV at mass, his "joyous entry" was clear evidence that keeping the *foy de Bourgogne* alive for the previous 118 years had as much significance for French identity as for Burgundian. Catholic identity had certainly shifted during that period, most notably during the Wars of Religion, and particularly under the domination of the League in the 1590s, when foreign domination by another Catholic power—the crown of Spain—became a distinct possibility. It was the traditional Gallican Catholic identity that Burgundians such as Bégat, St.-Julien, and Bernard had helped keep alive during the civil wars, however, that ultimately prevailed.[61] Perhaps Henry recognized this himself, for later on the very same day that he entered the Burgundian capital and heard mass, he made a personal visit to the charterhouse of Champmol just outside town. Constructed by Duke Philip the Bold in the 1390s as a Burgundian Saint-Denis, this mausoleum contained the remains of the Valois dukes in the intricately carved tombs of Claus Sluter. There Henry paid homage to them by praying alone for more than half an hour.[62]

Notes

Apologies to Eugen Weber for having appropriated the title of his *Peasants into Frenchmen: The Modernization of Rural France, 1870–1914* (Stanford: Stanford University Press, 1976). An earlier version of this essay was presented at a meeting of the Society for French Historical Studies in El Paso, Texas, in March 1992; I am grateful to all those present for their many useful suggestions and criticisms, particularly William Beik. Some of the themes of this essay are underscored in a recent collection of essays: Mark Greengrass, ed., *Conquest and Coalescence: The Shaping of the State in Early Modern Europe* (London 1991). I received a number of useful ideas from this collection, particularly from the editor's introduction; the essay by Christian Desplat, "Louis XIII and the Union of Béarn to France," pp. 68–83; and the esssay by R. J. W. Evans, "The Habsburg Monarchy and Bohemia, 1526–1848," pp. 134–54.

1. Nancy Lyman Roelker, *One King, One Faith: Heresy and Tridentine Catholicism in the Sixteenth-Century Parlement of Paris* (Berkeley: University of California Press, 1996), chap. 10. See also Mack P. Holt, *The French Wars of Religion, 1562–1629* (Cambridge: Cambridge University Press, 1995), chap. 6.

2. See Archives Municipales, Dijon [hereafter AMD], I 6 (liasse), for the original documents. See also Henri Chabeuf, "Charles le Téméraire à Dijon en janvier 1474," *Mémoires de la Société bourguignonne de géographie et d'histoire* 18 (1902): 79–349; Pierre Quarré, "La joyeuse entrée de Charles le Téméraire à Dijon en 1474,"

Bulletin de l'Académie Royale de Belgique: Classe des Beaux-Arts (1969): 326–40; Richard Vaughan, *Charles the Bold: The Last Valois Duke of Burgundy* (New York: Barnes & Noble, 1974), pp. 168–69; Vaughan, *Valois Burgundy* (New York: Longmans, 1975), pp. 182–83; Joseph Calmette, *The Golden Age of Burgundy: The Magnificent Dukes and Their Courts* trans. Doreen Weightman (London: Weidenfeld & Nicholson, 1962), p. 191; and Pierre Gras, ed., *Histoire de Dijon* (Toulouse: Privat, 1987), p. 83.

3. Mary of Burgundy and her supporters claimed that the duchy of Burgundy was a fief and not part of the royal domain, and thus inheritable by her from her father, Charles the Bold. This ran counter to the views of Louis XI and even most legal-minded Burgundians, who accepted the French claim that the duchy of Burgundy was part of the royal domain and was given as an appanage by King John to the Valois dukes. As an appanage of the royal domain, the duchy was not inheritable by a female due to the Salic law, and thus should revert back to the crown automatically on the death of Charles the Bold. See Paul Saenger, "Burgundy and the Inalienability of Appanages in the Reign of Louis XI," *French Historical Studies* 10 (1977): 1–26.

4. AMD, B 164, fols. 84–85, January 1476–77; André Leguai, *Dijon et Louis XI, 1461–1483* (Dijon: Bernigaud et Privat, 1947), pp. 50–55; Leguai, "La conquête de la Bourgogne par Louis XI," *Annales de Bourgogne* 49 (1977): 87–92; Pierre Champion, *Louis XI,* 2 vols. (Paris: H. Champion, 1927), 2:281–89; Dom Urbain Plancher, *Histoire générale et particulière de Bourgogne,* 4 vols. (Dijon, 1739–81), 4:268–74; and A. Voisin, "La mutemaque du 26 juin 1477: Notes sur l'opinion à Dijon au lendemaine de la Réunion," *Annales de Bourgogne* 7 (1935): 337–56.

5. Leguai, "La conquête de la Bourgogne par Louis XI," especially p. 92; and Marie-Josèphe Reynes-Meyer, "Dijon sous Charles VIII," *Annales de Bourgogne* 50 (1978): 85–102.

6. I thus take issue with the older view that under the Valois dukes a *distinctive* national identity emerged. Many authors could be cited who propagate this view, but see Otto Cartellieri, *The Court of Burgundy: Studies in the History of Civilization* (New York: Knopf, 1929 ed.), especially the introduction, pp. 1–23.

7. R. Vaughan, *Valois Burgundy,* pp. 23–26.

8. It was Henri Pirenne who suggested nearly a century ago that the States-General of the Netherlands brought a sense of unity to the Burgundian state, though this view has long been discounted. Even in the Netherlands, the role of the States-General was negligible until the later sixteenth century; see Henri Pirenne, "The Foundation and Constitution of the Burgundian State (Fifteenth and Sixteenth Centuries)," *American Historical Review* 14 (1908–9): 477–502.

9. Vaughan, *Valois Burgundy,* p. 28; and Richard Vaughan, *Philip the Good: The Apogee of Burgundy* (New York: Longmans, 1970), pp. 303–33, 379–91.

10. See Yvon Lacaze, "Le rôle des traditions dans la genèse d'un sentiment national au XVe siècle: La Bourgogne de Philippe de Bon," *Bibliothèque de l'École des Chartes* 129 (1971): 303–85, especially the sources cited on pp. 361–62, n. 6;

Lucien Febvre, "Les ducs Valois de Bourgogne et les idées politiques de leur temps," *Revue bourguignonne* 23 (1913): 27–50; Vaughan, *Philip the Good,* pp. 205–38; Cartellieri, *The Court of Burgundy,* p. 57, for the articles of the Toison d'Or; John Bossy, *Christianity in the West, 1400–1700* (Oxford: Oxford University Press, 1985), pp. 154–55, for the allusion to Jan van Eyck; and the sources cited in note 3 above for Charles the Bold's "joyous entry."

11. This entire episode is discussed in Henri Hauser, "Le traité de Madrid et la cession de la Bourgogne à Charles Quint: Etude sur le sentiment national bourguignon en 1525–1526," *Revue bourguignonne* 22 (1912): 1–182. The remonstrance addressed to Francis by the Third Estate of Burgundy is printed on pp. 164–68.

12. I chose these three men because their views were published and widely disseminated throughout France; Bégat's remonstrance was even translated into Spanish, Italian, German, and Latin.

13. I discuss this opposition to Protestantism in Burgundy in Holt, "Wine, Community and Reformation in Sixteenth-Century Burgundy," *Past and Present* 138 (February 1993): 58–93.

14. Bibliothèque Nationale, Paris, Fonds français 22304, fol. 14 (copies of the registers of the Parlement of Dijon).

15. For a study of Bégat's background and career, see P. Viard, "Études sur la Réforme et les guerres de religion en Bourgogne: Le président Bégat," *Revue bourguignonne* 15 (1905): 1–105.

16. Jean Bégat, *Rémonstrances faictes au Roy de France, par les Députez des Trois Estats du Païs & Duché de Bourgongne, sur l'Edit de la Pacification* (Antwerp, 1564). I used an eighteenth-century edition printed in the *Mémoires de Condé, ou recueil pour servir à l'histoire de France* (The Hague, 1743), 4:356–412.

17. Ibid., pp. 360–69 (quote on p. 361).

18. Ibid., pp. 371–72.

19. Ibid., pp. 398, 405.

20. Ibid., pp. 397–400.

21. Ibid., pp. 403–4.

22. AMD, B 199, fols. 1r–10r, June 21, 1561; Mack P. Holt, "Popular Political Culture and Mayoral Elections in Sixteenth-Century Dijon," in *Society and Institutions in Early Modern France,* ed. Mack P. Holt (Athens: University of Georgia Press, 1991), pp. 98–116; and James R. Farr, "Popular Religious Solidarity in Sixteenth-Century Dijon," *French Historical Studies* 14 (1985): 192–214.

23. Bégat, *Remonstrances* (1743 ed.), p. 404.

24. Ibid., pp. 411–12.

25. See Myriam Yardeni, *La conscience nationale en France pendant les guerres de religion, 1559–1598* (Louvain: Nauwelaerts, 1971), pp. 104–6.

26. Pierre de St.-Julien, *De l'origine des bourgognons, et antiquité des estats de Bourgogne* (Paris, 1581). The introduction and preface are unpaginated, and references to them are given by the signature. The rest of the work (674 pp.) is cited by page number.

27. Arnay-le-Duc, Buncey, Is-sur-Tille, and Volnay were the only towns with a Protestant presence by the end of the century, though there were doubtless individual Protestants who practiced underground in most of the larger towns.

28. For St.-Julien's career and writings, see the short work by Léonce Raffin, *Saint-Julien de Baleure, historien bourguignon, 1519–1593* (Paris: H. Champion, 1926).

29. St.-Julien, *De l'origine des bourgognons,* introduction, fols. aii, eiiij, Ai.

30. See the chapter by J. H. M. Salmon in *The Cambridge History of Political Thought, 1450–1700,* ed. J. H. Burns and Mark Goldie (Cambridge: Cambridge University Press, 1991), pp. 219–41.

31. St.-Julien, *De l'origine des bourgognons,* pp. 63–65. The estates of Burgundy did not actually exist until the fourteenth century. See Joseph Billioud, *Les États de Bourgogne aux XIVe et XVe siècles* (Dijon: Académie des sciences, arts et belles lettres, 1922); Henri Drouot, *Mayenne et la Bourgogne: Étude sur la Ligue (1587–1596),* 2 vols. (Dijon: Bernigaud et Privat, and Paris: A. Picard, 1937), 1:94–102; Georges Weill, "Les états de Bourgogne sous Henri III," *Mémoires de la Société bourguignonne de géographie et d'histoire* 9 (1893): 121–48; and J. Russell Major, *Representative Government in Early Modern France* (New Haven: Yale University Press, 1980), pp. 80–89.

32. St.-Julien, *De l'origine des bourgognons,* p. 74; and p. 178 for the inclusion of the motto, "Tout par amour, et par force rien," with the cat.

33. Ibid., pp. 74–75.

34. Ibid., p. 102.

35. Ibid., pp. 111–13, 135.

36. Ibid., p. 148.

37. Ibid., pp. 154–55.

38. Ibid., pp. 168–69.

39. AMD, B 117, fol. 120. The articles of the confraternity are printed in Edmond Belle, *La Réforme à Dijon des origines à la fin de la lieutenance générale de Gaspard de Saulx-Tavannes, 1530–1570* (Dijon: Revue bourguignonne, 1911), pp. 215–19; for more about this confraternity, see pp. 109–18; Holt, "Wine, Community and Reformation in Sixteenth-Century Burgundy"; and Robert R. Harding, "The Mobilization of Confraternities against the Reformation in France," *Sixteenth Century Journal* 11 (1980): 85–107, which deals primarily with the confraternity in Mâcon.

40. For these histories, see St.-Julien, *De l'origine des bourgognons:* for Autun, pp. 185–226, for Mâcon, pp. 227–367; for Chalon, pp. 369–491; and for Tournus, pp. 493–537.

41. Ibid., pp. 643–44.

42. Ibid., p. 663.

43. Ibid., p. 664. Twentieth-century historians point out that the silence and paucity of the sources make it very difficult to determine the exact nature of Clotild's religion (Arian or orthodox), what Clovis's religion was before his conversion (Frankish paganism, Roman paganism, Arianism, or some combination), or even if Clotild had anything to do with her husband's conversion, despite the claims

of Gregory of Tours. For a full review of this issue, see Patrick J. Geary, *Before France and Germany: The Creation and Transformation of the Merovingian World* (Oxford: Oxford University Press, 1988), pp. 82–86; and Ian Wood, "Gregory of Tours and Clovis," *Revue belge de philologie et d'histoire* 63 (1985): 249–72.

44. See Mack P. Holt, *The Duke of Anjou and the Politique Struggle during the Wars of Religion* (Cambridge: Cambridge University Press, 1986), pp. 205–6, and the sources cited therein.

45. William F. Church, *Constitutional Thought in Sixteenth-Century France* (Cambridge: Harvard University Press, 1941), pp. 77–97.

46. For Bernard's career and background, see Drouot, *Mayenne et la Bourgogne,* 1:194–96, 374–77; and Yardeni, *La conscience nationale,* pp. 227–30.

47. Three editions were published in Dijon, Paris, and Lyon in late 1589; and a slightly revised and updated edition was published at Troyes in early 1590: Étienne Bernard, *Advis des Estats de Bourgongne aux françois touchant la resolution prise aux estats de Blois, l'An 1588. Fait à Dijon le premier iour de Ianvier, 1590, Contre Henry de Bourbon, soy disant Roy de Navarre* (Troyes, 1590). I cite this last edition, in the modern reprint edition of Henri Chevreul, ed., *Pièces sur la Ligue en Bourgogne,* 2 vols. (Paris, 1882–83), 2:1–39. For a discussion of the different editions, see Drouot, *Mayenne et la Bourgogne,* 2:374, n. 3.

48. Bernard, *Advis des Estats,* pp. 3–10 (quote on p. 10).

49. Ibid., pp. 11–13.

50. Ibid., p. 14.

51. Ibid., pp. 23–24.

52. Ibid., p. 25.

53. Ibid., p. 28.

54. Ibid., p. 29.

55. Ibid.

56. See Michael Wolfe, *The Conversion of Henri IV: Politics, Power, and Religious Belief in Early Modern France* (Cambridge: Harvard University Press, 1993).

57. Drouot, *Mayenne et la Bourgogne,* 2:385–428.

58. For the younger Berbisey's role in these negotiations, see Joseph Garnier, ed., *Journal de Gabriel Breunot, conseiller au Parlement de Dijon,* 3 vols. (Dijon, 1866), 2:530–42.

59. AMD, B 232, fol. 190, June 5, 1595, deliberations of the city council, the most complete account of Henry's entry; see also *Journal de Gabriel Breunot,* 2:552–53; AMD, L 20 (liasse), 1595; and Bibliothèque Municipale, Dijon, MS 1070, fols. 313–22, "Journal de ce qui s'est passée à la réduction de la ville de Dijon en l'obéissance du Roy Henri IV. MDXCV."

60. See Holt, "Wine, Community and Reformation."

61. Jonathan Powis, "Gallican Liberties and the Politics of Later Sixteenth Century France," *Historical Journal* 26 (1983): 515–30; and Holt, *The French Wars of Religion,* chap. 6.

62. Bibliothèque Municipale, Dijon, MS 1070, fol. 318.

Michael Wolfe

Protestant Reactions to the Conversion of Henry IV

The difficulties French Calvinists encountered in coming to terms
with Henry IV's 1593 abjuration marked a crucial turning point in
their quest for recognition in Catholic France. Although the king's conversion was not the foregone conclusion that Catholics at the time and nationalist historians later construed it to be, it always remained an option for
Navarre as he tried after 1584 to realize his dynastic claim to the French
throne.[1] The Huguenot polemic surrounding the royal conscience essentially foreshadowed the ideological dilemma facing the Reformed community later during its struggles against Richelieu and Louis XIII in the
1620s, down to Louis XIV's revocation of the Edict of Nantes in 1685. At
the heart of the Huguenots' sad story was the impossibility of reconciling
traditional royalism with religious dissent in a country where the popular
majority and major institutions still remained committed to confessional
uniformity defined by Catholicism—a situation that was hardly changed, as
we shall see, by the Edict of Nantes. Rather than leading to the New
Jerusalem, the path of loyalism embraced by Huguenots after 1584 brought
them steadily diminishing political options once their protector became
heir presumptive to the French throne. Ultimately, French Calvinists suffered so tragically in the next century because they had tied their existence
to the sufferance of the crown worn by their *bon* Henri. In the 1580s,
however, few dared to contemplate, let alone ask, whether Henry (never
mind his successors) could still be *bon* if he became a Catholic.

The inconsistent behavior of kings and princes during the Wars of Religion, Henri de Navarre included, demoralized a people whose historic royalism ran very deep. Part of the problem for the Huguenots stemmed from
Calvin's shortcomings as a political analyst. Despite mounting persecution,
Calvin had taught his followers to obey even wicked rulers, although French
Calvinists had abandoned this admonition within a decade of his death in
1564.[2] This erosion of confidence in princely leadership was not confined to
the Reformed community, and can perhaps best be seen in the local self-help
groups, such as the Protestant assemblies and Catholic leagues, that sprang
up so abundantly during these bloody years.[3] The presbyterial organization

adopted by the French Reformed churches after 1559 announced early on the Huguenots' deep aversion to the hierarchical order of the Gallican church and the monarchy.[4] Although predicated on principles very different from French royal tradition, these organizations after 1584 devoted enormous attention to Navarre's personality and the various attributes of ideal kingship. As public respect for Henry III's person sank in the 1580s, contemporaries—Huguenots included—labored to formulate and then realize a monarchical ethic that limited abuses of power by an evil-minded king, yet safeguarded the full authority of the benevolent sovereign they all hoped one day would govern them.[5] As a result, each of the three major factions—Huguenot, loyalist Catholic, and Leaguer Catholic—generated their own competing myths of Henry IV, which helped to define their positions in the clash over France's future.[6] The Huguenots' vision of Henry as a courageous man of his word, steadfast to God's cause and his family's dynastic rights, would be sorely tested after 1589.

Henry's character was not without its blemishes, even in the eyes of the *réformés,* however. A lingering mistrust had colored Huguenot attitudes toward Navarre ever since his forced conversion in September 1572. The Béarnais gave little indication over the next three years that he was anything but a practicing Catholic, especially given his involvement in the siege of La Rochelle (1572–73). His intrigues with Alençon's Malcontents, so often cited by historians, reflected political ambition, not crypto-Calvinism.[7] Bereft of princely leadership after 1572, Huguenot communities across France began to organize independent elected assemblies and republican ideologies that became a source of trouble for Navarre after he recanted in February 1576. His leadership of the Reformed movement did not go undisputed in the years ahead; powerful competitors, such as the hard-nosed prince de Condé until 1588 and, later in the 1590s, the clever duc de Bouillon, stood ready to assume this mantle should Navarre fail to do the assemblies' bidding.[8] A fatal contradiction developed after 1584 between French Calvinism's cooperative paramilitary institutions and the monarchical tradition that its princely protector hoped to inherit. Although few appreciated it at the time, this incongruous situation seriously undermined the Huguenots' case against Navarre's conversion.

It was commonly believed that a king's religious and moral character influenced, or perhaps even determined, the probity of his subjects. Huguenot leaders after 1584 therefore took the crown's repeated calls for Navarre to embrace Catholicism very seriously. As they saw it, Navarre's accession as a Protestant could pave the way for France's evangelization; if he abjured the Reformed faith, however, the days of French Calvinism would most certainly be numbered. Alençon's sudden death in June 1584 put Navarre in a very ticklish situation because it brought his dynastic claim to the Catholic throne into direct conflict with his role as protector of the Reformed churches. The calculated ambiguity of Navarre's numerous declarations in the 1580s stemmed from his need to encourage Catholic hopes for his conversion while allaying his coreligionaries' suspicions about his commitment to the Protestant cause.[9] He tried to bridge the divergent aims of the two groups by emphasizing patriotic themes like peace, defense of the crown, and succoring the people. He likewise focused on the subversive nature of the Holy League and denounced religious persecution in any guise. He even offered to protect Catholic churches in areas he controlled. Overall, he worked hard to portray himself as a *bon françois* who stood above faction and whose deepest concern was for the monarchy's welfare. This stratagem obviously impressed René Lucinge, Savoy's ambassador to France, who wrote in 1584 that "most Catholics who sympathize with Navarre do so because they think it pleases the king."[10]

Although French Calvinists eagerly disavowed the radical ideas of the 1570s and followed the traditional loyalism invoked by their leader, they failed at first to recognize the potential pitfalls that came with this change of course. Most worrisome for French Calvinists was the fact that since his return to Calvinism in 1576, Navarre had never publicly rejected the possibility of another confessional change. Even in early 1586, as leaguer Catholics pushed Henry III toward another religious war, Navarre announced his readiness to convert to Catholicism should a national church council declare him to be in doctrinal error.[11] This astute display of openmindedness (some *réformés* called it budding treachery) brought Navarre several dividends. It allowed him to keep his distance from Protestants, such as Philippe Duplessis-Mornay and Vincent Ferrier, who saw a national church council as a way to vindicate the Reformed position.[12] Navarre was also able to separate himself from the militant Calvinists known as the *consistoriaux,* who utterly rejected negotiations with the papists. It also presented Catholics a more attractive image of him as an errant believer who only sought religious truth.[13]

Navarre's call for a settlement of all confessional differences was, of course, merely a smokescreen to hide his indecision. It nevertheless created a quandary for militant Huguenots and Catholics alike since both sides measured such a colloquy's success by how well they vanquished their opponent; conversely, to lose any portion of the debate necessarily tainted the proceedings. This vicious circular reasoning had wrecked earlier rhetorical efforts, beginning at Poissy in 1561, to bring about a conciliar solution to religious strife.[14] The alternative to discussion was religious war—a course that since the 1560s had proved equally nugatory. By the 1580s, polemical strategies mirrored the confusion wrought by a generation of civil war and the hazards of royal succession. For no group involved was this more true than for the Huguenots, particularly after 1584 as they confronted the dreadful prospect of Navarre's conversion.

Henry's apparent willingness to consider another confessional change sharpened the existing divisions in the Reformed community, differences that roughly corresponded to the movement's mixed social makeup and regional character.[15] Militancy ran hottest in the urban churches, particularly in the west and in scattered areas in the Midi, while moderate conciliation with the crown found adherents among the Huguenot nobility, especially in Languedoc, where ties to Damville's *politiques* counted for so much. When these ties began to matter less in the 1590s, Huguenot noblemen tried to wrest concessions from the crown by fanning the local churches' fears, though never enough to force a showdown with Henry IV, who was now a Catholic.[16] In short, the latent rifts that later proved so fatal to French Calvinists in the seventeenth century could have been patched over if only they had convinced Navarre never to convert. The struggle over the king's conscience thus became one of controversialist argument rather than a test of arms once it entered the public domain through print and oratory.

The inherent and paralyzing limits of Huguenot loyalism can further be seen in the well-known shift that took place after 1584 in the political writings of such Protestant luminaries as Duplessis-Mornay, François Hotman, Theodore Beza, and a host of lesser publicists. Almost overnight, they dropped the radical theories of legitimate resistance and constitutional monarchy elaborated after the Saint Bartholomew's Day massacre and became staunch champions of France's royal tradition—a tradition they considered to be shorn of Catholic attributes.[17] This proviso gave their royalism a crucial difference which debates over France's fundamental laws simply masked with a veneer of Gallicanism rather than dispelled. At the core of

Huguenot loyalism in the 1580s and 1590s lay two distinct visions of the monarchy's role in French society. The first, as exemplified in the writings of Agrippa d'Aubigné and Beza, believed that Henry's claim to the throne represented a key step in the evangelization of France; for them, the crown's sacred mission now became a Calvinist, not a Catholic one.[18] The other view, less conventional but perhaps politically more realistic, offered a secular justification of absolute monarchy based on natural law, not divine right. François Hotman's *Brutum Fulmen* (1585) and the anonymous *De la vraye et légitime Constitution de l'Estat* (1590), for example, reflected this new tendency in Huguenot legal circles.[19] From this perspective, the accidents of royal succession that eventually brought Navarre to the throne in 1589 began to give the monarchomach forebears of Locke's *Two Treatises* paternal claims to Hobbes's mighty Leviathan. Secular justifications of civil authority and religious toleration were the last things that Henry IV wanted associated with the debate over his faith, because they invited charges of atheism. When seen in this light, Huguenot loyalism—be it along the path of evangelism or secularism—did not have much to recommend it to the embattled Henri de Navarre.

From the start, French Calvinists realized that the movement's future depended on Navarre's unswerving commitment to the Reformed faith—a commitment Huguenot assemblies had him periodically reaffirm during the 1580s.[20] Agrippa d'Aubigné's bitter denunciation in the late 1590s of Henry IV's apostasy was not far from the lips of many Huguenots in the 1580s who feared the seductiveness of a Catholic conversion.[21] They bit their tongues, however, and took refuge in the hope—indeed, the myth—of Henry as a man who preferred death over betrayal of lifelong friends and convictions. As time passed, Protestant anxiety rose by degrees as the temptation to convert became increasingly irresistible. It can be measured in the changing polemical strategies Protestant writers used to deal with the possibility of the king's conversion.

One of the earliest and most thoroughgoing Protestant attacks appeared in 1585 in a pamphlet entitled *Double d'une lettre envoiée à un certain personnage*. Although often attributed to Duplessis-Mornay, it is most likely the work of his close associate Vincent Ferrier, a well-known Protestant minister.[22] The pamphlet purportedly relates a heated debate that took place in July 1584 between Duplessis-Mornay and the sieur de Roquelaure, one of a small but growing number of Catholics whose support of Henry lent substance to the claim that his cause transcended the confessional partisanship. For Ferrier, however, their presence near the Protestant protector threatened to undermine Henry's allegiance to the Reformed faith.[23]

Echoing the crown's own case for Henry's abjuration, Roquelaure argued that Navarre could safeguard his eventual authority as king only by upholding the monarchy's sacred traditions. From a *politique* perspective—Ferrier used this pejorative term when relating Roquelaure's discourse—he urged Henry to go through with a public conversion to satisfy Catholics, even if his conscience bade him do otherwise. This blatant distortion of Catholic arguments for Navarre's conversion was, of course, intentional since it left the moral high ground to Duplessis-Mornay, who wasted no time in attacking the lamentable gap between external appearance and inner conviction approved by Roquelaure as good policy. Better to trust in God than in this wily bastard son of Machiavelli, Duplessis-Mornay warned. Even if Navarre sincerely converted, he could never escape Catholic suspicions of hypocrisy. A conversion therefore would give the papists an added excuse for sedition and also alienate his Protestant allies at home and abroad. This implicit threat of Huguenot resistance haunted Henry over the next thirteen years until he finally settled the matter—at least for his lifetime—in the Edict of Nantes.[24] While such warnings no doubt delayed Navarre's conversion, they did so at the price of poisoning relations with the *réformés* to the point where he thought them no less rebellious than the Catholic Leaguers.

Curiously enough, the polemical boundaries between Huguenots and Leaguers, so well defined on most issues, virtually disappeared on the question of the king's conversion because each thought it impossible for Henry to combine religious conviction with a change to Catholicism. This common ground was rather narrow, to be sure, since Leaguers refused to recognize Henry's claim to the throne because of his faith, while Huguenots generally refused to concede that faith had any bearing on the legitimacy of his claim.[25] Their rhetorical strategies against a possible conversion nevertheless shared a common moral vocabulary about the dangers of hypocrisy that was unsettling to Navarre and his supporters, particularly after the assassination of Henry III in August 1589. Both sides believed that the temptation to convert grew even greater following the regicide. Some Protestants felt especially uneasy given Henry IV's decision in the Declaration of Saint-Cloud (August 4, 1589) to set what appeared to be a timetable for his instruction.[26]

These heightened fears after 1589 affected Protestant responses to the conversion question in ways that further soured Henry IV's relations with the Reformed movement. In late 1589, for example, Jean de Sponde, a prominent Huguenot adviser to Navarre who himself became a Catholic in 1593, published a tract that offered Henry IV strong political reasons not to convert.[27] Sponde avoided the pious platitudes that Duplessis-Mornay and Ferrier had voiced in the mid-1580s and instead painted a gloomy picture of the disasters that awaited the king should he sacrifice his good name and his soul for worldly gain. Rather than end the wars, a Catholic conversion would only prepare the way for their perpetuation because Catholics would demand that the king prove his sincerity by upholding his coronation oath to extirpate heresy. French Calvinists, of course, would be forced to elect another protector to defend their communities and faith. These dire predictions, which almost came true after 1593 (and indeed would after 1620), probably gave the undecided Henry IV reason enough to hesitate before embarking on the perilous road to conversion.[28] In the end, Sponde added to Duplessis-Mornay's righteous opposition the specter of armed resistance against Henry IV should he decide to embrace Catholicism.

Other Protestant pleas against a Catholic conversion returned time and again to the themes of betrayal and disaster. One remonstrance delivered privately to the king in 1592, for example, upbraided him for losing sight of the true faith by his wanton love affairs. This shrill attack also derided the king's clever handling of the conversion question, suggesting that perhaps Henry believed in neither confession. This veiled charge of atheism stole a page from leaguer polemics about Navarre's lack of faith. Again, like the Catholics, Huguenots offered a moral critique of Henry IV's wavering which justified opposition should the king's spiritual evolution go against their perceived interests.[29]

One last strategy used to dissuade Henry IV from going through with a Catholic conversion can be found in the lengthy letter sent to him on June 20, 1593, by a longtime associate, the Calvinist minister Gabriel Damours. Damours couched his appeal to the king's spiritual welfare in terms of the highly personal relationship that Henry IV had long enjoyed with him and with other Huguenot leaders. A Catholic conversion, Damours argued, would lose him not only God's grace, but also lifelong friends. Damours recalled past occasions when Navarre had fought alongside his Calvinist comrades, many of whom had died in his service. Had they died in vain? he poignantly asked. The king risked dishonoring their memory—and himself—unless he remained steadfast in his religious convictions. Such emotional blackmail sometimes took on a picaresque flavor of sentimental reminiscence, as when Damours remembered the joyous thanks they had both given to God under an oak tree after the victory at Coutras. According to Damours, the source of the king's apparent ingratitude, now that he seemed ready to receive Catholic instruction, was his carnal lust for Gabrielle d'Estrées. To go through with a Catholic conversion smacked of cowardice and womanly domination, Damours averred, as he struck at the very core of Henry IV's self-image as a man and king.[30]

This menacing tone had found no place in François de la Noue's eloquent analysis of the conversion question in 1591, one year before his death. A fearless Huguenot captain committed to his faith, La Noue discussed what no Huguenot had so far dared to breathe openly: the possibility of Henry IV's eventual return to the Catholic church. He warned his fellow Protestants not to resist the king should he one day convert lest they bring on themselves the war they so dreaded. Intimidation—be it by Huguenots or Catholics—would corrupt Henry IV's relationship with God by injecting secular concerns into a delicate question of conscience.[31] Without public calm, Henry IV would never have an opportunity to read Scripture, confer with saintly men of the cloth, and meditate on God's will. Only under these circumstances could the Holy Spirit move the king to see the light—a light La Noue purposely refrained from characterizing as either Calvinist or Catholic. In short, the road to Henry IV's conversion would begin once all subjects had returned to obedience. La Noue held out hope that the two confessions could one day be reconciled, given their common belief in Christ and the Apostles' Creed, though such a settlement could never be made a precondition for the king's decision one way or the other. Again, as for Catholics, sincerity was the key issue at stake in the debate. Yet whereas Duplessis-Mornay and Sponde assumed it was impossible to join religious conviction with a conversion, La Noue left the matter of religious truth open. Much like Montaigne, La Noue found in skepticism a refuge from the theological disputes tearing the country apart; instead, he affirmed the fideist position that rejected warring over religious belief because the grounds of faith could never be rationally demonstrated. Citing the principle of liberty of conscience, La Noue argued that the Huguenots had no right, let alone the power, to force Henry IV *not* to become a Catholic should his conscience so dictate. Although not widely shared at the time, this admission of impotence went to the very core of the Huguenots' dilemma.

Two years later, in late February 1593, when Leaguers from the Estates-General in Paris and Catholics in the king's party prepared to meet together in the village of Suresnes to discuss a possible settlement, Henry IV held a series of not so secret nighttime meetings with the duc de Sully during which—at least according to the *Oeconomies royales* written twenty-five years later—the king allegedly asked Sully if now was not the time convert.[32] Sully picked up where La Noue had left off, arguing that he could not make such a weighty decision for the king. After prodding by the king, however, he did venture his opinion that the time for a decision was drawing near. Sully then went on to present a detailed analysis of a conversion's advantages, provided Henry could undertake it in good conscience. As Sully saw it, true piety and salvation could be achieved in either faith so long as one lived morally and let God be his guide. By trivializing doctrinal disputes, Sully probably helped Henry IV—if help he needed—to reconcile himself to the idea of a Catholic conversion. There is no reason to doubt the sincerity of Sully's irenicist views given his own conscientious resistance to following his beloved master back to the mother church.[33] As Sully saw it in early 1593, the king could either be saved as a Protestant and lose his crown, or be saved as a Catholic and reunite his realm. Whether these conversations ever took place as Sully recorded them cannot be confirmed, though it is clear that during the next few weeks into March, Henry IV set the wheels in motion for his conversion at Saint-Denis on July 25—an event Catholics, except embittered Leaguers, received with alacrity, but one that dismayed most Huguenots, who, unlike Sully, could not greet a future ruled by a Catholic Henry IV with confidence.

In the months that followed his alleged conversations with Sully, Henry IV kept up the fiction that Calvinist ministers would have a role in his public instruction. Informal meetings in Mantes during March, where Protestants reportedly took on the king's Catholic *convertisseurs,* raised Huguenots' hopes of an all-encompassing settlement of religious differences and an edict fixing their favored status in the realm.[34] On May 16, on the eve of Renaud de Beaune's momentous announcement of Navarre's willingness to receive Catholic instruction, Henry IV persuaded prominent Catholic noblemen in his entourage to sign a letter promising never to raise arms against the French Reformed community.[35] Despite misgivings over

Henry's intentions, especially the king's recent prohibition of Calvinist services at court, Duplessis-Mornay sent off a detailed memorandum in June to Huguenot divines outlining strategies to be used in the upcoming debates with Catholics. These meetings never took place, however.[36] In fact, controversialist experts summoned from Huguenot communities across the realm waited patiently—and, as it turned out, vainly—in Mantes until July 23, two days before the king's Catholic conversion at Saint-Denis. These frustrations help to explain the rumors that circulated later that summer that the Huguenots might move to elect another protector given Henry IV's betrayal of their cause.[37] Excluded from the king's instruction and uncertain of their future, French Calvinists displayed the kind of nervous dread and resolve that had led them in the 1570s to take matters into their own hands.

Over the next five years, Protestant assemblies, which had fallen into abeyance after Henry IV's accession, began to meet regularly again to prepare for possible conflict with their erstwhile protector. Many feared that French Catholics as well as the pope would require Henry IV to wage war on the *réformés* to prove his sincerity; the king's coronation oath at Chartres in February 1594 to extirpate heresy seemed to bear out such awful expectations.[38] Another cause of concern were the restrictive measures against Calvinist worship found in Henry IV's peace treaties with leaguer cities.[39] An outspoken minority among the Huguenot nobility and *consistoriaux* came to the fore over the next three years, suggesting that the *réformés* choose a powerful foreign prince, like the Elector Palatine or Elizabeth I of England, to be their protector. Although these plans came to naught, the Huguenot assemblies did agree in 1597 to withhold all military assistance from Henry IV in his struggle to expel Spanish troops from Amiens.[40] Ironically, these agitations by French Calvinists, though understandable in the light of past experience, brought about precisely what they feared most: Henry IV's increasing reliance on loyalist Catholics as well as repentant Leaguers. Some observers thought it likely that the converted king, once he had taken care of the Spanish menace, would turn his attention to the internal threat posed by the Huguenot "state within the state." In a brief to Pope Clement VIII, the duc de Nevers wrote in November 1593 that whatever else might be said about the loyalist Catholics, they had "succeeded in removing the leader of the Huguenots, thus taking away from them their chief support and protection."[41] Matters were not helped by the sarcastic tone of the letter to the king sent by Huguenot leaders assembled in Mantes in late 1593. In it, they lauded him for his successful dissimulation, since they could not imagine that in changing the external aspect of his devotion he had in any way altered his true, heartfelt faith. This was precisely the perspective adopted by leaguer critics of the king's conversion, who saw in it nothing but rank hypocrisy.[42]

Henry IV's promise at Chartres to ensure a Catholic succession was another blow to Huguenot hopes. Over the next few years, the king commenced the slow, but quite deliberate, recatholicization of the Bourbon household and its collateral lines, particularly the Condé family. Plans were already afoot as well for Henry IV's eventual divorce from Marguerite de Valois, with whom he shared a mutual animosity, but not a conjugal bed. The king hoped he could then wed Marie de Médicis—a union first proposed secretly prior to his conversion in 1593. After considerable difficulty, the marriage finally took place in 1600.[43] In the meantime, Henry IV had entrusted the young Henri II de Condé, the heir apparent until Louis XIII's birth in 1601, to Catholic tutors who hoped to sow the seeds of another conversion. They were not to be disappointed.[44] Similar efforts in 1599 toward the king's sister, Catherine de Bourbon, proceeded less smoothly as she stubbornly adhered to her Calvinist beliefs. Like her mother a generation before, Catherine became a symbol of respectability and a source of financial support for Huguenot divines until her sudden death in 1606.[45]

Henry IV's decision to recatholicize the royal family formed part of a larger confessional change taking place after 1593 in the royal government and at court. Though he had much less control here, Henry IV nevertheless exercised an important influence over the growing number of Protestants who followed his lead by recanting their Calvinist faith and embracing Catholicism.[46] Among these converts were a conspicuous number of the king's Huguenot advisers, men such as his childhood tutor, Victor Pierre Palma Cayet (1593), Jean de Sponde (1593), the sieur de Morlas (1594), and the sieur de Sancy (1596).[47] Efforts to win Sully over to Roman orthodoxy proved less fruitful, however. All these newly Catholic councillors cited high on their lists of reasons for converting the sterling example set by the king. Other resonances of Henry IV's conversion can be found in the apologia these men wrote defending their abjurations. In them, they took up and elaborated on many of the themes used in the king's own Catholic instruction. These recent converts helped deflect Protestant attacks on the king's apostasy, too. As a result, Huguenot influence at the Bourbon court slowly withered away after 1593 as relations between Henry IV and the French Reformed community became mired in mistrust and verbal abuse. Sully, of course, was exceptional in this regard only because he steadfastly refused to serve as the Huguenots' advocate at court.

French Calvinists thus faced an uncertain future, rendered doubly vulnerable because they could not invoke, without appearing to be treasonous, the brave words and novel political theories that had helped to rally the movement after the massacres of the 1570s. Rather than resolving the problem of Catholic intolerance, the Huguenots' decision to embrace royalist obedience after 1584 had gradually eliminated the viability of independent action without explicit support by the crown. Unable at first to imagine another confessional change by their protector, French Calvinists could only watch impotently as Navarre moved toward a Catholic conversion in early 1593. The ceremonies eventually celebrated at Saint-Denis later that July ratified their exclusion from the Most Christian Kingdom that Gallican Catholics hoped would be reborn as a result of Henry IV's return to the Catholic church. Such hopes no doubt received a boost when, less than two weeks later, the king sent word through Bellièvre to leaguer representatives that he "desired nothing more than to see all his subjects reunited in the Catholic religion . . . knowing full well that otherwise the realm would forever be in danger of renewed civil strife."[48] Over the next five years, the Huguenots' understandable fears of renewed persecution risked igniting another civil war until Henry IV restored a measure of confidence among them in April 1598 by issuing the Edict of Nantes.

Or so, at least, it seemed. While certainly crucial for his overall pacification of the realm, the Edict of Nantes did not represent the momentous breakthrough for toleration that historians have so frequently assumed it to be. Indeed, the edict must be seen in light of the king's worsening relations with the Huguenots as well as his earlier treaties with Leaguers in 1594–95. In these, Henry IV reaffirmed many of the barriers that had long existed between Catholic France and the Huguenot minority, barriers that virtually foreclosed any eventual integration between the two except by conversion to the dominant religion. The Chambers de l'Édit erected to implement the decree's provisions, for example, channeled sectarian conflict into the king's courts, thus forming a sort of bureaucratic containment which purposefully isolated the French Reformed churches as a recognizable corporate entity whose identity and rights the crown increasingly defined.[49] As a result,

Protestant rhetoric of conciliation and combat was shifted from the public domain of print culture, where it had been so potent since the 1550s, to the juridical confines and legal briefs of the sovereign courts, where it could, of course, be more easily controlled. In this light, the Edict of Nantes domesticated the Reformed community by removing from it both the necessity and the ability to appeal to public opinion in the name of either Scripture or conscience. All appeals for safeguarding Reformed interests had to be framed by reference to the king alone. After all, any other sort of behavior would be inappropriate for *bons françois* during the so-called age of absolutism. The quest for Huguenot confessional recognition, seemingly achieved after 1598, thereafter gave way to a search for political respectability. Duplessis-Mornay's efforts to integrate the Huguenot community into France's corporative structure, along with Pierre du Moulin's attempt to move the Reformed churches toward a more episcopal organization, reflected the general desire among most Reformed leaders in France to work within the strictures set by the crown in 1598.[50]

As violations of Huguenot liberties mounted during Marie de Médicis's regency and the early reign of her son, Louis XIII, some Huguenot leaders like the duc de Rohan began to reconsider the merits of conformity. By 1620, it was possible for the Reformed community to mount resistance against the crown, but not—as in the past—to sustain it indefinitely. Certainly, this renewed resistance lacked the accompanying elevated discourse about rights of resistance and toleration that had nourished Huguenot militancy in the 1570s. English intervention, while militarily necessary perhaps, undermined the Huguenots' long efforts to play the role of *bon françois*. This explains why, as Daniel Ligou recently argued, the Huguenots after the Grace of Alais (1630) became even more royal than the king, developing a "theology of royal power almost idolatrous when it came to the king's person . . . totally confusing all values by mixing together God, Caesar and Louis."[51] This narrowed polemical—and thus political—horizon went back, as we have seen, to the fateful choice made by French Calvinists after 1584 to strike out on the path of dynastic loyalism, confident that their confessional triumph would soon follow. Henry IV's conversion to Catholicism permanently wrecked these hopes, however. As ratified in the Edict of Nantes, the king's abjuration virtually ensured that the Huguenots would remain a minority whose loyalty to the crown would never be above suspicion no matter how strongly or consistently it might be expressed.

Far from toleration, therefore, Henry IV instead predicated confessional coexistence on separation and exclusion mitigated only by those "liberties" specifically guaranteed for the Huguenots by the crown, and nothing more. The most immediate objective achieved by the Edict of Nantes was to allay Huguenot fears of the conversion's repercussions. From the vantage point of 1598, it was a definite improvement compared with the past treatment Huguenots had received from France's Catholic kings. And the peace promised to endure given the defeat of Catholic hardliners, whose ascendancy since the 1570s had helped to feed confessional strife. Yet dependence on the crown was the price Huguenots had to pay for protection from the Catholic majority, whose animus toward them remained high. Granted, the concessions contained in the Edict of Nantes probably represented more than the *réformés* could have realistically expected under the circumstances, though such magnanimity was typical of Henry IV, who—if given the chance— much preferred to defeat his enemies with kindness rather than violence.[52] By making them an offer they could not refuse, Henry IV was able to quarantine, not liberate, the Reformed community in Catholic France. Huguenot congregations also found themselves slowly cut off from international Calvinist synods held during the years ahead—the 1618 Synod of Dort being the best example—lest they be accused of conspiring with foreign powers.[53] Thus, the Edict of Nantes institutionalized rather than resolved the underlying conflict between Huguenot loyalism and religious dissent that had plagued French Calvinists ever since their protector had become heir presumptive in 1584. French Calvinists remained safe only so long as the crown refused to exploit this implicit contradiction. Luckily for them, their *bon* Henri never pushed the issue; under his successors, however, the *réformés* would not be so fortunate.

Notes

All translations are by the author unless otherwise indicated.

1. After 1593, Catholic writers fitted Henry IV's conversion into what they considered to be a logical, if not divinely inspired, sequence of events which began with Navarre's birth in 1553. Modern historians, too numerous to cite, invariably present the king's abjuration as a politically inevitable act crucial for France's later greatness. See Michael Wolfe, *The Conversion of Henri IV: Politics, Power, and Religious Belief in Early Modern France* (Cambridge: Harvard University Press, 1993), pp. 59–63.

2. W. Fred Graham, "Calvin and the Political Order: An Analysis of the Three Explanatory Studies," in *Calviniana: Ideas and Influence of Jean Calvin,* ed. Robert V. Schnucker, Sixteenth Century Essays and Studies 10 (Kirksville, Mo.: Sixteenth Century Journal Publishers, 1988), pp. 51–61.

3. For Protestant assemblies, see Léonce Anquez, *Histoire des assemblées politiques de la France, 1573–1622* (Paris, 1859); E. Haag, *La France Protestante,* 10 vols. (Paris, 1846–1859; reprinted in Geneva: Droz, 1966); and N. M. Sutherland, *The Huguenot Struggle for Recognition* (New Haven: Yale University Press, 1980), especially chap. 7. Recent literature on the Catholic League includes Élie Barnavi, *Le parti de Dieu: Étude sociale et politique des chefs de la Ligue parisienne (1585–1595)* (Louvain: Nauwelaerts, 1980); Robert Descimon, *Qui étaient les Seize?* (Paris: Hachette, 1984); and Denis Crouzet, *Les guerriers de Dieu,* 2 vols. (Paris: Champ Vallon, 1990).

4. Glenn S. Sunshine, "Reformed Theology and the Origins of the Synodical Polity: Calvin, Beza and the Gallican Confession," in *Later Calvinism: International Perspectives,* ed. W. Fred Graham, Sixteenth Century Essays and Studies 22 (Kirksville, Mo.: Sixteenth Century Journal Publishers, 1994), pp. 141–58. Jean de Morély's proposal in the late 1560s to establish a more popularly based congregational church system, although ultimately repudiated, reflected this tendency toward local self-determination among the Reformed churches. See Robert M. Kingdon, *Geneva and the Consolidation of the French Protestant Movement, 1564–1572* (Geneva: Droz, 1967).

5. In general, see François Dumont, "La royauté française vue par les auteurs littéraires au XVIe siècle," *Études historiques à la mémoire de Noël Didier* (Paris: Editions Montchrestien, 1960), pp. 61–93; Michel Tyvaert, "L'image du roi: Légimité et moralité royales dans les histoires de France au XVIIe siècle," *Revue d'histoire moderne et contemporaine* 21 (1974): 521–47; and Orest Ranum, *Artisans of Glory: Writers and Historical Thought in Seventeenth-Century France* (Chapel Hill: University of North Carolina Press, 1980).

6. Christian Desplat, "Le mythe d'Henri IV: Nouvelles approaches," *Bulletin de la société des amis du château de Pau* 72 (1977): 81–103; and Jacques Hennequin, *Henri IV dans ses oraisons funèbres ou la naissance d'une légende* (Paris: Presses Universitaires de France, 1977).

7. Raymond Ritter, "Le roi de Navarre et sa prétendue fuite de la cour en 1576," *Bulletin philologique et historique* 2 (1972): 667–84; and J. J. Supple, "The Role of François de la Noue in the Siege of La Rochelle and the Protestant Alliance with the Mécontents," *Bibliothèque d'humanisme et Renaissance* 42 (1981): 107–22.

8. For Alençon, see Mack P. Holt, *The Duke of Anjou and the Politique Struggle during the French Wars of Religion* (Cambridge: Cambridge University Press, 1986); for Condé, see J. Garrisson-Estèbe, *Protestants du Midi, 1559–1598* (Toulouse: Privat, 1980), pp. 177–93; and duc d'Aumale, *Histoire des princes de Condé pendant les XVIe–XVIIe siècles,* 2 vols. (Paris, 1885), 1:108–12.

9. A typical case is the "Déclaration d'Henri de Navarre," dated November 30,

1585, Bergerac, printed in *Édits des guerres de religion,* ed. André Stegmann, 2 vols. (Paris, 1979), 2:214–16.

10. René de Lucinge to Charles-Emanuel, October 3, 1585, Paris, in *Lettres sur les débuts de la Ligue (1585),* ed. Alain Dufour (Geneva: Droz, 1964), pp. 201–2.

11. Henri de Navarre to MM. le Clergé, January 1, 1586, Montauban, in *Recueil des lettres missives de Henri IV,* ed. Berger de Xivery, 9 vols. (Paris, 1843–76), 2:165–68.

12. See C. Blum, "De la méthode de resoudre les controverses: Le 'Traité de concile' de Duplessis Mornay," in *La controverse religieuse,* ed. B. Dompnier, 2 vols. (Montpellier: Presses Universitaires de France, 1980), 1:116–30. The *Traité de concile* appeared anonymously in 1590.

13. Wolfe, *The Conversion of Henri IV,* pp. 32–33.

14. Donald Nugent, *Ecumenism in the Age of the Reformation: The Colloquy of Poissy* (Cambridge: Harvard University Press, 1974); and Mario Turchetti, *Concordia o tolleranza? François Baudouin (1520–1573) e i 'moyenneurs'* (Geneva: Droz, 1984).

15. The social tensions within French Calvinism are explored in Henry Heller, *The Conquest of Poverty: The Calvinist Revolt in Sixteenth-Century France* (Leiden: E. J. Brill, 1986).

16. Sutherland, *The Huguenot Struggle,* pp. 283–332.

17. Donald Kelley, *The Beginning of Ideology: Consciousness and Society in the French Reformation* (New York: Cambridge University Press, 1981); and Myriam Yardeni, *La conscience nationale en France pendant les guerres de religion, 1559–1598* (Louvain: Nauwelaerts, 1971).

18. Tadatake Maruyama, *The Ecclesiology of Theodore Beza: The Reform of the True Church* (Geneva: Droz, 1978), pp. 239–42; and Raoul Patry, *Philippe Du Plessis-Mornay: un huguenot homme d'état (1549–1623)* (Paris: Fischbacker, 1933).

19. H. Kretzer, "Remarques sur le droit de résistance des Calvinistes français au début du XVIIe siècle," *Bibliothèque de la société d'histoire du protestantisme français* 78 (1977): 54–75.

20. Sutherland, *The Huguenot Struggle,* pp. 283–92. As she so succinctly phrased it on p. 265: "His interests, whether as first prince, heir apparent or king, never fully coincided with those of the Protestant party, and this was already apparent" in 1571!

21. Samuel Kinser, "Agrippa d'Aubigné and the Apostasy of Henri IV," *Studies in the Renaissance* 2 (1964): 245–68; and Marguerite Soulis, "Les idées politiques d'Agrippa d'Aubigné de 1580–1590," in *Les écrivains et la politique dans le sud-ouest de la France autour des années 1580: Actes du colloque de Bordeaux 6–7 novembre 1981* Bordeaux, 1982), pp. 163–68.

22. Henri Hauser argued that it was Duplessis-Mornay who penned the pamphlet, though I am inclined to agree with Villeroy, who attributed it to Ferrier. See Hauser, *Sources de l'histoire de France,* 8 vols. (Paris: A. Picard, 1912), 3:291; and Villeroy, *Mémoires d'estat,* 3 vols. (Sedan and Paris, 1622–23), 3:22–28. Biblio-

thèque Nationale [hereafter BN], Cinq Cent Colbert, MS 489, fols. 181–207, imputes it to a certain pastor named Marius. I have relied on the copy in BN, Fonds français, MS 4683, fols. 71–90, entitled "Dialogue entre le sieur de Roquelaure et M. de Mornet." The place of publication for the original 1585 edition is given as Frankfort, though that may be spurious.

23. BN, Cinq Cent Colbert, MS 489, fols. 181–209, gives July 15 as the date and Nérac as the place where the debate took place, though it is known that Henry was at Pau at the time. See Robert, "Voyages et séjours d'Henri de Navarre en 1584," *Revue de Pau et Béarn* 12 (1984): 67–94.

24. See below, p. 382.

25. Jean de Serres, in his *Recueil des choses memorables avenues en France pendant les années 1547–1596* (n.p., 1598), pp. 761–65, for instance, attacked Henry IV's conversion in virtually the same terms used by the radical Seize preacher Jean Boucher in his *Sermons de la simulée conversion d'Henri de Navarre* (Paris, 1594), going so far as to repeat the leaguer charge that not only Paris, but "son Royaume . . . valoit bien une Messe" (p. 762). The opposition of both Huguenots and Leaguers to Henry IV's conversation sometimes makes it difficult to determine which party was behind the publication of certain pieces. An excellent example of this polemical ambiguity can be found in Anonymous, *Discours sur une question d'estat de ce temps. Question: Que le Roy ne se faict-il Catholique? S'il se faisoit Catholique son royaume seroit incontinent en paix* (n.p., 1591), which can be read as a warning to Navarre by the Huguenots of the dangers of conversion or as an exposition by Leaguers of Navarre's duplicity toward loyalist Catholics.

26. *Le serment et promesse du Roy à son advenement* (n.p., 1589), pp. 3–4. Navarre agreed to convoke an assembly for his instruction within six months, though he deliberately left its confessional makeup unclear. See Ronald Love, "Winning the Catholics and the Religious Dilemma in August 1589," *Canadian Journal of History* 24 (1989): 361–79. On Huguenot agitations at Saint-Cloud, see Duplessis-Mornay to Henry IV, undated memorandum, in *Mémoires et correspondance,* ed. Anguis and Fontenelle de Vandorie, 12 vols. (Paris, 1824–34), 2:394.

27. Jean de Sponde, *Advertissement au Roy où sont déduites les raisons d'Estat pour lesquelles il ne luy est pais bien séant de changer de religion* (n.p., 1589). Alan Boase, in *Vie de Jean de Sponde* (Geneva: Droz, 1979), p. 66, offered strong arguments in favor of Sponde's authorship. Palma Cayet, in *Chronologie novenaire,* p. 169, stated that the pamphlet was published in La Rochelle.

28. Sutherland, *The Huguenot Struggle,* pp. 304–13.

29. L.B., *Remonstance au Roy,* delivered August 2, 1592, published in Ernst Stähelin, *Der Übertritt König Heinrich IV zur römischen katholischen Kirche* (Basel, 1856), app. 1, pp. 783–95.

30. BN, Collection Dupuy, MS 322, fols. 295–97, Gabriel Damours to Henry IV, June 20, 1593, Saint Jean d'Angély.

31. Henri Hauser, "François de la Noue et la conversion du Roi," *Revue historique* (1888): 313–29. Hauser included a transcription of the letter, which he saw as

evidence of La Noue's patriotic principles—a view recently thrown into question by William H. Huseman in "François de la Noue (1531–1591) au service du libéralisme du XIXe siècle," *Renaissance and Reformation/Renaissance et Réforme* 9 (1985): 189–208.

32. Sully, Maximilien de Béthune, duc de, *Oeconomies royales,* ed. Joseph-François Michaud and Jean-Jacques-François Poujoulat, vol. 16 of *Nouvelle collection des mémoires relatifs à l'histoire de France* (Paris, 1881), pp. 105–8.

33. BN, Fonds français, MS 2945, fol. 50, "Bref du pape Paul V à M. de Sully pour l'inciter à se faire catholique," Rome, October 9, 1605, and fol. 51, "Réponce de M. de Sully au bref du pape Paul V," Paris, November 27, 1605.

34. Sully, *Oeconomies royales,* p. 109.

35. Palma Cayet, *Chronologie novenaire,* p. 467; and BN, Fonds français, MS 3275, fol. 140, "Promesse des Seigneurs Catholiques du Conseil du Roy en faveur de ceulx de la Religion," May 16, 1593.

36. Duplessis-Mornay, *Mémoires,* 5:450–53. On the prohibition of Calvinist services, see BN, Collection Dupuy, MS 322, fols. 306–8.

37. BN, Collection Dupy, MS 753, fols. 240–48, "Copie de certains Mémoires dressés par ceux de la Religion Réformée lors que le Roy Henry le Grand allant à la Messe."

38. For the coronation, see Nicolas de Thou, *Cérémonies observées au sacre et couronnement du très-chrestien et très-valeureux Henry IV, Roy de France et Navarre* (Paris, 1594).

39. Wolfe, *The Conversion of Henri IV,* pp. 181–82.

40. Sutherland, *The Huguenot Struggle,* pp. 324–26.

41. BN, Cinq Cent Colbert, MS 31, fols. 462–65, and Collection Dupuy, MS 753, fols. 240–48. See Henry IV's response in BN, Fonds français, MS 4019, fols. 247–48.

42. BN, Fonds français, MS 5045, fols. 379–82, discusses these rumors of conflict between Henry IV and the Huguenots. Nevers's comments can be found in BN, Fonds français, MS 3987, fols. 147–52.

43. P. Feret, "Nullité de mariage de Henri IV avec Marguerite de Valois," *Revue des questions historiques* 11 (1876): 77–114.

44. BN, Fonds français, MS 3449, fol. 17, Soissons to Henry IV, early December 1595, n.p. Soissons was peeved that the king had not consulted him concerning the young Condé's future. The dowager princesse de Condé also objected to the king's plans for her son. Henry IV responded by bringing her before the Parlement of Paris on charges that she had poisoned her husband in 1588. Although never convicted, she lost custody of her child as a result. BN, Fonds français, MS 2751, fols. 252–54. She also converted to Catholicism the next year. See P. Garreta, ed., *La conversion de la princesse de Condé à Rouen en 1596* (Rouen, 1901).

45. Anonymous, *Conférence tenue à Nancy sur le different de la Religion. A l'effet de convertir Madame soeur unique du Roy, à la Catholique et Romaine* (n.p., 1600). See also *Lettres et poésies de Catherine de Bourbon,* ed. Raymond Ritter (Paris: H. Champion,

1927), p. 16; and Abbé Jean Fonda, "L'infortunée Catherine de Bourbon, soeur unique d'Henri IV," *Revue de l'Agenais* 93 (1967): 137–50.

46. Jean de Sponde, in *Déclaration des principaux motifs qui ont induict le feu sieur de Sponde, conseiller, maistre des requestes du Roy, à s'unir à l'Eglise Catholique. Adressée à ceux qui sont séparez* (Paris, 1595), pp. 27–28, spoke for many when he wrote: "I had no other example but Your Majesty's conversion . . . I have to admit that God's miraculous favor toward you deeply affected me." For Sponde, see also Florimond de Raemond, *Le tombeau de feu sieur de Sponde* (Bordeaux, 1595); Raemond was himself a convert to Catholicism. Sponde died soon after his conversion.

47. V. P. Palma-Cayet, *Copie d'une lettre ecrite par Victor Pierre Palma-Cayet contentant les causes et raisons de sa conversion* (Paris, 1595); Anonymous, *Discours de la conversion et mort du sieur de Morlas* (Paris, 1595); Agrippa d'Aubigné, *Confession catholique du sieur de Sancy* (n.p., 1597). Aubigné's tract ridicules these courtly converts. See also Michel Peronnet, "Confession catholique du sieur de Sancy," *Réforme, Humanisme, Renaissance* 5 (1979): 24–33.

48. BN, Fonds français, MS 15893, fols. 130–31, "Responce de Bellièvre à Jeannin du party contraire," August 12, 1593.

49. Georges Pagès put it well years ago when he wrote: "No religious peace during this period ever originated as a reconciliation between two rival confessions. Such accords must instead be seen simply as acts of state, which imposed on each confession a reciprocal toleration, circumscribed territorially and according to conditions set down by the state" ("La paix de religion et l'Édit de Nantes," *Revue d'histoire moderne* 25 [1936]: 393–413, p. 398).

50. Arthur L. Herman, "Protestant Churches in a Catholic Kingdom: Political Assemblies in the Thought of Philippe Duplessis-Mornay," *Sixteenth Century Journal* 21 (1990): 543–57; and Brian G. Armstrong, "The Changing Face of French Protestantism: The Influence of Pierre Du Moulin," in *Calviniana: Ideas and Influences of Jean Calvin,* ed. R. V. Schnucker, Sixteenth Century Essays and Studies 10 (Kirksville, Mo.: Sixteenth Century Journal Publishers, 1988), pp. 131–49.

51. Daniel Ligou, "Pourquoi la Révocation de l'Édit de Nante?," in *Un siècle et démi d'histoire protestante: Théodore de Bèze et les protestants sujets du roi,* ed. Léo Hamon (Paris: Éditions de la Maison des sciences de l'homme, 1985), pp. 29–51; and Elisabeth Labrousse, "La doctrine politique des Huguenots, 1630–1685," *Études théologiques et religieuse* 47 (1972): 421–29.

52. Wolfe, *The Conversion of Henri IV,* pp. 182–84; see also J. Garrisson, *L'édit de Nantes et sa révocation: Histoire d'une intolérance* (Paris: Gallimard, 1985); and F. Baumgartner, "The Catholic Opposition to the Edict of Nantes, 1598–1599," *Bibliothèque d'humanisme et Renaissance* 40 (1978): 525–36. A copy of the Edict of Nantes can be found in Roland Mousnier, *L'assassinat d'Henri IV, 14 Mai 1610* (Paris: Aubier, 1964), pp. 294–334.

53. This growing conservatism in the Reformed churches also became evident in the shift away from rhetorical defense of doctrine through flexible *persuasio* to a more analytically logical, and thus rigid, scholasticism, which, according to Brian

Armstrong, brought to an end the idea of reform as a continuous process of change. See his essay *"Semper Reformanada:* The Case of the French Reformed Church, 1559–1620," in *Later Calvinism: Internal Perspectives,* ed. W. F. Graham, Sixteenth Century Essays and Studies 22 (Kirksville, Mo.: Sixteenth Century Journal Publishers, 1994), pp. 119–40. See also the magisterial work by François Laplanche, *L'Écriture, le sacré et l'histoire: Érudits et politiques protestants devant la Bible en France au XVIIe siècle* (Lille: Presses Universitaires de Lille, 1986), which traces the internal breakdown of Calvinist orthodoxy in France during the seventeenth century.

Index

Contributors

Charmarie Blaisdell is Associate Professor of History at Northeastern University. She is currently completing a study of French female religious communities during the early modern era.

William Bouwsma is Professor Emeritus of History at Berkeley and the author of nine books on Renaissance and Reformation Europe. Among these are *Venice and the Defense of Republican Liberty* (1968), *The Culture of Renaissance Humanism* (1973), and *John Calvin: A Sixteenth-Century Portrait* (1988).

Lawrence M. Bryant is Associate Professor of History at Chico State University in California and the author of *The King and the City in the Parisian Royal Entry Ceremony: Politics, Ritual and Art in the Renaissance* (1986).

Denis Crouzet is Professor of History at the Sorbonne and the author of several works on sixteenth-century French religious and political culture, principally *Les Guerriers de Dieu* (1990) and *La Nuit de Saint Barthélemy* (1994).

Robert Descimon is Research Fellow at the Centre National des Recherches Scientifiques in Paris. He has published several books on the history of the Holy League and France during the Fronde, including *Qui étaient les Seize?* (1983) and *Le juge, la potence, et le pouvoir* (1986).

Barbara B. Diefendorf is Associate Professor of History at Boston University, and the author of *Paris City Councillors in the Sixteenth Century: The Politics of Patrimony* (1983) and *Beneath the Cross: Catholics and Huguenots in Sixteenth-Century Paris* (1991).

Richard M. Golden is Department Chair at North Texas State University and the author of *The Godly Rebellion: Parisian Curés and the Religious Fronde* (1981) and editor of *Church, State, and Society in the Bourbon Kingdom of France* (1982) and *The Huguenot Connection: The Edict of Nantes, Its Revocation, and Early French Migration to South Carolina* (1988).

Sarah Hanley is Professor of History at the University of Iowa and the author of *The Lit de Justice of the Kings of France: Constitutional Ideology in Legend, Ritual, and Discourse* (1983).

Mack P. Holt is Associate Professor of History at George Mason University. His books include *The Duke of Anjou and the Politique Struggle during the Wars of Religion* (1986) and *Society and Institutions in Early Modern France* (1991), for which he served as editor.

Donald R. Kelley is Professor of History at Rutgers University and author of numerous studies on early modern law and politics, including *Foundations of Modern Historical Scholarship: Language, Law and History in the French Renaissance* (1970), *François Hotman: A Revolutionary's Ordeal* (1973), *History, Law, and the Human Sciences: Medieval and Renaissance Perspectives* (1984), and *The Human Measure: Social Thought in the Western Legal Tradition* (1990).

Kristen B. Neuschel is Associate Professor of History at Duke University and the author of *Word of Honor: Interpreting Noble Culture in Sixteenth Century France* (1989). She is currently studying gender roles and values in early modern French aristocratic culture.

J.H.M. Salmon is Professor Emeritus of History at Bryn Mawr College and the author of six books on the history of early modern France. Among these are *The French Wars of Religion in English Political Thought* (1959), *Society in Crisis: France in the Sixteenth Century* (1975), and an annotated edition of the *Francogallia* (1972).

Zachary Sayre Schiffman is Associate Professor of History at the University of Northeastern Illinois—Chicago and the author of *On the Threshold of Modernity: Relativism in the French Renaissance* (1991).

Silvia Shannon is Assistant Professor of History at St. Anselm's College. She is currently completing a study of the Guise family during the Wars of Religion.

Alfred Soman is Research Fellow at the Sorbonne and the author of numerous articles on deviance, criminal law, and the Parlement of Paris. Some of these have recently been published by Variorum.

Michael Wolfe is Associate Professor of History at Pennsylvania State University—Altoona and the author of *The Conversion of Henri IV: Politics, Power and Religious Belief in Early Modern France* (1993) and the coeditor of *The Medieval City under Siege* (1995).

Library of Congress Cataloging-in-Publication Data

Changing identities in early modern France / Michael Wolfe, editor.

p. cm.

Includes index.

ISBN 0-8223-1908-X (alk. paper). — ISBN 0-8223-1913-6 (pbk. : alk. paper)

1. France—Civilization—1328–1600. 2. French—Identity.

3. Social classes—France. 4. Renaissance—France.

5. Enlightenment—France. I. Wolfe, Michael.

DC33.3.C45 1997

944'.025—dc20   96-33335   CIP